THE MISSIONARI

'I go back to Africa to make an open path for commerce and Christianity!' said David Livingstone in 1857, at the height of his fame. What manner of men and women were the missionaries? Why did they go out to Africa in such vast numbers? Was it chiefly to take the Bible to 'degraded heathen'? Or were their motives complicated by personal ambition and by the greed of the countries from which they came?

The missionaries who marched across Africa in the nineteenth and twentieth centuries are the subject of Geoffrey Moorhouse's book. He has reached behind the caricatures, following closely the unfolding pattern of missionary enterprise in the 'Dark Continent', to find heroism, hypocrisy and honest endeavour in almost equal proportions. And much racial prejudice. Long before the imperialistic scramble for Africa, some missionaries were in the habit of summoning gunboats to wipe out 'heathen' towns. At the same time the missionaries, more than anybody else, were responsible for ending the slave trade in Africa. If there had been no missionaries, there would have been no Battle of Mengo between Catholics and Protestants in Uganda in 1892; but there might not have been a modern Africa, either. Almost every man who led his country to independence after the Second World War had been educated by missionaries.

The missionary movement is enormously rich in characters. Livingstone himself emerges with his greatness set in a perspective which Sunday School teachers usually neglect. Then there is Cardinal Lavigerie, founder of the White Fathers, who actually forbade his men to preach Christianity; Robert Arthington, the miser of Headingley, who secretly spent a fortune supporting the missionary societies; Robert Ashe, who first demonstrated the art of swimming to the Baganda. And a host of others, explorers and men and women of God, as well as Samuel Crowther, the first African bishop of the Church of England, and Mtesa and Mwanga, rulers of the Baganda.

Above all, this book is an assessment of a phenomenon which only one other great religion has rivalled. Geoffrey Moorhouse

Continued on back flap

by the same author

THE OTHER ENGLAND
THE PRESS
AGAINST ALL REASON
CALCUTTA

Continued from front flap

journeyed across 5,000 miles of Africa in the course of his researches. He has made use of source material from black Africa as well as from white Europe and North America, including the missionary societies themselves. He has written a history, but it comes a full and ironic circle right up to the present day, with an African indigenous Church establishing a missionary outpost in London.

Geoffrey Moorhouse

THE MISSIONARIES

J. B. LIPPINCOTT COMPANY
PHILADELPHIA AND NEW YORK

Printed in Great Britain

U.S. Library of Congress Cataloging in Publication Data

Moorhouse, Geoffrey, birth date
The missionaries.
1. Missions—Africa—History. I. Title.
BV3500.M6 266'.0096 72-6052
ISBN-0-397-00801-5

To Jan, *in gratitude*

CONTENTS

ILLUSTRATIONS

Acknowledgments and thanks are due to the Trustees of the British Museum for plates 1, 2, 3, 4, 8, 9, 10, 11, 12, 13, 14, 15, 16, 17 and 18; to the Church Missionary Society for plates 5 and 7; to the Africana Museum, Johannesburg for plate 6; to the Department of Religious Studies, Makerere University, Kampala for plates 19 and 23; to the Dr A. T. Schofield Collection of Photographs, Makerere University, Kampala for plates 20, 21 and 22; to Fr Louis Facq, W.F., by permission of Fr F. Payeur, W.F., for plate 24; and to the Clarendon Press for plate 25.

LINE DRAWINGS

Acknowledgments and thanks are due to the Trustees of the British Museum for nos 1, 4, 5, 6, 7, 8, 9, 10, 11, 12, 13, 14 and 15; to the Church Missionary Society for no. 2; and to the Mansell Collection for no. 3.

MAPS

ACKNOWLEDGMENTS

Most of the work for this book was done in London and I am particularly grateful for the help given me on a number of occasions by Miss Jean Wood and her staff in the library of the Church Missionary Society, and by Miss Eileen Fletcher, Librarian of the London Missionary Society.

I also spent nearly three months in a journey across Africa, where many people gave me a great deal of assistance, one way and another. Above all I have to thank Dr M. Louise Pirouet, of Makerere University, not only for offering me invaluable advice while I was in Uganda, but for giving me access to a great deal of original material which forms part of her own outstanding research upon the Church in East Africa. In the Congo, life would have been rather more difficult in Kinshasa had it not been for the kindness and help of the Rev. Angus MacNeill, his wife and colleagues at the Baptist Missionary Society headquarters; and my explorations up the river would not have been possible without the base which the Rev. D. Norkett and his colleagues of the BMS station at Bolobo offered me. My thanks to all of them, and to the people of the villages I visited, whose kindness not only included taking me into their homes, but sent me downstream again in a canoe loaded to the gunwales with a variety of presents ranging from dead crocodile meat to live turtles. No kindness, however, exceeded that of the Rev. Peter Burch and his wife in Sierra Leone, who not only acted as guides and instructors around Freetown and its hinterland, but who nursed me when I had briefly and idiotically crippled myself with badly burned feet.

I should also like to thank Professor E. A. Ayandele for his readiness to welcome me to Ibadan. Unfortunately, I never got there. Even after three months of persistent application, the Nigerian authorities had still not granted me a visa by the time I flew into Lagos. After a few hours I was obliged to fly out again, for reasons which were never disclosed. Lastly, I am most grateful to Professor Roland Oliver for reading the manuscript, for saving me from at least two monumental errors of fact, and for making a number of helpful criticisms. The responsibility for what has emerged is, of course, entirely mine.

THE MISSIONARIES

INTRODUCTION

This does not pretend to be the full story of the Christian missionaries in Africa. To attempt that, one would have required several volumes of this size. The omissions are obvious. There is the barest acknowledgment of Catholic efforts to proselytise the continent before the nineteenth century, little enough is said of Catholic missions even in the period which has been scrutinised, and Protestants may well think that scant attention has been paid to such celebrated figures as Robert Moffat, Mary Slessor and Albert Schweitzer. I have not attempted to assess the nature and quality of Christianity *per se* which has been implanted in Africa; that is still a matter – and seems likely to remain so for many years to come – for slow and extensive academic research. I believe, however, that all these omissions can be justified. A very fine historian of Africa has written that 'all worthwhile historical writing is primarily an artistic exercise, consisting in an attempt to master a large body of facts and to present a small selection of them in the proportion and form that seem most meaningful at a particular moment in time'.* This is the principle I have tried to follow in this book.

It is, therefore, primarily the story of Protestant missionaries who were working in Africa during the nineteenth and early twentieth centuries. And, with the exception of David Livingstone, the most celebrated figures in the missionary pantheon have been somewhat neglected because it has seemed important to portray the norm rather than the outstanding. The norm was a desire by pious Christians of Europe and North America, in a movement which gathered enormous momentum as the nineteenth

* Roland Oliver, *The Missionary Factor in East Africa*, p. vii.

century proceeded, to bestow upon other races of the world the articles of their faith and what they took to be the benefits of their civilisation. With the exception of Islam, no other great religion has ever produced such a motivation, none has appeared in such a colonising role. So ardent was this Christian desire, starting from the most exalted of motives, that the gift was sometimes indistinguishable from an imposition even at the beginning of the modern missionary enterprise. By the end of the nineteenth century it had become inseparable from the purely secular motives of straightforward imperialism. In none of the fields to which the white Christians sent their missionaries, moreover, was this pattern clearer, was this enterprise more effective, was the transformation wrought more radical, than in Africa. The Dark Continent was a very paradigm of the missionary story.

In India, the excursions of the white men began with commerce, not religion. In China and Japan, the local cultures proved enduringly resistant to the importation of alien strains based upon Christianity. In the Pacific islands, the conflict of cultures and the agonies this produced were comparatively small, perhaps because no community, isolated from its neighbours by vast expanses of ocean, was large enough or strong enough to withstand outside pressures once these had been applied with all the weight of the white man's world behind them. South America alone offers close parallels to Africa. The history of Catholic missionaries there is not dissimilar to the history of Protestants in this other field: except that what they achieved, what they transformed, was the work of a much more extended period of time.

The Protestant missionaries who took their Bibles to Africa in the nineteenth century therefore represent in the most acute form the prescriptions of a faith and the spirit of an age. They came from every white nation whose social and moral values had been sculptured by the descendants of the Christian Reformation in the sixteenth century. They came, significantly, in proportions approximating to purely national instincts for expansion and appetites for colonisation. Of these missionaries, it was the men and women representing the British societies who bore most of the burdens in the nineteenth century, who took most of the spoils, who were supported most extensively by their kinsmen at home. Much of Africa as we know it today, to a degree which cannot yet be assessed, is their legacy.

And he said unto them, Go ye into all the world, and preach the gospel to every creature.

MARK 16 XV

I go back to Africa to make an open path for commerce and Christianity; do you carry out the work which I have begun.

DAVID LIVINGSTONE, *4 December 1857*

The Church in the colonies is the white people's Church, the foreigner's Church. She does not call the native to God's ways, but to the ways of the white man, of the master, of the oppressor. And as we know, in this matter many are called but few chosen.

FRANTZ FANON, *The Wretched of the Earth*

I
TO SPREAD MILD TRUTHS

London had not known a public meeting like it. From early morning the streets around the Strand had been crowded with people anxious to get a good view of the high and mighty, as they made their way by carriage to Exeter Hall, though the doors would not be opened until ten o'clock and the first speech was not due until after 11 am. The demand for tickets had been so great that, two or three days before, large sums of money had been offered by those hoping to gain admission. That idol of the gods, Charles Kean, had just played his first night as Hamlet at the Haymarket Theatre before a packed audience, but the interest he aroused was as nothing compared with the general fervour attending this first anniversary meeting of the Society for the Extinction of the Slave Trade and for the Civilisation of Africa.

It was a warm summer's day, in June 1840 and London was fairly bursting with a zeal and an excitement and a righteous self-assurance that all ran in several different directions at once. A great deal of it, the society's subscribing members had to concede, had nothing to do with moral indignation against the slave trade or with an earnest desire to bless and lighten the darkest continent with the benefits of civilisation. Most of the citizens packing the pavements of the Strand were there, above all, because they wanted to catch sight of Queen Victoria's new German consort *en route* to his first public engagement in Great Britain; what *The Times* was to call, within a day or two, 'the scene of Prince Albert's matriculation in the business of a free and deliberative people'. These free and deliberative people, moreover, had good reason to be stimulated by a glittering and potentially courageous enterprise. For almost a year now, since the society's foundation, the Government had been laying plans to despatch an expedition of three steamships to West Africa, where it was known that slavery still lingered almost half a century after its official abolition, where cannibalism and other horrors were said to flourish. These vessels were to sail up the river Niger, pacifying and civilising as they went, and few people doubted that they would sail bravely down again, with the Union Jack fluttering gloriously from each masthead, with yet another epic tale to be added to the story of this island race. The Exeter Hall meeting was merely a splendid opportunity for the public to ratify and acclaim what was already certain and about to be launched.

Essentially, however, and in its origins, this was an intensely moral occasion. It was Christian through and through and its real significance was that it marked the beginning of unparallelled growth and development in the missionary venture in Africa. For nearly half a century this had been a comparatively stunted thing, full of pious hopes and dogged persistence and awful self-sacrifice, with little to reward those who bent their energies and wills and sometimes their lives in its service. But from that June morning onwards, it must have seemed in missionary circles as though some great shadow had fallen away from the understanding of a Christian people. Henceforth, they were to need little persuasion of their deep obligation to go forth and proclaim the message of the Gospel to the poor degraded heathen in Africa and elsewhere. For the best part of a century now, they were to rally to this cause with obsessive enthusiasm, sending their agents out across the world in an increasing flow, supporting them with money, with goodwill and with esteem on a lavish scale. It is doubtful whether, in the history of any nation, there has ever been anything to match the concentrated interest of the British people in their Christian missionaries which now began to form and take shape; for on the face of it, this was an entirely selfless preoccupation.

The drive against slavery and the sharpening of the missionary instinct were as inseparable in 1840 as they had been in the last decade of the eighteenth century, which had seen the foundation, one after another, of three great Protestant missionary societies in Britain. The men who had so pledged themselves, all those years ago, had done so partly out of an awareness of man's inhumanity to man, particularly in Africa, where the traffic in human beings was at its most extensive and repulsive. It was no accident that William Wilberforce had been one of the founding fathers of the Church Missionary Society.

In its early years the CMS had been faced with a struggle even for recognition by the Established Church of England which it represented. Now that struggle was over, though Wilberforce was no longer there to witness the beginning of fruitfulness. In his place, since 1822, had stood Thomas Fowell Buxton as leader of the crusade against slavery; and Buxton, too, was deeply engaged in the work of the CMS. It was under his leadership that this society for the civilisation of Africa had been formed. It was he who had germinated the idea for a Niger Expedition upon which the Government was now about to act. He wanted a more extensive preventive force against the slave trade operating in West Africa than the Royal Navy had yet managed to provide; for in spite of anti-slaving legislation now stretching back over several decades, the traffic still went on. But beyond such immediate and specific steps as the operation of gunboats in African waters, Buxton had a vision of something grander and more enduring. 'The real remedy', he argued, 'the true ransom for Africa, will be found in her fertile soil.' And in a phrase which was to become a battle-cry of the missionary for some time to come, he declared that 'It is the Bible and the plough that must regenerate Africa.' The profiteers in human flesh and misery would have their trade undercut by the introduction of a commerce based upon Christian standards and Western commodity. Treaties to this end must be made with local chieftains and explorations must be made into the agricultural and commercial potential of Africa, and a beginning must be made under the protection of the Union Jack. There must be a settlement of some kind and, in proposing this, Buxton added the hasty qualification that while 'this necessarily calls to mind our vast empire in India . . . I entirely disclaim any disposition to erect a new empire in Africa'. This was the plan to which the British Government at once gave its ready assent. And while the Comptroller of Steam Machinery was making his preparations for the fitting out of the required three vessels, the anti-slaving lobby and the missionary interests were grooming themselves for a new peak in their endeavours, the meeting in Exeter Hall on 1 June 1840.

There was such a press of people waiting to get in so early in the day that the doors had to be opened quite one hour before it was intended, 'and long before ten o'clock every part of the hall, exclusive of the seats reserved on the platform for the committee and leading friends and supporters of the institution, was densely filled by a highly respectable audience. The number of ladies greatly predominated and their personal beauty and elegance of costume enhanced the *tout ensemble* of a truly interesting *coup d'œil.*' By half past ten this assembly had started to get a little restive, so the Exeter Hall organist amused them by playing a

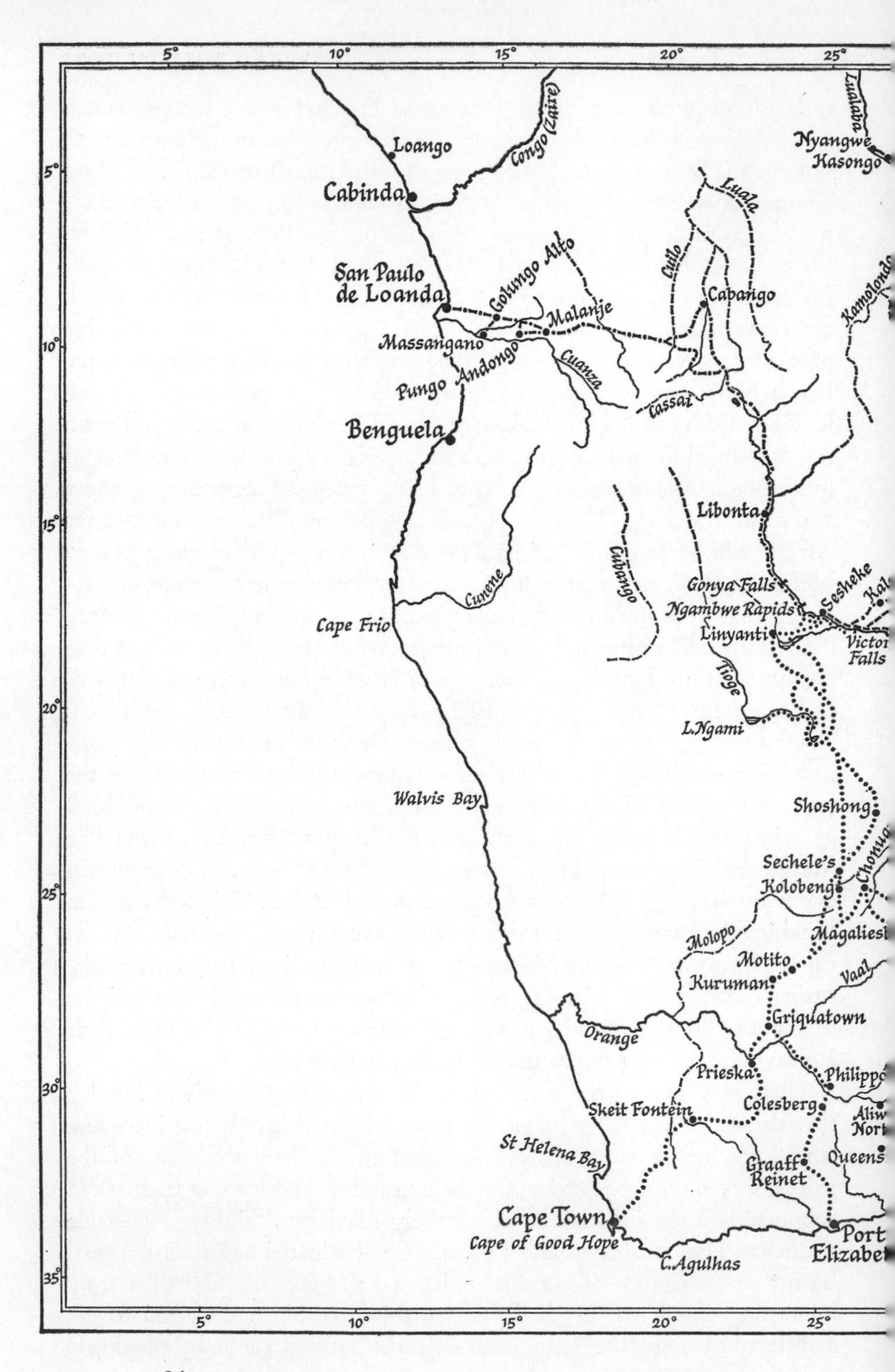
Loango
Congo (Zaire)
Cabinda
Lualaba
Nyangwe
Kasongo
Luala
Cuilo
San Paulo de Loanda
Golungo Alto
Cabango
Malanje
Massangano
Pungo Andongo
Cuanza
Kamolondo
Cassai
Benguela
Libonta
Cubango
Cunene
Gonya Falls
Ngambwe Rapids
Sesheke
Cape Frio
Linyanti
Tioge
L.Ngami
Walvis Bay
Shoshong
Sechele's
Kolobeng
Molopo
Motito
Kuruman
Vaal
Griquatown
Orange
Prieska
Colesberg
Skeit Fontein
St Helena Bay
Graaff Reinet
Cape Town
Cape of Good Hope
C.Agulhas

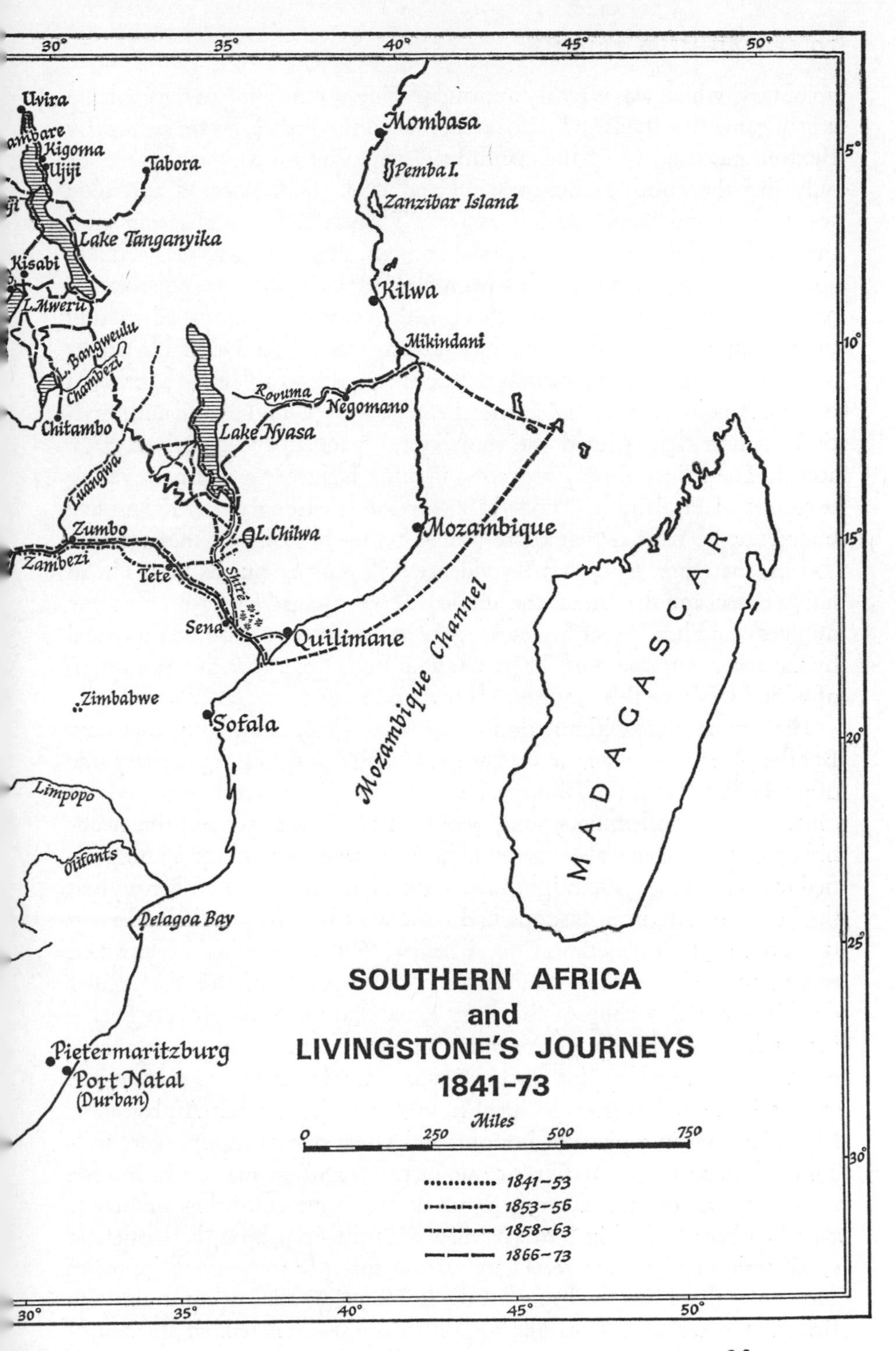

SOUTHERN AFRICA
and
LIVINGSTONE'S JOURNEYS
1841-73

voluntary, which was warmly applauded. This was nothing to the applause which came shortly after he had done, when the Prince, accompanied by Buxton and the rest of the committee, appeared on the platform. Not only did the entire audience stand and clap. They cheered and they waved hats and handkerchiefs as well. There was more cheering after the organist had played the national anthem. Prince Albert was scarcely able to utter a sentence in his opening address without a punctuating cheer. He had propped his speech upon the brim of his upturned hat and the vibration from one round of applause was so great that his papers dropped into the crown, leaving the Consort quite wordless for a moment or two. An observer said he seemed to feel the truly English and enthusiastic reception that greeted the remarks he made in his slightly foreign accent. The Prince deeply regretted that the benevolent and persevering exertions of England had not yet succeeded in ending the African slave trade; but he trusted that there would be no relaxing of these efforts. 'Let us, therefore, trust that Providence will prosper our exertions in so holy a cause, and that under the auspices of our Queen' (cheering for some minutes) 'and her Government we may at no distant period be rewarded by the accomplishment of the great and human object for the promotion of which we have this day met.' (Loud and long-continued cheers.)

The Prince was, without doubt, the society's greatest coup that day. But the platform as a whole was weighty with distinction from every side of public life. True, the Bishop of London had begged to be excused because he was confirming young people in Hertfordshire, and the Archbishop of Canterbury also regretted his inability to attend for an unspecified reason; and a cynic might have been forgiven for remembering that the bench of Anglican bishops had been very loth to put their blessing upon the CMS a generation or so before. But seven other bishops had turned up and appeared to be sitting quite easily among the secular notabilities. The darling of the Tory Party was there, Sir Robert Peel, a man who had already given much of himself to reform, but whose greatest years now lay just ahead. Young Mr Gladstone was present and some said he had a great political future, too. The French Ambassador, M. Guizot, sat in a place of honour, and when one of the speakers welcomed him as representative of one of the mightiest nations in Europe there was more wild cheering from an audience consisting of people who had been locked in bitter conflict with the French on the battlefield of Waterloo and elsewhere. There were a dozen or so peers of the realm and one of them was the leader of the Roman Catholic lay community in Britain, the Duke of Norfolk; for this was a cause in which all men of goodwill could forget their sectarian differences and act together. The society had from the beginning included every shade of Christian opinion in Britain within its ranks. Indeed, so great was the determination of British Christians to right wrongs wherever they might be found, that this very week had seen them making representations on behalf of the Jews of Damascus, who were being persecuted by the Moslem Mehemet Ali; the Bishop of Ripon and Lord Ashley, both of whom were on the platform this day, had just waited upon Lord Palmerston with a memorandum expressing deep sympathy 'for all the cruelty inflicted upon that inoffensive people' and asking Her Majesty's Government 'if not to obtain redress, at least to prevent a recurrence'.

There were two men in Exeter Hall who between them marked the occasion for what it was in the history of missionary enterprise. One of them was William Wilberforce's son, the Venerable Archdeacon, who received his ration of applause when he rose to speak from the platform because of his noble lineage and who was cheered again when he spoke grandly of the concepts which had brought them all together on this rousing day. Archdeacon Wilberforce reminded everyone that their purpose was to ensure 'that every ship laden with commerce might also bear the boon of everlasting life, that from no part of the earth should they receive only, without giving for the gold of the West and the spices from the East the more precious wealth – the more blessed frankincense of Christ their master'. Tremendous applause at that.

And among those fervent, patriotic, well-meaning, committed and slightly hysterical Christians, was a man who was destined much more than anyone else in Exeter Hall, in London, in the whole world, to exemplify the spirit which was now being proclaimed and released as a benison upon degraded Africa. Somewhere down in that audience, unremarked by the reporters covering the meeting, unnoticed by anyone at all, making no contribution to the proceedings, was a twenty-seven-year-old medical student from Charing Cross Hospital, who had come down from Scotland armed with a great deal of native tenacity and a very complex missionary instinct that was all his own. He was David Livingstone and he was very close to an ordination ceremony that would transform him into a Christian minister as well as a doctor of medicine. Before the year was out he would have sailed for Africa, to a lifetime's obsession of such heroic, such epic proportions, that alone he would do more to kill the slave trade and exalt the Christian missionary profession than all the glittering meetings of nobility, of bishops, of politicians and of enthusiastic well-wishers that might be held in Exeter Hall or anywhere else on the face of the earth. If this day's work marked the real beginning of the missionary success story, it was Livingstone who translated it into a fable.

There were many speeches and they all ran to considerable length, for it was a verbose age and these people had much righteous virtue and indignation to express. No more than three or four speeches had been made by one o'clock, at which point Prince Albert decided that he had done his royal duty, bowed to the assembly and left amidst further enthusiastic cheering from all parts of the hall. Fowell Buxton had made the longest speech by this time, a highly impassioned piece of oratory which struck precisely the emotional and horror-stricken note natural to this time when people discussed the plight of Africa.

What was the state of Africa, exclaimed Buxton. Why, it was one universal slaughterhouse, as was proved upon evidence that could not be disputed. What was its trade! A trade in the bodies of its inhabitants. (Cheers.) Its religion was human sacrifice. (Loud cheers.) Its trade swept off and mowed down multitudes every day in the year and every hour in the day. Multitudes, did he say! Why, thousands were destroyed in the nightly combustions which took place – thousands fell by day travelling the burning sands; and as to a slave-ship, it was impossible to describe, except in the words of Scripture, which said: 'A pestilence walketh upon the waters'; nay, the very shark knew the slave-ship to be a barque of blood, and expected from it his daily sustenance. (Loud cheers.) Buxton said that he and his companions in the crusade against slavery wanted peace for Africa. They wanted to establish industry, that industry which should till the land and out of the land extract a ransom for that unhappy country, that industry which would cultivate the land and by availing itself of the bounty of nature should transform the face of the country. They wanted commerce for that country, by which they should carry away the superfluities of Africa, and take to her the produce which the skill and machinery of this country afforded. They wanted, above all, to establish religion in Africa. (Loud cheers.)

Apart from the regular volleys of applause, one other thing interrupted the flow of Buxton's speech. He had been on his feet for half an hour or so when there appeared on the platform the person of Daniel O'Connell, Member of Parliament for Dublin. He was, of course, pressing the claims of Catholic Emancipation upon the House of Commons at this time, but he was a man who took a warm interest in the predicaments of many besides the Catholic Irish. Only a day or two before, he had moved two resolutions in the House, and while one was for an inquiry into the iniquity of Irish taxation, the other had been for an inquiry into the state of prison discipline. His arrival at Exeter Hall this day, therefore, was genuinely in the character of the man's broad sympathies. But Buxton and others were well aware of his principal reputation and of its possible detraction from their most pressing business. There were evidently O'Connell supporters in the hall and 'he was slightly cheered', until his presence became more extensively known, when the applause became general, and was met by some expressions of disapprobation, and cries of 'Chair, chair'. Buxton moved swiftly to prevent his meeting collapsing into an O'Connell demonstration, to forestall the risk that this occasion might be used obliquely in aid of the Irish Home Rule movement. He knew, he said, the honourable gentleman who had just entered, and he verily believed that a more strenuous advocate of the abolition of slavery did not exist; and he must take leave to say that if these interruptions were to be repeated or anything likely to injure the cause of Africa should arise, he pledged himself that Mr O'Connell would instantly retire. It was an acute manoeuvre and it succeeded in its basic purpose. From time to time, as the long meeting lumbered into the June afternoon, there were cries for O'Connell's voice to be heard, but he tactfully held his tongue. They were still calling for him to speak when the last single-minded society spokesman had finished; until the organist pulled out all the stops of his instrument and 'amidst its rolling thunder the disputants and the friends of the society quitted the scene of the action'.

Peel spoke, and only the Prince had been received more warmly, for hats and handkerchiefs were again flourished with enthusiasm as the baronet arose. He made a diffident remark about his own very small part in the work to which the society had pledged itself. He created a sensation when he read the contents of a document issued by the shipping companies, which logged commercial transactions earlier in 1840 on the East African coast. Sir Robert's extract reported how a Spanish brig containing nine hundred slaves had been hit by a storm off Mozambique, how six hundred of these wretches had been suffocated when the hatches were battened down, and how another one hundred had perished before the vessel could return to harbour. And why, asked Sir Robert icily, had the brig put about to the safety of Mozambique? Merely to obtain a fresh supply of cargo (renewed sensation). 'Until this country rescues Christianity and the character of the white people from the grievous infamy of these sins,' declared Peel, 'it never will be able to convince the black population of Africa of the moral superiority of their European fellow-men.' There were loud cheers from all parts of Exeter Hall when he said that.

But it was not Sir Robert Peel who concisely expressed a thought that was perhaps uppermost in more minds than would have cared to admit it openly. It was a Mr Gurney, a member of the society's committee, who followed him, who enlarged upon the commercial opportunities that might follow from cleansing Africa of all pagan practices. He paid his respects to the missionary instincts that were abroad that afternoon by suggesting that there was no worldly policy so sure as that which was based on Christianity. And then he began to consider the commercial opportunities that might follow from the Niger Expedition the Government now had in hand. He anticipated the day when they might obtain wool and indigo in great quantities from Africa. There were other points to be borne in mind which Mr Gurney deemed favourable. Africa was populous and the population was unsophisticated; might not artificial wants be created for them? Such wants would produce civilisation and increase commerce. And then, amid more cheers, Mr Gurney recollected that he was speaking on behalf of a cause which originated in a noble premise. The olive branch, he said, would do more to produce civilisation than the musket and the sword and they might anticipate that their exertions would be the means of hastening that day when Christianity would cover the earth as the waters covered the sea.

It was mid-afternoon by now, and but three of eight resolutions had been laboriously put to the meeting, seconded and carried unanimously, with only sporadic cries for O'Connell to impede their progress. Fowell Buxton, however, made his own interruption as Mr Gurney sat down. He had, he said, just received a letter from Buckingham House, informing him that Prince Albert had subscribed £105 to the society's funds and had also directed that his name be put down as an annual subscriber of £10. Not only did Mr Buxton have this princely sum to report; other donations had also been promised since the day's proceedings began. The Duke of Northumberland had offered £50, the Bishop of London £25, the Bishop of Lincoln £20, the Primate of Ireland £25. Lord Ripon (who since the Prince's departure had been sitting as chairman of the meeting) had offered £50. Anyone wishing to add to these donations would be warmly received in the committee room and at the bottom of the stairs.

The remnant of the afternoon dragged on, with Mr Langdale, the Earl of Chichester, Lord Ashley, the Rev. Mr Clayton and the Rev. J. W. Cunningham, following each other laboriously on the platform. Nothing that anyone had to say now was remotely original, and it is scarcely surprising that the shouts for Daniel O'Connell became ever more insistent in the last weary half hour. Indeed, there was a sense in which every speech made since Buxton's had been superfluous. For he had summarised almost completely in one minute, every sentiment that was so earnestly repeated in Exeter Hall that packed and ponderous summer's day. He had even capped it with a verse that went closer, maybe, to the heart of the matter than he could have dreamed of at the time.

Buxton had not forgotten, he said, the military triumphs of the British nation, but there was now open to it a road to glory more illustrious, noble and pure than the battles of Waterloo or Trafalgar had opened. 'To arrest the destruction of mankind, to throw a blessing upon a continent now in ruins, to give civilisation and to spread the mild truths of the Gospel over a region in comparison with which the British empire was but a speck upon the ocean, was a higher and nobler road, and his desire and prayer was that Her Majesty might tread it (cheers) and that, crowned with every other blessing, she might

> 'Shine the leader of applauding nations,
> To scatter happiness and peace around her,
> To bid the prostrate captive rise and live,
> To see new cities tower at her command,
> And blasted nations flourish in her smile.'

This was a text that was to inspire the missionary enterprise for a hundred years to come. It was to drive these men and women of God across Africa in the face of hardship, hostility and indifference, almost as much as any divine injunction extracted from the New Testament.

2

TO CONVERT THE HEATHEN

It had taken a long time for the missionary movement to reach a point at which it could rely upon the most distinguished patronage in the land. The Exeter Hall meeting was the culmination, in Britain, of a half century's fairly isolated commitment to an ideal. And even before that quite remarkable last decade of the eighteenth century, which had seen the foundation of the Baptist Missionary Society, the London Missionary Society and the Church Missionary Society, one after the other, there had been a long and slow development of instinct before the moment of commitment.

These three were all Protestant organisations, like similar missionary bodies that were to follow them on the continent of Europe and in North America; they were, moreover, Protestants with a profound belief in a literal interpretation of the Bible and a deep distrust of institutional additions to the Word of God, as represented most blatantly by the Church of Rome. True, the Anglicans of the Church Missionary Society had their own episcopal claims to defend, and in this they formed an uncomfortable bridge between fundamental Protestantism and red-blooded Catholicism. Even though it was possible for them to hobnob with Catholics on an anti-slavery platform by 1840, they still retained an inbred suspicion of Papacy and anything that seemed to make concessions in that direction, as the Anglo-Catholic wing of their own Church was now beginning to do.

The missionary zeal of these Protestants, which was codified by the events of the 1790s, was to some extent a logical progression in the history of Christianity and, in particular, a natural stage in the development of Protestant Christianity. Their forefathers had broken away from Rome, there had been a long period of struggle throughout Europe for survival, followed by an equally long period of consolidation. It is scarcely surprising that not until almost the end of the eighteenth century were they confident enough of their own security, strong enough in their self-assurance, to re-examine their fundamental texts and take heed of the literal injunction to go out into all the world and preach the Gospel to every creature.

In England there were purely local factors which tended to fortify their zeal. The period after the English Restoration had vitiated the religious life of the country to the extent that Bishop Joseph Butler, in 1726, refused the Archbishopric of Canterbury because he thought the decline in the Church of England was so great that it was too late to be saved. The Protestant reforming zeal which was about to break in a torrent of righteousness was but a natural reaction to this sorry state of affairs.

Elsewhere, the Protestants had gone forth to proselytise the heathen in only a tentative way. In 1732 four missionaries of the Moravian Church of the Brethren had set out from Germany to live among Negroes in the Dutch West Indies and among Eskimos in Greenland. Another Moravian, George Schmidt, was despatched by the Dutch Reformed Church in Amsterdam to the Cape of Good Hope in 1737, shortly after his release from a German prison, where he had spent six years as a penalty for his Protestantism. Christianity had been introduced to South Africa with the arrival of Jan van Riebeck and his 126 followers, in 1652, in the first permanent colony of the Dutch East India Company. These were pious Dutchmen who were eventually to father bigoted Boers and it was inevitable that, although they certainly saw nothing inconsistent in their profession of Christianity and their possession of slaves, they should wish these as far as possible to be Christianised slaves. Van Riebeck noted in his log how the Ziekentrooster (Comforter of the Sick) proposed to run a school for juvenile slaves who were not yet strong enough for hard work. 'In order to animate the said slaves diligently to attend to be instructed in learning Christian prayer,' he wrote, 'he has been ordered at the end of the lesson to give each slave a quid of tobacco and a nip of brandy.'

George Schmidt was not a welcome intruder into this situation, in spite of his credentials from Amsterdam. There were already Dutch clergy in the settlement at the Cape, acting as chaplains to their own people, and they were much offended when they saw Schmidt infringing what they took to be their exclusive rights. He was making progress with the Hottentots, in spite of his inability to master their language with its manifold clicks and other alien sounds. Worse, he was starting to baptise them. The Dutch clergy believed they alone had the authority to administer sacraments and this sturdy Moravian refused to hand over his converts to them for the actual rite of baptism. So they laid charges against him in Amsterdam, one of which mentioned heresy, and Amsterdam replied with a blank condemnation of Schmidt's work, and the Moravian returned to Europe in 1744 a broken man.

The British themselves had dabbled in a kind of missionary activity. In 1648, their elected representatives recorded in their official journal that 'the Commons of England assembled in Parliament, having received intelligence that the heathens of New England are beginning to call upon the name of the Lord, feel bound to assist in this work'. Thus the Society for the Propagation of the Gospel in New England was established, and it was very largely Oliver Cromwell's doing. It was to concentrate its efforts eventually not only in New England but also among the rising colonies in the West Indies, just as a sister body, the Society for Promoting Christian Knowledge, was within a few years to spend itself largely on work in India. The SPG's chief concern was to maintain Christian standards among the European colonists across the Atlantic. These were generally so fragile that when John Wesley went to Georgia on behalf of the society he found that he had to abandon his cherished plan of preaching to the Indians and concentrate instead on the white settlers of Savannah.

Just once, in this period, the British made an attempt to reach the African on his home ground. A young Fellow of Christ's College, Cambridge, had resigned a curacy in England to work for the SPG in New Jersey. This was Thomas Thompson, who spent five years working among Negro slaves on the plantations there and then asked the society if it would send him to Guinea 'to make a trial with the Natives and see what hopes there would be of introducing them to the Christian religion'. His letter to the society, in which he applied for the transfer, expresses precisely the tone of missionary zeal that was soon to become prevalent among many men of burning piety in Britain. 'In an ordinary way,' wrote Thompson, 'one Labourer can do but little yet . . . no Doubt it must be of divine Grace that the Conversion of that people is wrought, whether it be by many or by few; but if ever a Church is founded among them, some Body must lay the first Stone . . . and should I be prevented in my Intention, God only knows how long it may be before any other Person will take the same Resolution.' So in 1751 the SPG despatched him to the Gold

Coast at a salary of £70 a year and at Cape Coast* he settled down to turn Africans into Christians.

Thompson also found himself trying to make spiritual inroads into the small settlement of European traders there, where the laxity traditional to colonies without a supervising man of God was evident. The going was hard. Thompson discovered that the Africans would not assemble to hear his teaching more than once a week and some demanded a tot of liquor as the price of their attendance.

After four years Thompson left for England, a sick man, but not before he had sent three Negro lads ahead of him for education. They were put to school in London where, within seven weeks, 'one of them could say the Lord's Prayer and the Apostles' Creed and the other two answered well'. A few years later one had perished of consumption, a second had died in the madhouse. But the third, Philip Quaque, survived to become the SPG's 'Missionary School Master and Catechist to the Negroes on the Gold Coast'. And Thomas Thompson, his work in the mission field concluded, wrote a tract entitled *The African Trade for Negro Slaves shown to be consistent with the Principles of Humanity and with the Laws of Revealed Religion.*

This seems a shocking hypocrisy to twentieth-century man; it was soon to become repellent to men of sensitive piety in that age. But until the last half of the eighteenth century it was but the way of the world at large. In spite of a succession of Popes who castigated slavery and slave ownership, the Catholics who sailed with Henry the Navigator's captains around Africa in the fifteenth century, who established various Portuguese colonies there (and whose missionaries had lost heart and turned to more apparently fruitful fields in the New World by the start of the nineteenth century), had also maintained the right of the white man to possess and use Negro slaves. A Jesuit monastery in Loanda in the sixteenth century was rumoured to be endowed with 12,000 slaves; and when the slave trade was developed between Angola and Brazil, the Bishop would sit on his throne by the quayside, blessing each cargo as it went aboard, and promising each member of it happier times in the eternal life to come. When William Hawkins of Plymouth, father of the more famous Sir John, went slaving to Sierra Leone in 1562, the Christian Queen Elizabeth of England saw nothing incongruous in lending him one of her own ships, the name of which was *Jesus.*

The turning of the tide against the slave trade can first be detected in a protest recorded by a group of Quakers at Germantown, Pennsylvania,

* Modern Accra.

in 1688. It was to be repeated by other groups of American Friends periodically throughout the eighteenth century. But it was in England in 1772 that the first significant blow against the traders was struck by the Chief Justice, Lord Mansfield, in a judgment which thenceforth prohibited the forcible detention of a slave in England. From that moment, the abolitionists of Britain began to organise a lobby whose aim was to banish slavery wherever it might be found and in whatever form. They were soon deeply involved in a plan to found an African settlement for freed slaves in Sierra Leone. This was a by-product of the Mansfield judgment, for London was now the wasteland of many destitute Negroes, who had been cast adrift by their old masters, who were free men, but who were without the means for survival. A Committee for Relieving the Black Poor was set up, the Government was persuaded of its responsibility to help, and boatloads of these destitutes were shipped off to West Africa to live in a kind of liberty at last.

The men most committed to the abolition lobby, the men who made it work, were without exception Evangelical Christians with an extraordinary sense of purpose. One of them was Granville Sharpe, whose study of the law on relations between master and slave had led to the test case brought before Lord Mansfield. Another was Zachary Macaulay, father of Thomas Babington Macaulay, who returned from several years in Jamaica disgusted with what he had seen of slavery there, and who became the first Governor of Sierra Leone. Another was Henry Thornton, a wealthy banker, who was in the habit of donating six-sevenths of his income to the needy. The most famous of all was William Wilberforce, Anglican admirer of Methodism and friend of William Pitt, who was to spend more than half his life battling for the freedom of black slaves. The eventual triumph of these men, shared by successors like Fowell Buxton, was much more in the nature of a long siege than a series of fixed battles. Under Wilberforce's guidance, one resolution after another was to be moved in the House of Commons, meeting with no success until 1807, when the British interest in the slave trade was officially ended. Yet it was not until 1834 that slavery ceased to exist in Britain's dominions; and still there were to be decades spent in fighting slavery in Africa.

There were people of several denominations involved in the abolition lobby, none more than Quakers, but its backbone was constructed out of the Clapham Sect. These Anglicans acquired their name because they circulated round the parish church of Clapham, whose rector, John Venn, had come south from the evangelical belt of the Yorkshire woollen manufacturing towns, full of the fundamentalist fervour that he had learned from his celebrated father, the Rev. Henry Venn.* Without exception they were soon to be as dedicated to the ideals of the missionary movement as much as to the anti-slavery crusade; indeed, the two things were quite obviously indistinguishable in their eyes. It was from their ranks that the Church Missionary Society of the Anglican Evangelical wing arose, which was eventually to become the most powerful, the most widespread and the wealthiest missionary body in the world. In point of time, however, they were relatively slow off the mark.

The founding fathers of the modern missionary movement were English Baptists. Apart from the general spirit of those Protestant times, a number of other influences caused them to act when they did. An American Congregational minister called Jonathan Edwards, of Northampton, Massachusetts, had written in 1747 a tract entitled *An humble attempt to promote explicit agreement and visible union of God's people in extraordinary prayer for the revival of religion and the advancement of Christ's Kingdom on earth.* Its argument was as general and slightly vague as its rambling title suggests, but when it fell into the hands of English Baptists of the Northamptonshire Association, it stimulated them to set aside one day a month, from 1784 onwards, for prayer and divine guidance on the advancement of Christianity. Gradually there emerged from this English group the dominating personality of William Carey.

Carey was a man of extraordinary talents, especially considering his background. His father was a weaver-cum-schoolmaster, and he himself was a shoemaker, but it is said that he could speak Latin, Hebrew, Greek and Dutch fluently by the time he was fifteen. At about the time that he and the other Northamptonshire Baptists were digesting the Edwards tract, England was engrossed in the more picturesque topic of Captain Cook and the voyages he had recently made round the Pacific and down to Antarctica. A totally new world, half savage, half Arcadian, had just been opened up by the great navigator, and its exotic qualities had been recorded by William Hodges and other artists who had travelled with Cook. Carey seems to have been as susceptible as any of his fellow-countrymen to the appeal of the South Seas and its inhabitants, but in his case it clearly suggested a field in which the philosophy aired by Jonathan Edwards might partly be exercised. In 1786 Carey submitted to his local Baptist preachers' conference, as a subject for discussion, 'Whether the commandment given to the Apostles to teach all nations in all the world

* John Venn's son, the second Henry Venn, was to be one of the great architects of the Church Missionary Society, serving as its secretary from 1842 to 1872.

must not be recognised as binding on us also, since the great promise still follows it?' For the moment his missionary instinct was out of place. The president of the conference told this young man to shut up and sit down for 'Nothing certainly can come to pass in this matter before a new Pentecost, accompanied by a new gift of miracles and tongues, promises success to the commission of Christ as in the beginning'.

So Carey sat down and shut up for the time being, but privately began to compose his own tract, which was published in 1792 under the heading *An Enquiry into the Obligations of Christians to use means for the Conversion of the Heathens*. It started from the basic argument that Christians were bound to propagate the Gospel, not out of charity or mercy, but from an obligation to God and their fellow-men. It reviewed the work done as missionaries by the Apostles and St Paul. Then it turned to the present state of God's creation. Carey had drawn up a long table of every known country in the world, and its religious condition, together with rudimentary knowledge of its size and population. Thus, under Africa, he noted that Abyssinia was nine hundred miles long, eight hundred miles wide, inhabited by 5,800,000 people, most of whom were Armenian Christians. 'Negroland' (and he did not specify just where this area came on the map of Africa) was 2,200 miles long, 840 miles wide, with eighteen million people, all of them Pagans; so were the inhabitants of the Congo and several other lands. 'This, as nearly as I can obtain information, is the state of the world,' wrote Carey. 'The inhabitants of the world according to this calculation amount to about seven hundred and thirty-one millions; four hundred and twenty millions of whom are still in Pagan darkness, an hundred and thirty millions the followers of Mahomet, an hundred millions catholics, forty-four millions protestants, thirty millions of the Greek and Armenian Churches, and perhaps seven millions of Jews.' It must, he thought, strike every considerate mind what a vast proportion of the sons of Adam there were who remained yet in the most deplorable state of heathen darkness, without any means of knowing the true God except what was afforded them by the works of nature. 'In many of these parts also they are cannibals, feeding upon the flesh of their slain enemies, with the greatest brutality and eagerness.'

At least Carey was prepared to give these savages the benefit of any doubt that might be going about their savage condition. 'Barbarous as these poor heathen are, they appear to be as capable of knowledge as we are; and in many places, at least, have discovered uncommon genius and tractableness; and I greatly question whether most of the barbarities practised by them, have not originated in some real or supposed affront and are therefore, more properly, acts of self-defence, than proofs of inhuman and bloodthirsty dispositions.' Carey was rather less forbearing about some of his fellow-Christians. 'There are Christians, so-called, of the greek and armenian churches' – carefully distinguished by no capital letters – 'in all the mahometan countries; but they are, if possible, more ignorant and vicious than the mahometans themselves . . . Papists also are in general ignorant of divine things and very vicious. Nor do the bulk of the Church of England much exceed them, either in knowledge or holiness; and many errors and much looseness of conduct are to be found among Dissenters of all denominations . . . the face of most Christian countries presents a dreadful scene of ignorance, hypocrisy and profligacy.'

In the face of crying need on all sides, Carey's readers might have been forgiven for wondering just where the missionary front ought to be opened up. Carey himself was in no doubt that, hapless as some other Christians might be, they would mostly have to manage as best they could while missionaries spent themselves on the heathen, bringing them civilisation and making them useful members of society. Carefully he considered what this might mean in practical terms. It would evidently be impossible, in the South Seas, Africa or elsewhere, to obtain European food, but there seemed no reason why the missionaries should not eat as the natives did. He took the view that it would be best if missionary parties consisted of two married men, accompanied by two or more other Christian families who should be wholly employed in providing necessities of life for them. One other obstacle he dismissed rather breezily, even for a man who had been a prodigious linguist in his adolescence. 'As to learning their languages,' said Carey, 'it is well known to require no extraordinary talents to learn, in the space of a year, or two at most, the language of any people upon earth.' This was almost the only false assumption he made about the manner of man he was proposing for the Lord's service among the heathen. The missionaries, he observed, must be men of great piety, prudence, courage and forbearance, of undoubted orthodoxy in their sentiments. They must be willing to leave all the comforts of life behind them and to encounter all the hardships of a torrid or a frigid climate, an uncomfortable manner of living and every inconvenience that could attend their undertaking. Clothing, a few knives, powder and shot, fishing tackle and the articles of husbandry must be provided for them. They must be very careful not to resent injuries which might be offered to them, nor to think highly of themselves, so as to despise the poor heathen and by these means to lay a foundation for their resentment or rejection of the Gospel.

It was, basically, an intelligent appraisal of a new form of Christian vocation, full of common sense and care. But its purpose soared high above any mundane needs to live off the land like a native and avoid being too sensitive to insults. 'What a heaven will it be,' declared the Northamptonshire shoemaker, 'to see the many myriads of poor heathens, of Britons amongst the rest, who by their labours have been brought to the knowledge of God. Surely a crown of rejoicing like this is worth aspiring to? Surely it is worth while to lay ourselves out with all our might, in promoting the cause and kingdom of Christ?'

This time no one told Carey to shut up and sit down. Instead, he was encouraged to preach sermons on his missionary theme, to congregations who were urged to open subscriptions at 1d. a week per person for the support of missions; individuals were also asked to tithe their incomes for the same purpose. On 2 October 1792 a dozen men met in the back parlour of the Widow Beeby Wallis's house in Kettering, signed seven resolutions and appointed a committee to regulate the affairs of the new Baptist Missionary Society. Within six months, Carey, accompanied by his four sons and his psychotic wife, together with a small group of other Baptists, had sailed from London aboard a Danish Indiaman. By the end of 1793 they had established themselves in the Danish settlement of Serampore, a few miles up the Hooghly river above Calcutta. The modern missionary movement had begun.

Carey, in fact, had a distant hand in the second British missionary foundation. It was commonplace in those days for Protestants of various sects throughout Europe and North America to maintain contact with each other; it was a natural reflex, if nothing else, springing from their common suspicion of the Catholic Church. Soon after the Northamptonshire Baptist had settled down in India he entered into correspondence with a Dr Ryland of Bristol. Ryland, together with friends from a number of Protestant connections, began to meet in 1794 to consider the need for foreign missions and one of these, David Bogue, a Congregational minister, published an article directed at all 'Christian Brethren'. 'A survey of the state of the world,' it said, 'presents to us more than one-half of the human race destitute of the knowledge of the Gospel, and sitting in darkness and in the shadow of death. Their deplorable condition it is utterly impossible for words to describe ...'

At almost the same time a book was published by Melville Horne, the Anglican chaplain of the colony in Sierra Leone, asking for missionary service, and it was well reviewed in the *Evangelical Magazine* and elsewhere. A group of Protestant ministers – Congregationalists, Evangelical Anglicans, Presbyterians and Methodists among them – began to meet regularly at the Castle and Falcon public house in Aldersgate, London, whose owner, Mr Dupont, was a regular attender at the Spa Fields Chapel and the Moorfields Tabernacle. On 17 February 1795 the thirty-four men who had gathered at the Castle and Falcon declared that they were pledged to 'an extensive and regularly organised society, to consist of Evangelical ministers and lay brethren of all denominations ... for promoting the great work of introducing the Gospel and its ordinances to heathen and other unenlightened countries ...' The actual foundation meeting of the new body had to wait until September, when the Castle and Falcon's clientele was swollen for the occasion by 'a synod of Burgher Seceders from Scotland'. It was decided to call the new foundation the Missionary Society, though within a few years this was to be changed to the London Missionary Society. Members had to subscribe one guinea or more a year or else they had to pay a lump sum of £10.

Like Carey, these people were also acting under the immediate influence of Captain Cook's voyages and their first thought for a field of work was the South Seas. The rules they had drawn up for the examination of missionaries stated in part that 'Godly men who understand the mechanic arts may be of signal use to this undertaking as missionaries, especially in the South Sea Islands and other uncivilised parts of the world'. They were not averse to recruiting ministers of religion, by any means, but ministers of religion did not seem to be over-enthusiastic about leaving their home congregations. There may well have been a certain amount of rationalising in David Bogue's mind when he wrote, of his plan for the training of missionaries, that 'as our design is not to form mathematicians, philosophers or even linguists, it would be unwise to appropriate a greater proportion of their limited term to these inquiries'. And a friend of his, Dr Bennett, was within a year or two observing that 'There have not ceased to be men of influence in the society who sincerely think that the best education for missionaries is none at all; and the next best, that which consists in teaching them to make wheelbarrows, and plant turnips, rendering them useful mechanics and agriculturists, rather than good divines or preachers'.

The first consignment of missionaries from the society was very well loaded in favour of men who understood the mechanic arts. In 1796 the vessel *Duff* sailed for Tahiti with thirty representatives of the Missionary Society aboard, and with a special flag at its mast bearing the peaceful device of a fluttering dove. There were, to be sure, four ministers on the passenger list, but these apart the missionaries included six carpenters, two shoemakers, two bricklayers, two weavers, two tailors, a shopkeeper, a harness maker, a gentleman's servant, a gardener, a surgeon, a blacksmith, a cooper, a butcher, a cotton manufacturer, a hatter, a draper and a cabinet maker.

The voyage to Arcadia was subject to strains from the outset. Some of the missionaries aboard 'entertained a suspicion that Brother Jefferson and Brother Cock were not quite sound in their religious principles. Knowing that both of them had been members of Armenian Societies, they were fearful that the old leaven had not been thoroughly purged out.' Poor Brothers Jefferson and Cock were forthwith excommunicated by their fellows after cross-examination, though they were graciously readmitted to 'the Church of Christ on board the *Duff*' somewhat later. The stumbling block appears to have been a passage in St Paul's Epistle to the Romans, with its tricky propositions about predestination. At which 'Brother Cock, not unwisely, asserted that the interpretation of the passage was too difficult for him!'

There were greater and graver hazards ahead. One of the first things the missionaries decided, upon arriving in Tahiti, was that to marry a heathen woman was directly contrary to the Word of God. Within a month or two brave Mr Lewis, one of the ministers, stated that it was his fixed determination to marry a native; and was promptly excommunicated. Some time later Mr Broomhall, the harness maker, 'began to act in a way that aroused first the fears and then the anxious sympathy of his colleagues', and finally announced that he had ceased to believe in the immortality of the soul and declined to submit any longer to the restraints of the Gospel; he too, naturally enough, took a native woman as wife.

Writing a century later, the historian of the LMS was to be found attempting to produce a reasonable excuse for the apparently curious anathema placed by these first missionaries upon the native women of the South Seas. 'It was not,' he wrote, 'a case of a missionary marrying a native convert, but of a Christian man uniting himself to a heathen woman, and that on an island where the testimony of the missionaries, after a residence of eighteen months, was that in all probability not one single female on the island over ten or twelve years of age had escaped pollution.' Venereal disease, introduced by whalers and Cook's seamen, was not the only factor weighing against the success of that maiden voyage. Soon after arriving, a few of these godly Europeans had been beaten and stripped by the native populace.

No one in England was to know of this by the time the *Duff* returned in July 1798, after a voyage home by way of Canton. The news that it had successfully landed its missionaries was enough to insure a second expedition in the same vessel, but this was a total disaster. The *Duff* was first of all captured by a French privateer cruising off the South American coast. With its prize, the Frenchman was itself captured by a Portuguese fleet and everyone aboard both privateer and *Duff* was conveyed to Lisbon. It took some time for the English among them to make their way laboriously back to London, 'the great majority of the missionaries reasoning, as imperfectly educated men not unnaturally might in such circumstances, that God meant in this way to teach them that it was not His will for them to go to Tahiti'. And by then, in Tahiti itself, twenty out of the thirty men first deposited there, had abandoned their mission 'under circumstances that did them little credit'.

Nor was there more encouraging news from the inaugural Missionary Society voyage to Africa. Six men had sailed in the *Calypso* for Sierra Leone at the end of 1797 and even before they weighed anchor in the Thames there had been theological disputes between them, so serious that the directors of the society had planned to go ahead to Falmouth and intercept the *Calypso* to smooth things out. But bad weather had prevented the vessel from putting into Falmouth, the disputes continued and worsened all the way to West Africa, and within six months the infant mission was in ruins, with three men dead of fever and a fourth recalled to England for indiscipline.

By this time, the missionary instinct was stirring in the Church of England. Since 1783 an Eclectic Society of clergy and laymen had been meeting once a fortnight in London to discuss topics of Christian ethic and principle. It was three years before a missionary subject crossed their minds; but in 1786 they collectively wondered 'What is the best method of planting and propagating the Gospel in Botany Bay?' – a place they had recently become aware of as a result of Captain Cook. After another three years they were to be found considering 'What is the best method of propagating the Gospel in the East Indies?' Missions then vanished from their agenda until 1796, by which time both the Baptists and the interdenominational Evangelicals had founded their societies. These eclectic Anglicans now addressed themselves to the proposition 'With what propriety and in what mode should a Mission be attempted to the Heathen from the Established Church?' The title of their debate suggests a degree of caution which they were certainly feeling. Both the SPG and the SPCK, after all, had a missionary intent, though it was not exclusively directed at any heathen; and both these bodies were parts of the Church of England. The eclectic gentlemen had no wish to be the source of jealous frictions within their own Church. They were, moreover, well aware that it would be impossible to create a viable force of any description within the Church unless it had the support of the bishops. And Anglican bishops of the time were not given to blessing easily the bright ideas of men whose role in the Established Church was subordinate to their own. There were other reasons for a tentative approach to the subject. Some of the group's members doubted the possibility of obtaining suitable men for such spiritually and physically hazardous work, or urged the overriding claims of the Church at home, which clearly had plenty of missionary work to undertake among the poor if it wanted. And so, for yet another three years, these men considered privately and talked together but did not actually do anything.

On 12 April 1799, however, in the stimulating atmosphere of the Castle and Falcon public house, where other pious men had taken heart before them, they acted. John Venn was in the chair and sixteen of the clergy together with nine laymen of the Church of England were with him to inaugurate what they immediately called the Society for Missions to Africa and the East, though by 1812 this had been translated into the Church Missionary Society for Africa and the East. They passed four resolutions at that first meeting, and the second of these said that 'as it appears from the printed reports of the societies for Propagating the Gospel and for Promoting Christian Knowledge that those societies confine their labours to the British plantations in America and to the West Indies, there seems to be still wanting in the Established Church a society for sending missionaries to the continent of Africa, or the other parts of the heathen world'.

The priority these men gave to Africa can be explained by the fact that most of them were involved in the anti-slavery lobby, as their missionary predecessors of the BMS and the LMS were not. There was also far less of an artisan flavour to the origins of the CMS than there was in either of the two earlier foundations. These were mostly middle-class men of substance and conscience, and of the twenty-four people who sat on the first CMS committee, thirteen were clergymen of the Established Church, three were merchants and the others included a solicitor, an upholsterer, a skinner, a banker, a surgeon, a tea broker, a silk merchant and even a sculptor (the Royal Academician John Bacon). A number of them were shareholders in the Sierra Leone Company which had been set up to colonise West Africa.

John Venn, the first secretary of the CMS, soon formulated what manner of men the society was seeking. The missionary, he wrote, 'is one who, like Enoch, walks with God, and derives from constant communion with Him a portion of the Divine likeness. Dead to the usual pursuits of the world, his affections are fixed upon things above, where Christ sitteth at the right hand of God. He is not influenced by the love of fame and distinction, the desire of wealth or the love of ease and self-indulgence. Deeply affected by the sinful and ruined state of mankind, especially of the Heathen, he devotes his life, with all its faculties, to promote their salvation.' This was a prescription for a Christian monk or a martyr, and the early missionaries to some extent saw themselves as a self-sacrificial cross between the two, with a distinct emphasis upon the second.

There was to be much more of a struggle ahead than these founding fathers imagined in their moment of dedication to their purpose. But on the threshold of a new century a floodgate of proselytising righteousness was slowly and cumbersomely being cranked open. Between 1792 and 1835, throughout Europe and North America, more than a score of missionary societies appeared and even more came later. Berlin, Paris, Leipzig and Bremen supplied their quota of foundations; so did the Swedes, the Norwegians and the Rhinelanders. Across the Atlantic the American Board of Commissioners for Foreign Missions was born in 1810, the General Missionary Convention of the Baptist Denomination in 1814, and three other organisations followed before 1820.

And from the outset almost everyone looked to Sierra Leone, as to a beacon in a dark night, from which illumination might spread across a world full of heathens.

3
THE GERMAN SALVATION

The enthusiasm of the missionary societies was all very well, but for a start it was almost all they had to offer the heathen of Africa; and this was especially so in the case of the CMS. One of the first things those careful men did was to send a deputation to Lambeth Palace, to wait on the Archbishop of Canterbury, Dr Moore, and solicit his approval. It consisted of Venn, Wilberforce and Charles Grant, who was a Member of Parliament as well as a director of the powerful East India Company. They were ambushed and kept waiting by the archiepiscopal chaplains and it was a couple of months before His Grace consented to see Wilberforce alone; and even then he did nothing but take note of the reformer's news. It was to be another full twelve months before Wilberforce was allowed a second meeting, what time the Archbishop was said to have been consulting the other bishops of the Church of England. And even then the news for the CMS was that 'His Grace regretted that he could not with propriety at once express his full concurrence and approbation of an endeavour in behalf of an object he had deeply at heart'. It was to be 1815 before any bishop of the Anglicans would have any official connection with their missionary body.

Nor were the clergymen lower down the class-conscious ranks of the Church more eager to commit themselves to this new work of God's. The members of the committee wrote round the land to all the parsons of their collective acquaintance, but not one replied with much hope of producing likely candidates for missionary work. Mr Jones of Crediton knew of one young shopman, 'a staunch episcopalian, somewhat contemptuous of Dissenters, and aiming at ordination', but doubted if he would do. Mr Fawcett of Carlisle knew two men who were apparently suited but asked 'Could it be right to break the hearts of their mothers?' Mr Dikes of Hull knew no one. Mr Powley of Dewsbury knew no one. Mr Vaughan of Bristol knew no one. Dr Hawker of Plymouth protested against the sending of laymen at all, even if they could be found. It looked as if they would have to be found, given the clergy's unwillingness to offer themselves to Africa. One of the few who gave the CMS committee even a glimmer of hope that here they might have a recruit, was a bright young curate from Shropshire, with hopes of an early preferment from a position worth £200 a year. He believed that he might be prepared to consider a missionary vocation in Africa if the inducements were substantial enough; an income, say, of at least £700 a year 'in order to do missionary work effectively'. The committee declined his offer.

Salvation came to the Church of England from Germany. A pious Lutheran, the Baron von Schirnding, had been much stimulated by news of British missionary foundations, particularly of the LMS. He had persuaded 'Father' Janicke, preacher at the Bohemian Church in Berlin, to start a school which would train missionaries who might be placed at the disposal of any society that needed them. Two of the Berlin students, Melchior Renner of Württemberg and Peter Hartwig, a Prussian, were soon offered to the CMS and were gratefully accepted. They arrived in London at the end of 1802 and when they met the committee it was discovered that none of the Englishmen could speak German, that the two Germans had not a word of English between them. A Dr Steinkopf was summoned to act as interpreter and the two newcomers were sent to lodge at Clapham while they learned a little of the missionary language. They acquired enough, over the next twelve months, for Hartwig to court and then marry Sarah Windsor, who was governess to the Venn family. Yet on the occasion of the official Valedictory Dismissal to them, on the eve of their departure to West Africa, the two young Germans were still so stumbling in English that they felt unable to reply to the farewell speech; so they presented a letter expressing their sentiments instead. The proposal was that they should found the nucleus of a Christian community of both sexes, thereby 'exhibiting to the Natives the practical influence of Christianity in regulating the tempers and the life, and in thus increasing the domestic felicity'. The venture was only partly successful. Renner was eventually to serve the CMS in Africa for seventeen years. But Hartwig abandoned his mission not long after his arrival and became a slave trader: whereupon his wife left him and came home.

The result of this setback was that the CMS resolved that no one should be sent out again until he had been fully trained under the eyes of the committee. A seminary was started in Buckinghamshire, a very rudimentary affair, with a former chaplain from Sierra Leone as Rector and a country parson, the Rev. Thomas Scott, a founding member of the CMS, charged with teaching Arabic and Susoo (a West African language); though he did not, in fact, know a word of either. A second party of Germans arrived in time for the opening of the Bledlow school in 1806.

The German strain in the CMS was growing. To the Berlin Seminary there was now added a similar forcing house for missionaries, based at Basel in Switzerland. Its inspiration was a journal called *Gatherings for Lovers of Christian Truths*, which had been started by Augustus Urlsperger, the Dean of Augsburg, and which carried much news of the infant missionary societies of England throughout the Continent. It was a short step from producing propaganda to turning out propagandists and the forcing house at Basel was eventually to evolve into an independent missionary society in its own right. But by 1822 it had already produced eighty-eight pupils for the benefit of the English CMS alone. And by the time 'Father' Janicke died in 1827, the Berlin Seminary had turned out eighty missionaries for work on behalf of Dutch and British societies, its connection with the English having become so firm by then that Baron von Schirnding had been made a Continental director of the LMS.

Such was the flow of Germans into the ranks of British societies, such was the dearth of local manpower willing and able to give itself to God's work among the heathen, that there were Englishmen close to despair at the shortage of divine grace so evidently hampering their finest expectations. It was bad enough to suffer guilt feelings about the wrongs done by Europeans and particularly by Britons to Africans. The guilt was clearly there in the instructions of the CMS to Renner and Hartwig, with its assertion that 'the British nation is now, and has long been, most deeply criminal. We desire, therefore, while we pray and labour for the removal of this evil, to make Western Africa the best remuneration in our power for its manifold wrongs.' It was a torture, on top of this admission, to discover that none of the guilty was ready to make the reparation.

And so, in 1811 Melville Horne preached a frenzied sermon designed to shame the British into a missionary instinct. This leading Evangelical was appalled to find that Germany was 'advancing with the sacred Cross of Christ and reviving the drooping zeal of the Church of England . . . Where are our own ministers?' he asked. 'What happy peculiarity is there in the air of Germany?' he wondered. 'What food is it that nourishes these pious Lutherans? I cannot allow these good men to stand in our place. Let us assert our own dignity and that of the Church to which we belong.' Dignified or not, Melville Horne asserted something most vehemently. 'Christian matrons!' he cried, 'from whose endeared and endearing lips we first heard of the wondrous Babe of Bethlehem, and were taught to bend our knee to Jesus – ye who first taught these eagles how to soar, will ye now check their flight in the midst of heaven?... what more laudable ambition can inspire you than a desire to be Mothers of the Missionaries, Confessors and Martyrs of Jesus? Generations unborn shall call you blessed. The Churches of Asia and Africa, when they make grateful mention of their founders, will say "Blessed be the wombs which bare them, and the breasts which they have sucked!" Ye Wives, also, learn to rejoice at the sound of battle. Rouse the slumbering courage of your soldiers to the field and think no place so safe, so honoured, as the Camp of Jesus. Tell the missionary story to your little ones, until their young hearts burn, and in the spirit of those innocents who shouted Hosanna to their lowly King, they cry "Shall not we also be Missionaries of Jesus Christ?"'

Long after the Christian matrons of England had started to produce good English missionaries, there were still Germans going off to Africa on behalf of the CMS. Two of the most famous, men who spent their lives in the service of an alien Church, were J. Lewis Krapf and Johannes Rebmann, products of the Basel Seminary, who were sent off to East Africa when the CMS started work there in the 1830s. Krapf was a farmer's son whose life was charted for him by a series of coincidences in his childhood. He had been badly beaten by a neighbour at the age of eleven and for the next six months was ill in bed, a convalescence in which 'my thoughts dwelt much upon eternity; and the reading of the Bible and devotional books became my delight'.

Krapf discovered a flair for languages at school, and when he was in the lowest form his father bought him an atlas. He at once experienced the thrill of cartography and the pull of the unknown horizon. By the time he was fourteen there was a serious discussion in the Krapf household about a future for young Lewis as a sea captain, but his father could not afford the fees of a nautical college. This, said Krapf, years later, was a great disappointment. 'Neither law nor physic were to my mind; divinity was less objectionable; but I dreaded the learning of Hebrew, with its repulsive-looking characters and unfamiliar sounds. I still continued zealously the study of Greek and Latin and of general knowledge, adding to these also the commencement of French and Italian.'

When he was fifteen his headmaster read an essay to the school on the spread of Christianity among the heathen. 'It was the first time I had heard of missions among the heathen, and the idea assumed a definite form in my mind so that, boy-like, I asked myself "Why not become a missionary and go and convert the heathen?" ' His family favoured the idea, and he went off to Basel as soon as he had finished school. At Basel he experienced what would now be called a crisis of faith, and was very ready to end his studies and return to work the family farm; but his family persuaded him to go on to ordination, largely because they thought it would be a disgrace to lower himself to manual labour after so much education. So he plodded on, took a curacy after ordination, and on meeting an old friend just back from missionary work, offered himself to the CMS.

The Church of England by this time had obtained a foothold in West Africa. Now it was looking hopefully for a similar opportunity in East Africa. It sent Krapf off to pioneer a Christian route down the continent from Abyssinia. His earliest experiences were in a pattern which was to be repeated time and again by every missionary who left England for a heathen land. The voyage out to the eastern Mediterranean was perhaps less of a penance to Krapf than it would be to many who followed him, though a tremendous storm hit the ship as it was passing Crete and he consoled himself with the thought that St Paul had been through all this before, in these very waters. Prayer 'so strengthened me that I was enabled to sustain my terrified fellow-voyagers, among whom was a French actress, greatly by reading aloud the narrative of the prophet Jonah'. When he arrived in Adowa, he discovered that there were Catholic priests in the district; on being expelled by the local prince he decided that this was because the priests had offered bigger and better presents than he had brought with him.

The Abyssinians already practised a form of Christianity, the mass of the people belonging to the Coptic faith, which had survived in this mountainous region and along the Egyptian stretch of the Nile since soon after the age of the Apostles; the other early Christian settlements along North Africa, which had appeared in the Roman heyday, had long since been swept away by the advancing tide of Islam. Europeans, however, regarded the Copts with a great deal of condescending reserve. In the 1890s Lord Cromer spoke for many of his co-religionists when he remarked that the only difference between a Copt and a Moslem was that whereas a Moslem was an Egyptian worshipping in a mosque, a Copt was an Egyptian worshipping in a church.

Krapf was much less patronising than that, though he noted several things that would have made the CMS committee members recoil with Protestant mortification. No Christian people on earth, he found, were so rigid in their fasting as these. Immorality was the order of the day and even priests and monks broke the seventh commandment. True, the Coptic Church had established monogamy, but concubinage was habitual and Sahela Selassie even hoped for a consorting English princess to consolidate his alliance with Great Britain. The lusty atmosphere of Abyssinia evidently left its mark on Krapf, for 'my experiences . . . convinced me that an unmarried missionary could not eventually prosper'. And although he had left Europe without the faintest notions of marriage, he now proposed to a young lady from Basel, who promptly took ship to Egypt, where he joined her for the wedding.

With Rosine he travelled south again, their baggage heavy with a large supply of Amharic Bibles and testaments, and before they had finished their long journey to Zanzibar, Rosine gave birth to a daughter prematurely in the wilderness of Shoa. The child lived for only a few hours, and Krapf christened her Eueba, a tear, before burying her under a tree by the side of the track. Within a year the mother was to be dead, too, and another child which survived her for only a few days. And Krapf was to continue his mission single-handed and single-mindedly for the better part of twenty years. There were to be many missionaries in the century ahead, who lost wife and children in such a way, sacrificial victims to the obscure promises of God and the white man in Africa.

In Zanzibar, Krapf made friends with the Imam of Muscat, the Sultan Said-Said. Indeed, the spontaneous friendship that Moslems very often offered Christians in pagan Africa is a curious phenomenon of the times, given the many things which divided them, particularly the slave trade, in which Moslem Arabs were deeply involved and which the Christian missionaries were determined to uproot. It is partly to be explained, no doubt, by a degree of common religious experience; partly by a feeling of affinity in an alien environment. The Sultan was so evidently taken by the German that he provided him with a letter of recommendation that was intended to ease the missionary's passage along East Africa, wherever he might encounter Moslems. 'Greetings to all our subjects, friends and governors', it said. 'This letter is written on behalf of Dr Krapf, the German, a good man who wishes to convert the world to God. Behave well to him and be everywhere serviceable to him.'

Krapf now began to spend himself almost entirely on the study of Swahili; for the next couple of years he was engrossed in the translation of the New Testament and started a Swahili dictionary with four thousand entries under the first two letters alone. He was a man of the very widest perspectives, well aware that he could be no more than an instrument of preparation for an enterprise in which he was unlikely to take part himself. He used to calculate, he said later, how many missionaries and how much money would be required to connect eastern and western Africa by a chain of missionary stations. He estimated the distance from Mombasa to the river Gabun in West Africa at some nine hundred leagues. If stations with four missionaries each were established at intervals of one hundred leagues, the cost of the thirty-six missionaries and their dwellings would come to between £4,000 and £5,000 a year. If progress were made from both sides of the continent the chain of missions would be completed in four to five years.

Krapf also thought that England might profitably establish on the East coast a colony for liberated slaves like the one in Sierra Leone, that each might be used as a springboard for the conversion of the African races inland. And if more attention were paid to the formation of the mission chain across Africa, the slave trade with America and Arabia would be quickly and thoroughly ended. 'Till Christianity becomes the ruling faith in Africa', he wrote, 'however great and noble may be the exertions of the Government of Great Britain, and however liberal its expenditure in sending out squadrons to intercept slave-ships, the slave trade will continue to flourish. Christianity and civilisation ever go hand in hand; brother will not sell brother; and when the colour of a man's skin no longer excludes him from the office of an evangelist, the traffic in slaves will have had its knell. A black bishop and black clergy of the Protestant Church may ere long become a necessity in the civilisation of Africa.'

Krapf wrote those words when his African work was over, in 1860, when a black Protestant bishop and clergy were about to become a small reality in the Christian enterprise. During his time along the East coast they could have been no more than the distant vision of an astute and sympathetic man, whose own labours were much more those of the geographer and explorer than of the preacher. His journals are copious with notes on tribal habits and native existence. He observes that the houses of the Wanika are like haycocks in Europe, with grass roofs stretching down from a central stake. At night the inhabitants of these huts lie round their fires on cow-hides and do not trouble themselves about the smoke, the heat and vermin such as fleas, lice and bugs, being only afraid of serpents. The huts stand so close together that when one catches fire the whole village is sometimes in flames. These are a people steeped in superstition, much impressed by natural coincidences attending the arrival of the white man. Krapf was particularly well received by one tribe because it started raining just as he entered their village and, much against his wishes, his servant Abdallah did what he could to strengthen their conviction that he was responsible.

It was while he was in this village of Rabai, just behind Mombasa, that Krapf spoke with the elders about the real purpose of his journey. While the rains came down he sat and explained that the object of his visit was to teach them the words of the Bible he held in his hand. 'One of the elders asked me if I was an enchanter, who could tell out of the book how long he was to live; or whether I could heal the sick chief by a prayer from it. I answered that this book could make them live in everlasting joy, if they accepted and believed what was read to them; that they would be cured of the worst of maladies, sin, if they believed in the Son of God. I then narrated to them some of the chief facts in the life of Christ, and pointed out in conclusion that God so loved the world that He gave His only begotten Son, that whosoever believeth in Him should not perish, but have everlasting life. One of the elders said that it was really true that God loved man, for he gave the Wanika rain, tembo (cocoa-nut wine) and clothes. I rejoiced that these were certainly proofs of Divine love, but that, after all, they were only earthly gifts, and would not avail them, if God had not taken care for their souls, and had not sent His Son to free them from sin and Satan. Another elder, who seemed to understand me better, repeated my whole address, and that with tolerable accuracy. After the rain had ceased, they all dispersed quietly, to go and sow their rice, but heartily shook me by the hand and offered me a goat by way of a gift. I refused it, however, being determined to hold aloof from the system of giving and taking, the receipt of a present among these people always entailing the bestowal of one. On the whole, I could not avoid seeing that the people were somewhat shy of me for fear that I should convert them to Mohammedanism; for they could not draw any distinction between Christianity and Islamism. Mothers removed their children as soon as they saw me in the streets of the village, a practice not uncommon among the Wanika, arising out of the apprehension that strangers merely come to steal the children and sell them into slavery.'

In spite of the fact that women and children ran in fear from Krapf, whose shoes seemed to be made of iron, whose hair was like an ape's and whose spectacles were 'objects of astonishment and ridicule', his relationship with the Wanika became so congenial that he settled among them and made his East African base at Rabai. It was here, in 1846, that he was joined by his fellow-Württemberger, Johannes Rebmann, who was destined to spend an even longer time in Africa than Krapf – twenty-nine years without one single period of relief in Europe.

Together Krapf and Rebmann built a church for public worship and on the first Sunday after it was finished, a dozen or so people assembled inside while Krapf explained why it had been built and invited them to come again each Sunday to listen to God's holy word. The response to his invitation was automatic, and it was to be the despair of Christian missionaries for generations to come. One of the men promptly asked what Krapf and Rebmann would give the Wanika if they attended church. If the missionaries were prepared to supply a cow and rice, then the people would attend; if not, they would stay away, for no Wanika ever went to a palaver without eating and drinking. 'This,' wrote Krapf, 'was rather a humbling experience on our little church's consecration; but we consoled ourselves with the thought that the Jews preferred to look upon our Divine Master rather as upon an earthly king than as upon a king eternal, the only wise God.'

So Krapf started to make house-to-house visits, to prepare the Wanika for public worship and to announce the day when Christians kept their Sabbath. Every Sunday morning the church service was signalled by firing a gun once or twice and by ringing a bell which had been sent out from London. The two missionaries also tried to introduce something of the Sabbatarian spirit by buying nothing on that day, by forbidding their servants to do any work then, by wearing what Krapf called 'holiday clothes'. Even so, it was an uphill struggle. They made almost no headway against pagan notions of the universe, where the earth finished in a great morass in West Africa, being buried there, and there an end to it. Even the most tractable of these people were terribly discouraging to the two good men who had come to help them. The son of Chief Jindoa, a lad of ten, learned to read fairly well and to write a letter, but gave it all up on growing older when he discovered that the missionaries could not or would not satisfy his desire for clothing or other material possessions.

Krapf was a tolerant and understanding man, far more so than many who would follow him, but even his patience began to wear thin under the pressure of perpetual cadging. No one, he swore, who had not personally experienced it, could imagine what annoyance was caused to the missionaries by these mendicant propensities of the heathen, who begged everything they saw. One senses a sort of wry relief in the way his journals turn again to an anthropological examination of the natives after a fruitless attempt to proselytise them. Carefully he distinguished the various oaths and ordeals used by the Wanika: the *kirapo ja zoka*, the ordeal of the hatchet, which is passed red hot four times over the hand of the accused, who is deemed guilty if he is burned; the *kirapo ja jungu ja gnandu*, the ordeal of the copper kettle, which is heated by the magician till it glows, whereupon a stone is put inside, which the accused must retrieve without being burnt if he is to be exonerated. There were many such ordeals in this savage land, which Krapf had been sent to transform into something gentler and full of Christian love. He was eventually charged with nothing less than the creation of twelve mission stations along the banks of the Nile from Alexandria to Gondar, the capital of Abyssinia; and other stations were to proceed south from here, and to the east and the west. The line of stations was to be called the Apostles' Street, that in Alexandria being named St Matthew's, that in Cairo, St Mark's, the one in Assuan, St Luke's and so on.

Krapf and Rebmann began a series of journeys into the interior, designed to prospect the lie of the land for this chain-laying. Between them they were to make eight expeditions in the space of five years. Rebmann had no less of the explorer's instinct than Krapf, and his, in the end, produced the greatest exploring coup. Inland from their base at Rabai were uplands and Rebmann at once felt at home in them. 'How splendid the whole landscape,' he wrote, 'with its rich variety of mountain, hill and dale, covered by the most luxurious vegetation! I could have fancied myself on the Jura mountains near Basel, or in the region about Cannstadt in the dear fatherland, so beautiful was the country, so delightful the climate.' This was, in fact, the Chagga country and lying across Rebmann's path, a few days' march ahead, was a mountain the like of which he had never encountered before even in his beloved Swiss Alps. He had heard native rumours of this peak ever since arriving in Africa. It was said to glitter whitely towards its summit and Runga, king of the Majame tribe, had once sent an expedition to investigate it. He had hoped it might prove to be made of silver or something equally valuable. But only one of the party returned, his hands and his feet mutilated with a curious stiffness which eventually turned, like leprosy, to the shedding of fingers and toes. He reported appalling cold in the ascent of that mountain but this, he said, was not what had killed his companions; they had died of their fear and terror. Other natives had told Rebmann how they had ventured some way up the mountain to collect the silver substance in a vessel; but, miraculously, it had turned to water by the time they had reached the bottom again.

Now Rebmann found himself within sight of this awful mountain, in a range which gradually became more distinctive with its spurs and ridges, its gullies and its buttresses. 'At about ten o'clock I observed something remarkably white on the top of a high mountain,' Rebmann logged in his journal, 'and first supposed that it was a very white cloud . . . but having gone a few paces more I could no more rest satisfied with that explanation; and while I was asking my guide a second time whether that white thing yonder was indeed a cloud, and scarcely listening to his answer that yonder was a cloud, but what that white thing was he did not know, but supposed it was coldness, the most delightful recognition took place in my mind of an old well-known European guest called snow. All the strange stories we had so often heard about the gold and silver mountain Kilimanjaro in Jagga, supposed to be inaccessible on account of evil spirits, which had killed a great many of those who had attempted to ascend it, were now rendered intelligible to me.' He sat down and read Psalm 111, and was especially moved by the sixth verse, with its promise that 'He hath shewed his people the power of his works, that he may give them the heritage of the heathen'. It was 11 May 1848, and Rebmann was the first European to clap eyes on Africa's highest mountain, and to identify it as a snowbound peak at 19,000 feet.

When the news reached Europe the idea was ridiculed, for snow a mere two hundred miles from the Equator was a mighty preposterous suggestion. But Rebmann replied that he had not spent years with the Swiss Alps on his doorstep for nothing; and Krapf, whose own geographical claim to fame was the first sight of Mount Kenya, was later able to vouch for Rebmann's accuracy, passing Kilimanjaro himself several times on his wanderings.

Although the journals of Krapf and Rebmann seem more often than not to be the log-books of travellers than the memoranda of missionaries, they never lost sight of the essential reason why they were in Africa, discouraging though attempts at conversion were. Sir Richard Burton may have taken to Rebmann, when the two met briefly in East Africa, as a fellow-traveller worthy of respect (though he sketched him as a preacher, standing on a rooftop with a crowd of natives below), but the Germans did not forget that they were men of God before everything else. They were dedicated to the destruction of paganism, which had its own vague idea of a Supreme Being. This, it seemed to the two CMS men, was a constant factor in East African mythology, though there were tribal variations lower down the divine scale of things. Among the Masai and the Waknafi, for instance, the Supreme Being was called Engai and dwelt on a white mountain, from which descended the vital water and rain. There was an intermediary between Engai and the people, the Neiterkob, to whom the tribes first turned in their prayers for rain, health, victory or cattle. Later and more sophisticated generations of Christians might find in this relationship a curious similarity to the position held by the Virgin Mary and other saints as a means of intercession with Christ. To Krapf and Rebmann it was simply a formidable though understandable ignorance of Truth, and thoughtfully they applied themselves to the task of demolishing it by tackling its by-products one by one. Krapf, for example, records how he dealt with a boy who visited him for instruction and who on one occasion stole a servant's fishing rod. The servant, with the consent of the boy's father, tied the young thief to a post and flogged him soundly. Krapf, carefully watching this punishment, let it continue for a while. For one thing, he believed the lad deserved a thrashing. 'But at last I ordered him to be set at liberty, promising the servant that I would make good the loss of the fishing rod. The boy was untied and dismissed in the presence of a number of Mohammedans, who were standing around. "See," I then said, "this boy has been restored to liberty because I mediated for him, and made good the damage he had done; in a much higher sense has Jesus Christ, the Son of God, borne and made compensation on the Cross for your unrighteousness." '

Krapf was very conscious of the Moslem influence in East Africa, as he had reason to be. To the north of Rabai was Harar, a city of learning and missionary work, sacred to Moslems as was no other place outside Mecca and Medina. From here, Islam had trickled down the East coast and Krapf bethought himself one day of a curious way in which the flow might be staunched. He had observed how imported French brandy had started to spread among the Moslems he encountered. He must be the only Christian missionary of the nineteenth century who did not shudder with horror at the prospect of alcohol circulating among people he had come to convert. 'What,' he asked himself, 'if this increasing love of ardent spirits did eventually break up the false religion of their prophets, and so great good come out of evil?' For Krapf had a sharp sense of history, which told him that the Christian Gospel generally reached a nation when it was on the brink of destruction.

Harar, besides being a Moslem holy city, was also a centre of the East African slave trade. This was another reason for anathema besides its false religion. Between ten and twelve thousand captives a year passed through the country of Krapf and Rebmann, on their way from a number of slave markets to various ports on the Swahili coast and Arabia. They were marched in small gangs of six to ten men, chained to each other, carrying a variety of burdens upon their heads. Many of them had been caught at night in snares and when they had been trapped the slavers bound them, jammed their necks into forked pieces of wood, and took them off to the market at Kiloa. It led Krapf to wonder, just a little, why God in His mercy placed no limits to such horrors and such violations of the laws of humanity. In the end he was forced to assume that the slave trade, like much else which was nasty, was part of God's inscrutable purpose.

By the time Krapf's journals were published the missionary enterprise in Africa was well under way. He had himself returned to Europe for a rest before going back to his work and the Prince Consort had received him at Windsor, as well as the King of Prussia in Berlin. He continued his explorations until 1852, when his health finally gave way under the strain of recurring malaria and he left Africa for the last time. He had gone there in the 1830s as a pathfinder, he had never really been anything more than this in the most literal sense, but he had discharged his task magnificently. His major achievement, apart from the physical breaking of new ground, was to send back to the CMS information which would be of inestimable value to those who followed him. He pointed out that in times of tribal peace a missionary could roam safely around Africa provided he had secured the friendship of the local king. It was important, though, that the white man should at all times conduct himself with great respect towards African kings, avoiding all semblance of political interference in the affairs of the country. They should be ready occasionally to give presents to these monarchs, and Krapf himself had never travelled without a quantity of knives, beads and coloured articles which he had picked up from Muscat; one king had asked him, as a farewell gift, for an emetic, because he felt unwell – whereupon Dr Krapf presented him with twenty-seven grains of ipecacuanha. At the same time, Krapf reported to London, a missionary must show deep gratitude for every benefit conferred upon him, however trifling, 'and he must distinctly show his gratitude by deeds'.

The missionaries who followed this careful and perceptive German were too frequently to neglect his advice. Even more did the missionary nations of Europe disregard his thoughtful conclusions on the whole relationship between Africa and the countries which were soon dedicated to transforming her. 'Expect nothing, or very little,' wrote Krapf, 'from political changes in Eastern Africa. Do not think that because East Africans are "profitable in nothing to God and the world" they ought to be brought under the dominion of some European power, in the hope that they may bestir themselves more actively and eagerly for what is worldly and, in consequence, become eventually more awake to what is spiritual and eternal. On the contrary, banish the thought that Europe must spread her protecting wings over Eastern Africa, if missionary work is to prosper in that land of outer darkness. Europe would, no doubt, remove much that is mischievous and obstructive out of the way of missionary work, but she would probably set in its way as many and, perhaps, still greater checks.'

Doubtless this advice had too negative a ring in the ears of the CMS committee in London. Perhaps it was regarded as unsound because, worthy though Dr Krapf most evidently was, he was not, after all, an Englishman. Much more to their taste were a few sentences he had written as a justification for efforts which to some extent, to the purist proselytiser, had appeared barren. 'The friends of missionary labours . . . should obtain some knowledge of this unexplored portion of the East African coast, and thus become better acquainted with the various routes by which messengers of the Gospel may press forward to some common centre.'

Now, that had a fine and challenging tone to it, to any man with a spark of Christian manhood in him.

4
TO THE CAPE

It was 1817 before those Christian matrons of England had responded to Melville Horne's clarion call sufficiently for the CMS to dispense with the services of the Berlin Seminary, though the institution at Basel continued to produce missionaries for years to come. While the bishops of the Church of England had been taking their time to lend their weight to foreign missionary work, the members of the CMS had been attempting to stimulate matronly and other zeal in every part of the country. They sent their representatives round the parishes for sermons and hearty hymn-singing, which invariably included 'Jesus shall reign, where ere the sun . . .' Typical of these recruiting campaigns was an excursion around Yorkshire lasting two and a half months by the Rev. Basil Woodd.

Woodd's expenses came to £150 but he collected in return £1,060. And in exchange for fifty separate sermons on the missionary theme he had the satisfaction of starting twenty-eight missionary support organisations. His was judicious propaganda, designed to excite the young Christian man with the prospect of exotic experience just as much as to stimulate him with the anticipation of heathen souls saved. 'I brought two Hindoo gods with me,' Woodd reported of one stop. 'One has a snout like an elephant. I find they entertain everybody, and plead the cause of Missions as well as if they were Missionaries themselves.' And however reluctant the English were at first to offer themselves for missionary work, they do not seem at any time to have been reluctant to turn out and hear about the missionary field. One CMS man preached three times on one Sunday in Bradford; his first congregation consisted of two thousand, his second three thousand and his third of four thousand people.

But as soon as Englishmen were enticed from their pews and on to the boats sailing for the heathen lands, they discovered what a desperate enterprise they had committed themselves to in many ways. The hazards they faced were far greater than many could possibly have foreseen. They were certainly not setting out in expectation of an easy life, and they were prepared for the most unpleasant manifestations of degraded and vicious humanity, for cannibalism and perhaps even worse. But this, after all, was what they were sworn to fight in their shining Christian armour; this was the recognisable foe who could be overcome by God's grace and the sturdy devotion of the pilgrim hero. There were more insidious obstacles to be faced than slave traders and heathen libertines, however, and in many ways they were to be a far greater test of Christian faith and courage.

The business of living off the land, like a native, which William Carey had so blithely anticipated, required both will-power and constitution, as Lewis Krapf had discovered. He could enjoy giraffe steaks, but found elephant meat peculiar and unpalatable. This was not the lowest point in his diet, however. His stores on one expedition were so reduced that in his hunger he ate the young shoots of a tree mixed with gunpowder. This he found bitter and unwholesome, so he tried ants instead. Not many who followed Krapf were as resilient as he. Even among the few who preceded him to Africa were people much less prepared to take the place as they found it. Zachary Macaulay was still in Sierra Leone when the first Methodist missionaries arrived, and he reported that 'This morning there was nothing to be heard among the Missionary ladies but doleful lamentations or bitter complaints. To their astonishment Freetown resembled neither London nor Portsmouth; they could find no pastrycooks' shops, nor any gingerbread to buy for their children. Dr Coke had deceived them; if this was Africa they would go no farther, that they would not. Their husbands were silent; but their looks were sufficiently expressive of chagrin and disappointment.'

Worse by far than the crude living conditions of Africa was the climate of Africa, and the diseases that flourished in it. The East African uplands might be splendidly bracing but the coastlands were hot and humid; and West Africa was infinitely worse than anywhere on the other side of the continent. There was rain of proportions unknown anywhere in Europe and when there was no rain there was steamy heat which left a man as limp as a wrung dishclout. In the East the tsetse fly produced sleeping sickness and everywhere there was the terrible malaria. The word was Italian, it literally meant bad air, and until Ronald Ross in

India at the very end of the nineteenth century discovered that it was transmitted by the bite of a mosquito, it was thought to be the product of a miasma hanging over the swamps of Sierra Leone, Nigeria and elsewhere. Scarcely anyone went to Africa without succumbing to this fever, with its alternate bouts of sweating and shivering, with its delirium and its dreadful debilitation which wasted a body away unto death unless the victim was very fortunate.

Malaria was especially rampant in Sierra Leone, which soon earned the grim title of the White Man's Grave. Out of twenty-six men and women who had gone there on missionary work before 1816, sixteen had died, apart from several of their children. In 1823 seven new schoolmasters and five wives arrived in the colony. Six died that year and ten were dead within eighteen months. Conditions were no better elsewhere along the coast. By 1826, out of a total of seventy-nine missionaries and their wives who had been in West Africa during the previous twenty-two years, only fourteen were still at their stations; most of the others had died. Typical of the missionary experience in those years was the case of Henry Palmer and his family.

Palmer had fought at Waterloo and on the battlefield had felt those first comforting tremors of Christianity familiar through many ages to men in the middle of war. He had come home to marry a clergyman's daughter and together they had offered themselves as missionaries. They arrived in Sierra Leone and within three months Palmer was stricken with fever and died. His widow was pregnant, but in the midst of her lonely grief she found the dogged courage to write: 'He who cannot ever, whose love to His people can never fail, has seen fit to take my beloved husband to Himself. Can I reply against God? I cannot. I will not. The hour was come and His name was glorified.' Three weeks later her child was born and died almost at once. Six days later Mrs Palmer was dead, too, and buried beside her husband and child amidst those beautiful bush-covered hills that roll away in a great arc behind Freetown. It required considerable fortitude for missionaries to follow where people like the Palmers had perished before them from an ailment for which there was no cure. Yet still they came, in a small trickle at first, but by every boat, knowing that their chances of survival and return to their families in England were exceedingly small. There can never have been a finer or more sustained demonstration of the courage that can be mustered out of faith.

The greatest agony of all, however, was very often not the pain of loss, or the fear of a mysteriously inexorable death, but the spiritual torture which followed when faith was in danger of being shattered upon blank incomprehension. Throughout Africa, wherever the missionaries now began to go, they found that the natives did not succumb easily to the great blandishments of the Christian Gospel. Worse, they had endurance, diabolical endurance, to resist persuasion and enlightenment. They had the cunning to make use of the missionaries where and when they would, to seem biddable and anxious to learn these new and shining truths, and then to turn round and laugh in the faces of these solicitous white men when their heathen purposes were no longer served by an appearance of infantile acquiescence.

Robert Moffat arrived in South Africa on behalf of the LMS when he was twenty-one in 1817. Five years later he was writing in his journal: 'No conversions, no enquiry after God; no objections raised to exercise our powers in defence. Indifference and stupidity form the wreath on every brow; ignorance – the grossest ignorance – forms the basis of every heart. Things earthly, sensual and devilish, stimulate to motion and mirth, while the great concerns of the soul's redemption appear to them like a ragged garment, in which they see neither loneliness nor worth ... We preach, we converse, we catechise, but without the least apparent success. Only satiate their mendicant spirits by perpetually giving, and you are all that is good; but refuse to meet their endless demands and their theme of praise is turned to ridicule and abuse ... The prospect is neither calculated to encourage nor cheer, but we labour in hope ...' Faith and hope and very little else sustained many men and women through many a dark night of the soul once they reached this darkest of continents. And sometimes this was simply not enough, great though it might be, to achieve the purpose that had inspired the godly venture.

The Rev. Francis Owen was one who battled with paganism in South Africa, some little time after Moffat's despairing entry. Owen was a young Anglican curate from a parish in Yorkshire, a highly intelligent man who had graduated sixth Senior Optime in the Mathematical Tripos at Cambridge. He was among the first of such clergymen to offer himself for missionary work and he decided on this course after attending a CMS anniversary meeting in 1836. One of the speakers was Captain Allen Gardiner, late of the Royal Navy. Gardiner had become a missionary after spending many years at sea, he had been a rollicking atheist before he had returned to the Christianity of his origins and, as very often is the case in such circumstances, he had returned to it with a piety and commitment that far outstripped that of most contemporaries who had never wavered in their faith. By 1836 he had tasted the harsh realities of missionary life at the Cape and he could speak of it with an eloquence and a throbbing fervour that promised ultimate triumph in the face of difficulties that most men might regard as insuperable. It was this eloquence that moved young Francis Owen to abandon his Normanton curacy and present himself to the CMS. On Christmas Eve of the same year, he sailed with his wife, his sister and a maid for the Cape.

It was decided that Owen and his womenfolk, together with local servants and guides, should proceed by wagon inland, preaching and attempting to convert wherever they went. They soon established a pattern of work. Owen and his interpreter would sit on chairs in an open space beside the wagons, between the men and the women of the local population. Owen would bid them all to rise and he would then recite the 136th Psalm, which begins 'Oh give thanks unto the Lord for He is good; for His mercy endureth for ever'. The natives would then be told to sit while Owen gave a short account of the creation of man, the covenant of life, the formation of women and the institution of marriage; for morality weighed as heavily upon the missionary conscience as Divine revelation. Sometimes he would proceed from the institution of marriage to the temptation of the serpent, the fall of man and the promise of a deliverer. Then he would tell his audience to rise again while he blessed them; and they would disperse 'as quietly and orderly as they had assembled'.

Occasionally Owen would detect, at these gatherings, someone who seemed unusually attentive to what he was being told. There was a Sabbath in 1837 when seven natives came to the wagons before the time for service. They immediately accepted Owen's invitation to stay for the missionaries' *al fresco* matins 'and behaved with the strictest propriety'. Owen read the 'Te Deum' and other prayers in Kaffir and gave a short analysis of the first three chapters of Genesis. One man was observed to listen to all this without his attention once wavering. When the service was over Owen took him aside and asked what the man thought of the Word of God which he had just heard. The man confessed his ignorance but said he was glad to have heard it.

Owen then inquired whether the man knew Jesus Christ, the Son of God, who shed blood for him. The man confessed ignorance on this subject. Owen asked whether the man knew himself to be a sinner and the man said that while Owen was speaking to him he most certainly felt a sinner. It was a moment that any missionary would gladly wait for, the moment when a heathen man would submit himself meekly as a penitent. And Francis Owen, his heart overflowing with the generous consolations of the truly Christian victor, forgot the weariness he must by now have been feeling, and the prospect of a Sabbath dinner his wife was cooking by the wagon, and proceeded to the salvation of one lost soul. 'I told him,' he wrote that night, 'that to feel ourselves sinners was the first step to salvation and then read and enlarged upon a variety of texts of Scripture, containing promises to the penitent; also such passages as were calculated to awaken as well as to encourage him. He listened standing with fixed attention for about two hours; during which time I brought a large portion of the Word of God before him.' At which point Francis Owen discovered, as so many missionaries did, that the Word of God and the promise of salvation had not been entirely responsible for the man's rapt attention and apparently receptive spirit. After more than two hours of earnest endeavour 'the man rather disappointed me by asking for a present'. But this custom, Owen bravely added, 'is so general with the natives that it was not so discouraging a circumstance as might at first sight be imagined'.

Missionaries found that chiefs, no less than their tribespeople, were liable to be engaged in Christian conversation up to a point. Francis Owen had an encounter with one of the mightiest chiefs in the whole of Africa when he moved into the lands of Dingaan, who had succeeded the terrible Chaka as leader of the Zulus. He met Dingaan on his first Sunday in Zulu country and was immediately impressed by the alacrity with which the chief's commands were obeyed by his people. As usual a crowd of natives had gathered by the Owen wagons, with the warrior chief sitting in the middle, facing this gentle young Englishman. Owen began his preaching with prayer. Then he enlarged upon Christ's life, character, doctrines, miracles and death. He recounted how Christ was laid in his grave until, three days later, God had raised him up again to be seen by the Apostles, with whom he ate and drank. 'I said that what the Prophets, Christ and his Apostles taught was written down in books, and that those books were all after a time made into one book, which book I had in my hand; that my people had received this book and had sent me to his people to teach them the same; that this book contained also a history of the life of Jesus Christ. I then stated the blessedness of those who believed and practised what was contained in the book and the misery of those who did not practise it, that they would be cast into Hell, a place of everlasting fire.

'I was proceeding to speak of it in Scripture language, as a place where the fire is not quenched, when he again interrupted me and asked where Hell was. I said the Word of God did not tell where Hell was, but only that there was such a place. I then glided into the solemn account of the Last Judgement in those words "when the Son of Man shall come into His glory etc." After I had read a few verses, he said he wanted to have the word more explained. I then enlarged on every clause in this description. The design of Christ's second coming, the glory with which he would come, the throne on which he would sit and all nations coming before him. He asked what sort of throne? I said a great white throne. He asked who were they who would rise up again, whether we, pointing to his women, shall rise again, what bodies we shall come with, whether we shall see one another and know one another again. Some of these questions he repeated and I gave such answers as the Scriptures furnished me with. He seemed to think it incredible that the dead should be raised again, not knowing the power of God. Finally he said, why don't the dead get up now, that we may see them? To which I replied that God had appointed the day and now he commanded all men everywhere to repent. I read also part of the third chapter of Peter II, concerning the Last Day; and am persuaded that, though he does not believe, yet he cannot venture to deny the truth of the resurrection.'

Owen's conversations with Dingaan were not always totally biblical in character. On one occasion Owen pointed out that Britain had not been at war for twenty years, that the British never went to war except in self-defence, because Jesus Christ had taught all men to love one another. This must have sounded a very strange doctrine to Dingaan, who was perpetually at war, and he asked whether the countries on his side of the sea were the greatest or those on Owen's side. Seasoning his natural patriotism with diplomacy, Owen told him that the European countries were by far the greatest, though Dingaan was the greatest of the African chiefs he had yet seen. Dingaan then ordered one of his men to produce an old print picturing the Kings of England since the Norman Conquest and invited Owen to read out their names; which the missionary did, seizing the chance to remark that Elizabeth's was the reign in which the English had started to worship God truly, since when their country had been greater than ever before. Then Owen brought out an encyclopaedia from his baggage, showing Dingaan some of the illustrations and spending much time explaining to the king the principles and use of the diving bell.

Besides their periodic battles with other tribes, the Zulus at this time were engaged in a running war against the Boers. Owen's first encounter with Dingaan, indeed, came only a few months before the massacre of Piet Retief and his column of sixty men in the king's kraal. The years following 1836 were the years of the Great Trek, when some seven thousand Dutch settlers crossed the Orange river out of the Cape Province in search of freedom from increasing British influence at the Cape. Blocking their way in Natal were the Zulus, who resented the incursion of these arrogant Europeans. The reputation of the Boers was already one of total contempt for Hottentots and other black men. They were, moreover, farmers and to them cattle meant wealth and life just as much as to the Zulus. All the ingredients of racial tragedy were there in the confrontation of two excessively proud peoples, both with fighting instincts standing sharply above natural toughness, both prepared to struggle unto death for the possession of land and cattle.

Retief and his men wanted to settle in Natal after their long haul over the Drakensberg mountains and they were prepared to parley amicably with Dingaan for his token permission. The king required, as proof of their amicable intentions, that they should recapture on his behalf seven hundred head of cattle that had been stolen from the Zulus by a rival tribe. Retief and his men rounded up the cattle and drove them to Dingaan's kraal, where they were received warmly. The king even prepared a document which would transfer a block of territory to the Boers, with Retief named as Governor. A celebration was prepared to ratify this transfer. Beer was brewed specially for the occasion and the Boers were so much at their ease that they had even left their weapons in their laager at the bottom of Dingaan's hill. They were drinking contentedly when Dingaan suddenly gave a signal to his men. Every Boer was seized and dragged off to a neighbouring hill, and there beaten to death with knobkerries. Francis Owen was in Dingaan's kraal at the time, though he had not taken part in the treaty celebrations. His curious relationship with Dingaan had developed to a point at which he was acting as a kind of secretary to the king; almost all the letters which passed from Dingaan to the Boers were in his hand. And he watched the massacre from the little house in which Dingaan had installed him and his family.

'My attention was directed to the blood-stained hill nearly opposite my hut, and on the other side of my wagon which hides it from view, where all the executions at this fearful spot take place, and which was destined now to add sixty more bleeding carcases to the number of those which have already cried to heaven for vengeance . . . I laid myself down on the ground. Mrs and Miss Owen were not more thunderstruck than myself. We comforted one another. Presently, the deed of blood being accomplished, the whole multitude returned to the town to meet their sovereign; and, as they drew near to him, set up a shout which reached the station and continued for some time . . . Dingaan's conduct was worthy of a savage, as he is. It was base and treacherous, to say the least of it.'

Missionaries were very frequently to be placed in the appalling dilemma which confronted Francis Owen during the massacre of Retief's column. They went to Africa expecting to deal with savage man and from their very first contact they witnessed the savagery in action. Owen records in his diary a commonplace event in the experience of many men of his profession, the execution of a native, in this case a woman who had been charged with 'having been somewhat saucy to an Indoona'. She was brought before Dingaan, examined and sentenced to death. 'The King pronounced sentence in the following terms: "Take her away; we will kill thee." Four executioners then hurried her away to the place where she was doomed to fall another victim to barbarous severity! When will the mild reign of the Prince of Peace put an end to these cruelties?'

Missionaries never intervened on such occasions. They allowed native justice to take its course, they wrung their hands as they composed their diaries that evening, they wondered when the Prince of Peace would transform the savage mind to something milder and more humane, they settled next day for gentle talk with the executioners, they hoped that their descriptions of Christ and their moral conclusions from his life might turn these bloodthirsty men into penitents. If their behaviour seems cowardly in retrospect, conceivably hypocritical, it is as well to remember that it was also realistic; that adding a martyr's death to a hapless native's would have done nothing to shift the course of native justice; that it might well have led to a general animosity against the missionaries and a total rejection of everything they stood for. As long as they could maintain contact with the heathen, then there was some chance that he could be turned from his heathen ways. They, after all, were engaged upon a way which stretched forward timelessly into eternity.

Few of the missionaries, though, exposed the contorted agony of their consciences more than Francis Owen. Few were as sensitive as he, not many were more naïve than this young man, who could be knotted almost comically by some of Dingaan's demands upon him. There were, for example, the occasions when Dingaan asked him for gunpowder. At first Owen's instinct was to refuse with a lie, saying that he had only enough to shoot birds for the pot. Dingaan countered by claiming that he only wanted gunpowder in order to shoot elephants. 'Being convinced that this was his real object, and in order to save myself the unpleasant office of giving him an article of this nature, I told him it was sold in Port Natal and he could get it there if he pleased. But I hereby got myself into another dilemma, for now he wanted *me* to purchase some and give it to him; and he said he would give me an elephant's tooth to purchase it with.' Owen declined the gift, pointed out that he was a teacher, not a trader, and suggested that Dingaan should give the tooth to Owen's driver, who was about to go into Port Natal. 'He, however, renewed his request so earnestly that on reflection I thought it proper to grant it to him, being quite satisfied in my own mind that the object for which he wanted the powder was an innocent one.' In spite of the fact that Owen acknowledged to himself that the people of Port Natal would realise he was ordering powder for Dingaan, he consented to write a letter seeking supplies ostensibly for missionary use.

Dingaan, who was not at all averse to playing off one white man against another, now asked the credulous Owen to add a postscript to the letter, pointing out that the chief had supplied the tooth. This Owen did, 'though, I must confess with some reluctance, on account of the disguise which I was apparently assuming. Yet, as the thing itself was true, and I was not accountable for any lawful use I might choose to make of the gunpowder, and it appearing to me that I might as innocently give it to Dingaan, being convinced that this was the only object he had, and that I was not obliged to say what use I intended or did not intend to make of my purchase, fully believing also that Mr Maynard's agent would not have the slightest objection to the powder . . . I could not feel that I was, God forbid, practising any deception, but merely assisting Dingaan to procure an article which he innocently wanted but which he could not get for himself, through his deep-rooted objection to apply for any. This I did certainly to please him, but without violating (as I trusted) any principle, though a full statement of all my feelings and views seems necessary to clear me from the suspicion which a partial statement might occasion, that I departed in this instance from that path of Christian simplicity, which it has always been my earnest desire and aim to walk in. And if, after all, I erred from the path of plain dealing, at the thought of which my soul shudders, I throw myself on the compassion of that Being who knew the integrity of my heart, and his people, who can make all allowance for the circumstances in which I was placed and the want of all time for consideration.' Within a few years David Livingstone would be having dealings with men like Dingaan in the same part of the world, but without any agonies about the path of Christian simplicity. He would recognise that natives needed arms to fight the Boers as well as to shoot for the pot, and he would supply them without much compunction.

The massacre of Retief and his men, however, brought Francis Owen and his conscience-stricken writhings to an end. He remained in the kraal for only a few days longer and then, fearful that the Zulus' taste for blood might impulsively be turned in the direction of the English missionary party, he asked Dingaan for permission to leave for Port Natal. It was granted, on condition that the missionaries left behind every possession not vital for their journey, and the Owen wagons rolled down the hill in retreat. They drove out of Natal and back to the Cape, and there Francis Owen settled to a parish ministry for a time.

This was not what the CMS expected of its men in South Africa or anywhere else in the world. A letter was soon on its way from London, pointing out that Mr Owen, in more than three years of endeavour, had not produced one single native convert ready for baptism. Not only was there nothing tangible to show for his time overseas, but his had been a costly venture as well; and, indeed, between January and April 1839, working as a parish parson between Port Elizabeth and Grahamstown, Owen had drawn £1,362 15s. 11d. on the CMS account. Taking all things into consideration, Salisbury Square had now decided to abandon its mission in South Africa. And so Francis Owen, his wife and his sister, set sail for England, where he settled to a quiet parish life in Sheffield.

Much sterner material than this was at work in South Africa by the time Owen left and some of it was American in origin. The antecedents of these missionaries were almost as deeply involved in a reaction against the slave trade as those of their counterparts in Britain. In 1775 Samuel Hopkins, the pastor of a rich congregation in Rhode Island, whose members had grown wealthy upon the proceeds of slavery, and Ezra Stiles, who was later to become President of Yale College, issued a joint appeal for funds to train young American blacks to go to Africa as evangelists. The plan was stillborn because at that moment the War of Independence broke out. But with the war over and independence from Britain achieved, a fresh impulse came out of the Andover Theological Seminary in Massachusetts. A group of young seminarians had started, in good Protestant tradition, to meet in a field for their joint prayer time. On one occasion a thunderstorm broke while they were on their knees, they took refuge in the lee of a haystack and thenceforth they were identified among their fellow-students as the Haystack Brethren. By September 1808 they were seriously discussing the possibility of starting a mission to the heathen and at first their intentions were only vaguely formed. They talked among themselves of 'cutting a path through the moral wilderness of the West to the Pacific'. Sometimes they thought of shipping themselves off to South America. Once or twice they wondered whether they should venture to Africa. Like every other missionary nucleus before them, the chief preoccupation was the salvation of heathen souls; but they also thought in terms of reparation to Africa for the sins inflicted upon it by a generation or two of American slave owners. Within a few years a nephew of George Washington was to be installed as the first president of a body dedicated to the settlement of freed Negro slaves on the West coast of Africa, in Liberia. Reparation was much in the air of the newly independent colonies across the Atlantic, and doubtless their own recent release from a form of bondage had something to do with it.

The Haystack Brethren and their friends had been in contact with the LMS in England. They had subscribed to its literature since its foundation and one of them even crossed the Atlantic to inquire of the LMS committee whether they might join forces in missionary work. The LMS thought this unwise, arguing that it would be difficult to act with unity and decision. So the seminarians lobbied their academic and religious tutors, transmitted their own enthusiasm, and on 29 June 1810 the American Board of Foreign Missions was instituted by the General Association of Massachusetts, meeting at Bradford. For a time it struggled, as missionary bodies in Britain had struggled. There was difficulty in obtaining a charter from the Senate and House of Representatives of Massachusetts. There was public indifference to evangelical piety. The Boston newspapers did not even bother to report the new foundation. But at least a start was made by the ordination of five young men in the Salem Tabernacle at the beginning of 1812, who before the year ended had sailed for Calcutta.

It was to be another twenty years before the board decided to send a mission to Africa. By then the Americans were succouring the heathen in India and Ceylon, in the Sandwich Islands, in Palestine, Malta, Syria, South America, Turkey, Greece, China, Siam, Sumatra and Singapore, as well as spreading the Word among the Cherokee and Choctaw Indians on their own continent. But in 1833 they packed the Presbyterian John Leighton Wilson off to Cape Palmas with what doubtless seemed soundly inspired advice. 'The fact is, dear brother,' he was told at the gathering to send him on his way, 'that the malaria of western Africa will not much longer frighten the Church from the performance of its duty. . . . The great fact is coming out, that natural evils, to a far greater extent than has been supposed, are punishments for violating natural laws. . . . The development of this fact is what is disarming the cholera of its terrors to all virtuous and temperate men. And the progress of this development, no doubt, will ultimately furnish a life preserver for every man, whose duty calls him to plunge into the pestiferous vapours of tropical climes.' Thus armed, Mr Wilson embarked for the dreadful West coast and happily survived the pestiferous vapours for the next twenty years.

The board now turned its attention to South Africa. The Andover seminarians had years before allowed their thoughts to stray in that direction. One of them had gone so far as to write to Dr John Philip, superintendent of the LMS at the Cape, for helpful advice. 'Has it been found best,' he asked, 'for the missionaries to conform to the customs of the natives in dress or manners of life?' And Dr Philip had promised that the land of the Zulus offered a noble field for missionary labour, without requiring the European to yield too much of his civilised habits. In December 1834 the barque *Burlington* sailed from Boston for the Cape, with six missionaries and their wives aboard. Their first sight of Africa was Table Mountain, and when the lookouts had shouted news of the landfall the missionaries gathered on deck and sang the hymn 'O'er the gloomy hills of darkness, Look my soul, be still and gaze'. Missionaries usually broke into hymnody whenever they reached the end of a voyage and stood on deck with that dark and ominous but strangely palpitating continent before them at last.

At the Cape the party divided. The Champions, the Grouts and the Adamses mounted their wagons and drove off to the east, to Dingaan's country in Natal. The Wilsons and the Venables were bound for Matabeleland. So was the man destined to leave a greater mark than any of them upon the Christianity of South Africa, and he was Daniel Lindley.

Lindley was one of those rigid, inflexible men of colossal pride whom it is possible to admire but not easy to like, and in coming to a land inhabited by Boers as well as natives he was in many ways discovering his spiritual and his temperamental home. He had been born at the turn of the century of frontier stock in Washington County, Pennsylvania. His father, Jacob, was a minister belonging to the strictest Protestant sect of all in North America, the Cumberland Presbyterians, who prohibited whistling and much else on the Sabbath and even postponed the beating of children until a Monday. It produced in Daniel a lifelong teetotaller and non-smoker, though Jacob used both drink and tobacco as relief from the austerities of his creed. At Ohio University – which Daniel attended without a ha'p'orth of help from his father – this withdrawn and rather cold young man decided to become a minister, too. He was appointed to a church in North Carolina, deep in the corn-liquor country, and he at once set about organising a local temperance society. There was a special gallery in the church for slaves, who had to enter the building by a separate entrance from the one used by their masters. Not once did Lindley preach against slavery. He would not have been popular if he had tried to, for the Southern Presbyterian Synods had consistently discouraged agitation against slave-owning. Too much of the Presbyterian income came from men who believed slave labour an important element in the natural order of things.

When the American Board of Missions began to appeal for men, Lindley decided to offer himself. His reasons for going, he had put rather abruptly in his letter of application to the board. First, he wrote, God in the goodness of His providence had opened many doors of entrance to the heathen. Second, it was evident that more men from somewhere ought to take the Gospel to the heathen. Third, Lindley's connection with the things of this world did not forbid his going. Fourth, he was willing to make every sacrifice that his going would cost him. Fifth, his going from the south might have some good effect on the southern Churches with regard to the work of foreign missions. If the board deemed him worthy of its patronage, he would be ready to go anywhere it sent him, 'only as regards climate I would prefer a latitude not above 40 . . .'

A few weeks before sailing he married Lucy Allen, a Sunday School teacher to whom he had become engaged after only three weeks' acquaintance; she was to bear their first child in an ox-cart on the way to Griqua Town, where they were to spend several months learning the Sichuana language.

The Lindleys soon found themselves swept up in the turmoil which attended the Great Trek from the Cape. They had been given permission by Chief Umsiligazi to settle in Matabeleland, in the township of Mosega.

On a January morning in 1837 this was attacked by one of the Boer commandos that were now skirmishing and foraging northwards, led by Andres Potgieter. Normally, Matabele warriors would have been there to repulse the enemy but on this day they were some distance upcountry and the Boers had no difficulty in plundering what cattle and wagons they wished. They also set fire to the town. Reasoning prudently that they would get little mercy from the enraged Matabele on their return, the Lindleys and the other missionaries with them spanned their own oxen as soon as the Boers had left and set off across country to Dingaan's Zulu territory, to join forces with the other group of Americans.

Dingaan, who had recently acquired the missionary services of Francis Owen, agreed that these Christian reinforcements might also bide a while on his lands. And there they remained until the time of the Retief massacre, when again they uprooted and moved south. It was at this point that Lindley decided that he must throw in his lot with the Boers. At the end of 1837 he had written of them to the American Board at home in these terms: 'They are, in truth, as much objects of Christian charity as the people to whom we have come. They have no minister, no teacher for their children, almost no books and almost nothing to keep them from sinking into the depths of heathenism. They express a strong wish to be supplied with books and teachers such as they need. As a body they are ignorant and wicked. There are among them some orderly, well-behaved persons, a few who may be pious . . . The Boers are all matter-of-course members of the Reformed Church to which they have a bigoted rather than intelligent attachment . . . Unless they come under religious instruction they will overturn everything in this country . . . Some of the English Churches may offer them help. Should this be done I am afraid they would reject it, as they seem determined to quit the English geheel en al (entirely, altogether).'

Eighteen months later, after his experiences among the Zulus and after withdrawing under the cloud of the Retief massacre, he is writing of the Boers in different terms. He now sincerely believes that the cheapest, speediest, easiest way of converting the heathen is to convert the white ones first. The whites emphatically must be provided for, or the missionaries will labour in vain to make Christians of the blacks. The two groups will come so much in contact with each other that the influence of the whites, if evil, will be irresistible without a miracle to prevent it. 'To their own vices the aborigines will add those of the white men, and thus make themselves two-fold more the children of hell than they were before.' It is easy enough to see this as a rationalisation of an inbred and temperamental sympathy for the Boers. But it should be remembered that Lindley was writing it after five years in South Africa in which, just like Francis Owen, he had accomplished nothing in missionary terms. He was in that most discouraging situation of the man who feels he is not wanted; worse, that he never will be wanted if he continues with the company he has been keeping. Certainly there were characteristics in Lindley that could be observed in any representative selection of the emigrant Dutch farmers. He could never, as some Boers could, shoot down some innocent black woman on the strength of an obscure verse in the Book of Joshua, but he was capable of writing about Africans in general like this: 'The great majority of the heathen in this country would as soon consent to send their cattle as their children to school. In Africans the elements of improvement are, it seems to me, fewer and feebler than in any other portion of mankind. Their degradation is unfathomable – it has no bottom. But Christ died for them. His love, too, is unfathomable – this is enough for us to know.'

It was at about this time that he began to grow a long beard, like every Dutch predicant at the Cape. And when the Voortrekkers, whose own Reformed ministers had refused to accompany them on their epic wanderings north, invited him to become their pastor in the newly settled township of Pietermaritzburg, Lindley accepted. It was there that he confirmed the young Paul Kruger, who had been a lad in Potgieter's commando at Mosega and who was to become President of the South African Republic. It was there that he presented a copy of the United States Constitution to the infant Volksraad (People's Council) of the new Boer Republic of Natal. It was there that he became officially a minister of the Dutch Reformed Church and severed his connection with the American Board of Missions, though he never lost sight of his homeland. After a couple of decades in Africa, the Lindley family went back to the American South for a holiday and Miss Martha Lindley, who had never been there before, registered some amazement (which seems to have been mutual) at the society she was now plunged into.

'Miss Q,' she reported, 'is a *young lady* of fifty years. She is exactly what I always imagined old maids in America would be. She asked us *in English* if we spoke English or the African language. I said, "We speak both languages." She opened her eyes *wide* and exclaimed, "Indeed! I am surprised." And, turning to Miss P, she said, just as if she thought we could not hear: "How well they speak English! Are you not surprised?" "Yes, indeed." And then they both stretched their eyes as wide open as they possibly could, and looked first at us and then at each other, then smiled and nodded their heads and exclaimed: "I am surprised. How strange. They appear so well. Why, for all I can see, they are just like other folks! You don't mean to say you have lived in Africa all your lives...?"' And if the ladies of North Carolina were astonished at the degree of civilisation still clinging to the missionary girls after an upbringing on the Dark Continent, the Lindley daughters, for their part, were somewhat scandalised by the good southern habit of shouting in church 'when they got happy'.

Then it was back to Africa, which was home for the Lindley family much more than North Carolina could ever be now. And there, after years as a Dutch Reformed predicant, Daniel Lindley's initial missionary instinct possessed him again. At the age of fifty-four he and Lucy moved out of Durban and started a new station on the Zulu reserve at Inanda, and returned to the old and backbreaking way they had known so many years before, when they had first trekked inland from the Cape. They were become pioneers again and there was much in their life of Old Testamental force and perseverance, of resignation to the will of God and the laws of Nature. Mrs Lindley kept a journal which reads more like a log-book than a diary; it is no more than the jottings of the trail-breaker's wife, noted while her man has gone foraging for sustenance as she calmly awaits his return.

'*May 8, 1857:* Mr L started off with a load of fancy articles; viz. work table, wheel-barrow, tools etc. etc. for his new place.
May 9: Mr L returns for Sabbath.
May 10: Sunday. An interesting day with us. Five women were baptised... after which the Lord's Supper was administered. Dreadful coughing still among the babies.
May 11: Mr L returned to his waggon and work.
May 12: Two green snakes killed in the smoke house.
May 13: Mr L came for a visit.
May 18: Commenced making a warm night shirt for Mr L at 8 o'clock, and finished it at half eleven, Lottie and Sarah each making a sleeve.
May 21: Prayer meeting. Two bad snakes killed.
May 22: Lute was lying on the bed, talking to himself, and said:

"The wind blows
And thirteen goes"

Who knows but that he may be the poet of the Inanda?'

So it goes on, recording the most stilted bones of a missionary existence. There are days when bricks have to be made and are finished just in time to escape a good downpour of rain. There are days when Mr L kills a couple of fat hogs, when he has a boil behind his knee that prevents him from preaching one Sabbath, when he rises to give an interesting sermon on John the Baptist. There is the day when a delightful letter comes from dear Mary, nineteen pages of it, together with two pictures of herself; and another day when news comes distantly of the Indian Mutiny.

One has to remind oneself with an effort sometimes that those daily entries, the commonplace events they are recording, belong to a colossal enterprise that was beginning to sweep Africa from end to end, that was essentially part of some numinous work of God's. Yet this was so; it was not just the case of a man and his wife beating an austere existence out of the veldt in an effort to create a new life for themselves. The American Board of Missions which had sent Lindley to this corner of the world in the first place, had been very clear about the grandeur and sweep of their own part in it all. They had been crudely candid about the nature of the missionary task they had taken in hand. The missionary's duties, they owned, were peculiar. 'He is an evangelist. When he gathers churches, it is not to be their pastor; he raises up others to take this charge and burden. True, he may act as a pastor for a time; but it is simply from necessity. His sphere is aggression, conquest.' He was, in short, a Christian soldier marching on to war, in company with many others. Before very long, an Englishman would be composing a hymn, expressing precisely those sentiments.* When the American Board had sent John Leighton Wilson to West Africa in 1833, it had pictured the entire field of battle.

'Having made a successful beginning among the tribes of the coast,' it declared, 'we shall, as our labours increase and the roads are opened, advance into the interior with our permanent establishments . . . Our European brethren of different denominations, whose line of march already extends across the continent to the South, will advance from that quarter; the English Episcopal Missions will advance from the mountains of Abyssinia, and our brethren from the same denomination at Sierra Leone, and those of various names in Liberia, will move with us from the West; and our children may hear of the meeting of these upon some central mountain, to celebrate in lofty praise, Africa's redemption.'

* S. Baring-Gould wrote 'Onward Christian Soldiers' specifically for a children's church festival in Yorkshire in 1864. The rousing tune to which it is usually sung came a few years later from Arthur Sullivan, who shortly afterwards forsook hymnody for comic opera.

Missionary bodies on either side of the Atlantic were by then thinking of their obligations to the heathen in much the same way. The American vision of the future was almost identical with that of Lewis Krapf in East Africa. It was an order of battle, almost as much as any that was ever issued by a military commander in time of war. The troops were re-recruited, the enemy was clearly recognised, the strategy was devised, the ultimate victory was sure, the scouts had reported back and the first few skirmishes had mettled the Christian soldiery. Now the army began to march forward in earnest.

5

THE ADVANCE IN THE WEST

The Christian army's first advance upon that mythical, panegyric mountain was planned to take place from the west. This was the British expedition to the river Niger, which was ratified so rapturously at the Exeter Hall meeting in London in the presence of Prince Albert and that galaxy of distinguished public figures. That day in June 1840, preoccupied as it was with much Christian fervour against the slave trade, was an intensely moral one. But even then, undercurrents of other interests could be detected among the great eddies and swirls of Gospel rhetoric. The Niger Expedition, indeed, justified itself on purely Christian principles; but it cannot really be mistaken for anything other than a great imperial excursion for the acquisition of British influence in West Africa.

It was part of an expanding climate of interest in the subject. A couple of years before the Baptists had founded the first of the big missionary societies, an Association for Promoting the Discovery of the Interior of Africa had been established in London. It was organised by men of science who had resolved that 'as no species ofinformation is more ardently desired, or more generally useful, than that which improves the science of geography; and as the vast continent of Africa, notwithstanding all the efforts of the ancients, is still a great measure unexplored, the Members of this Club do form themselves into an Association for Promoting the Discovery of the Inland Parts of that quarter of the World'. These men, too, declared their abhorrence of the slave trade, but their primary aim was simply to find out what this unknown region consisted of. By 1840 they had sent several expeditions from the North African coast towards the interior, with varying degrees of success. The first one saw the joint leader dead of dysentery before he had even left his starting point in Cairo. But others had actually crossed the great Saharan desert. That magnificently attractive man Hugh Clapperton – ex-cabin boy, ex-pirate, ex-explorer in Labrador, ex-hunter with a Red Indian tribe, ex-fiancé to an Indian princess, now Captain RN – had struggled south to Lake Chad. Major Gordon Laing, after a journey of appalling privation and sadness, had finally reached the fabled city of Timbuctoo. The news that they had sent back to England had whetted the appetites of men who were not concerned with scientific research in even its vaguest forms, and who did little more than doff their hats as a respectable reflex action whenever the fight to end the slave trade was mentioned.

The effect of the missionary interest in the same area was similar, and a few wise men in Government were well aware that behind the high moral purpose of the missionary societies and the anti-slavery lobby, lurked the anticipations of men who were not chiefly dedicated to an end of man's inhumanity to man in Africa. After Fowell Buxton, of the Church Missionary Society and the Society for the Extinction of the Slave Trade, had presented his great project for the Civilisation of Africa, Lord Palmerston observed to a colleague that 'No doubt the extension of commerce in Africa is an object to be aimed at, but I am inclined to think that such extension will be the effect rather than the cause of the extinction of the Slave Trade'. And thus, in its usual sidelong fashion, the Government itself became committed to a venture that really paid no more than very loud lip service to Christian ideals. It did not even have to accept the responsibility for originating ideas which were only auxiliary to the business of converting heathen souls to God and rescuing savages from degradation. Fowell Buxton had already done this for Her Majesty's Ministers when he presented his proposals in 1839.

His new society, it appeared, had no intention of opening missionary stations or even of starting schools in the region at the present time. If the Government was prepared to back an expedition up the Niger, this should concentrate its efforts on a variety of other projects. It should start a survey of the leading languages and dialects, and translate the most important ones into written scripts. It should introduce the printing press to West Africa and initiate the local manufacture of paper. It should thoroughly investigate the climate in various areas and introduce medicine to relieve the worst of the hardships the climate caused. It should take the first steps towards the engineering of roads and canals for transport and of drainage for health. It should share with

Africans any available knowledge of agriculture and it should provide implements and seeds, as well as advice on the best crops to grow for a world market. This document reads like a highly ambitious product of some United Nations office in the middle of the twentieth century; coming from a man starting out with the haziest information from the field in the middle of the nineteenth century, it is quite astonishingly sophisticated.

It took the Government only a few days to make up its mind. It decided to back the expedition and to put up £79,143 for the initial costs and a year's running expenses. It appointed Captain Trotter RN to command an enterprise which was to be directly responsible to the Admiralty. The expedition would sail for the Rio Nun, which was one of several estuaries of the Niger proper, that tantalising river which had first been sighted by Mungo Park at the end of the eighteenth century, but whose course was still known only as far as the mighty bend where it turned away from the edge of the Sahara and disappeared into apparently endless swamps south-west of Timbuctoo. The Admiralty fell to the planning with a will that indicates the high excitement the expedition now produced in all circles connected with it. The age of steam had scarcely started to smudge its way across the oceans of the world; the year of the Exeter Hall meeting was the year in which the Atlantic was crossed for the first time by a regular steamship service. Nothing less than this exciting new method of propulsion would do for the Niger Expedition. The newly appointed Comptroller of Steam Machinery at the Admiralty was instructed to prepare three steamships for the voyage, all constructed of iron, named *Albert*, *Wilberforce* and *Soudan*. They were fitted with equipment specifically designed for the conditions under which they would be operating. This included a novel system of ventilation, in which a chemical filter would neutralise the dreadful swamp gases which were thought to produce malaria; it was to prove a devastating failure.

In the spring of 1841 the expedition sailed from England. It was loaded with professional sailors and with scientists. It included a group of agriculturists, who were intending to establish a model farm somewhere along the route, for which a number of Quakers had put up £4,000. It took with it only two men directly concerned with missionary work, both of them there on behalf of the Church Missionary Society, with the permission of Her Majesty's Government. One was J. F. Schon, yet another of the German seminarians from Basel, who had been chosen for his linguistic abilities. The other was a very promising young Nigerian called Samuel Adjai Crowther, who had been rescued from slavery himself, and transformed into a missionary catechist, or native lay teacher. Both Schon and Crowther were working for the CMS in Sierra Leone, and they joined the expedition as the three steamships called at Freetown on their way round the West coast, together with a number of liberated slaves who would act as interpreters among the Niger tribes and work the model farm. And as the vessels plodded on towards the Niger mouth, there could have been very few people at home in Britain who were not at least quietly exhilarated by the prospect of the glorious enterprise to which the nation had committed itself. A few there certainly were, for William Simpson, a clerk aboard the *Wilberforce*, had been told by some of his friends that he ought not to accept an engagement with the expedition. It was not, they argued, in accordance with the will of God, whose divine priorities were first the restoration of the Jews to Palestine, then light flowing from Jerusalem to the whole world, and only as a consequence of this, a turning of Africans towards God.

The small squadron arrived at the Rio Nun by the middle of August and by the end of the month the dreaded delta had been passed without a single case of malaria on board. But by 4 September the expedition's chief medical officer, Dr McWilliam, was logging that 'Fever of a most malignant character broke out in the *Albert*, and almost immediately in the other vessels, and abated not until the whole expedition was paralysed'. A fortnight later, some men had died and the general situation had become so bad that Captain Trotter seriously considered turning his vessels round and heading back to the sea. Instead, it was decided that the *Soudan* should be loaded with sick and be despatched south alone. She left with forty fever cases aboard. Two days later the *Wilberforce* followed her. By the beginning of October the *Albert* was still forging upriver and had actually accomplished some of the things set out in the expedition's instructions. Two treaties had been concluded with tribal chiefs and these had nominally secured their permission to allow missionaries to teach Christianity in their areas; they had also promised to forbid the traffic in slaves to the coast through their domains. In addition to the treaties, the model farm had been located on the west bank of the Niger, facing the junction with the Benue river. But by 3 October, with one man after another falling sick, and with the risk of running aground increasing because the river was now falling rapidly with the end of the wet season, Captain Trotter submitted to the inevitable and put his little flagship about, three hundred miles or so up the Niger.

It took the *Albert* a fortnight to reach relative safety and that headlong retreat was a nightmare from start to finish. No sooner had the ship turned south again than Captain Trotter went down with fever, which by then meant that the only officer left to navigate was Mr Willie, the mate. The three engineers were also out of action and Dr Stanger, one of the medical officers, had to do their job single-handed. At ten o'clock one night the captain's clerk rose sweating from his delirium and flung himself overboard, but an African sailor swam after him, hauled him back aboard and lashed him into his hammock to prevent him doing the same thing again. The same precaution was taken with the second engineer, who was fast losing his wits; but somehow he struggled out of his strait-jacket, leapt into the river and was not seen again. Mr Willie now became too ill to navigate, and Dr McWilliam took charge of the *Albert*. Another officer, Mr Kingdom, died and the missionary Schon buried him on the marshy banks of the river. Then Mr Willie died, and within an hour the purser's steward had gone, too, and after him Captain Allen of the Marines. In the space of a week three other officers and a marine were also buried by the enfeebled remnant of the ship's company. By this time the *Albert* was swinging and swerving downstream, all but out of control, its decks strewn with sick and dying men. Dr McWilliam was doing his best to con the ship from a textbook he had discovered in the dead captain's cabin; but he had to leave the bridge repeatedly to attend to some fellow who was screaming in delirium. And from time to time Dr Stanger in the engine room had to abandon his pistons and his pinwheels, to do the job for which he had been trained, too. It was while they were still drifting dangerously down the river that this ghastly wreckage of the glorious Niger Expedition was met by the trading steamer *Ethiope*, whose crew patched them up, and helped them to the shelter of Fernando Po.

The expedition had been an almost total disaster. Of the 145 Europeans who had taken part, no fewer than 130 had been stricken with malaria, and forty of them were now dead. From now on another grim epithet was added to the lore of West Africa. Sierra Leone had for decades been known as the White Man's Grave; now the Rio Nun was to be called the Gate of the Cemetery. Nor were those who had just passed through that gate the only casualties of this monumental failure. By January 1843 the African Civilisation Society was discredited in Government circles and dissolved by its members. On his way to that last meeting Fowell Buxton, the man really responsible for the Niger Expedition, said that 'I feel as if I were going to the funeral of an old and dear friend'. He rarely referred to the expedition afterwards. He survived it only three years himself, and a missionary historian later concluded that 'The failure of the Niger Expedition killed Fowell Buxton as surely as the Battle of Austerlitz killed Pitt'.

A few things were rescued from the wreckage. True, the treaties lapsed and the model farm collapsed after it had started to grow cotton. But the Church Missionary Society was not simply whistling to maintain its own spirits when – instead of calling a disaster a disaster – it allowed that the expedition's immediate objects had been 'imperfectly accomplished'. For in J. F. Schon they had sent to the Niger not only a missionary with eight years' experience in West Africa and proven ability with languages; the journal which he kept up the Niger showed him to be a careful observer and a man of sound judgment as well. He suggested that the society should not contemplate a mission staffed by Europeans anywhere along the three hundred miles of the river that had been navigated, for no suitable sites had been detectable. Moreover, it would be as well to throw greater emphasis upon the training of African catechists to preach the Gospel in areas with such a devastating climate as this. People could only guess what peculiarity in the West African air it was which caused the frightful rate of sickness among Europeans; Samuel Crowther, the Nigerian, was inclined to believe that the great casualty figures aboard the three ships had resulted from the storage of green wood for the boilers in the holds of the vessels, where they had decomposed into malarial germs. Whatever the reason the fact was that the Africans whom the British recruited to work with them had not suffered to anything like the same extent. Out of 158 black men, only eleven had been taken ill and not one of them had died.

Schon's observations led to a small but important change in the policy of the CMS. He reported that in the course of the expedition, brief as this had been, the liberated African slaves who had sailed with the British were warmly welcomed by their own people as prospective teachers; and from his experience in Sierra Leone he could promise the CMS that the colony of ex-slaves there – men who had originated in various parts of West Africa and who had been given Christian sanctuary, training and employment around Freetown – would be equally happy at the prospect of returning to their homelands. Schon considered the possibility of training native catechists in England, but rejected this in favour of extending the scope of the Fourah Bay Institution in Freetown, which had so far been limited to the education of natives for work in Sierra Leone. At the same time, Schon argued, suitably equipped Europeans should be set to intensive study of African vernacular languages, so that translations of Scripture might be made available for the local preachers to take into the interior of the continent. His report was adopted by the CMS almost in its entirety and a special fund was launched for the extension of Fourah Bay. And within four years of the Niger disaster a foundation stone was laid for a new building, which was to be erected on a spot where, forty years before, a factory had stood that engaged in the slave trade. And the rafters of its roof, when finished, were to be made mostly from the masts of redundant slave-ships.

The disaster of 1841 was, in the event, no more than a temporary setback. British missionaries certainly believed they had a divine purpose to fulfil in West Africa, and the British Government was quite as convinced of its temporal obligations in the same area. In 1854 the Government sent the steamship *Pleiad* up the Niger, with a dozen Europeans and fifty-four Africans aboard, who succeeded in sailing 250 miles up the tributary Benue river and returned without a single death from malaria. Samuel Crowther represented the CMS on this venture and reported that 'The reception we met with all along from kings and chiefs of the countries was beyond all expectation. I believe the time has fully come when Christianity must be introduced on the banks of the Niger: the people are willing to receive any who may be sent among them.'

Three years later, the Government felt confident enough to launch yet another expedition on the lines of its first attempt of 1841. The steamship *Dayspring* was specially constructed and sailed from Liverpool under Admiralty command, with instructions to make treaties, prospect for missionary openings and chart fresh stretches of the Niger. Again Crowther sailed, this time in the company of another African catechist from Sierra Leone, J. C. Taylor. The voyage began well. The *Dayspring* got through the 120 miles of the Niger delta without a single casualty and after a month on the river it reached Onitsha, where Taylor was put ashore to start a mission. Crowther made arrangements for three other missionary sites to be established, as soon as men could be sent to run them, and by the beginning of October, three months after entering the delta, the *Dayspring* was prospecting confidently high up the river near Jebba. Then disaster struck again. Here the river narrowed and navigation was made difficult because the current swept strongly round a bend at this point, with large and jagged rocks on either side.

The *Dayspring* was a comparatively small boat, of only seventy-seven tons, deliberately designed with a draught of only 5 ft 8 in. to get over shallow water. Her engines were no more than 30 hp, and though they were adequate for the normal flow of the Niger, they were hopelessly underpowered for passage through really turbulent water. As *Dayspring* butted uncertainly round the bend the current took charge and the little vessel was swept on to the largest of the rocks, badly holed and soon squatting on the river bed with only masts and funnel showing. No one was killed, although most of the stores and equipment was lost, and when the survivors got ashore they discovered from a group of surly tribesmen that they had lost their ship upon the notorious Ju-Ju rock of Jebba, the abode of the god Ketsa. The sinking had, in short, been a form of divine vengeance, for the god abhorred the colour red above most things and the *Dayspring* had been plentifully decorated with it, from Lieutenant Glover's tunic downwards. In propitiation for this unwitting insolence, the tribesmen removed the *Dayspring*'s engines and placed them in Ketsa's shrine on the rock, where engineers found them more than half a century later, when they were building a railway bridge across the Niger.

There was remarkably little hostility to the ship's company of the *Dayspring*, considering what had happened. They were allowed to set up a camp in peace, where they proposed to wait the arrival of a relief vessel, which had been planned to follow them up the river several months later. In the event, the *Sunbeam* had been detained and the shipwrecked party spent a year in the area before being taken back to the sea. They made good use of their time. Lieutenant Glover marched ninety miles upstream, to the place where Mungo Park had died fifty years before. Samuel Crowther scouted out more missionary territory and actually started to build a station, which he could see as an excellent springboard for a Christian advance from the coast into the totally Moslem lands of northern Nigeria and beyond.

The three Niger Expeditions, then, produced a fusion of missionary and political effort that was to become more binding as time went by. The 1841 disaster might have persuaded the CMS to throw great weight into the training of African representatives for the most difficult conditions, but this did not mean a withdrawal of British manpower. By 1846 the white man and his Bible had been introduced at opposite ends of the Nigerian coast, at Badagry and Old Calabar, and was rapidly becoming indistinguishable, among the local populace, from white men who arrived with trading goods and white men in cocked hats bearing treaties and regal authorisations. The mixture was not at all unpalatable to the

Africans with whom they had dealings. The tribes, after all, were perpetually at war with each other. In turn, in varying degree, they saw great advantage to themselves from an alliance with the Europeans, whether these were bent upon spreading the boundaries of God, Mammon or merely Queen Victoria. The Egba in Yorubaland particularly welcomed the missionaries with open arms, for they had suffered much at the hands of rival tribes for many years, and they were well aware that behind each missionary there lurked the power of the steamboat and the ultimate sanction of the naval gunner's mate.

The missionaries themselves, although they came in peace, were not at all indifferent to the protective cover provided by Her Majesty's sailors and marines; and they had good reason to fear that the whim of a chief might change overnight from warm support to blazing hostility. It was in this frame of mind that Hope Waddell, of the United Presbyterian Mission, refused to sail from Britain to Old Calabar in 1845 unless the Admiralty guaranteed the protection of his party; and My Lords Commissioners ordered the Royal Navy to accompany the missionaries to their destination, and to keep a watchful eye upon proceedings ashore until the men of God were well established. The Admiralty really had no choice, even if it had regarded the missionary requirement as a piece of damned impertinence; not with so many high and mighty personages in the land, from the Prince Consort downwards, so deeply interested in this particular method of civilising Africa.

The tortuous relationships that now began to develop along the coastal strip of Nigeria between the local potentates, the missionaries and the British Government are exemplified in the happenings within the province of Eyo Honesty II, king of Creek Town in Old Calabar. When the missionaries first arrived there, Eyo Honesty's rule was confined to the island on which Creek Town stood. He welcomed them warmly, seeking in them potential allies for the extension of his ambition to add Duke Town and Old Town on the mainland to his realm. For their part, the missionaries found him an attractive figure. He spoke English intelligibly (he even acquired an English clerk to his court), he did not smoke or drink, he provided all facilities without question. 'King Eyo is undoubtedly a ruler,' Hope Waddell reported back to Edinburgh, 'and the principal ruler in the country; and as such must be respected by us. Our Christian principles, the interest of the country, the welfare of the Mission stations, require of us to respect him as a ruler of his people.' And Eyo Honesty, his eyes firmly fixed upon the education and the industry that would elevate his Efik people from their comparative poverty and insecurity, declared that 'Every good thing that we have comes from the white people, because they know more than we'.

Within a couple of years, Creek Town had become the base camp for missionary work in Old Calabar. The king's own courtyard was turned into an open-air church for Sunday services and he very often acted as the interpreter between the white missionaries and their black congregations. In his zeal to befriend the missionaries and to be supported by them in his own aims, he even ordered that the *ekpeyong*, the guardian god of every Efik household, should be destroyed throughout his kingdom. By 1850 Eyo Honesty controlled the territory he desired because the enormous wealth he had acquired in the course of his relations with the missionaries and white traders had transformed rival monarchs into his debtors and eventually his agents. This did not make him independent of the white men. They pressed him to use his power, now apparently unlimited in Eyo Honesty's eyes, to end the sacrifice of slaves on the death of their masters. This was asking much of any Efik, for in common with tribes throughout Africa, they believed that slaves must accompany their masters to another world for perpetual support and servitude. Nevertheless, Eyo Honesty obliged the missionaries and declared that henceforth only criminals could be put to death, and this not by their masters, but only after proper trial. This was a breach in the traditional social structure, the consequences of which were far-reaching. It was a weakening of the cultural defence system that extended from one end of Nigeria to the other and which the missionaries had so far been unable to penetrate. But now they pressed Eyo Honesty for more reforms. They formed a Society for the Abolition of Inhuman and Superstitious Customs and for Promoting Civilisation in Old Calabar, which was particularly dedicated to a riddance of infanticide, the murder of twins, the punishment of slaves for the misdemeanours of their masters – a substitution which was commonplace here and elsewhere in Africa. Eyo Honesty had never intended to surrender local customs so completely to the directives of the white man but now he had little choice but to acquiesce, for Consul Beecroft had been enrolled by the missionaries as a founding member of their new society, and behind Consul Beecroft cruised all the power of the Royal Navy. The Consul, indeed, started to impose fines on Efik tribespeople who were deemed guilty of insulting behaviour to the missionaries, which more often than not meant that they were registering a protest against some local custom which had been vilified and then demolished at the behest of the white men.

Eyo Honesty, in short, found that he was now obliged to learn more

of Christian teaching and habits than he really wished to know. Even his own slaves, who had eagerly embraced the philosophy that had relieved them of their heaviest burdens, now began to disobey him. After a few years, these were almost the only people along the coast who wholeheartedly welcomed the missionaries and their interfering ways. Friction began to increase in Creek Town. In Eyo Honesty's more recent acquisitions of Old Town and Duke Town, there was even greater hostility between the native Africans and the colonising Europeans. The people of Old Town, particularly attached to their customs, had been implacably opposed to the missionaries from the start. As for Duke Town, Consul Beecroft doubtless declared the general missionary attitude when he described it as 'an African Sodom and Gomorrah'. In spite of Old Town's deep aversion to proselytes, one of Hope Waddell's men had been stationed there, to make what headway he could against its heathen rites.

Samuel Edgerley was about the worst choice possible for such a posting. He was congenitally tactless and intolerant, without any sympathy at all for the cultural background of what he was habitually pleased to refer to as these 'degraded and heathen people'. Almost as soon as he arrived in Old Town, in 1849, he marched into the Palaver house and kicked over the Egbo drum. This was not only a gross desecration of a sacred object, but an insult to the highest judicial authority in the land, and any Efik would have been executed on the spot for the same action. There was uproar throughout Old Town and it subsided only when Hope Waddell apologised and promised that Edgerley would not repeat his offence. But by 1854 the atmosphere had so changed that almost anything Edgerley did could be sure of the moral support of the other missionaries, as a gesture of solidarity against the increasing antipathy of the Africans. By then he had become so truculent that he went to the shrine of the guardian god of the town and smashed several of the images, including the sacred egg. He took others as personal souvenirs. For a few hours, only Eyo Honesty and his rapidly diminishing loyalty to the Europeans stood between the missionaries and a massacre, for the townspeople took up arms and marched on the mission house. The king appeared in person and dispersed them, but this did little to relieve the feelings of the missionaries and their countrymen, the traders, who felt humiliated when Eyo Honesty chastised them for Edgerley's gross insensitivity and criminal vandalism. From now on, the Europeans began to look for ways to redress a balance of power which they felt was more and more putting them at a disadvantage.

They found it when they brought to the Consul's attention the slaughter of fifty slaves which had recently accompanied the death of the deposed king of Old Town. True, Eyo Honesty had passed a law forbidding this practice, but as the deposed king, Willie Tom, had not been present at the palaver which ratified it, under Efik custom no one could consider it binding upon him, as the missionaries were well aware. But now they lobbied the consulate for action to put down these insubordinate people of Old Town, and adduced the slaughter as evidence in chief of the need for reprisal. Among the other so-called crimes of the Old Towners, they listed innumerable instances of insult which had been offered them since the time of Edgerley's first desecration of shrines. They urged the Consul that he would be 'forwarding the work of Civilisation' if he suppressed in an 'effectual way' the dreadful practices of Old Town. The European traders added their own arguments to those of the missionaries and the Consul had little option but to act upon what was clearly his duty as the representative of a mighty Christian state. He passed a message to the Admiralty and HMS *Antelope* was despatched with all haste from its cruising station just over the horizon. And with one or two full broadsides from the naval gunners, Old Town was razed to the ground. This was not a unique event. Only a few years before, HMS *Antelope* had performed a similar service in bombarding Lagos, farther up the coast, and the CMS missionary in the area, the Rev. C. A. Gollmer, had written exuberantly to London that 'I look upon it as God's interposition for the good of Africa and may we not hope that now the word of God will gain free course among the Jebus, too?' By 1856 Mr Gollmer had acquired such a taste for this method of converting the heathen that he was asking the naval authorities to sail up and attack the intractable Ijebu people as well. And once more, the Admiralty obliged.

The Efik had no answer to the firepower of the British man-o'-war, any more than the Ijebu or any other tribe along the West African coast. The struggle for the cultural supremacy of the tribes, between the traditional tribal authorities and the white missionaries, continued for years; indeed, it was never to end. But from now on the missionaries were almost certain of victory on any issue they cared to push to the limit, as long as they were operating within range of the naval gunners. In Eyo Honesty's territory, one such issue was raised over the question of sanctuary in the mission house at Duke Town. The Europeans claimed that any African who broke a tribal law which was deemed unChristian, could take refuge with them and there be safe. When African outlaws began to seek sanctuary, their chiefs at once demanded that the missionaries should surrender them. The missionaries naturally refused, whereupon the chiefs invoked what sanctions they had at their own disposal. They declared that there must be no more contact between any of their people and the missionaries, that any Efik who had children or slaves attendant upon the mission house must withdraw them, that the local people must not even supply the missionaries with provisions. Before long HMS *Scourge* steamed up the coast and put a landing party ashore, which summoned the local chiefs to a conference on board. There they were told that by inviting the missionaries to their country they had entered into a perpetual obligation to help them, that they must never again take any measures against the missionaries, that if they molested the missionaries and the Africans who were being educated by the missionaries, they would incur the extreme displeasure of the Queen of England. And doubtless, when this advice was offered, the commanding officer of the *Scourge* allowed his eyes to dwell significantly for a moment upon his range of armament. At any rate, with the memory of Old Town's destruction still well in mind, the chiefs sheepishly declared their gratitude for an opportunity to discuss matters, and swore that in future they would make no more palaver against the missionaries.

Their resentment, once they had returned home did not, of course, vanish. By now, in 1856, there were missionary ladies as well as men in Creek Town and surrounding districts, and they had started to clothe the converted slaves in European gowns, which gave them an air of superiority over the free and almost naked women who had not yet been converted to a belief in the Christian god. Mrs Robb was not only intent upon bringing modesty and decorum to her female converts; she instructed them to ignore all tribal customs into the bargain. The tribal authorities reacted by trying to persuade people of their blood not to attend church services. The persuasion failed completely and Agnes Waddel in her journal noted the bitter comment of one old man when he realised that no longer could the traditional sanctions of his people be expected to have their ancient effect. 'Fine ting dis be,' he said, 'white woman come and make law for we.'

From now on, there was no holding the missionary expansion in Old Calabar. It was gradual but it was also very steady. In 1851 there had been two hundred converts but by 1875 there were to be 1,671. Slaves gained more freedom. More people were married according to Christian rites and buried beneath Christian gravestones. And gradually a climate of social custom was changed into a polyglot assembly of institutions in which neither the African natives nor the British missionaries could feel entirely at home. Within a generation of Eyo Honesty's openhanded welcome to Hope Waddell and his assistants, the authorities in Creek Town had passed the following law: 'Henceforth on God's day no market to be held in any part of Creek Town territory; no sale of strong drink, either native or imported, in doorways or verandahs; no work; no play; no devil making; no firing of guns; no Egbo processions; no Palaver.'

6

'A VERY USEFUL INSTRUMENT'

Away from the West African coast, beyond the range of British master-gunners, the land was much less promising for the spread of the Christian Gospel. While Eyo Honesty in Old Calabar was being coerced into accepting a completely new range of social and moral ethics, the inland chiefs were still powerful enough and independent enough to lay down their own laws before any missionary who visited them, and he was well aware that he was allowed to preach his faith upcountry on sufferance. It was to be two or three decades before the sanctions of the British military could be invoked beyond the coastal fringe to fortify the sanctity of the missionary. And yet one of the most spectacular advances in the Christianisation of Africa was taking shape in those years in just such unpromising circumstances. Samuel Adjai Crowther, the Nigerian who travelled as representative of the CMS on the three official Niger Expeditions, was quietly working away in the hinterland of Abeokuta, over one hundred miles from the sea, and producing results that were to send the CMS into paroxysms of gratification and win for Crowther himself an audience of Queen Victoria and a bishop's mitre and crozier.

It was quite a feat for the Yoruba child who had been captured with his family by slavers so many years before. He was saved for his place in missionary history by a British man-o'-war, cruising off the West African coast on anti-slaving duties, and put ashore at Freetown together with the rest of the rescued cargo. He was placed in the care of a schoolmaster, who found this child so bright and promising that he sent him to England for a year's education at the CMS school in Islington. In 1825, at the age of nineteen, when he was back in Sierra Leone as a teacher for the

1. The German missionary Johannes Rebmann, who served the English Church Missionary Society for thirty years in East Africa, preaching from the roof of his house. The sketch was by Captain (later Sir) Richard Burton.

2. 'The death of Captain Allen Gardiner, Sailor and Saint' – from Jesse Page's biography of 1897. The nineteenth-century missionary was always portrayed as an heroic figure to the public in England, in highly sentimental terms.

3. Daniel Lindley and his family, photographed in Rochester, New York, about 1861. This early American missionary became a member of the Dutch Reformed Church in South Africa, and baptised the infant Paul Kruger.

4. By the end of the nineteenth century missionary churches were frequently indistinguishable from their models at home. Interior of the Wesley Church at Cape Coast (Accra) West Africa

5. Samuel Adjai Crowther, the first African bishop, a former slave boy who was eventually consecrated in Canterbury Cathedral, under the patronage of the CMS.

Government, this emancipated young slave was baptised with the names of the Rev. Samuel Crowther, the vicar of Christ Church, Newgate Street, in London, who was a prominent member of the first committee of the CMS. It was common practice for young Africans at their baptism to be saddled with alien names in honour of someone in England who had a reputation that counted in missionary circles, though the habit did not always produce the anticipated results. Many years later a missionary worker wondered aloud 'why could not the late Bishop Crowther have been known by his own native name? It is distressing to read in the local papers of Sierra Leone or Lagos that a man named Henry Venn or William Wilberforce has been sent to prison for felony.'

Crowther was no disappointment, however. He had been teaching with a quiet effectiveness that impressed the Europeans in Freetown, when the missionaries there decided that a native must be sent to London for special training as a catechist who would eventually work among his own people. Crowther was the obvious choice, and his old teacher Mr Davey said so. 'He would, I have reason to believe, prove a very useful instrument for carrying on the work in Western Africa. He has abilities far surpassing any that I have met with before and added to this he appears to be truly pious. Our only fear respecting him might be that he should be lifted up too much by a second voyage to England. He has improved very much under the assiduous care of Brother Haensel . . .'

Brother Haensel was the Rev. Charles Haensel, one of the German Lutherans from the Basel Seminary, whom the CMS had installed as Principal of its school at Fourah Bay. He was a very strict disciplinarian, a man of such austerity and cold Protestant zeal that even the merchants of Freetown were wary of incurring his anger at any misdemeanour, real or imagined. Years later Crowther was to describe him as 'a peculiar person altogether . . . a man of very penetrating qualifications'. Brother Haensel's cast of mind was clearly set out in something he wrote himself during his years at Fourah Bay, before Crowther was sent to England for the second time. 'It has been my endeavour,' he wrote, 'to prevent any sudden rise in the outward condition of the youths. Coming out of Government schools, or out of menial employ, they have mostly brought scanty clothing with them – a couple of shirts, a pair of trousers, a hat and perhaps a jacket, with a book of Common Prayer, and in some instances a Bible, constitute their entire possessions. I have, in the first place, where necessary, added a Bible to their stock, a pair of trousers, and a shirt after a little while, a jacket if necessary, after a month or two, and another pair of trousers after that. This for their full dress on Sunday and other particular occasions; at home they always go barefooted. Even Samuel Crowther does so at home, though his visit to England has raised him to the height of white stockings, a suit of blue cloth, a waistcoat and a beaver hat on Sundays . . . I send occasionally one or other on errands, just to remind them that they are not above carrying a basketful of rice or anything else on their heads. From Samuel Crowther I require only the inspection of these services. I have, however, pointed out to him the necessity of example accompanying precept in this as in all branches of our work, and he follows my suggestions. When Samuel Crowther first entered the Institution he brought with him a mattress with which he had been presented when in England, but as this was too great a luxury I at once forbade its entrance, to which he readily consented. I wish for the good of his own soul to see him in that state of lowliness of mind which Africans so easily lose by visits to England.'

It was thus in a proper state of humility that young Crowther was bundled off to England for a second time. And by the canons of missionary discipline he was still so unspoilt on his return that when the Fowell Buxton plan for the Civilisation of Africa materialised into the first expedition up the river Niger, and the CMS was given Government approval to send a couple of its men with the three exploring vessels, Crowther was quite the most qualified candidate among the Christianised Africans in Freetown. He kept a meticulous journal of what happened aboard the *Albert* and he was of inestimable value in acting as interpreter to the tribespeople. After the emaciated wreck of the expedition had spent some time recuperating at Fernando Po and then staggered off to England, Crowther was left behind at Freetown to continue his teaching there. Spreading the Christian Gospel, Crowther found, was not a particularly easy task even for a man who could speak to pagan Africans as one who shared their culture and their traditions, who had himself originated in the same background. On one occasion he was working among people who worshipped Shango, the god of thunder and lightning. 'I drew their attention to the character of their worship from the lewd expressions which had shamelessly been uttered in my hearing. This was sufficient to inflame the whole assembly. A man rose up with wrath and indignation at my rebuke, and with eyes vivid as lightning, spoke like thunder. He instantly referred me to nominal Christians, who, he said, were the greatest adulterers that could be met with in the Colony, and that he himself was formerly one of the churchgoers, but found no benefit from his connection with the religion of the Bible. To my great mortification, shame and regret I was silenced – the charge was too true.'

Within a few years the CMS had acted on J. F. Schon's recommendation that African catechists should be sent inland from the Niger delta, on the assumption that they would survive the malarial climate better than any European. Crowther was one of the first to be recruited for this role. The CMS had him ordained as a deacon and then sent him to establish a mission, if he could, among his own people in the region of Abeokuta. No area could have given Crowther a better chance of success. He was immediately reunited with the mother and sister he had not seen for almost a quarter of a century. And gradually he began to impress the Yoruba he met, with his own gentleness and goodness. This alone was not enough to explain the advance which Christianity now delicately began to make round Abeokuta. There was tribal factionalism, as there always would be throughout Africa, with one side seeing the advantages to be gained in some kind of alliance with anything that represented the power of alien Europeans. By 1848 Crowther had performed the first baptisms in Abeokuta, and one of the people who received his blessing was his old mother, whom he christened Hannah. But, significantly, it was in that year that the chiefs of the town sent a petition to Queen Victoria, asking her to open the road to Lagos for them for purposes which were entirely commercial. And Her Majesty, mindful of her duty as Defender of the Faith in a Christian nation, sent Lord Chichester out to Africa, together with two beautifully bound Bibles as her personal gift, and a steel corn mill donated by Prince Albert. She also sent a message with his Lordship, which said that 'The Queen and people of England are very glad to hear that Sagbua and the chiefs think as they do upon the subject of commerce. But commerce alone will not make a nation great and happy like England. England has become great and happy by the knowledge of the true God and Jesus Christ.'

Crowther's part in the pacifying process round Abeokuta should not be underestimated, however. The Alake of Abeokuta, the most powerful of the local chiefs, was highly impressed by the transformation wrought in his land by this black Christian missionary. The Alake, no Christian himself, declared that in ten years the people had been turned from war to peace. The missionaries, though a small and weak body in outward appearance, were stronger than any of the mighty men in the land. Before Crowther and his handful of helpers arrived, the roads to Ijaye, Ibadan, Ketu and Ijebu were so dangerous that a caravan of fifty could not pass along them peacefully. But now a woman travelling alone could make a journey of three days in perfect safety. Small children could play outside the walls of Abeokuta in the certainty that they would be unharmed, which had not been so before. If this was the result of Christian mission, then the Alake, heathen though he might be, was very ready to welcome more of these Christian missionaries.

Someone else was by now just as impressed by what he had heard of Samuel Crowther, and he was Lord Palmerston in London. The Government was toying with plans for the second Niger Expedition and it wanted sound advice from men who knew the area before committing itself, so that a repetition of the first failure could be avoided. Crowther was once more extracted from Africa and put aboard ship for the Thames, and after Lord Palmerston had picked his brains about the state of the slave trade and the lie of the land, the Nigerian was taken to Windsor Castle to meet the Queen. Crowther was always a copious diarist and a revealing one; he was far too uncomplicated a man, perhaps too innocent, to conceal or attempt to distort anything of his own feelings. And nothing that he ever wrote so revealed the fundamental awe and gratification he always felt when thrust into the company of his English superiors, as his entry for that November day in 1851.

The appointment at Windsor had been made for 4.30 pm and Crowther was accompanied by Lord Wriothesley Russell, one of the Court officials.

'On our arrival,' Crowther wrote later, 'Prince Albert was not in; the servants-in-waiting went about to seek him. While we were waiting in a drawing-room I could not help looking round at the magnificence of the room glittering with gold, the carpet, the chairs, etc., all brilliant. While in this state of mind the door was opened and I saw a lady gorgeously dressed, with a long train, step gracefully in. I thought she was the Queen. I rose at once and was ready to kneel and pay my obeisance; but she simply bowed to us, said not a word, took something from the mantelpiece and retired. After she left, Lord Russell told me that she was one of the Ladies-in-waiting. "Well," I said to myself, "if a Lady-in-waiting is so superbly dressed, what will be that of the Queen herself!" Soon we were invited to an upper drawing-room, more richly furnished than the first. Here we met Prince Albert standing by a writing table. Lord Russell made obeisance and introduced me, and I made obeisance. A few words of introductory remarks led to conversation about West Africa, and Abeokuta in particular. The Prince asked whether we could find the place on any map, or thereabouts. I then showed the position in the large map from the Blue Book, and brought out of my pocket the small one which Samuel [Crowther's eldest son] had made on the section of the slave trade influence, with the different towns and seaports legibly shown.

'About this time a lady came in, simply dressed, and the Prince looking behind him, introduced her to Lord Russell, but in so quick a way that I could not catch the sound. This lady and the Prince turned towards the map to find out Abeokuta and Sierra Leone, where the slaves are liberated. All this time I was in blissful ignorance of the Great Majesty before whom I stood, was conversing freely and answering every question put to me about the way slaves are entrapped in their homes or caught as captives in war. On inquiry I gave them the history of how I was caught and sold, to which all of them listened with breathless attention. It was getting dark, a lamp was got, and the Prince was anxious to find and define the relative positions of the different places on the map, especially Lagos, which was the principal seaport from which Yoruba slaves were shipped; and when the Prince wanted to open the Blue Book map wider it blew the lamp out altogether, and there was a burst of laughter from the Prince, the lady, and Lord Russell. The Prince then said, "Will Your Majesty kindly bring in a candle from the mantelpiece?" On hearing this I became aware of the person before whom I was all the time. I trembled from head to foot, and could not open my mouth to answer the questions that followed.

'Lord Russell and the Prince told me not to be frightened, and the smiles on the face of the good Queen assured me that she was not angry at the liberty I took in speaking so freely before her, and so my fears subsided. I pointed out Lagos, the particular object of inquiry, and told them that I with others was shipped from that place, and showed the facility which that port has, beyond all other ports, as a depot, being much nearer, and the port of the highway to the interior Yoruba countries. The Prince said: "Lagos must be knocked down, by all means; as long as they have the lake to screen themselves and the man-o'-war outside, it is of no use." The Queen was highly pleased to hear this. Lord Russell then mentioned my translations into the Yoruba language, and I repeated, by request, the Lord's Prayer in the Yoruba, which the Queen said was a soft and melodious language. Lord Russell informed the Queen of my having seen Sir H. Leeke, who rescued me and others from the slave-ship many years ago, which interested her very much. She was told that Mrs Crowther was recaptured in the same way that I was, and she asked whether she was in England, and was told no. She asked after Sally Forbes Bonetta, the Yoruba African young girl rescued from Dahomey. After these questions she withdrew with a marked farewell gesture.' And Crowther was whisked off to Cambridge, to address the undergraduates there, and appeal to them for more missionaries to preach the Gospel to his people in Africa.

The CMS had many African catechists working on its behalf now, but Samuel Crowther had become a man apart, a very paragon of the virtues to be recovered in fallen man if only he submitted his heart and soul to the missionary process. On his return to Africa now he is to be seen in various attitudes of patronage which had previously belonged only to white men in his country. He does not condescend to his countrymen; he has far too much genuine humility for that. But on a journey in the hinterland of Abeokuta he gives to a boatman who has helped him a small piece of Windsor soap, recording in his journal that night that 'possibly at some future date this unknown toilet requisite would be displayed to the admiration of his friends, if not to their adoration, too'. He presents the king of Ketu with another piece of missionary equipment he has acquired on his most recent excursion to London, a beautiful silk patchwork quilt, made by some missionary well-wisher in England, and two silk and velvet caps decorated with feathers and flowers. At which the king of Ketu claps his hands in delight and promises Crowther to make himself at home and to invite any of his missionary friends to do likewise. His journal becomes less the artless record of a naïve and unsophisticated man, much more the diary of a fellow who has acquired opinions of his own and the confidence to pronounce them with some authority; basically they are echoes of attitudes which Crowther must have heard expressed many times in the CMS headquarters in London and elsewhere in his widening experience.

When news of the Indian Mutiny reaches West Africa he is caught writing that 'The reputation of the unjust disparagement on the missionary work as being the cause of this barbarous mutiny . . . will open the eyes of those who opposed the conversion of the Sepoys, to see what advantage it is in any community to have converted natives mingled with it, who are like salt in the midst of a mass of corruption'. And yet Crowther, although he is steadily becoming less the pure African and more the hybrid Afro-European in outlook, never entirely loses his personal and native gentleness and shrewdness. The CMS, by the late 1850s, was pushing towards the north of Nigeria and thinking fondly of the graces that might follow the conversion of Moslems there. Crowther is astute enough to remark that a Moslem will never be brought round to Christianity if his own religion is abused as false and inferior 'but by kind treatment he may be lead to read and study the Christian's Bible, which by the blessing of God may lead him from the error of his ways'. By then Crowther has served on the second and third Niger Expeditions and has become much more than the very useful instrument of conversion which his old schoolmaster had envisaged. He has become the most notable black Christian in Africa, and if there is ever to be something of an indigenous Church there, he is clearly the man to lead it. And by this time the CMS in London is much under the influence of someone who devoutly believed that the missionaries must look forward to a time when Africans would run their own Church.

This was Henry Venn, a Prebendary of St Paul's Cathedral, a member of the Clapham Sect, son of one of the CMS founders, John Venn, and from 1842 secretary of the CMS for thirty years. In a series of minutes he produced during the 1850s, Venn manufactured a blueprint for missionary strategy in the Church of England. He decided that converts made in Africa and Asia should slowly be persuaded to pay for their ministers instead of accepting them as a charity from England. As soon as the churches in any area reached this stage they should be organised into a native pastorate, staffed by African ministers who had been carefully trained for this job by the white missionaries. As soon as the white missionary had accomplished this task in any area, he should move on to fresh territory, leaving the Africans to rule themselves under the general and regional direction of Europeans. Venn was a visionary, with the far-sightedness of Wilberforce before him, and his vision was not limited to an ideal of the Church in Africa staffed and governed by Africans. He sent instructions to his missionaries in the field, urging them to exercise their will-power and to respect African customs and traditions which were clearly unChristian by any European standards. He even suggested that there were circumstances when slavery perhaps ought not to be tampered with, coming as it did within Venn's definition of 'racial peculiarity'.

One thing Venn determined to initiate at the earliest opportunity was the African Church. Once again Samuel Crowther was brought to London, and this time it was to be consecrated as the first black bishop in the Church of England. The glowing optimism of the moment in CMS circles was conveyed by one of its journals as the day of the ceremony drew near. 'Already the African Christian,' wrote some anonymous contributor, who might well have been Venn himself, 'has shown himself not only capable of understanding and receiving the truth of Christianity, but of communicating it to his fellow-countrymen. On him the African climate exercises no malign influences, to him the languages of Africa present no impediment . . .' The moment had come for the African native, already raised to the ministry, to be further elevated to the episcopate, and the initial choice had fallen on one man. 'Nearly twenty-one years have elapsed since the Rev. Samuel Crowther was ordained a deacon by the Bishop of London. The Lord has given him grace during the period which has since elapsed to continue humble, consistent and useful. He has made full proof of his ministry.' Another Church periodical was a little more cautious in its approval of the new appointment, declaring that 'the future of the native Church depends on the manner in which its first Bishop shall administer its polity and organise its laws. It will be necessary also for him to exercise great discrimination in conferring Holy Orders on his brethren, and to take heed that he magnifies his office in the estimation of all by the exemplary consistency of his life and the holiness of his conversation.'

Cautious many people in the Church of England might well have been, but the Church produced all the pomp and circumstance at its command for the consecration of Samuel Crowther. It was such an event that special trains were run from London and elsewhere to take all the participants and well-wishers to Canterbury Cathedral. The nave and chancel were packed at eight o'clock in the morning, some time before the ceremony was due to take place. Dignitaries of Church and State were there, and so was Admiral Leeke, who had been the young captain of HMS *Myrmidon* when it rescued the child Crowther from the slave-ship off Lagos many decades before. The Archbishop himself led the consecration. The Bishop of Lincoln read the Epistle and the Bishop of Winchester the Gospel. The sermon was preached by a Professor of Philosophy from Oxford. And thus, on St Peter's Day, 1864, Samuel Adjai Crowther, once a totally obscure Yoruba child, was transformed by Divine Permission, into the Church of England's Bishop in western Africa. And the University of Oxford capped the achievement by making him an honorary Doctor of Divinity.

Within three weeks the new Bishop Crowther was on the boat for Lagos. There he established his episcopal headquarters, though he was always to be much more mobile than any bishop before him, travelling up the Niger to outlying parts of his diocese whenever there was a Government steamer going in the right direction. He established more outposts of the Church on some of these visitations, and the college at Fourah Bay in Sierra Leone kept him supplied with native catechists and schoolmasters to staff them. The fear that may have been entertained in some quarters of the CMS, that this black bishop might rush around his native land ordaining his fellow-countrymen without the most careful preparation and perfect discrimination was, however, groundless. In his first seven years as a bishop, Crowther turned only eight Africans into priests. And he discovered that his own rank and breeding, impressive though they might be to fellow-Christians in Africa, were by no means a universal guarantee that he would be welcome wherever he went.

In 1867 Abeokuta was no longer the peaceful place extolled by the Alake some years before, and Christian missionaries were no longer as welcome among the people generally there as he had been prepared to make them. There had been a rising against the Christians in the town, and some people had been killed. In September, Crowther was travelling up-river on one of his periodic journeys round the diocese when he came into the territory of Chief Abokko. They had known each other for a long time and they had always been on the most friendly terms. But now Abokko's men suddenly appeared and seized Crowther, together with all the stores and equipment in his boat. Part of the haul included £50 in gold and silver, with which Crowther was going to pay wages at a station farther upstream, and 16,000 cowrie shells, with which his party would buy provisions on the journey. The Bishop and his men were brought before Abokko, who at once flew into a temper and harangued his old acquaintance about a variety of grudges. British merchants, he said, who by now were trading high up the Niger, refused to recognise his sovereignty over that stretch of the river. He was constantly slighted, he claimed, by being given only small and paltry presents unfitting to one of such high rank as his. Four of Crowther's boatmen were at once put in irons and Abokko made it quite clear that the Bishop himself would not be allowed to leave unless ransom was produced. At first, the price asked was two hundred slaves. When Crowther declared that he would die rather than produce any such thing, Abokko demanded alternative terms. He would, he said, take nothing less for the release of the Bishop than 1,000 bags of cowries, which at that time would have been worth £1,000 along the Niger; he would also require another 1,000 bags for the release of Crowther's son Dandeson, who was also in the party. One of the processes of tribal justice in the region, however, required the presence of a mediator in difficult and intractable cases and the mediator on this occasion ruled that the whole of Crowther's party should be released on payment of coral beads, velvets, white satins and cowries to a total value of £1,000.

It was at this point, when the Bishop and his party were resigning themselves to an uncomfortable and anxious wait until the ransom goods could be brought up from the delta, that one of the British trading vessels, the *Thomas Bagley*, steamed into sight round the bend. It flew from its mast the flag of the British Consul in Lokoja, Mr Fell, and as soon as this gentleman stepped ashore he realised what was afoot. Quietly he told his men to gather up the Crowther possessions while he diverted the attention of Abokko and his people. Then he went into the chief's compound and began to palaver with him about the ransom. Abokko remained adamant that there would be no freedom for the Bishop until the agreed price was paid. Mr Fell turned to Crowther and told him to make for the steamer and, in pandemonium, the Europeans and Christian Africans raced down to the river, while Abokko's men grabbed weapons and tried to head them off. Crowther and Dandeson and the rest scrambled aboard the *Thomas Bagley*, but just before reaching the water's edge, Mr Fell was hit by a poisoned arrow and died shortly afterwards. 'I would, had such been the will of God,' wrote Crowther that night, when he was safely away from Abokko's stretch of the river, 'that I had been shot and my dead body taken to Lokoja instead of his.'

Crowther was rarely placed in such a humiliating position as that, partly, no doubt, because of his own character, which was a passport which won him tolerance even in regions where Christians were not particularly welcome; partly because he was, after all, a symbol of British power, and British power increasingly dominated the country. But he could never be free of the tension that was inseparable from his own hybrid position. He could instinctively see the tribal point of view and approach it sympathetically, but he now had responsibilities to a different tribal god, he was enmeshed in different tribal values, he was gratified by different tribal rewards and all of these in any conflict dominated his actions in the end. There was, for example, the business of the guanas at Bonny.

The people of this region worshipped the guana, or monitor lizard. Europeans who were living there, on missionary work or for trade, found that the guanas ate their chickens, their turkeys, ducks and geese with impunity. They lay across roads or in doorways, six feet long, and they lashed out with their long tails, which were flexible as whips, with sharp serrated edges, at anyone who tried to pass them. If a European wounded or killed a guana he was immediately in trouble. A crowd would gather, and if it did not assault the man and rob him, it would haul him off to the local authority. And before long, the indignant European would be brought before a consular official whose duty it was to advise that native susceptibilities should, wherever possible, be placated. The European must in future avoid giving offence in such a trifling matter as that of monitor lizards. And the European would not be much soothed by this advice.

It was largely because of Crowther's influence over many years, and his gentle persuasion, that the king of Bonny formally and for ever renounced the worship of guanas on Easter Day 1867. Christianity had been gaining a foothold in the area for years. King William Pepple had in 1848 invited the United Presbyterian Mission Board in Edinburgh to come to his domain, largely because he was jealous of the advance being made in Old Calabar under the combined influence of Hope Waddell and Eyo Honesty. He had offered to pay all the educational expenses of any Presbyterians who might come out to Bonny for a full twenty years, with the extra inducement of £500 per annum for the upkeep of one missionary. Edinburgh turned the offer down, because the king was not prepared to yield certain tribal customs that the Scotsmen regarded as obligatory. But by 1867 he had been succeeded by George Pepple I. This king had been educated in England, where he had become a Christian. He paid much more than lip service to a trinity of Cs, which were 'that civilisation, that commerce and that Christianity which I should like to see diffused among my subjects'. He was not prepared to forgo polygamy and a certain divine right of action residing in his office, but otherwise he was even more Anglicised than Samuel Crowther. He had been applauded in Britain for his after-dinner speeches, he was once received by the Prince of Wales, and he used to tell the children of Bonny, when he addressed them as their sovereign, that the Lord Mayor of London was his special friend.

It was a deeply embedded principle of Bonny that no king should ever travel outside his territory, but George Pepple would regularly go to the seaside and even to Madeira for a holiday in the best English tradition. He refused to take oaths or to perform rites incompatible with Christianity. He read *The Times*, whenever a new consignment could be brought to him from the coast, he wore a suit which had been tailored in St James's, he sported a moustache which he had waxed to fine and horizontal points. A British official who knew him well sometime later reported that he 'smokes cigarettes, scents his handkerchiefs with the newest essence, dilates on the acting of Ellen Terry and Irving, and criticises the comic operas of Gilbert and Sullivan'. He was also a Sunday school teacher and a member of that governing body which Henry Venn was intent on establishing in the native African Church.

And yet, on the very doorstep of this sophisticated dandy, half-naked tribesmen worshipped the monitor lizard with the savage devotion that had been bred into them through many generations. Nothing could better illustrate the incongruity that was now beginning to spread across Africa; which, indeed, is still there today. George Pepple soon stopped part of it.

Henceforth, he decreed, this example of paganism should cease. Crowther was there when the king made his pronouncement; indeed, it was Crowther who officiated at the Easter Day service in Bonny when George Pepple spoke. 'No sooner was this renunciation made,' wrote the Bishop, 'and orders given to clear the town of them than many persons turned out in pursuit of these poor reptiles . . . and now killed them as if it were in revenge, and strewed their carcases all about in open places and in the markets by dozens and scores; 57 were counted in one market place, where they were exposed to public view as a proof of the people's conviction and former error, and that they were determined to reform in good earnest in this respect . . . There was another decision made respecting the removal of the guanas. Lest any hereafter should say he had not had some share in the extinction of the sacred reptile, it was decided that some blood should be sprinkled into all the wells in Bonny town to indicate that they had concurred not only in its destruction, but also in its use as food.' For days after the massacre of guanas, there was only one well in Bonny which was unpolluted by their blood, and therefore usable. It was the well belonging to the Church, behind the mission house. And Samuel Crowther's response to the situation was an exact measurement of the distance he had come since his infancy as a child of Yoruba parentage and pagan ancestry. He said that the townspeople were welcome to draw water from the mission well, on one condition. They must be decently clothed.

In his writings as a bishop there is, until his declining years, now even more of the rather lofty, Anglicised observer of his fellow-Africans than when he was first finding his feet as a missionary and establishing his confidence as a man of authority. He remarks that unconverted natives are shrewd, artful and cunning, ready to prey on the stranger, to weigh up the extent of his ignorance before striking him down in commerce, charging him much more than a hundred per cent above the normal market price of things. These natives are never ashamed of themselves so long as they have gained their object, for strangers are considered their lawful prey. 'Deceitfulness and self-interest, again, are traits in their character . . . Time is to them of no value; after the seller has wasted about five hours in holding on to see whether you would call him back and accept his terms, he will come back and offer to accept your terms as a particular favour to you . . . They are passionate and revengeful; hence there is great difficulty in reconciling them. Nothing satisfies one who imagines himself wronged, unless retaliation. The propensity to theft may be classified as an instinct. When a stranger is robbed, it is considered a matter of course; by mutual agreement nothing is revealed by anyone privy to the theft, old or young . . .'

This is a man who is confident, beyond peradventure of any doubts, of his own mission and of the benefits that his faith will bring to his fellow-countrymen; benefits not merely spiritual but social and economic and political as well. He is a prince of the Church, moving among people who are almost invariably poor in every sense compared to himself. Crowther was continually being asked for scraps of the Bible, so that superstitious tribesmen could wear them as prophylactics to avoid ill-health. At a church service in Onitsha he records that the collection from the faithful consisted of a small piece of tobacco leaf, a bunch of trade beads, a reel of cotton, some fish-hooks and a silk pocket-handkerchief. He himself had climbed far above such things now. Without rising to the dandified heights of George Pepple I, he always dressed in English clothes, well-cut and clerically black. He refused to allow teaching in the schools of his Niger Mission to be conducted in anything but English.

It was inevitable that when a concerted reaction against the British presence in Nigeria occurred, Bishop Crowther should scorn it in the roundest terms. The reaction did not take place until he was an old man, when a generation and more of his people had been educated in mission schools, had tasted some of the benefits the British endowed them with, had been given some share in the administrative machinery of their land, but yet felt themselves to be dispossessed of a birthright. They had been given a vision of the possible, but they wanted to achieve it on their own terms and under their own control, without having to pay any subscription to a foreign overlord. This was one of the earliest manifestations of anti-colonialism, and Samuel Crowther had no sympathy with it at all. Africa, he declared, had neither the knowledge nor the skill to devise plans to bring out her vast resources for her own improvement; from want of Christian enlightenment, cruelty and barbarity overspread the land to an incredible degree. 'Therefore,' he said, 'to claim "Africa for the Africans alone" is to claim for her the right of continued ignorance to practise cruelty and acts of barbarity as her perpetual inheritance. For it is certain, unless help come from without, a nation can never rise much above its present state. "Hath a nation changed their gods which are yet no gods?" No, "for all people will walk every one in the name of his God".'

Nothing less than this could be expected of a man who had passed through Samuel Crowther's bewildering accumulation of experience. A slave child had been liberated by men who carried themselves like gods, who claimed divine inspiration, who had apparently supernatural powers of life and death. He had been cherished by them and their kinsmen, he had been exalted by them far above any other African he had ever heard of. They had liberated in him all his own natural powers. Their Queen, a demi-goddess herself, had received him in her own home, listening to him with breathless attention and smiling upon him graciously. Their Archbishop of Canterbury had placed hands upon his head, through which flowed a divine influx of grace, which gave him a god-like quality of his own. Everywhere he had travelled in that fantastic and marvellous land across the seas, he had been received with acclaim, while honours and wealth had been presented to him as of right. The Royal Geographical Society had given him a gold watch, valued at £40, in recognition of his valuable services to geographical science. All this to one who had been but a slave child in darkest Africa.

It would have required a god-like quality for any man not to speak with the voice of the white demi-gods in those circumstances. Samuel Crowther was a human being and so, in a sense, his voice could be taken for a treachery by some of his own people. They vilified him for this apparent betrayal. In the end, he would suffer betrayal himself.

7

THE GREATEST MISSIONARY

By the time Samuel Crowther had been raised from his ancestral obscurity and translated into a bishop of the Established Church of England, Queen Victoria's great and happy Christian nation was dazzled by a name far more glittering than his. Indeed, within a month of Crowther's consecration in Canterbury Cathedral in 1864, the heroic figure of David Livingstone was to emerge from Africa for a second time.

Livingstone was not, on this occasion, to be received with the delirious acclaim that had greeted him from one end of the British Isles to the other after his first period in the mission field, for in July 1864 he was returning from his expedition up the river Zambezi, and this had produced nothing at all for the British to make a great song and dance about. The Government, in fact, which had mounted the expedition and financed it largely in submission to Livingstone's own powers of persuasion and his colossal popularity, had become somewhat sceptical of his capacities and his advice. In 1864 the name which for several years had held a lustre for the British second only to that of Queen Victoria herself, was about to go through a slightly tarnished period which would not end until Henry Morton Stanley found Livingstone at Ujiji in those epic circumstances that fortified a living legend once and for all. After that, and particularly after his death and his burial in Westminster Abbey, David Livingstone's reputation was secure from assault by anyone but the most reckless heretic. Even in the middle of the twentieth century, historians would still acknowledge him as the greatest missionary of them all. For almost a hundred years he would take his place in the pantheon of English-speaking Christians as a figure of inspiring sanctity and devotion, to be considered in the same breath as St Francis of Assisi and St Joan of Arc. A great man he undoubtedly was, of uncommon and quite staggering devotion to a purpose of his own. He was also an exceedingly complex man, with weaknesses and sometimes unpleasant foibles that history has taken little account of. The David Livingstone who emerges from his journals and correspondence, from the diaries of associates and acquaintances, is not by any means the David Livingstone who was glorified by the missionary movement after his death, and deified for many generations in the Sunday School classrooms of Great Britain. Of those who knew him, only H. M. Stanley appears to have seen him as an immaculate human being, devoid of warts, elevated upon a plane much higher than that of any contemporary. And such is the need of any people to idealise totally its hero figures, that the image which the hero-worshipping Stanley presented to the world is the one which English-speaking Christians have popularly held ever since.

The year 1864 was not the only one in which the paths of Samuel Crowther and David Livingstone almost, but not quite, crossed. Their early lives were in a small way not completely dissimilar. The one had been rescued from an African obscurity and presented with an education that opened an unprecedentedly new world for him; the other had been reared at Blantyre, Lanarkshire, in a Scottish industrial poverty and had raised himself to the threshold of greatness with the aid of his Latin grammar and dogged attendance at night school after his shift in the factory.

By 1840 Crowther was being drilled to represent the CMS upon the first Niger Expedition; and the twenty-seven-year-old Livingstone was sitting in the audience at Exeter Hall that summer, when the expedition's plans were made public with such a fervent flourish. He had long since decided to become a missionary and he might well have been preparing to sail for China if the Opium War there had not barred the way, for he had been attracted by the possibilities held out in the writings of the missionary pioneer in China, Karl Gutzlaff. Instead, after consulting Robert Moffat, who was home on leave from the Cape, he offered himself to the London Missionary Society for work in Africa. Now he was almost at the end of his medical training at the Charing Cross Hospital. That November he was ordained a minister of religion at the Albion Chapel, London Wall, together with other men who were to serve the LMS, and within a fortnight he was on board ship, bound for South Africa.

Typically, he persuaded Captain Donaldson to teach him something of navigation and spent much of the voyage struggling with a sextant and compasses. Livingstone's appetite for knowledge verged on the pathological. There would be many men whose record in converting pagan tribespeople to Christianity was far superior to his, and there were certainly many doctors in his day whose practice of medicine was based more upon a detached observation of cause and effect, and less upon a brisk prejudice against all forms of hypochondria. There was no one at all to match David Livingstone in the breadth of his interests, or in his ability after a time to write at length and with enormous detail upon topography, botany, zoology, disease, linguistics and anthropology. It is a professional voice from the twentieth century which has remarked that 'for his own period he is by far the most comprehensive source of information on South-Central Africa'. Up to a few days before his legendary death at Ilala, Livingstone was still making his customary notes about new fishes, animals and plants he had just seen.

That outward voyage displayed another side of Livingstone's character. When he had laboured as a piecer in the Blantyre cotton mill, his workmates had discovered what a spiky fellow he could be. They had heard that he was planning to get out of the factory as soon as he could, that he was set on something bigger and better for himself; the Latin grammar propped up on his looms was intended as a passport to something much more rarified than mill management. His mates were sceptical, of course. Some of them even ventured to suggest that they thought he would do better to forget his big ideas and stay put with them. At which Livingstone would become tight-lipped and snap round at them: 'You *think*! I don't need anyone to think for me, I assure you.' As he was to tell his brother-in-law years after, David Livingstone never followed anyone else's views in preference to his own judgment. And on the boat to South Africa he turned his caustic tongue once more upon colleagues.

Travelling with him on behalf of the LMS were William Ross and his wife. Ross was a former schoolmaster, he was eleven years older than Livingstone, but they had been ordained together at London Wall the previous month. There was an inevitable basis of friction from the start, for while Livingstone came from the orthodox Presbyterian Church of Scotland, the Rosses belonged to the United Secession branch of that Church, and a number of wafer-thin but none the less bitterly contested principles divided the two sects. The Rosses themselves were clearly willing enough to patronise the serious young bachelor accompanying them. When the three discussed the prospects of the life that lay ahead of them, the married couple would sigh a little heavily and quote that passage from Ecclesiastes whose essence is that two are better than one. Unfortunately for the Rosses, the voyage to the Cape was a rough one, neither of them was a good sailor, and when they were in the throes of seasickness one day young Dr Livingstone breezily quoted the passage back to them. This was to develop into an abiding animosity when these missionaries had settled down to their African work, with the Rosses telling enlarged tales of Livingstone's cruelty and Livingstone heatedly declaring that 'the only cruelty I was guilty of was quoting the same text to him when both he and his spouse were turning their stomachs out into one basin'. He never forgave the Rosses for the rumours they spread about him. When Mrs Ross died of dysentery a few years later, Livingstone wrote to one friend that she was 'a loss to her husband and children, that's all. She may, however, have been useful sometimes'; and to another he wrote 'No loss certainly, not even to her own children. They were left to grow in unrestricted heathendom.'

From the outset of his work in South Africa, Livingstone had little taste for combining his own talents with those of other missionaries. After a month or so in Cape Town he sailed on to Port Elizabeth and then trekked upcountry to the most northern of the LMS outposts at Kuruman. There was already a quarrelsome atmosphere when he arrived, for while two of the missionaries there believed in making use of native teachers whenever possible, their two colleagues were adamantly opposed to this. One of the latter was Robert Moffat, under whose influence Livingstone had come before leaving Britain and who was to be the only missionary with whom the young doctor got on really well. Livingstone's own highly individualistic temperament could have done nothing to soothe whatever frictions were in the air on his arrival. He never would yield anything of his judgment to anyone, even to men with much greater experience than himself, and time did nothing to soften his craggy nature. Years later he wrote to Moffat, by then home in Britain, that 'there is no more Christian affection between most if not all the "brethren" and me than between my riding ox and his grandmother'.

Not all the strains that occurred in Livingstone's relations with colleagues followed from his intolerance of advice. He was deeply critical of the narrowness that most of the LMS representatives in South Africa practised in their interpretation of the Christian Gospel. They were almost entirely rigid men, with dogmatic aversions to breaking the Sabbath and the nudity of the natives, convinced that those who did not follow their teachings meticulously would be damned for all eternity.

Livingstone himself was remarkably flexible at such points. He had an instinct for African tradition and behaviour, for the psychology of the tribesman, which far surpassed that of almost every European who had so far made contact with these heathen. He certainly did not regard the African as in any way his equal except before God, and it is conceivable that he did not even accept that qualification. He could generalise about the Bechuana chiefs as 'hereditary asses, born idiots or little better, good at nothing but begging'. He treated them, as often as not, in much the same way that a brisk sergeant-major might handle a new platoon of rather obtuse and raw recruits. 'I tell my Bakwains,' he wrote to the secretary of the LMS on one occasion, 'that if spared ten years I shall move on to the regions beyond them. Now is their opportunity and if they do not learn, the guilt will rest on their own heads.' In fact, he spent less than six years with them, and in that time he was very often away, scouting out the regions beyond the known territory of the white man, responding much more to his own personal devil than to the vocation which was ostensibly derived from the God of the Christians. Yet in spite of his peremptory paternalism, Livingstone had a genuine regard for the native virtues of the African. He dealt honestly with them when this was by no means common among Europeans. And there was in his own nature that which they could admire. He was tough and he was apparently without fear of man or beast. He inspired in them high devotion and in the end it became something little short of worship.

After only a couple of months at the mission station in Kuruman, Livingstone and his colleague Roger Edwards set off for the north, to prospect for new openings there. Some 250 miles or so upcountry they found the people evidently eager for the assistance of missionaries and Livingstone decided that he must stay among them alone, to study their tribal life and language before he could be of any use to them as a teacher. It was here that he had his first encounter with Chief Sechele. At once, the two men established a rapport that was to develop into firm friendship some years later when Livingstone went to live among the Bechuana people.* Sechele was a man of acute intelligence, with a capacity to acquire new skills that impressed this persevering Scot, with his own addiction to study and absorption. He mastered the alphabet in a single day, soon learned how to read, and after that was inseparable from the Bible which Livingstone presented to him. Isaiah was his favourite section and he would wander round his compound, shaking his head in gratification, saying, 'He was a fine man, that Isaiah; he knew how to speak.' Sechele had, of course, a number of wives, and even Livingstone's

* The Bakwains of Livingstone's references.

flexibility did not extend to offering the Christian sacraments to a chiefly polygamist. Yet he did not once attempt to browbeat Sechele into renouncing his multiplicity of consorts. Instead he quietly pointed out Christian precepts which Sechele could accept without too much personal discomfort and in the end the chief decided to make a settlement upon all but one of his women and henceforth to live with her alone. It was a short-lived renunciation. Within six months he had seduced another woman, and in doing so deeply hurt the man who had so carefully steered him into monogamy. 'He never denied it,' wrote Livingstone to Robert Moffat, 'but confessed he had fallen before temptation on that occasion. The confession loosened all my bones. I felt as if I should sink to the earth, or run away . . . When I thought of the reproach to the name of Christ, no one except yourselves can imagine the lancinating pangs. They fell on the soul like drops of aqua fortis on an ulcerated stomach. I suppose we thought too much of him and too little of Him whose grace we ought to have magnified in him.' Sechele was, nevertheless, a small and unique triumph for Livingstone. During those six months of grace he had been baptised and no one else among the Bechuana tribes achieved that condition under Livingstone's tutelage throughout the six years that the Doctor spent among them.

By this time his friendship with Moffat had been cemented by marriage to Moffat's daughter Mary. Livingstone could never by any stretch of the imagination be regarded as a warm man; but, even so, there is something peculiarly bleak in the way he announced his betrothal to the world; it sounds like the calculation of someone for whom marriage was little more than an important detail in a grand strategy of action. 'Various considerations connected with this new sphere of labour,' he wrote to the LMS in London, 'having led me to the conclusion that it was my duty to enter into the marriage relation, I have made the necessary arrangements for union with Mary, the eldest daughter of Mr Moffat, in the beginning of January 1845 . . . I may mention that I do not regret having come out single. I rather think it would be advantageous if many of our young missionaries would spend at least as much time previous to marriage as would enable them to acquire the language and become acclimatised. In cases where young men would be kindly cared for by older brethren, a much larger delay would be advantageous for the mission, but when there is an almost total deprivation of European society and civilisation, long delay would be improper.'

Livingstone was certainly not impervious to sexual attraction. Missionaries generally avoided remarking on the blatant sexuality of African women so pointedly, that one comes to the conclusion that a great deal of stern Victorian will-power was applied to subdue their own natural reactions. Not so in the case of Livingstone. He notes in one of his journals that he has not yet met any beautiful woman among the black people and that 'I cannot conceive of any European being so far captivated with them as to covet criminal intercourse'. It is possible, indeed, that the sexual drive in this strong-minded and aggressive man was powerful enough for him to appreciate the lusty Sechele's predicament far better than most missionaries, and accordingly to treat him with much more sympathy in the first place than Sechele would have obtained from any other representative of the LMS.

The Livingstones settled for the start of their marriage among Sechele's tribe of the Bechuana peoples. It was an isolated existence, made even more lonely than it need have been by Livingstone's inability to work well with people of his own race. At the beginning, Roger Edwards shared the mission with them; he was, in fact, the senior man in the region. But so frequent were the arguments that Livingstone provoked by his plain speaking and his intolerance of anyone else's viewpoint, that the partnership soon dissolved and the Livingstones moved with Sechele and his people to build a new township on the Kolobeng river, nearly three hundred miles above Kuruman. His only contact now with his fellow-missionaries in South Africa was to be with his father-in-law, upon whom he depended for much besides the only advice he was ever pleased to take from Europeans. Constantly messengers would travel south from the tiny mission, bearing requests to Moffat down in Kuruman. Could Moffat procure some heifers for his daughter and son-in-law? Had he any paint-oil to spare? Would it be possible to get a bullet-mould sent out from Birmingham? Please would he arrange for some new axles to be sent upcountry without delay? The Moffats usually obliged at once and seem to have generously discharged their duty as Christian in-laws. They even kept the Livingstones regularly supplied with subscription copies of a popular Church journal from England, though after a time the Doctor became impatient of some of the contents. 'I felt glad,' he scribbled one day, 'to hear that you, or rather Mrs Moffat, had put a stop to *The Patriot*. It has of late become excessively nauseous to me. The filthy quack advertisements stuck at the bottom of some of the pages create an unpleasant feeling in my mind every time I reach them. Holloway, a Jew I believe, draws thousands of pounds annually from the public purse by falsehood, and the editors of *The Patriot*, for the sake of a rather higher rate of payment, admit his lies into the news part of the paper and thereby become the vehicle by which a portion of the religious world too is drawn into the vortex of deception.'

Livingstone had much weightier things on his mind than Mr Holloway's advertisements in *The Patriot*, however, and chief among them was his relations with the Boers. On one matter he differed from his father-in-law and this was in the use of native Africans as evangelists. Livingstone had come to believe that carefully schooled tribesmen could be an asset to the missionary purpose, and he set out to find suitable candidates. This at once brought him into collision with Hendrik Potgeiter's men, who firmly believed that the Doctor was secretly an agent of the British Government and was organising native opposition to their own God-given aims of expansion to the north of the Cape. Livingstone records how on one occasion a Boer commando led by Potgeiter descended upon the Kolobeng settlement to harangue him about his presence and his suspicious activities. 'We could scarcely get an opportunity to reason with him on the absurdity of this supposition,' he told Robert Moffat, 'for an individual from Holland, whom I take to be a Jesuit, would scarcely allow us to speak three words without screaming out at the top of his voice that missionaries were like a cancer and ought to be shot and a thousand other things which, perhaps happily for me, I did not understand.'

The noisy individual from Holland was, in fact, Potgeiter's secretary, Hendrik Buhrmann, and certainly no Jesuit. Nevertheless, his performance on that occasion indicates the temper of the Boers towards Livingstone. In particular, the Boers accused the Scot of supplying Sechele and the other natives with arms in order to fight them out of their lands. And it is symptomatic of Livingstone's standing with his own fellow-countrymen that a number of them in South Africa were not slow to accept the Boer assertions and repeat them as something more substantial than rumour. The talk of Livingstone as a gun-runner for the natives became so widespread, indeed, and he resented it so fiercely that eventually he made a statement which was published in the *Cape Town Mail*. It said that 'My reply to both Missionaries and Boers was and is, if you can prove that I either *lent* or *sold* or *gave* a gun . . . to Sechele, I shall willingly leave the country'.

This was a very curious defence for him to make. For just six months earlier, a Boer commando had raided Sechele's settlement. The purpose of this excursion was to capture a chief they wanted for cattle-stealing, to whom Sechele was giving sanctuary. Sechele refused to yield him, whereupon the Boers attacked and sent the tribesmen headlong into the veldt. Livingstone and his wife were absent at the time and when the commando entered the settlement, the mission house was broken into (and it is not clear whether the natives or the Boers did the damage). In reporting the raid to his superiors, the leader of the commando, Acting Commandant-General Scholtz, noted that inside the Livingstone premises 'we found several half-finished guns and a gunmaker's shop with abundance of tools. We here found more guns and tools than Bibles, so that the place had more the appearance of a gunmaker's shop than a mission-station, and more of a smuggling-shop than of a school-place.' That, undoubtedly, was the observation of a prejudiced witness. Livingstone himself can be mistaken for no such thing. As early as 1848, four years previously, he had written to Moffat about how he had presented a native with a gun which 'gave great satisfaction'. Later correspondence with his father-in-law makes it clear that this was not an isolated practice, that he did indeed supply Sechele with arms and ammunition from time to time. His attitude – and in the circumstances no detached observer could think it unreasonable – was that the African natives could very well make use of firearms, both to hunt for food and to defend themselves against the manifest hostility of the Boers.

Another curiosity about this highly complicated man was his attitude to his own name. He had been born David Livingston, in 1813, without benefit of a final 'e'. Towards the end of September 1852 he wrote to his parents in Scotland and signed himself, for the first time, David Livingstone. It was to be another three years before he changed his style in letters that he wrote to the LMS in London, and it is conceivable that the alteration in his domestic correspondence was a first small manifestation of the crisis that was now beginning to materialise in his life. Possibly he was now attracted for the first time by the chance of lonely grandeur, and saw in the translation of his name to something synonymous with living stone, a small but supremely important piece of symbolism. He had only just written to his parents a letter which is remarkable both for its lofty tone and its embittered content. 'I could,' he told them, 'become a merchant tomorrow with a fair chance of making a fortune . . . Then again I could become a doctor in the Colony. They are well paid and not very numerous . . . But we have never had a renegade in our Society. We become poor to make others rich . . . I know of two of the Wesleyan Society who have turned renegade. One, a Mr Archbell, is one of the greatest land speculators in Natal and has about 18,000 acres still in hand. He still has the impudence to go occasionally into the pulpit, but the Natives move out in a body when he does. He is rich, much good may it do him.' A man whose salary from the LMS as a husband and father of four children amounted to no more than £100 a year, might well feel envious of a fellow-missionary who appeared to have sold something of his soul for 18,000 acres of land. But Livingstone's discontent was compounded of more elements than straightforward financial embarrassment. The marriage itself and the accumulation of children had become something more than an economic burden to him. Mary's zeal for the missionary life had never matched his own and she had been ill since losing a fifth child at birth. Livingstone was perpetually away from the family on exploratory journeys upcountry and this doubtless produced its own frictions, for the Moffats could be quite as strong-minded as the Livingstones. There was at least one occasion when Livingstone had taken the entire family with him on a venture into the bush, which was utterly wasted by their presence as far as he was concerned. He had badly wanted to make an ascent of a hitherto unknown river, but the children had gone down with fever and so the project had at once been abandoned. He was conscious enough that his own rambling nature was the subject of criticism by his missionary colleagues. 'Some of the brethren,' he wrote to Arthur Tidman, the LMS secretary in London, 'do not hesitate to tell the natives that my object is to obtain the applause of men. This bothers me, for I sometimes suspect my own motives.'

He could easily justify his own perpetual urge to be moving off into unknown territory where white men had not been before. He had told the Moffats that the contrast between the well-staffed missions of the colony and the empty lands to the north, east and west made his heart sore. 'In one place the people are crammed, in the other starved,' he said. As early as 1847 he had written to Tidman that 'The Colonial market is literally glutted with missionaries. I do not believe that equal advantages are enjoyed by any town or village in the United Kingdom as those which are pressed upon the people of Algoa Bay, Uitenhage, Graaf Reinet and Colesburg.' Somewhere in the centre of his thinking was a conviction, not unlike that of Henry Venn of the CMS at the same time, that it was important for Africans to minister the Christian Gospel to their fellows and that the search for such men, and their training, should take precedence over the perpetual importation of yet more white missionaries from Britain.

He saw his own missionary vocation in these terms: he would be the man who went forth into the lost places of Africa to seek out her native sons, who might build where he was by temperament unfitted to build. He was, some time later, when he had returned to England, to illustrate his private concept of the missionary, and it was not an image which until then had generally been acceptable by those with the missionary interest at heart. 'Nowhere,' said Livingstone on that occasion, 'have I ever appeared as anything else but a servant of God, who has simply followed the leadings of His hand . . . My views of what is missionary duty are not so contracted as those whose ideal is a dumpy sort of man with a Bible under his arm. I have laboured in bricks and mortar, at the forge and carpenter's bench, as well as in preaching and medical practice. I feel that I am "not my own". I am serving Christ when shooting a buffalo for my men, or taking an astronomical observation, or writing to one of His children who forget, during the little moment of penning a note, that charity which is eulogised as "thinking no evil".'

He might also have added that he believed he was serving Christ when he was responding to one of the deepest needs in his nature, which was simply to find out about things unknown. Ever since coming to Africa Livingstone had succumbed periodically to what in another context would have been called wanderlust. His was such a gripping need in this form that the attendant hazards which would deter most men were either unrecognisable or regarded as totally insignificant beside the reward of discovery and, perhaps even greater, the satisfaction of knowing that the achievement was unique. Before he married Mary Moffat, Livingstone had been free to wander where he would, provided he did not attach too much weight to the disapproval of his colleagues; and although this stung him, he saw himself on a plane above such jealous criticisms. He had trekked north from Kuruman with Roger Edwards in response to his private devil and had been very nearly killed by a lion in the process. After the initial pleasures of family life had worn off he had gone out into the wilderness again, this time crossing the Kalahari desert and, with his two companions, the hunters Oswell and Murray, had been the first European to sight Lake Ngami. A river had stretched tantalisingly north from the lake, drawing Livingstone like a magnet. It was not in the man to resist the challenge it presented to his powers of resourcefulness, to his physical and mental toughness, to his courage. He wrote to the LMS directors, suggesting that it was imperative he should go north. And they agreed that the river 'seems to open a highway for the progress of the Gospel in the interior of Africa'.

First he had to make arrangements for his family, and he decided to pack them all off to England. 'The reports circulated and made by natives would render my wife miserable,' he told Tidman. 'She is again threatened by symptoms of paralysis, but now they extend down the whole side even to the toes. Frequent pregnancies will in all probability aggravate the complaint. And as the children must go home for education, I believe it would be the best policy for her to take them to England herself . . . Nothing but a strong conviction that the step will tend to the glory of Christ would make me orphanise my children. Even now my bowels yearn for them. They will forget me. But I hope that when the day of trial comes I shall not be found a more sorry soldier than those who serve an earthly sovereign.' It was necessary, of course, to justify himself in the name of Christ. It was inevitable that he should do so before his children, though the stern father allowed himself to speak before the anguished absentee. 'If your sins and naughtiness are not forgiven,' he wrote to them soon after they had reached England, 'blotted out by Jesus, then you will go away into Hell like the rich man in the Bible . . . I have separated myself from you all, my dear children, and from Mamma whom I love very much, too, in order to please Jesus and tell sinners who have never heard about him.' And then, a little later, he gave them more advice. 'Don't speak Scotch. It is not so pretty as English.' Whatever yearning David Livingstone may have felt in his bowels for his children, there is little sign of it in communications with his wife after this. One of the first letters she received from him after she had reached England, although addressed to 'My dearest Mary', continued: 'I have very little to write about. Nothing but Africa news and these of no interest. I am thankful that you are where you are, and if you improve your opportunities you may have cause for gratitude throughout life. Hope you give much of your time to the children. You will be sorry for it if you don't . . . With kind love to you I must conclude this uninteresting letter . . . Yours very affectionately, D. Livingston.'

By the time Mary received that letter, her husband had started the epic journey that was to last two and a half years and secure for him a place in history. In the missionary strategy for Africa it was virtually a one-man advance upon the interior from the south, to balance that great drive from the west through Nigeria and to complement the penetration from the east which Lewis Krapf was contemplating from his mission at Rabai. The specific objects of Livingstone's share in this vast enterprise he had set before the LMS directors and they had agreed upon his order of priorities. First he was to establish a new mission in Barotseland or beyond and after that he would concern himself with an investigation of the slave trade in the regions to the north. He would 'also find a way to the sea on either the east or west coast'. Later, when his venture had made him famous, his published journal would reveal another reason for embarking upon his enterprise that came nearer to explaining it, perhaps, than anything he had told the LMS directors. 'The Boers,' he wrote, 'resolved to shut up the interior, and I determined to open up the country; and we shall see who have been most successful in resolution – they or I.' At any rate, the settled priorities were to become reversed between November 1853, when Livingstone went on trek, and the end of May 1856, when he reached the sea on the East coast of Africa. In that time he spent only nine weeks in exploring the Barotse lands for a site suitable for missionary expansion, and then abandoned the project without success and headed north again.

The historic journey was made in the grand tradition of exploration. Livingstone's party was lightly but carefully equipped to travel with the maximum speed that men on foot could manage. Nothing superfluous was taken, and this was partly to reduce the chances of being attacked and plundered by rapacious tribesmen. For although the Livingstone legend, from the moment it was recognised and ever since, has tended to imply that his was a lonely journey into country where no man had ever been known to tread, the fact is that his party was never far from routes which had been well known to local natives from ancient times; Livingstone was merely the first white man ever to have traversed them. In his baggage were three muskets, a rifle, a double-barrelled smooth bore and ammunition to hunt with. In case these failed to provide enough food, there were 20 lb. of beads, worth 40s., for barter, a few biscuits, a few pounds of tea, sugar and coffee. There was a small gipsy tent, a sheepskin mantle for use as a blanket and a horse-rug for a bed. Captain Donaldson's assiduous pupil on the voyage to Cape Town had also packed a nautical almanac, Thomson's Logarithm Tables, a sextant, an artificial horizon, a thermometer and compasses. He had a bag containing medicines. He carried a magic lantern, and he would not be the first European in Africa to discover that this device was of enormous value in impressing the uncivilised mind of the native with apparent and very useful powers of sorcery. In a small tin canister he had a change of shirt, trousers and shoes, to be worn when he eventually reached civilisation again. He had more spare clothes to be used when those he was dressed in had worn out. He had a Bible. Nothing else. Thus equipped, he and his twenty-seven Makololo bearers moved off into the bush on a feat of endurance and courage that was to intoxicate the British nation more than anything since Francis Drake had voyaged round the world. Across the Atlantic, Livingstone's journey made much less of an impact. The *New York Times* reprinted a small report from a Liverpool newspaper, announcing the Doctor's safe arrival at the end of his long march, and the great honours that awaited him at home, but this appeared at the bottom of a page, beneath a paragraph about a railroad hoax in Georgia; the trial of Charles B. Huntingdon for forgery was given much more prominence. And while London was honouring its hero, New York was very largely ignoring him. Twenty years later, however, the Americans were to lament Livingstone's death almost as much as the British. The American Geographical Society held a commemorative meeting in the New York Academy of Music, at which the entire wall behind the stage was covered with a map of Africa surmounted by a picture of Livingstone between the Union Jack and the Stars and Stripes. Some 1,500 people packed the hall, and many of them were among the most distinguished citizens in the land, like Harriet Ward Beecher, Cyrus W. Field, General George Cabot Ward and Chief Justice Daly. And while they paused to reflect on this panegyric to the great missionary's courage, or that expression of regret that he had never visited America, the Governor's Island Band provided music to fit their mood, with the Miserere from 'Il Trovatore' and Rossini's 'Crucifixus'. It was a long, long way, in time and place and feeling, from the extraordinary journey which had first inspired this great homage.

For a start Livingstone aimed for the West coast, and it took him almost eighteen months to get there and back. Every hardship inseparable from African travel in the middle of the nineteenth century, Livingstone experienced. Equipment was damaged or lost. There were days on end when the party plodded on, drenched by torrential rain. Negotiations were carefully carried out with chiefs through whose territory the party wanted to pass, and whose temper and amicability were uncertain. Food ran short. Guides became rebellious and had to be browbeaten or cajoled into service. The Makololo themselves had to be gently chivvied along when their spirits began to fail as their homelands receded into the agonising distance. Livingstone went down with fever on some twenty occasions, but with that invigorating belief of his that the best antidote to any illness was simply to get up and march on, he pulled himself through each time, with some support from the medicine chest. 'I was determined to succeed or perish in the attempt,' he later told the hero-worshipping Britons at home. He was in the throes of dysentery and severely depressed after the long months of intermittent illness, when he and his men finally arrived at San Paulo de Loanda on 31 May 1854. Not one bearer had been lost on the way, and that, as much as anything, was the measure of Livingstone's achievement so far. Nothing comparable had been known in Africa before and doubtless Livingstone was the only man alive at the time with the temperament and the care to manage it.

For three and a half months the expedition recuperated among the Portuguese of Loanda, who offered them much kindness. In spite of his inherent suspicion of Papists, which automatically led him to apply the despised label of Jesuit to individuals of hazy origin who displeased him, Livingstone was impressed enough to observe that the Bishop of Loanda was 'a man of great kindness and benevolence of heart'. And then this dogged Scot, his supplies replenished, began to retrace his steps so that he could restore his bearers to their own people. The outward journey had taken six and a half months; the return trip took nearly twice as long. But still they finished without a man lost after covering three thousand miles of the most intractable country on earth. Within a couple of months Livingstone was off again, this time to look for the sea route to the east. This time he was provided with an escort of two hundred men and it is a measure of his charisma in the eyes of Africans that not only did the Makololo chief Sekeletu insist on travelling the first stages of the journey with him, but that the party was infinitely better supplied than its predecessor. Sekeletu insisted that riding oxen must be taken, together with cattle which would be killed for food, hoes and beads in order to purchase any necessities on the way, and such luxuries as butter and honey.

Almost at once Livingstone had another outstanding success, for less than a fortnight up the trail his column arrived at the fabulous waterfalls which had so far been no more than a rumour to Europeans. He named them on the spot after his Queen. The hardships now were more of a tribal nature than on the westward journey, and from the moment Livingstone struck the Zambezi and began to edge along the south bank, there was great risk of ambush by natives hostile to the Makololo. Any plans for missionary expansion in this part of the world, receding though they might now have been in Livingstone's mind, would clearly have to deal with difficulties that had long since been overcome farther south, and Livingstone was aware of them. His will-power was as strong as ever, though. 'Felt much turmoil of spirit in view of having all my plans for the welfare of this great region and teeming population knocked on the head by savages tomorrow. But I read that Jesus came and said, "All power is given unto me in heaven and in earth. Go ye therefore, and teach all nations – and lo, I am with you alway, even unto the end of the world." It is the word of a gentleman of the most sacred and strictest honour, and there is an end on't. I will not cross furtively by night as I intended to. It would appear as flight . . . Nay, verily, I shall take observations for latitude and longitude tonight, though they may be my last.' Thus fortified, he made his observations and plunged on. By the beginning of March 1856 he had reached Tete, the most inland Portuguese settlement on the river. He stayed some weeks to recover from fever, and then made his last drive to the sea. On 20 May he and his men rambled wearily into Quilimane, with the Indian Ocean surging and seething just beyond its fringe of huts and palm trees. They had travelled 1,300 miles and had completed the fable which now belonged to the man at their head.

It was a fable which the missionary world claimed as its own as well as Livingstone's, though there had been precious little missionary activity, in any sense the world generally recognised at the time, attached to it. Livingstone himself by now was well aware that his days as a representative of the London Missionary Society were almost over, though for inscrutable reasons of his own he preferred to keep the LMS in the dark about his future plans for many months to come. Some two and a half years earlier, just before starting his trek to Loanda, he had informed his parents in Scotland that if the society should object to his plans for interior exploration 'I would consider it my duty to withdraw from it'. In September 1855, as he was about to set off for the East coast, he wrote to Mrs Moffat, his mother-in-law, that 'if it is decided that this field be left still and I must go to the South, my missionary career will be ended'. He was thus anticipating a breach with the LMS that was clearly foreseen as a possibility by Arthur Tidman when he wrote to Livingstone on behalf of the LMS in August 1855. The letter was awaiting the Doctor when he reached Quilimane, and it ran to six long sheets of foolscap.

At first it gave news that would have warmed the heart of any man who had just completed such a journey as his. The Royal Geographical Society, wrote Tidman, had awarded its Gold Medal to Livingstone for his unprecedented exploits in reaching Loanda on the West coast, and then returning to base safely with all his bearers. But then Tidman came to the less palatable matters that his directors had been threshing out between them for months while this highly individualistic employee of theirs was fulfilling himself with exploration across the length and breadth of Central Africa. 'The Directors,' he said, 'while yielding to none in their appreciation of the objects upon which for some years past your energies have been concentrated, or in admiration of the zeal, intrepidity and success with which they have been carried out, are nevertheless restricted in their power of aiding plans connected only remotely with the spreading of the Gospel.' They were entirely confident of the importance which Livingstone's researches and adventures would have upon the interests of science, not to say common humanity, and they believed that these ultimately might be harnessed to the diffusion of Christian truth. But Livingstone's own reports, they felt, made it obvious that the nature of the ground, the variable weather, the prevalence of malaria 'and other adverse influences, constitute a very serious array of obstacles to missionary effort, and even were there a reasonable prospect of these being surmounted – and we by no means assume they are insurmountable – yet in that event the financial circumstances of the Society are not such as to afford any ground of hope that it would be in a position, within any definite period, to enter upon untried, remote and difficult fields of labour'.

This was a blow to Livingstone's pride, which saw the conclusions of the LMS – even though they were similar to his own, arrived at by somewhat different reasoning – as the basest ingratitude after what he had been through. And he was not at all mollified when Tidman rather tactlessly reminded him, at the end of the letter, that Livingstone owed the LMS some money: as he did. The LMS had been paying £120 a year for the maintenance of Mary and the children in addition to his salary of £100. Indeed, he was very angry at the reminder. If he had held any doubts about his future through the long trek across Africa, they were now completely banished. On his way home to England he wrote to a friend in Cape Town. 'As these statements are embalmed in some flattering sentences of approbation respecting my late efforts to open up the continent to the sympathies of the friends of Christianity, I suppose that it is intended to send me to some of the tried, neat and easy fields where I can wax fat and kick like Jeshurun . . . The proposition to leave the untried, remote and difficult fields of labour as they have been ever since Our Saviour died for man, involves my certain separation from the LMS.'

He arrived in London on 5 December 1856 and the nation rose to the occasion as only a very proud people can when they find they have produced an indisputable hero. 'The greatest asset that the reputation of Great Britain has ever possessed in Africa is the respect felt by natives of every grade for the manhood of David Livingstone.' That, as it happens, is the observation of a Livingstone biographer writing some seventy years later; but it codifies what the British instinctively felt when Livingstone returned to them after travels which someone reckoned to have stretched over 11,000 miles of Africa. First there was a reception given by the Royal Geographical Society, at which its President, Sir Roderick Murchison, presented the coveted Gold Medal. Next day the LMS mounted its own public welcome, under the presidency of Lord Shaftesbury, and whatever tensions had been bubbling to the surface while Livingstone was away, they seemed to be quite forgotten now. Indeed, such was the warmth of public affection and esteem automatically reflected upon the LMS from its luminous protégé, that the directors must have bitterly regretted ever having despatched the querulous letter that awaited the Doctor in Quilimane.

He, however, showed no sign of rancour as he made a kind of royal progress around the land, and so no damage appeared to have been done. Early in the New Year he was made a Freeman of the City of London. Glasgow gave him its own Freedom and £2,000 into the bargain. The Royal Society elected him a Fellow. The Universities of Oxford and Glasgow awarded him honorary degrees. He was received first by Prince Albert, later by the Queen. He spoke at meetings up and down the country, which were packed with people anxious to hear the fantastic tales he had to tell. At Manchester, the Chamber of Commerce listened entranced, while Livingstone told those ranks of calculating North country businessmen about oils they had never heard of before, of dyes that were the product of secret native formulae, of fibres that could be used for the manufacture of paper, of sheep that were hairy but not fleeced.

As soon as the initial wave of engagements freed him a little from the constant speaking and travelling expected of a new hero when received by his own, he settled down to produce a book out of his journals. By the time *Missionary Travels and Researches* appeared in November 1857, it was certain to be the biggest best-seller within living memory. The publishers printed 12,000 as a first edition, but orders for 13,800 copies had been received before it appeared. Charles Dickens reviewed it for *Household News* and assured its success among subscribers to the journal by writing that 'I have been following a narrative of great dangers and trials, encountered in a good cause, by as honest and courageous a man as ever lived . . . The effect of it on me has been to lower my opinion of my own character in a most remarkable and most disastrous manner.' That was the peculiar thing about Livingstone. He made you feel so humble and second-rate; but at least he gave you a shining ideal to which you might staggeringly aspire; he made you want to set forth, Bible clenched firmly in your hand, to be good and direct and unswerving, to lead lesser mortals into the Light, to be strong. Within a few weeks of publication, *Missionary Travels and Researches* had sold 30,000 copies at one guinea a time, and Livingstone took an agreed two-thirds of the publisher's profits. It made him rich.

6. Robert Moffat preaching to a group of Bechuana. Moffat persuaded Livingstone to follow him to southern Africa, and his daughter Mary eventually married Livingstone.

7. David Livingstone, in his uniform as British Consul in East Africa. After achieving this rank, following his breach with the London Missionary Society, he was rarely seen without the peaked cap, with its yellow band.

8. A halt in the forest somewhere in West Africa, late in the nineteenth century. Even then, movement about the country was at an expeditionary level.

9. Miss Ellenberger and her pupils at the Aburi Girls' School on the Gold Coast in the 1890s. Education was perhaps the greatest achievement of the missionaries in Africa.

In some excitement, the directors of the LMS abandoned all their earlier caution and began to lay plans for expansion in Central Africa. When they had written that reluctant letter they had been going through a bad patch, with a financial deficit of £12,000 and the Crimean War deflecting public interest from their work. But now Livingstone had turned a great tide in their affairs. At a special meeting early in February 1857 they resolved that two new missions should be opened up. One should be in the country of the Makololo, under Livingstone and an assistant, the other among the Matabele people. They launched an appeal for £5,000 to start this new work and immediately donations began to pour in; by the end of the year £6,400 had been subscribed. No longer was there talk of financial difficulties, and the directors voted Livingstone a special grant of £200 on account of the heavy expenditure he had incurred in their service. Nearly two months later Livingstone curtly declined the gift, saying that it had given rise to rumours that he was not in need of money, and adding that he would be obliged if the LMS would keep quiet about his financial resources.

He was, alas, no longer interested in the LMS, though he was certainly not yet ready to tell the directors this. His closest associate now was the President of the Royal Geographical Society, Sir Roderick Murchison. In those first few days after his return, they had spent much time in each other's company. Murchison had a vision of his own for Africa and it was one of discovering the unknown, both for the increase of geographical knowledge and for the glory of his country. He was delighted to find in Livingstone a man willing to bend himself to both these tasks in future, to a degree he would not have expected a little time ago from one who had always been a dedicated missionary above all things. If Livingstone was to return to Africa, and both men agreed that he must, he would be in need of a patron to take the place of the LMS. Government was the obvious possibility, and so Murchison immediately made contact with Lord Clarendon, the Foreign Secretary, to sound out the ground. As early as 16 January, Livingstone made his own formal offer of service to Lord Clarendon. By 15 April, a week after he had turned down the LMS gift of £200, Livingstone was writing to Murchison, 'I have been thinking since we parted that it may be better to defer the application for an appointment till nearer the period of my departure. I fear if it got out now, my friends at the Mission House will make use of the fact to damage my character in the public estimation by saying I have forsaken the Mission for higher pay.' The appointment which by then was being formulated for Livingstone within the Foreign Office was that of Consul in East

Africa at a salary of £500 per annum, and leader of an expedition up the river Zambezi. On 2 May this proposal was so far advanced that Livingstone was writing to Clarendon to set out his own ideas for work as Consul. He spoke of how his efforts in the post would tend, he hoped, to the benefit of trade and the increase of his country's good name. He outlined a policy which he believed would not encroach upon the rights of the Portuguese in the area. He added, 'As I do not intend to accept gratuity from my former employers, the LMS, I venture to accept such a salary as your Lordship may deem suitable, should you approve of my suggestion and think me worthy of employment in a public capacity.'

There is no record that the LMS directors were given the slightest hint of what was afoot until the autumn of that year. On 12 January he had told them that if there were to be a Makololo Mission 'the result would be promoted by the residence of himself and Mrs Livingstone amongst them and, with God's blessing, almost certainly secured were Mr Moffat to commence a Mission at the town of Moselekatse'. He was present at their February meeting to settle the plans for his return to Africa. He attended the society's annual general meeting on 14 May, gave a long address, said nothing at all to suggest that he was not going to lead the mission which had just been publicly announced from the same platform, and was generally received with tremendous expressions of goodwill. It was not until a year later, in May 1858, that the LMS made any reference to a breach with Livingstone in any of their published statements. Their annual report then briefly remarked that he was no longer a missionary.

The public announcement of the Zambezi Expedition and Livingstone's new role was made just before Christmas, when Parliament had decided that it could support this new venture to the tune of £5,000. Livingstone was now riding at his highest point in the popular estimation. His book was breaking records in the shops and he was still speaking to overflowing audiences wherever he appeared. These performances tended now to become more and more select. First he was in Dublin, lecturing to the British Association for the Advancement of Science. Then he was in the Cambridge Senate House, speaking to a mass of people from the University. An eye-witness to that occasion remarked on the difference between the Christian explorer and the distinguished academics who shared the platform with him. 'In marked contrast to them, we saw a man of moderate height, very plainly dressed, his face tanned to a dark brown by long exposure to sun and wind, and furrowed by deep lines which spoke of anxiety, hardship and disease, endured and overcome. I think I never saw any man whose appearance told its own tale as Livingstone's did. We all felt that we were about to hear a wonderful narrative of personal experiences, and that every word would come true.' When the first cheering at Livingstone's introduction had subsided, he began what was not so much a lecture as a series of halting notes on various aspects of Africa; its physical features, its inhabitants, its languages, on the way to deal with Africans.

'His language, for which he apologised on the ground that for seventeen years he had spoken the native language of Africa, and had in consequence almost forgotten his own, was peculiar to himself. He used short, jerky sentences, expressive of thoughts which he could not arrange in set periods, but which he did not wish his hearers to lose. But the most carefully ordered speech would have been far less effective, and when he suddenly shouted, "Do you carry on the work which I have begun. I leave it with you," and sat down, there was silence for a few seconds, and then came a great explosion of cheering never surpassed in this building.'

It was, indeed, a speech which ended on an heroic note, whatever technical deficiencies it might have had in the delivery. 'I beg to direct your attention to Africa,' Livingstone had urged before that last passionate shout. 'I know that in a few years I shall be cut off in that country, which is now open; do not let it be shut again! I go back to Africa to make an open path for commerce and Christianity.'

He went back in March 1858 and, not long before his departure, the Royal Geographical Society laid on a 'Farewell Livingstone Festival' in his honour. Mary Livingstone made one of her rare public appearances alongside her husband and was generously applauded. But for more than twelve months now, any event at which the Doctor was present had belonged to him alone, by acclaim and by right. He had, after all, accomplished his heroic journey without the help of a single civilised being. At this farewell gathering his friend and patron Sir Roderick Murchison put into rhetoric what everyone in the country felt in his heart and soul about the man who had risen from the obscurity of a Scottish cotton mill to a transcending nobility, by dint of his own resources and a trust in Almighty God. 'Sitting by my side,' exclaimed the President of the Royal Geographical Society, 'is the man who, knowing what he had to encounter – who, having struggled twenty or thirty times with the fever of Africa, who, knowing when he reached the Western coast at St Paul de Loanda, that a ship was ready to carry him to his native land, where his wife and children were anxiously awaiting his arrival – true to his plighted word, threw these considerations, which might have influenced an ordinary

man, to the winds, and reconducted those poor natives who had accompanied him through the heart of that country, back to their homes! Thus, by his noble and courageous conduct, leaving for himself in that country a glorious name, and proving to the people of Africa what an English Christian is!'

The cheering rolled round the building for minutes at that. It was to echo, like the sentiment itself, for a century, wherever two or three gathered together in the name of the Christian British Empire.

8

TO CREATE AN ENGLISH COLONY

Essentially, the Zambezi Expedition was intended to achieve in East Africa what the ill-fated Niger Expedition of 1841 had set out to achieve in the West. Twice, in those last few months before the expedition sailed, David Livingstone had publicly uttered his stirring cry about opening up a path to commerce and Christianity in Africa. On both occasions he had put the two aims in that order and, though that may be of some psychological interest, the linking of these purposes so closely together was not at all alien to the general missionary philosophy of the time. From the days of Fowell Buxton it had been accepted that the fastest way to destroy the wicked slave trade was to provide some alternative form of profitable enterprise which would undermine its hold upon local speculators. Livingstone, however, had not disclosed to the public another purpose he had in mind in returning to Africa. It would, indeed, have sounded rather odd from a man whose whole vocation so far had been one of converting heathen to a belief in the Christian God, however individual his own interpretation of that vocation might have seemed to some. And Livingstone was a man more sensitive than most to what others might think of him.

He was prepared to divulge his secret to a few carefully picked and select acquaintances and friends, though. Not long before his departure he wrote to Professor Sedgwick, who had acted as chairman at the meeting in the Senate House at Cambridge. 'That you may have a clear idea of my objects,' he said, 'I may state that they have more in them than meets the eye. They are not merely exploratory, for I go with the intention of benefiting both the African and my own countrymen. I take a practical mining geologist to tell us of the mineral resources of the country, an economic botanist to give a full report of the vegetable productions, an artist to give the scenery, a naval officer to tell of the capacity of river communications, and a moral agent to lay a Christian foundation for anything that may follow. All this machinery has for its ostensible object the development of African trade and the promotion of civilisation; but what I can tell to none but such as you, in whom I have confidence, is this. I hope it may result in an English colony in the healthy high lands of Central Africa.' Livingstone added a portentous postscript to this letter. 'I have told it only to the Duke of Argyll.'

No one, presumably, could have been better fitted for the role of moral agent to lay Christian foundations than Livingstone himself, the ordained minister of religion. Yet the man selected was his brother Charles. He was nine years younger than David and of notorious instability. He had emigrated to America in 1840 and after acquiring a college education, had taken a variety of jobs before entering the Union College in New York and emerging as a religious pastor with a congregation in Massachusetts. He had hoped to become a missionary for the LMS like his elder brother, but his application had been turned down. When the Doctor had proposed him to the Government as his personal assistant on the expedition, with special responsibility for spreading the Gospel among the Africans, no one could think of a good reason why this choice should not be made. It was, in fact, a disastrous appointment. The expedition's doctor, John Kirk, whose loyalty to David Livingstone endured through many sore trials and who reads like a generous witness, early on characterised the difference between the two brothers thus: 'Dr Livingstone, straightforward, honest, rather shy unless engaged in his great scheme for opening Africa. Mr CL base, hypocritical, preferring underhand to open means, without any great guiding scheme but acting from day to day for his own interest, devoid of all personal interest but ready to plume himself from anyone else.' After creating a great deal of trouble up the Zambezi, Charles Livingstone was sent home, ostensibly on the grounds of ill-health. He continued to flourish in the Government service, however, being appointed subsequently as British Consul in Bonny, where he pursued strangely anti-missionary policies and created as much ill-feeling in his region of Nigeria and beyond as he did on the Zambezi Expedition. Had his name not been Livingstone he might well have ended his days in the obscurity of an American pulpit. He had an historic role to play, however. It was to permit his elder brother to sail up the river Zambezi, not as a professional Christian, but as the self-promoted leader of an imperial expedition.

David Livingstone began to exercise his authority as the expedition's unquestionable leader from the start. The journey to East Africa involved a stop at Sierra Leone *en route* to the Cape, and there a dozen men of the Kru tribe were taken aboard for service on the Zambezi. They had scarcely reached their destination when the Doctor packed them off home again, in favour of his loyal Makololo. Before long, a European was also on the boat for home. This was Commander Bedingfeld RN, who had been appointed to survey the river for its transport capacities. He was not the best choice that could have been made, having twice been reprimanded during his naval career and having once been dismissed his ship, for various failures in the line of duty. By the time the expedition's small steam launch, the *Ma Robert*, had made its first excursion, both he and Livingstone were at daggers drawn with each other. 'Bedingfeld,' wrote Livingstone in his log, 'turned out an unmitigated muff, thought we could not move a mile without him and thereupon assumed all manner of airs. I mounted the paddle box and sent him home to nurse his dignity there.' The Commander doubtless behaved like a pompous ass, but he was not much accustomed to being ordered about like a midshipman on what he took to be his own quarterdeck, which was how Livingstone was beginning to treat people he regarded as subordinates.

A much more wretched episode than this was taking shape. Livingstone's peremptory eye was now cast with growing disapproval upon the activities of Thomas Baines. He had been apprenticed to an ornamental painter during his youth in King's Lynn but at the age of twenty-one had emigrated to the Cape and set himself up as portrait painter. When the Zambezi Expedition was being planned he was recruited as official artist, to provide illustrated evidence of the country and the people, just as William Hodges had done generations before on Captain Cook's voyages round the Pacific. He seems to have been a likeable fellow, possibly slow-moving, doubtless a bit of a dreamer when set alongside a purposeful and highly practical Scot. There was no question, however, of his unwillingness to apply himself to the tasks in hand on the expedition. On three separate occasions John Kirk mentions him with approval, either in his journal or in letters. 'Mr Baines,' he declared, 'is a trump and does more than anyone else.' Later he remarked that Baines was 'the hardest worked member of the expedition'. Nor was Baines merely putting in his quota of activity as artist. Kirk says that he 'is the great carpenter for the launch and is hard at work all day'.

Dr Livingstone was apparently unimpressed by this diligence. His attitude to the artist became more and more grudging, and he certainly took a poor view of the fact that, in his spare time, Baines would wander off and do some painting on his own account. It was while he was away from the others for a few hours on one occasion that Livingstone ordered Kirk and another colleague, Rae, to proceed to Tete. They were to rummage through Baines's possessions, which had been stockpiled there with other belongings of the expedition which were not immediately required. The Doctor made no secret of the fact to Kirk and Rae that they were to look for things which he suspected Baines of stealing. The two men found nothing, but the Doctor's mind was made up, it seemed. He told Baines to pack up and leave, though the artist was ill at the time and had no money or anything with which to barter his way back to civilisation. Somehow he struggled home to the Cape and eventually did rather well for himself on the South African goldfields. Livingstone had allowed no argument about rights or wrongs. Baines had not even been permitted to call anyone to speak for him, as Kirk would have been willing to. He was merely accused of making away with large quantities of public property and told to go. Some months later, a number of the missing things turned up where they had genuinely been mislaid. Livingstone never sent an apology to Baines. Indeed, when he eventually published another of his best-sellers, he coolly used some of Baines's pictures as illustration, without once referring to the artist in his text.

Somewhere near the bottom of this unappetising affair was Charles Livingstone, the malicious tell-tale. Well might Kirk write home to a friend that this was an unfortunate expedition for quarrels 'and of all that has happened, the disclosing of the horrible, childish and utterly false assertions of Mr CL would have been the worst . . .'. Charles was for ever taking grudges against people and forthwith seeding them into his brother's ear; and David, with nepotic loyalty, would listen and allow his own brooding soul to form the grudges in his turn. Very early in the expedition Kirk was remarking that 'The Doctor is a first-rate fellow when alone but he is easily put up to mischief by those who have the will and the knack'. Charles's shortcomings, it soon became clear, were not limited to malice. The glamour of his position on one of Her Majesty's expeditions soon wore off under the discomforts of expeditionary life. He was a congenital slacker and he gradually became a positive burden whenever some piece of work had to be undertaken which depended upon a full quota of willing hands. There were times when the party left the river to make excursions into the surrounding bush. These were usually crippled from the start, whenever Charles was in the team, because more than half the time was spent in stopping to let Charles have some sleep. It was this inability of his to work hard, as much as anything, that seems to have grieved Livingstone in the end. 'I am at a loss how to treat him,' he wrote one night in something close to despair. 'As an assistant he has been of no value. Photography very unsatisfactory, magnetism even more so. In going up with us now he is useless, as he knows nothing of Portuguese or the native language. He has often expected me to be his assistant instead of acting as mine.' Yet David would not get rid of him. Charles Livingstone remained with the expedition until he was invalided home not long before the whole enterprise was called off.

The Doctor himself did not do very much to lighten the heavy atmosphere that had persisted from the start. It was not in his nature to do so. And it was clear that he was at his very worst when travelling with other Europeans. As Professor Chadwick has remarked, 'he was inclined to regard discussion as insolence, disagreement as incipient mutiny, inefficiency as criminal negligence, prudence as cowardice'. Kirk had noted how 'Dr L, so remarkable in individual power, is deficient in administrative talent'. The trouble was partly that this inarticulate Scot found it difficult to convey to his subordinates precisely what it was he wished them to do. He would stand at the helm of the *Ma Robert*, wearing the peaked cap of his consular office, with its yellow band, from which he had been inseparable from the start, wrapped in his private and grandiose thoughts, saying nothing to anyone. 'When the weather gets foul or anything begins to go wrong,' said Kirk, 'it is well to give him a wide berth, most especially when he sings to himself. But the kind of air is some indication. If it be "Happy Land" then look out for squalls and stand clear. If "Scots Wha Hae", then there is some general vision of discovery before his mind which, having been puzzled how to realise, he is indulging in. But on all occasions, humming of airs is a bad omen.' In spite of his increasing detachment about Livingstone's character, Kirk never lost his admiration for the man's virtues, or his basic affection for him. Even after a couple of tense years in his company, when Kirk was due for home leave under the terms of his contract, he was writing that 'I should not think of leaving the Doctor alone at this time, that is, if he wishes me'.

That was a considerable tribute to Livingstone's virtues and to his magnetism, for Kirk was by no means starry-eyed at that point. Within a couple of months of remarking that Livingstone was a first-rate fellow, Kirk had conceded that 'he is a man who takes small, intense hatreds and is therefore a more dangerous enemy than useful friend'. His tenderest point, Kirk decided, was money. He was often 'very narrow, I should think mean, and he is ever ready to nurse suspicions when they have been suggested'. He was also totally sure of his own rectitude, with that surpassing certainty which convinces everyone else that what he says and does, in spite of some evidence to the contrary, must be right. His word, at this time, was something not much lower than Holy Writ as far as the British in general were concerned. Fairly typical of the esteem in which he was held was the matter of Livingstone's Rousers.

This was the name he had given, significant of his attitude to sickness, to a pill he had concocted. He thought it was an antidote to malaria. It was made up of resin of jalap, calomel, rhubarb and quinine and the prescription was, for a powerful man, eight grains of the resin, four or six of the rhubarb, four or six of the quinine. This 'discovery' so excited the Government that Lord John Russell immediately ordered the Admiralty to transmit the prescription to all vessels sailing in tropical waters – though the Royal College of Physicians was telling him that if diarrhoea accompanied the patient's fever, which was frequently the case, the results of Livingstone's Rousers would be disastrous.

The phenomenal will-power was still as strong as ever, driving the expedition up the Zambezi in a manner which was eventually to alarm Kirk seriously. Fifty miles above Tete was a gorge and a series of rapids, and Livingstone was well aware that this combination was a key to the triumph he had hoped for when he planned the expedition. His ambition was to open up the Zambezi from the sea to its source in the Central African Highlands. Unless the rapids could be negotiated, this ambition would fail, the triumph would be lost.

By the end of 1858 it was clear that there was no navigable way past the obstacle, though Livingstone's determination to succeed was such that he even contemplated blasting his way through with dynamite. 'Things look dark for our enterprise,' he logged on the night he acknowledged the impossibility even of this strategy. 'What we shall do if this is to be the end of navigation I cannot now divine, but here I am, and I am trusting him who never made ashamed those who did so . . . Spare me, good Lord.' It was not, in fact, the end of navigation, though it was the end of the Zambezi as a main thoroughfare.

Livingstone now turned to an investigation of the river's chief tributary, the Shiré, but even that was blocked by rapids after an early passage which made Kirk think it was potentially another Nile. Naming the obstruction after Sir Roderick Murchison, they took to marching inland and soon they began to smell some of the success Livingstone was seeking. They traversed the Shiré Highlands, and he was able to persuade himself that this was precisely the area in which Europeans could comfortably settle. He decided that its climate was perfect, that it was well-watered, that it could grow an abundance of crops. In rising spirits the party moved on to what must have seemed a consummation of their hopes. On 17 September 1859 they sighted Lake Nyasa, and they knew it for a major discovery.

Livingstone now did what he had never ceased to do, intermittently, from the moment he had first arrived in Africa, almost twenty years before. It was, above anything else, his saving grace and his real magnificence. He took thought for his African followers and put their own interests ahead of his own, in a way that no European had ever been known to do before him, that few were to match even after the world had applauded his example. He marched back from Lake Nyasa and down to Tete, where a group of his faithful Makololo had been left since Livingstone's departure for England. Some of them, after three years of absence, were ready for home and the Doctor promptly dropped everything he was doing and spent the next six months conducting them half-way across the breadth of Africa. 'We have,' he wrote to Murchison, when he had returned to base, 'kept faith with the Makololo, though we have done nothing else.'

One of the difficulties which Livingstone had been faced with in his river excursions, was the inadequacy of the *Ma Robert*. It had been badly designed, for one thing. It took all hands one and a half days to cut enough fuel from the bush for one day's travel by boat. It had also been constructed with a greater eye to economy than sturdiness. Some of the plates were no more than one-sixteenth of an inch thick, and after eighteen months' service Livingstone was reporting 'a worn-out steamer with 35 patches, covering at least 100 holes'. Eventually it broke up after grounding on a sandbank and had to be abandoned. But shortly after Livingstone returned from his escort duties with the Makololo, a replacement arrived. HMS *Sidon* sailed into the estuary of the Zambezi, bringing a new steam launch, the *Pioneer*. Aboard the warship were other reinforcements, members of the Universities Mission to Central Africa, under the leadership of Bishop Mackenzie.

In a sense the UMCA, though separated by a great deal of dogma and Christian politics from Livingstone's native Presbyterianism, was his own protégé. It owed its birth to those rousing meetings he had held in the Senate House in Cambridge and the Sheldonian Theatre in Oxford.

'Do you carry on the work which I have begun,' he had cried, and within a few months Churchmen in the two universities had formulated plans of their own to follow in his footsteps. They were men of the Church of England, and their tastes ran to high Anglo-Catholic ritual which Livingstone inherently suspected, but they were willing enough to work and so they were welcome to take part in the Zambezi enterprise. It was intended that they would travel up the river to some place chosen by the Doctor and there settle down to creating an agricultural village. Here they would show the natives how to export cotton, they would lead an exemplary communal life, and this combination would commend the entire range of Christian practice and morality to the minds of the simple savages. Charles Frederick Mackenzie had been made a bishop especially to lead this branch of the Zambezi project.

Mackenzie was an engaging man, with a fine mind. He had graduated at Cambridge with mathematical honours as Second Wrangler, and with a Fellowship at his old college, Caius, he had seemed set for an academic career. But he had become ordained and had shortly afterwards left for the Cape, where he had served as Archdeacon of Pietermaritzburg. On a visit to Cambridge in 1859, at which plans for the UMCA project were completed, he was invited to lead the party which would join Livingstone up the Zambezi and he had agreed to go, even though he had some misgivings about the jubilee atmosphere surrounding the preparations. 'I am afraid of this,' he told someone. 'Most great works of this kind have been carried on by one or two men in a quieter way, and have a more humble beginning.'

Given the sectarian and other differences that lay gapingly between them, Mackenzie and Livingstone got on surprisingly well together. Even after a month or two of each other's company, the Doctor was describing the newcomer as 'quite a brick of a bishop'. He was, no doubt, impressed by the Bishop's willingness to accept advice, even to take orders, from someone infinitely more experienced than himself. Mackenzie had been anxious to set out from base to a chosen location at once, but Livingstone had other plans at the moment. He badly wanted to explore the Rovuma river, which was almost in the opposite direction from the proposed site of the mission, near the Murchison Cataracts. So Mackenzie quietly complied. He repacked his books – Stephens' *Essays in Ecclesiastical Biography*, Samuel Wilberforce's *Addresses to Ordination Candidates*, Darwin's *Origin of Species* and a few others – and boarded the *Pioneer* with the rest of his party.

He was a man full of youthful zest at the age of thirty-six, and he was interested in new things, wanted to try his hand at every fresh opportunity. He was allowed to skipper the *Pioneer*, though he did not always produce a smooth passage; he was liable to ground the launch upon sandbanks because he had put the gear lever into reverse when he really wanted to go full ahead. There were always many sandbanks in those rivers and even for a skilled navigator like Livingstone, they could make the going desperately difficult. It took eight days to pass one of them, because everything had to be unloaded, including the boilers, so that the launch's own winches could haul the hull across. After a while they quit the Rovuma and went nosing up the mainstream and into the Shiré.

They then did what it is always necessary to do in Africa, sooner or later. They left the relative ease of the launch and they began to march into the highlands, to Livingstone's promised land. They had a long train of local porters, as well as sixteen Makololo that Livingstone had brought back with him from the Upper Zambezi, but Mackenzie did his share of donkey work. He marched along sturdily, with a can of oil slung round his neck in front and a bag of seeds on his back, with a loaded gun in one hand and a crozier in the other. This had been presented to him by the clergy of Cape Town for liturgical purposes, but he now used it to jab the lazier porters into greater action. They thought it was a new kind of musket and so it was generally effective.

The march lasted for a couple of months and in that time they had acquired an entourage of a hundred or so Africans, who had been picked up *en route*. For they were in territory where tribesmen were in rivalry for a profitable share in the slave trade. They would prey upon weaker villages, capture the inhabitants and march them towards the coast for sale to the Arabs. This party of Europeans had marched into a village that was under siege by one of the slaving tribes, and had at once done what any group of Christians with a spark of manhood between them would have done in the circumstances. They had settled down to fight off the slavers, though the Bishop had misgivings about his own role in the hostilities. It was not that he shrank from the notion of combat. In a way he thoroughly enjoyed it all. His journal records the incident with the relish of a boy to whom the tales of ancient and heroic Greece, upon which he has been brought up, have just come to life before his eyes. But he did not care, certainly, for the possibility that he himself might actually kill someone during the otherwise exciting skirmish. He never used the gun he was carrying. Indeed, he rapidly seized an excuse to get rid of it. 'Seeing Livingstone without one,' he wrote, 'I asked him to use mine, rather than that I should – on the principle that I *preferred* not to use it, and that I thought it more seemly that his finger should pull the trigger than mine.' And the Doctor, who had no such qualms where slavery was about, took the gun and used it.

With their collection of liberated slaves the party reached Magomero, one thousand feet up in the highlands, where it was decided to establish a temporary mission until the land could properly be surveyed for a permanent site. One of Mackenzie's first actions was to write home to London with the urgent request for two hundred blankets which, he said, were intended for moral purposes rather than warmth, to prevent these almost naked people from huddling indecently together at night. He had other requirements. He wrote to the Oxford and Cambridge University Boat Clubs, inviting them to subscribe the money for a launch which the UMCA people could have to themselves, as Livingstone would obviously need to monopolise the *Pioneer*. There was a great variety of equipment that might also be profitably despatched, he told British well-wishers, if the mission was to succeed in its purpose. And soon Messrs Bartlett and Sons, of Redditch, were packing 50,000 fish-hooks free of charge for consignment to the Zambezi.

Not all the Bishop's requests were so speedily and generously answered. He had invited a gunsmith, John Crofts of Birmingham, to come out, together with his wife and six children. The UMCA committee refused to send the family, because it would cost too much. Unfortunately for them, Crofts had a letter from the Bishop which both appointed him to a mission post and asked him to present himself and his family to a London doctor for medical examination before sailing. When the committee refused to pay six half-fares to Africa, Crofts threatened to sue them and had to be bought off with a compensation of £40. But Mackenzie's enthusiasm for the success of his mission was boundless and he planned expansion from the moment he arrived. He decided that he would ask his two spinster sisters to join him, in order to help the moral stability of the people surrounding the new mission. Then he settled down to work.

For all his enthusiasm and his boyish zest, Mackenzie had the prudence of a scholar and a highly sensitive man. He decided that it would be folly, with the limited native vocabulary he then possessed, to try to explain Christian religious ideas in a language so shaped by primitive religious ideas. So he and his missionaries would not teach in any orthodox sense. They would simply try to relate their own morality to the notion of a mighty and supernatural law. They would try to demonstrate that adultery, stealing and other vices were not just sources of friction and pain to any community, but were anathema to the most powerful spirits, however you conceived these to be. To sophisticated man in the twentieth century, this might seem to be no more than an obvious and wise course for anyone to follow in the circumstances. Given the philosophical basis of most missionary activity in the middle of the nineteenth century, it was astonishingly enlightened and verging on the unique. It was, moreover, a deliberate collision between alien values and those which were indigenous and manifested most crudely and strongly in the activities of the native witch-doctors. Mackenzie records an occasion when a witch-doctor was summoned to dispense the form of justice which these people had been reared upon since ancient times, and which the Bishop was bent upon undermining by his own painstaking and thoughtful methods.

Some corn had been stolen and when the owner complained to the chief the most celebrated witch-doctor in the area was summoned. The people assembled around a great fig tree just outside the mission hut and there the witch-doctor produced his equipment. He had a couple of sticks, like broom handles, which he handed to four young men with a great flourish and some incantation. From a greasy goatskin bag he then took a zebra tail, which he gave to another young man, then a calabash full of peas, which he handed to a boy. The witch-doctor now began to roll about on the ground, chanting as he did so, while the man with the zebra tail and the boy with the calabash moved round the four men, who were each holding an end of the two sticks. The pace gradually quickened, the tail and the calabash were waved more vigorously, and the men with the sticks began to twitch in spasms. After a while, they were in convulsions, foaming at the mouth, their eyes starting from their heads glassily. They were possessed by the devil which resided in the sticks they were holding.

At first the sticks moved in rotation, the men holding them firmly. Then the movement became wilder, so that the men were hardly able to maintain their grip; in the end they were being whirled round, it seemed to the watching Mackenzie, by the sticks. Suddenly they leapt up and raced into the bush in a maddened flight, heedless of bushes and thorns that tore at their bodies and made them bleed from deep scratches. Back they came in a rush to the people, went through more rotary motions with the sticks, then jumped up once more and raced off again. This time they did not stop until they fell exhausted by the hut belonging to a slave wife of the chief. There the sticks rolled from the hands of the men, to the foot of the woman. She was thus denounced as the thief. In a great uproar she was led towards the people, protesting her innocence indignantly. 'The medicine-man,' writes Mackenzie, 'was appealed to. In triumph he was smoking his pipe under a tree and the only remark he vouchsafed was "The spirit has declared her guilty; the spirit never lies".'

The woman offered to take the *muari*, to demonstrate her innocence. The *muari* was water which had been poisoned; if you were guilty, you died; if you were innocent, you vomited and lived. This was a chief's wife, however, and local custom allowed the ordeal by *muari* to be delegated to someone on her behalf. The woman disappeared into her hut for a moment or two and she reappeared with a cockerel. The bird's mouth was forced open, the *muari* was poured in, and the people gathered closely to watch their justice take its course. 'The bird, after struggling for a few seconds, threw up the poisoned water, lay quiet for a minute or two, and then, hearing a lusty challenge from a rival bird in the village, stood upon its legs, flapped its wings and crowed. It was evidently none the worse for the ordeal it had gone through, and all the people pronounced the woman innocent.' She carried off her cock with a swagger. The medicine-man shrugged his shoulders and disappeared. 'In the end,' says Mackenzie, 'we succeeded among our own people in establishing trial by jury instead of these objectionable and, in most cases, unjust proceedings; and our method of proceeding so commended itself to the pockets as well as to the good sense of the natives about us, that before we left the country one or other of us had to sit in the administration of justice almost every day.'

The new mission gradually evolved its own compromise routine in these uncivilised surroundings. Matins and Evensong were recited every day, just as they were in every Anglican parish church at home. Holy Communion was celebrated every Sunday and on Saints' Days, and at Sunday services a collection was taken for the Church in other lands. The missionaries took it in turn to decide which branch of the Church insolvent was most in need of these small offerings. There were never any sermons, but Mackenzie conducted a seminar in Bible studies after lunch each Sunday. Having established this pattern, the missionaries were ready for the next stage in their work, which was to create an exemplary agricultural settlement. At the end of November 1861 three men arrived from England to reinforce the first party. Early in the New Year one of the Mackenzie sisters and a missionary wife were expected. Mackenzie and a colleague set off to meet them. They went down the river in a constant downpour of drenching rain and the canoe they were using sank, together with their precious box of medicines, without which no white man would travel far in Africa and expect to survive. They began to march along the river bank, but after a day or two both men fell ill with malaria. On 31 January Mackenzie died, and his colleague buried him, reading as much of the burial service as he could discern from the Prayer Book in the evening gloom. The Bishop's mission was over, after less than a year in East Africa.

The indestructible Livingstone, however, was still forging on. He had been cynical about Mackenzie's desire to bring his sisters out. 'He seems to lean on them,' the Doctor wrote at the time. 'Most High Church people lean on wives or sisters . . . I hope the Bishop will remain at his post; if he doesn't he is a muff to lean on a wife or a sister. I would as soon lean on a policeman.' No one could ever have accused Doctor Livingstone of that.

But now, by the same HMS *Gorgon* that had conveyed Miss Mackenzie and Mrs Burrup to the mouth of the Zambezi, Mary Livingstone herself arrived on the scene. It was not a happy reunion. That it took place at all was entirely at her insistence. She had been a sick woman for a long time and she had suffered a great deal of hardship as well as neglect by her husband. After her return to England with the children, when Livingstone was on the threshold of his lonely march out of South Africa, she had found herself not very welcome among the Livingstone family resident in Scotland. Her own family was at the Cape and, without friends or fixed home, with no more than the meagre LMS grant to maintain her and the four children, she had lived on the edge of poverty in a succession of cheap lodgings; first in Hamilton, near the Livingstones, later in Manchester, Kendal and Epsom. She never had a settled address for very long. She had become acutely depressed and resentful of the glorification of her husband on his own return from Africa; the more so, because it seemed to her that the reasons why the entire nation venerated him contrasted strangely with his own behaviour to her. The daughter of one missionary and the nominal wife of another, she had long since ceased to regard missionary activity as anything but a source of deep personal pain. But now, facing a crisis in her life, she had decided that she must come to David Livingstone, whether the prospect pleased him or not.

She was accompanied, on the voyage out, by James Stewart, of the Free Church of Scotland, who had been sent out to investigate the prospects for an industrial mission in East Africa. They arrived with a whiff of scandal attaching to them. John Kirk may not be the ideal witness on this occasion, for he clearly did not like Mary very much. He refers to her once as a 'coarse, vulgar woman' and elsewhere as 'that avaricious wife'.

But he is the only witness we have to what he calls 'the injudicious conduct' of Mary Livingstone and James Stewart. 'No doubt,' he writes, 'he hoped to gain influence with Dr L through her. Certainly he did so and as he knew her character and professes (confidentially to me, so don't speak of it) to have found out early in the day that she drank very freely, so as to be utterly besotted at times, I think any prudent man would have drawn off from such a person, instead of risking his character by going at late hours into a married woman's bedroom and to prevent the people becoming aware, studiously keeping even the landlady of the house out, lest she should find out the secret. Of course the truth soon became well known and Mr Stewart's visits had an interpretation placed upon them, and quite naturally, too . . . Stewart, like a fool, went and told Mrs L, of all people in the world, all that was said about them and that these things had found their way up here.' From the moment the gossip got out along the Zambezi and inklings of it reached Livingstone's ear, Mary went into a decline from which she did not recover; Kirk was in no doubt that it was this which killed her less than three months after her arrival. Livingstone himself was clearly hit hard by her death. James Stewart, with a tendentious flourish, says that 'The man who had faced so many deaths, and braved so many dangers, was now utterly broken down and weeping like a child'. Livingstone himself writes as movingly as any husband might be expected to on the loss of a wife he cared for. 'For the first time in my life I feel willing to die.'

He was not broken by Mary's death. Instead, he attacked his explorations along the river with even greater frenzy, aboard the new steamer brought by HMS *Gorgon*. In September 1862 the party was plunging upstream in the *Lady Nyasa* in yet another attempt to break through the natural obstacles that had so far halted them and thwarted the great ambition driving the expedition on. At noon one day they had reached a very wide and shallow part of the river. 'Still Dr L means to drag over it,' logged Kirk. 'The infatuation which blinds him, I cannot comprehend, getting the boats jammed up the river where they cannot float and where it will soon be impossible to return . . . I can come to no other conclusion than that Dr L is out of his mind.' But nothing mattered to Livingstone now beside this vision of opening up the interior. The UMCA mission upcountry was quietly settling into a pseudo-parochial existence, but where Livingstone and his main party were, the concessions to formal Christian community life were very scanty indeed. James Stewart was thoroughly shocked by what he discovered on his arrival. Dr Livingstone was more faulty in the matter of Sabbath observance than he had supposed. At noon, when everyone should have been praising God loudly in a service, the Doctor was writing, and it made little difference to Stewart whether the matter was a letter or a despatch. Charles Livingstone was doing the same. So was Rae. So was Young. Others were reading *Chambers' Journal*, *Dynevor Terrace* and *The Count of Monte Cristo*. Only one or two were thumbing their Bibles.

Livingstone was not allowed to go on like this much longer. Already the Government in London was becoming restless at the lack of results the Doctor had assured them of when he had canvassed the expedition to them. Lord John Russell was testily penning a memorandum to the effect that 'Dr Livingstone's information is valuable, but he must not be allowed to tempt us to form colonies only to be reached by forcing steamers up cataracts'. The people on the spot in East Africa were becoming even more disenchanted with the Doctor's performances and they certainly did not now believe he had much value as a source of reliable information. He had told the undergraduates of Cambridge that if they would only buckle to and follow him back to Africa, there awaited them a land of milk and honey in which a missionary could quite easily live and feed well if he took with him a gun. It was talk such as this which had stimulated the formation of the UMCA, but now one of its members on the mission in the highlands was writing that 'the vast plains covered with deer, the herds of eland, buffalo and gnu, which we dreamed would always be within reach of our rifles, we never found'. Livingstone had pictured the highlands of Shiré as the greatest cotton-growing area in the world; indeed, he had told the Government that towards Lake Nyasa there was a cotton belt some four hundred miles long. Mackenzie's party had, on account of this, specifically brought with them a second-hand cotton gin from Ashton-under-Lyne, which had been carried with great difficulty by bearers across one mountain range after another. On their arrival in the anticipated cotton belt, one of the party had to report that 'You cannot get as much cotton as would fill your hat, though you were to travel for days'.

In letters written in 1860, after his earliest excursions on the Zambezi Expedition, Livingstone had praised Mount Morambala, not far from the site of Mackenzie's mission, lyrically. 'Its top,' he had said, 'was large and well-cultivated, with hills and dales and flowing fountains; orange trees and lemon trees grow wild, and pineapples nearly so . . . the people were friendly, growing cotton and sugar cane and maize.' Had this been England, according to Livingstone, they would have had a sanatorium, possibly a college, on the mountain. But now someone else had scrutinised that mountain rather carefully. This was Bishop Tozer, who had come out to take Mackenzie's place, arriving not with a gun and a crozier in his hands, like his predecessor, but a plain black umbrella. After settling down, Tozer had gone to the mountain and spent three weeks moving about it. And when he came back he was rather indignant at having been led up a kind of elevated garden path. 'Doctor Livingstone's extravagant descriptions of this mountain . . . unhesitatingly written soon after a short visit of, I believe, an hour or two at the northern end, is but a specimen of all his writing. The top is not "large", nor from its nature can it be "well-cultivated". Lemons certainly grow wild, but "oranges" are unknown. Water is *scarce* and the inhabitants very few and very poor. The ascent is so difficult that the idea of making a sanatorium here is a good specimen of the way in which Livingstone leaps to any conclusion he may want to see adopted. I believe him to be a good man but, to use the phrase of one of our party, "a very dangerous one".' Two mornings out of every seven on that mountain were so misty that the sun did not appear before noon.

James Stewart was so incensed by Livingstone's misrepresentations once he had found his feet, that he hurled his copy of the best-selling *Missionary Travels and Researches* into the Zambezi. It was not, he declared, a pack of lies, 'but it would need a great many additions to make it the truth'. Not that many of these disillusioned criticisms were widely circulated in Britain. When one of Tozer's men sent a letter down to a clergyman in Cape Town, for eventual transmission home, the clergyman erased those sentences which attacked Livingstone for his deceptions and sent the bowdlerised version to a missionary newspaper, which published them in that form.

Government, however, did not depend upon the missionary press for an evaluation of events overseas. The expedition which had been drummed up mostly in response to Livingstone's reputation, which had set out with hopes at least as high as those entertained for the first Niger excursion a couple of decades before, had not been a disaster; but it had achieved almost nothing apart from more evidence about the wretched slave trade. It was called home after six years of fruitless expenditure. Ironically, the news reached Livingstone near the Murchison Cataracts, where his men had just taken the *Lady Nyasa* to pieces. They were about to carry the steamer in sections overland so that their leader could explore the lake after which it was named. He never made that voyage. Instead, he retraced his way back to Quilimane and sailed the vessel across the Indian Ocean to Bombay before boarding a steamer to England.

This time, there was no public euphoria on his return. Her Majesty's Ministers were no longer as accessible to him as they had been in 1857. He was not shunned, for he still had a great reputation with the people. He addressed the British Association again and this time he concentrated on vilifying the slave trade and particularly the Portuguese laxity in trying to end it. But there was no repetition, in 1864, of the triumphal progress from one end of the land to the other. No city offered him its Freedom this time. He retreated quietly for seven months to the old Byron family home at Newstead Abbey, which now belonged to an old friend of his Kolobeng days, and there he wrote another book. It was Sir Roderick Murchison who came to the rescue during this fretful period in Livingstone's life. The President of the Royal Geographical Society had never lost faith in him in spite of the Government's increasing coolness. There had been no reason to do so. Whatever his failings, Livingstone as an explorer was without rival, and exploration was Murchison's chief passion in life. He knew as well as any man at home, and far better than most, that you could not possibly hope to triumph on all your journeys into the unknown. He now came up with a proposal for Livingstone to go back to the scene of his great triumph, to examine and report on 'the watershed or watersheds of South Africa'.

Livingstone accepted, of course. For him there was no alternative. But it is significant that he felt obliged to enter a qualification. 'Answered Sir Roderick about going out,' he wrote in his journal for 7 January 1865. 'Said I could only feel in the way of duty by working as a missionary.' A wheel had come a full circle. He had enjoyed his greatest fulfilment under the auspices of a missionary society. On abandoning this connection he had suffered relative failure. Now he would revert to his original vocation, though there was no question of returning to the protective covering of the LMS. The breach had been too great for that. But merely to think of himself, above all, as a missionary again would be support enough now.

By the time his new book was ready for the press his plans were made, and he divulged them in his preface. 'I propose to go inland, north of the territory which the Portuguese in Europe claim, and endeavour to commence that system on the East which has been so eminently successful on the West Coast; a system combining the repressive efforts of H.M. Cruisers with lawful trade and Christian Missions – the moral and material results of which have been so gratifying.'

Within eighteen months of returning from the Zambezi, he was in Africa again. This time the Government had put up only £500 to support his venture. He still clung to his official status as Consul 'for that portion of the African coast lying between the Portuguese sphere of influence and Abyssinia'. A clergyman who saw him in Bombay on the way out remarked that Livingstone 'was dressed very unlike a minister – more like a post-captain or an admiral. He wore a blue dress coat, trimmed with lace and bearing the Government gilt buttons. In his hand he carried a cocked hat.' But a reversion had taken place. On his way across the Indian Ocean to Zanzibar, Livingstone attended evening prayers aboard the vessel and wrote afterwards, 'I mean to keep up this, and make this a Christian expedition, telling a little about Christ wherever we go.'

He reached Africa again towards the end of January 1866. After a couple of months' preparation at the coast, he plunged away into the interior. First he headed for Lake Nyasa, where he had been thwarted by the recall of his first expedition. Then he advanced on Lake Tanganyika. After that he was away past the headwaters of the Congo river *en route* to another lake in the central watershed of the continent. As the months slipped by and became one year, and then two, Livingstone himself slipped slowly out of the consciousness of the British public at home. Occasionally rumours would reach England. Early on it was reported that he had been murdered, and flags were flown at half-mast. But then the rumour was quashed; he had been seen again by credible witnesses.

Another long period of silence followed and the public, when they thought of him at all, began to assume that he had just vanished into the interior of Africa on some wayward errand of his own; indeed, a story began to circulate that he had gone native and taken an African princess as wife. In fact, Livingstone was still plodding on, driven by the old devil to discover, and enduring greater privations than he had known even on his great and lonely first journey across the continent. There were times when he and his men ran short of food and barely managed to survive. There were other times when Livingstone's travelling case of medicines was lost and he had to pull himself out of malarial bouts by his rousing old method of sheer will-power. There was, from time to time, some sickening new encounter with the slave trade, which weakened Livingstone spiritually, as the shortage of food and medicines reduced him physically.

At Nyangwe, on 15 July 1871, he witnessed a massacre of slaves, and his account of it was to stir the world as nothing had ever done before. Arab raiders had appeared in the village market-place and started firing on the crowd of natives. It was a strategy which usually frightened these people into a rapid submission, so that they could be shackled and trooped off without trouble. On this occasion it started them in a panic-stricken and headlong rush to the river. They jumped into the canoes, lined up along the bank and began to paddle into midstream. The pursuing Arabs stood along the water's edge and poured volley after volley into fleeing boats and the natives who were swimming out to scramble aboard them.

'Shot after shot,' wrote Livingstone, 'continued to be fired on the helpless and perishing. Some of the long line of heads disappeared quietly; while other poor creatures threw their arms high, as if appealing to the great Father above, and sank. One canoe took in as many as it could hold, and all paddled with hands and arms; three canoes, got out in haste, picked up sinking friends, till all went down together, and disappeared . . . By-and-by all the heads disappeared.' Some of these people escaped. But the Arabs themselves reckoned that between 330 and 400 had been killed. Livingstone said that his impulse was to pistol the murderers, but he was advised against getting himself into a blood-feud; and so he held his fire and marched wearily away. 'It gave me,' he said, 'the impression of being in Hell.'

By this time, Livingstone's long absence had engaged the attention of James Gordon Bennett, the effective head of the *New York Herald*. With the acumen of every newspaper tycoon, who can sniff a good story out even when there is some evidence to suggest that it does not really exist, he despatched his roving correspondent H. M. Stanley to look for Dr Livingstone, wherever he might have got to in Africa. This robustly hybrid journalist – born John Rowland, fugitive from a Welsh workhouse, soldier on both sides of the American Civil War, self-styled citizen of Missouri – had a number of assignments to attend to *en route* to his prospective interview with the Doctor. He had to report on the opening of the Suez Canal, then he had to sail up the Nile and write about Upper Egypt. After that he was to visit Jerusalem, Baghdad, Constantinople, the Crimea and India. But eventually, in the first week of November 1871, the historic meeting took place at Ujiji, on the shore of Lake Tanganyika, after a hazardous journey which some of Stanley's newspaper colleagues were at first inclined to disbelieve. With the American flag flying at the head of his small column, Stanley led his bearers into the market-place of the town, to where a pale and haggard white man was standing. Stanley was so overcome by the emotion of the moment that he wanted to run and embrace the Scotsman, but was too embarrassed to do so in front of

a native crowd. 'So I did what cowardice and false pride suggested was the best thing – walked deliberately to him, took off my hat, and said: "Dr Livingstone, I presume."'

Stanley had gone in search of a scoop; he found a father-figure as well, to take the place of the parent he had lost some ten years or so before. And there can be little doubt that in the devoted and sentimental Stanley, Livingstone himself discovered someone upon whom he could lean for a little while, as a father upon his son. He had not, after all, allowed himself such a relationship with his own children. They had become dispersed since he had first packed them home, ages ago, though he had done his best to maintain contact with them by letter. In Stanley, the Americanised Welshman, it is probable that he saw something of his eldest boy Robert, who had run away from home, emigrated across the Atlantic, and perished as a prisoner of the Confederate forces in the American Civil War.

Livingstone described himself as a mere 'ruckle of bones' at this stage. Stanley found him almost toothless, with stomach troubles so severe that he could scarcely manage solid food. Yet the image of nobility was the one which predominated in his reports. 'His hair,' wrote the journalist, 'has brownish colour yet, but is here and there streaked with grey lines over the temples; his beard and moustache are very grey. His eyes, which are hazel, are remarkably bright; he has sight as keen as a hawk's . . . When walking he has a firm but heavy tread, like that of an overworked or fatigued man . . .' He was a man who could endure all things and Stanley vividly described some of the Doctor's sufferings and his apparent indifference to them. He told of how Livingstone had been stung dreadfully by a swarm of bees which settled in his hair in handfuls 'but, after partaking of a cup of warm tea and some food, he was as cheerful as if he had never travelled a mile'. The most revealing thing he wrote about this fabulous figure was that Livingstone 'had lived in a world which revolved inwardly, out of which he seldom awoke except to attend to immediate practical necessities'.

Stanley had brought Livingstone badly needed supplies. He also urged the Doctor to return to civilisation with his own party. Livingstone would not hear of it. He still had work to do in Africa, he said. His obsession had now become to discover the true source of the river Nile and he would never quit until he had claimed this crowning glory of all his wanderings as an explorer. So they parted, after four months together, and Stanley wept as they clasped hands for the last time. Then Livingstone vanished into the bush again, with his faithful Africans. For almost a year he would march in growing weariness and sickness and despair. But he was with those to whom he had unfailingly given the very best of himself, from his earliest days on the continent. They did not fail him when at last he died among them, the source of the Nile still undiscovered, but the crowning glory long since achieved with and through them. Carefully they removed the heart from his body and buried it by a tree, so that some part of him might remain with them. Then they embalmed his corpse and carried it across several hundred miles of the most difficult country on earth, so that it should be restored to his own people. And his own people went into deep mourning, from one end of the land to the other, on the day they buried him in Westminster Abbey.*

* The mood of the British was precisely expressed in a couple of verses which were published in *Punch* at the time of the funeral:

Open the Abbey doors, and bear him in
To sleep with King and statesman, chief, and sage,
The Missionary, come of weaver kin,
But great by work that brooks no lower wage.

He needs no epitaph to guard a name
Which man shall prize while worthy work is known;
He lived and died for good – be that his fame:
Let marble crumble: this is Living-stone.

9
THE FLOOD TIDE

The years of struggle and public indifference to missionary work had ended even before Livingstone appeared out of Africa for the first time, in 1856, and one of the steepest rises in popularity occurred about the time of the Niger Expedition. The annual income of the Church Missionary Society is a representative guide to financial progress throughout the nineteenth century. Until 1812–13, a dozen or so years after its foundation, subscriptions had never amounted to £3,000. The following year they had gone up to £13,000. By 1823–4 they had risen to £34,000, the year after they had reached £40,000, and they never again fell below that figure. By 1843 the income of the CMS was £115,000, which made it quite the wealthiest of the British societies, a lead it was never to lose. By 1872 the committee in Salisbury Square had £150,000 at its disposal, quite beyond an increasing amount of capital, and by 1882 the income had gone up to £190,000, with a centenary fund in 1899 topping £212,000.

The other societies in Britain were not nearly so well off; they could not draw, to the same extent, upon privileged and commercial wealth as the Established Church of England could, with royalty at its head and the squire patronising the vicar in every parish in the land. Yet the nonconformist societies were buoyant, too. The LMS appeal to start the new Central African Mission which Livingstone should have led, in 1857, was oversubscribed by £1,400 within a few months of opening. When a Baptist mission station on the Congo was destroyed by fire in 1886, the BMS asked for an estimated £4,000 to rebuild it; the money was in within a couple of months and the appeal was closed with £5,943 in the bank.

Both LMS and BMS received more than £100,000 in subscriptions at their centenary years.

This does not mean that the missionary societies were now into a century in which money and manpower would flow annually in unceasing and equal abundance. Between 1862 and 1872, for example, the British were much concerned with improving life for the underprivileged in their own country, their Church people were intent upon expanding the home missions to their own poor, and there was a consequent drop in financial support for foreign missions. By 1872, also, the burst of enthusiasm in the British universities which had sent many pious young graduates off to the mission field, in the wake of Livingstone and even before him, had apparently abated. In that year Bishop Bickersteth spoke tartly of the reasons for this decline in manpower. 'There is,' he declared, 'a relaxation of discipline, an amount of luxury and self-indulgence, a disposition to countenance free thought, which is nothing better than a licence for unbelief; and these things are more than sufficient to explain the decay of that Christian life and zeal which underlie the missionary enterprise.' The decline was only temporary. The figures were to soar again after H. M. Stanley's despatches had ennobled Dr Livingstone once more, and after the nation had mourned the passing of its hero.

Apart from special appeals, when a new mission was to be established, or an old mission had been damaged by fire, there was by the middle of the century a steady flow of contributions from churches and chapels all over the British Isles. A curiosity of the early years had been that while Anglican clergy and the well-to-do generally had been slow to back the missionary societies, the poor people of Great Britain could always be relied upon to produce something, even if it was only a pittance. At Harrow, in the 1820s, five hundred labourers and servants put their names down as penny subscribers to one of the new artisan Missionary Unions; at Manchester, every meeting of a similar body in 1823 was attended by twelve hundred people of the working class. The poor never ceased to give. In 1866 a small and poor northern parish in the Church of England, with only five homes rated at £30, could boast of 305 regular subscribers to the CMS and eighty-five people who kept special collecting boxes in their homes. The Vicar reported that 'Our subscriptions have increased. The collectors have continued their patient, painstaking work. And work it really is. We have received, during the year, more than 1,513 distinct gifts. In L— Street alone, which contains 114 houses, 402 gifts have been gathered from sixty-two subscribers . . . Next, our Missionary Boxes have yielded a larger sum. We never have had more of these silent friends asking for the family offerings of the Christian household. And they have not asked in vain. They seem, like the hand of God, ever open to receive the first fruits of our increase. The sick child is restored, the ailing mother is strengthened, the father's health is mercifully continued, and there is the open hand ready to accept the thank-offering to God for his goodness. I should like to see a missionary box in every house in the parish, that some portion of our weekly earnings may find its way into the treasures of God.'

When the Baptist Missionary Society penetrated the Congo above Stanley Pool in the 1870s, a Staffordshire collier who had been praying every day for this success, wrote a letter to BMS headquarters in London. 'I have been putting on one side into my Congo box any little savings, and they have been only little, as work has been dull, and home expenses, owing to long sickness, many and heavy. Yet I have £5 and this I send at once as my thank-offering for the glorious news.' A domestic servant in the north of Scotland sent £1; a widow and her son 'out of their poverty' sent 10s.; a watercress seller sent 5s., a scavenger £5, a seamstress £1, a blind girl £2, a blacksmith £2. One letter said: 'You will find enclosed half a sovereign; it is all we have in the world, and it is for the Congo Mission. I am a crippled widow, and have been in bed with a bad spinal complaint for five years. My only child, a daughter 17 years old, works with me with her needle, and we only just earn enough to live by. It has taken me a year to save this ten shillings; but if you knew the joy I feel in helping this Congo Mission it would, I think, cheer and encourage you. We buy the "Herald" each month and read it with great delight – this is the only book we are able to buy. You will not mind this being a small sum, will you? The Lord knows we cannot do more.'

Missionary societies were mostly Evangelical in character, which meant that they took a disparaging view of worldly goods, and there were some areas of fund-raising which they were bound in all conscience to disdain. It was all very well to hold a Public Breakfast at the London Tavern, as the Wesleyan Missionary Society did in 1843, provided the alcoholic stock-in-trade of the premises was kept carefully out of sight during these temperate proceedings. It was more difficult to reconcile the raising of money for God's purposes overseas with such soul-destroying devices as games of chance and rather jolly entertainments, and some missionary writers had to twist themselves into knots of justification in order to explain away the unpalatable. This is a contorted perspective from the 1890s: 'Here, let a word be said about Sales of Work. There is, rightly, a strong feeling against "bazaars", with their usual concomitants, being held for the benefit of distinctly religious objects. But a Missionary Sale, though at first sight much the same, is in reality a totally different thing. The gay folk who frequent bazaars would vote it insufferably dull; no raffling, no theatricals, no variety entertainments, no comic songs. During the preceding twelve months, busy fingers have been employed in making articles for sale; those busy fingers, many of them, have belonged to the bedridden, the poor, the solitary, the young; not a few have been set to work by real love for the Lord and zeal for his Glory; many simple articles have been dedicated to His cause with prayer. Then these articles are gathered together, and displayed, and sold; and great is the joy in many a cottage or sick room when the news comes that a piece of work, which perhaps occupied hours of loneliness and weakness, has been sold for its full value, and the money handed to the missionary treasurer. Who would rob these quiet workers of their joy? Who would forbid those who can help in scarcely any other way from helping in this way? A Missionary Sale may be, and often is, a holy service for the Lord. And, let it be added, in just those Sales where the spiritual tone is highest, is the largest success achieved.'

By the time Livingstone had made his mark, the wealthy had been deeply drawn into the forces supporting the missionary movement. Royal favours flowed regularly, though with a decent regard for the proprieties; Prince Albert lent himself readily to the aims of the Niger Expedition, but declined to serve as patron of its successor up the Zambezi, because he had no wish to disturb the Portuguese with any political implications; the Queen donated £20 to the jubilee fund of the CMS Windsor Association, but never did fill the vacant patronage of the CMS itself, though the seat was left open to her till the day she died, because this might have offended the LMS, the BMS and the other non-Established missionary bodies in her realm. Where royalty led the way so graciously, subjects of substance followed loyally. Bishop Mackenzie could thus canvass the Oxford and Cambridge Boat Clubs for his steam launch with impunity; that Redditch firm parcelled off 50,000 fish-hooks out of sheer goodwill to the same mission; Messrs Sutton and Sons of Reading presented the Baptists with boxes of seeds for planting in the Congo. The very wealthy began to leave large legacies to the missionary societies and a handful of rich eccentrics were among them, secretly pouring thousands of pounds into the missionary organisations even before they died.

When H. M. Stanley returned to Africa a year after Livingstone's death, to begin an epic journey of his own that would take him down the Congo, he saw himself as a freelance missionary as well as a writer and explorer. He had been deeply affected by his four months with the Doctor and the encounter had marked him in more ways than he recognised. There is little doubt that subconsciously he was treading, step for step, where the great man had gone before him. It was in this frame of mind that he wrote a letter to the *Daily Telegraph* from Uganda in November 1875. 'Oh, that some pious, practical missionary would come here!' he declared. 'What a field and harvest ripe for the sickle of civilisation . . . It is the practical Christian tutor who can teach people how to become Christians, cure their diseases, construct dwellings . . . and turn his hand to anything – like a sailor – this is the man who is wanted . . . You need not fear to spend money on such a mission . . .'

Two days after the letter was published, the secretary of the CMS received an envelope containing a cheque for £5,000 and a note which explained that the money was intended to start a new mission on Lake Victoria. It was signed by someone calling himself 'An Unprofitable Servant'. The writer was not identified until many years later, by which time he had spent several thousands of pounds in supporting the Baptists and the LMS as well as the CMS. His name was Robert Arthington and he was quite the most extravagant and probably the most eccentric missionary supporter of the nineteenth century.

Robert Arthington had been born in 1823 into a family of Quakers in Leeds. His father was a brewer, who used to send up a barrel of ale to the quarterly meeting of Friends in Leeds, until he had a crisis of conscience in 1850 and closed the brewery down. His mother used to write the texts for children's picture books, under such titles as *Rhymes for Harry and his Nurse-Maid* and *The Little Scholar's first Grammar*. Robert went to Cambridge, but on coming down it was unnecessary for him to take a job, with a great deal of money in the family. He occupied himself with a huge variety of interests. He became an enthusiastic collector of shells and an authority on coins. He wrote papers on *The Fertilisation of the Soil*, *Preventable Accidents* and *The Maintenance of Health*. He composed and set to music three poems which he entitled 'The Song of Songs', 'The Song of Moses' and 'Thou King of the Ages'. He was a congenital magpie as well as a bounding dilettante: when the family home was eventually given up, the purchasers found it organised like a museum which contained, among other things, the most comprehensive collection of umbrellas and spectacles in the land.

At some stage after leaving Cambridge, Robert met a girl he wished to marry. She turned him down and from that day, in classic manner, Arthington became a recluse. When his parents died and his sisters married, he moved to a new home, where a chain was always fastened across the door. A loaf and a jug of milk were left on the doorstep each day and very few people ever got beyond that point. Those who did, reported bare floors littered with books and papers. A printer who knew him said that 'He was always sombre and sorrowful. If one did not agree with him or yield to his strange views, he would not argue, but give you a cold, long look and then silently walk away.' He was said to live on half a crown a day and he soon became known locally as the Miser of Headingley. He ignored all begging letters, saying that he was not greatly moved by poverty, as he knew that it was possible to live on very little. He was once persuaded to preside at a missionary meeting in Leeds, where he was expected to make a large donation to the funds. He put one shilling on the plate.

He had become interested in missions in much the same way that he had become interested in coins and in umbrellas. But missions became his overwhelming obsession. He subscribed to every missionary journal that was published, and for half a century all his other passions became subordinated to this one supreme interest. He started to put thousands of his fortune, secretly, at the disposal of missionary societies. Apart from the £5,000 he sent to the CMS for a new mission in Uganda, he provided the Baptists with a steamer for use on the Congo, and the LMS with another for work on Lake Tanganyika. He even started a mission of his own, to work among the aboriginal tribes of Assam, though the longest journey he made himself was to Italy. He told the men he employed for this work to 'Preach and pass on; three months is enough for one tribe. Use interpreters. Don't stop to learn the language or to translate the Bible, much less to teach the people to read, otherwise you will never reach all the tribes.'

Three years before Arthington died, in 1900, at the age of seventy-seven, he went to live in Devon. He had always been exceedingly shrewd in his investments and knew himself to be very wealthy; he now discovered that he had seriously underestimated his resources. He began to distribute his money with the prodigality of a drunken sailor; at once he sent an anonymous £10,000 to an Indian Famine Fund, while maintaining his regular disbursements to the missionary societies. Even this was not enough to keep pace with the growth of interest upon his investments. At his death, his executors found they had £943,130 at their disposal. Before they could distribute allotments of Arthington's will, they had £1,119,848 on their hands. Over £100,000 went to relatives, a few thousands to friends and institutions Arthington had been associated with.

But the vast bulk of his fortune went to missionary bodies. Preferring the evangelical zeal of nonconformity to what he regarded as the theological complexities of the CMS, he left £373,000 to the LMS and £466,000 to the BMS. And the Baptists were so delighted by his regular support that the first European name given to the Congolese village of Kinshasa, which later became Leopoldville, was that of Arthington. Nor were smaller missionary societies forgotten; a mission of Plymouth Brethren, working on the borders of Northern Rhodesia and the Congo, received money from the bequest. His will also stipulated that, if it were practicable, 'every tribe of mankind that has them not, and which speaks a language distinct from all others' should be given a copy of the Gospels according to John and Luke, together with the Acts of the Apostles; and ten or a dozen people from each tribe should be taught to read them.

When the executors were going through Arthington's papers, after his death, they came upon a letter which had been written to him ages before by a missionary in Africa, and which gave them, they believed, some clue to the benefactor's extraordinary conduct over half a century. 'Were I in England again,' wrote this George King, 'I would gladly live in one room, make the floor my bed, a box my chair, another my table, rather than the heathen should perish for the lack of Christ.' If this was indeed the genesis of Arthington's Millions, as his disbursements were eventually known, its author unwittingly acquired a vital place in missionary history. By the time the Arthington Trust was wound up in 1936, more than £1 million had been distributed to missionary societies throughout the world in the previous thirty years alone.

With a mounting flow of money into the missionary funds from the middle of the nineteenth century, there also came a growing wave of propaganda. No longer must every penny be spent upon paying for the passages of missionary families to Africa and elsewhere, and upon supporting them at their work until they could support themselves, or until their new converts would support them from local resources. A proportion of funds could now be allotted to the creation of a publicity apparatus and the missionary societies carefully began to create it. The CMS started publishing *The Gleaner*, at 2d a copy each week, in 1838. Soon afterwards it produced a counterpart for young people, the *Juvenile Instructor*, which cost only a farthing each week; and subscribers who belonged to Sunday Schools were given free copies of the *Quarterly Token*. There was an adult equivalent of this, the *Quarterly Paper*, which was unhappily responsible for Mr Gladstone's breach with the CMS.

Mr Gladstone had been interested in the missionary movement from his youth, he had been on the platform at the Exeter Hall meeting in 1840, and he had long been a subscribing member of the Church Missionary Society. The *Quarterly Paper*'s Christmas number in 1849 contained, among other things, a small and sketchy map of the world which was intended to show the deployment of missionary forces and the division of the globe into different religions and religious sects. This was illustrated by the use of varying shades and combinations of cross-hatching. The totally heathen world was demonstrated in black; Protestant Christianity came pure white. Islam was picked out in a dark shade and both the Roman Catholic and Orthodox worlds were depicted in a light shade. This deeply offended Mr Gladstone's sensitivity to sectarian distinctions. The Orthodox, he believed, should have been demonstrated in a lighter shade than that applied to the Roman Catholics. So he made his protest; and he promptly cancelled his subscription to the CMS.

The missionary magazines were flourishing by the time of Livingstone's death. And shortly after that, a new form of publicity began to expand at an unprecedented rate. This was the missionary biography, which found a ready market among a people who were moved and exalted by the story of the great Doctor's apparent martyrdom in the cause of Christianity and enlightening the darkest continent on earth. A spate of these books began to issue from the printing presses, and they were to be the best-sellers for at least a generation and a half in Britain. By 1898 *The Story of the Life of Mackay of Uganda, by His Sister*, rewritten for the benefit of young people from a more substantial work, had run to a seventh edition, completing 26,000 copies. A handful of writers made a small fortune out of this area of letters. S. W. Partridge wrote no fewer than thirty-six biographies for adults, with titles like *Thomas J. Comber, Missionary Pioneer to the Congo; James Calvert, or From Dark to Dawn in Fiji* and *The Slave and His Champions, or Missionary Heroines in Eastern Lands.* By the 1880s the LMS had produced a series of highly successful Missionary Manuals, like *Among the Cannibals of New Guinea; Christ or Confucius, which?* or *The Story of the Amoy Mission* and *City, Rice Swamp and Hill.* The books came in heavy board covers whose edges were usually bevelled, and they had deeply incised drawings on the front, picked out in gold leaf: a couple of crouching natives, spears in hand, looking towards a sun, was a typical reproduction. The title of *Mackay of Uganda* was set upon the cover at an angle of forty-five degrees and the lettering, for some exuberant reason, was quaintly oriental in mood. These were books that were made to last, to suffer much handling without noticeable deterioration. And they did.

Their contents were pious to a degree. They were also as extravagantly romantic as any cheap novelette. When Jesse Page composed *Captain Allen Gardiner, Sailor and Saint* in 1897, his first paragraph read, 'Some lives, radiant with high endeavour, are best remembered by the pathos of the things they failed to do. This is true of the man whose life is briefly sketched in the pages of this book. Never had Truth a more chivalrous knight errant. In his quest for the souls of men he bravely pressed through dark thickets of heathenism, fought the dragons of superstition and ignorance and for long; at last, with a song of triumph on his dying lips, seeing by a vision of faith the final victory.' They could be much more tendentious than this. Not a breath of criticism was allowed to disturb any page consecrated to a Christian soldier in the field. There was not a hint of mortal weakness in any man dedicated to the salvation of pagan souls. On the other hand there was sometimes a great deal of racial prejudice, and this was particularly true of the volumes produced for juvenile readers.

The young person's edition of *Mackay*, for example, begins, 'This book is written especially for boys, in the hope that Mackay's example may lead many of them to think of Africa, and devote their lives to its moral and spiritual regeneration.' By page sixty-one, the author is deep in a number of generalisations about Africa and the Africans. 'The moister the climate, the darker the complexion of the black. The inhabitants of Busongoru and Karague are black as coal, while the Bangoro are more of a chocolate colour, and the tribes from the hills of Busoga and Gambaragara are, some of them, not much darker than Arabs. It remains to be proved but is, I think, true, that the darker the skin, the deeper the degradation . . .' This was the environment in which A. W. Mackay was spreading the Gospel and his sister, the writer, gives a picturesque account for boys of how the missionary vocation was first heard of in the Mackay household, when both were children themselves.

' "Would you like me to go as a missionary to Africa, Mother?"

' "If God prepares you for it, my boy, but not unless. You must first *come to Him*, and if He has need of you, He will call upon you in a way you will not mistake. You can throw your soul into the missionary enterprise and yet stay at home; but if the message comes 'Depart, for I will send thee far hence', take care you do not neglect it. Remember what Jonah got for his pains. But, as I have heard Dr Duff say, 'The advancement of the missionary cause is not only our duty and responsibility, but it is an *enjoyment* which those who have once tasted would not exchange for all the treasures of the Indian mines, for all the laurels of civic success, for all the glittering splendours of coronets. It is a joy as rich as heaven, pure as the Godhead, lasting as eternity!' "

' "I do not think I could like *black* people."

' "Not pity the poor captives?"

' "Oh yes, I could pity them, and would like to help them, but to *love* them – I don't know." '

The narrative by Mackay's sister then continues, without interruption: 'Perhaps, considering whence the mother came, it is no matter for surprise that she was a diligent reader of "The Bulwark", and that she earnestly sought to impress on his youthful mind that the Reformation is a great trust handed down to us by our forefathers. She spent much time in explaining to him the prominent errors and the lying legends of Popery, so that when the occasion offered, he would have no difficulty in unmasking its face and exposing its craftiness.' That was the trouble with writing Protestant missionary propaganda. Even if it meant that you tumbled headlong into a devastating *non sequitur*, you simply had to make it plain to your young readers that there were other perils lurking in the African undergrowth apart from those inherent in coal-black degradation.

There were periodicals, there were books, and there were games to be played with a missionary purpose. Almost from the cradle, a child could be carefully nourished with this source of endless amusement. There was, for a start, *An African Picture Game*, to be made by 'the Littlest Ones'. This issued from a packet which contained cut-out figures of Baby Efu and other human beings which, with similar cut-outs of animals, could be slotted into a cardboard base against a background scene of bush huts and jungle. The back of the packet bore a commentary, 'Story Time in Africa', which went as follows: '. . . Best of all, Auntie is going to tell some stories. She knows a great many. Wait a minute, Auntie! Kofi's FRIEND is just coming. She wants to listen, too! Now, Auntie will tell stories of Jesus, the Friend of little children everywhere – stories *you* love very much. And other stories will be about white girls and boys who live a long way away. She is going to tell them about you and me – she really is! Isn't it nice that we hear stories of the black boys and girls, and they hear stories about us!

'Hush-sh-sh! it's bedtime. Efu will soon be fast asleep. Good night little black sister! Sleep well, little black brother! Good night!

'PS – if you want to know more about EFU, ask your Mummy to buy you *The Book of An African Baby*.'

There was a game called *What Next?*, which must have been played in half the Christian households of Britain towards the end of the nineteenth century. It contained thirty-six cards, divided into four series of nine cards each, and each series was devoted to the adventurous life of a famous missionary. There was a narrative running through each series, broken at intervals by a picture of something whose name the player had to guess. The series on Mackay began thus: 'Alexander Mackay was a young Scottish engineer who in 1876 went to Uganda as a pioneer missionary. Uganda is 700 miles from the east coast of (picture of a map of Africa) and in those days there was no (picture of a tent) at night and thousands of hungry (picture of insects) swarmed about. At last he reached the (picture of a native village) of the heathen king Mtesa, the throb of whose (picture of a drum) brought fear to the hearts of thousands. Mackay lived on the green hillside in a little grass-thatched (picture of hut) . . .' Another game was called *A Missionary Tour of India; a game for young people*, which somewhat resembled Snakes and Ladders, with its injunctions to 'Miss a turn to visit the great heathen town of Tinnevelly, with its vast Temple of Siva'.

The CMS issued its own collection of amusements, and among them was *Missionary Outposts – an instructive round game for children.* There were jig-saw puzzles galore with a missionary theme. There were picture painting books by the dozen. And while most of these products were aimed at the young, the wider circle of the family was most certainly not forgotten. Oddly, for a movement which had a temperamental aversion to gambling and needed to justify its sales of work with many tortured qualifications, there was even *Missionary Lotto; a Game for Winter Evenings.* Priced at 1s. 6d. (or 1s. 9d. post free). 'This interesting Family Game is designed,' its sponsors promised, 'to promote the knowledge of Missionary Facts in a pleasant manner. It admits of many variations in its rules and methods; so that it can be made simple enough for little children or difficult enough to puzzle parents.'

Another stimulus became available to the British missionary societies at the time of Livingstone's death, and they did not neglect to make use of it. The United States, in the years following the Civil and Spanish Wars, had witnessed the start of a great Revivalist phenomenon and in the middle of it was the impressive figure of Dwight L. Moody. This bricklayer's son from Massachusetts has been seen as a man 'representative of a new America emerging after the Civil War, earthy and dynamic, centred on the great cities, spawned by industrialism'. He had been a successful businessman in Chicago, he had also been connected with his local Sunday School, and he had turned his back on commerce to lend himself completely to the Evangelistic movement that was beginning to stir his country.

He was a shrewd man who carefully trimmed his Gospel-preaching to the needs of personal survival. At first he held multi-racial meetings in the southern states, but when he was heavily criticised he abandoned them and thereafter whites and blacks were always strictly segregated at his meetings or treated to separate services. Moody's reputation was small but substantial until he left for a tour of Great Britain in 1873. By the time he returned to the States, a couple of years later, he was a figure who never again left the public eye. He was thereafter inseparable from the person of Ira D. Sankey, the bank president's son from Pennsylvania, and the two of them for a quarter of a century swept back and forth across North America and the British Isles, whenever sponsors were lucky enough to secure their services. Moody was the preacher, while Sankey accompanied him at the organ, and led the singing of those rousing choruses which were to be immortalised in the Moody and Sankey Hymn Book, and transmitted injudiciously through every heathen land, by missionaries to whom the sentiment of hot-Gospelling was everything and upon whom the aesthetics of hymnody fell as upon almost tone-deaf ears.

The British had never before encountered anything resembling the manner and methods of Dwight Moody. At one of his first meetings in England, in the Victoria Hall, Liverpool, a special tabernacle, costing 17,000 dollars, was erected over the stage to improve the acoustics. From that moment, crowds were assured at every meeting even if at first they might have been drawn more by curiosity than piety. The charitable called Moody's methods vigorous, while the critical thought them crude, and Moody was twice given a very rough passage by the sophisticated young men of the senior British universities. He was opening an eight-day campaign in Cambridge on Guy Fawkes Day 1882 and 'At first, Sankey's music produced, instead of the usual deathly stillness and rapt attention, shouts of "Hear, hear" and a steady tattoo on the floor with umbrellas and canes. Moody's New England accent was mimicked.' At his first meeting in Oxford, the interruptions became so loud and so continuous that he was forced to stop reading from the Book of Ezekiel. But the man had a driving zeal and earnestness that wore down any opposition by sheer staying power. His battle-cry 'The evangelisation of the world in this generation' became the rallying point for vast numbers of young Christian men in Britain as well as in the United States. There was soon to be a regular flow of students across the Atlantic in both directions, to take part in missionary and collegiate conferences. And though Dwight Moody's message never ceased to stress the primary importance of missions at home, especially in the industrialised cities, it left an incalculable mark upon the course of missionary work overseas.

Under the mounting pressure of the missionary propaganda machine the public of Britain did what people always do when confronted with endless, apparently inexorable and very carefully planned publicity. They subscribed. They were formed into cells and clubs and supporting bodies of an infinite variety, which might solicit no more than their money and their prayers, but which were just as likely to require of them several hours a week in stitching shapeless garments for naked African women, the more rapidly to speed transition from tribal degradation to Christian virtue. The CMS periodical *The Gleaner* eventually spawned The Gleaners Union, whose first applicants for membership included a bishop, a theological student, a farm labourer, an engine driver and someone who was sick in hospital. Within ten months, six thousand people had been enrolled. And when Bishop Tucker of Uganda appealed for funds at a London meeting of the Gleaners Union in 1891, £8,000 had been promised within half an hour of his address.

The Gleaners Union was much concerned with training youth to a proper appreciation of the missionary spirit, and at a meeting in 1894 Miss Ellen Bazett, of Reading, offered her own brisk and well-scrubbed views on how this could best be attained. 'First, *what* is the material we have to work on,' she asked. 'Boys! Splendid stuff, too! Can we not see in our merry, noisy, fidgetty boys, with all their love of adventure and dislike of anything soft and weak, the very seeds of future spirit, manliness, energy and enthusiasm which, when sanctified, as Secretaries, we must *train* and not *restrain* this boy spirit.' No doubt, some of Miss Bazett's splendid boys eventually found their way into one of the flourishing Missionary Boards, which consisted of young men who undertook to give talks on missionary subjects to Sunday Schools, or whatever audience asked for them. Or eventually, in maturity, when their own dreams of missionary work in some far-flung outpost of God's Empire had faded under the weight of a wife and children and a steady job in trade and commerce, they might become subscribing members of the Missionary Leaves Association, which pledged itself to provide Anglican missionaries with things they needed but could not obtain from the stockpiles of equipment belonging to the CMS – harmoniums, lanterns, church furniture or bells. There was no end to the number of bodies you could be associated with, in order to demonstrate your support for the missionary purposes of Christianity.

And all of this, while it undoubtedly was gaining momentum by the middle of the nineteenth century, was propelled more vigorously forward by the legend of David Livingstone. It was his example which produced a national enthusiasm for the missionary movement which had not been known before, as pulpits throughout the land echoed with panegyrics about the Christian hero who had died on his knees at prayer for Africa. It was his own professed faith which left another mark that was to last. His death cemented a relationship between commerce and Christianity, which was to produce a kind of profit for both. Five years after he had been buried in Westminster Abbey, with Stanley and Kirk and his old exploring friend Oswell among the pall-bearers, the Livingstonia Central Africa Trading Company Limited was formed with a capital of £20,000, mostly raised by Glasgow businessmen. Its avowed object was to 'lift from the missionaries' shoulders the burden of transport and the general trading concerns inevitable in a country without a recognised currency'. It was to work hand in hand with missions established by both the Free and Established Churches of Scotland. It would supply the missions with goods they needed, but it would also bring ivory out of the bush at a price that would undercut the Arab slavers. Before long, it had a network of trading posts running throughout East Africa. Before long, too, the effect of this enterprise and of its many successors would be detectable in Britain outside the meetings of shareholders. The missionary periodical press would soon be garnished with advertisements from nurserymen offering African grasses for sale, from furniture stores wishing to sell firescreens embossed with tropical beetles.

Livingstone had dramatically pointed this way ahead. At first light one morning in October 1875 his challenge was resolutely taken up by a parcel of Presbyterian missionaries and Livingstonia entrepreneurs, as they eased their boat into the waters of Lake Nyasa, bound for a new venture on the far shore. They sang the metrical version of the Old Hundredth Psalm as their boat slid along 'All people that on earth do dwell, Sing to the Lord with cheerful voice'. A new dawn was indeed breaking over the lake as they came. Over all Africa.

10

THE CHRISTIAN SOLDIERS

It is possible that no breed of men and women can be so safely assessed as the nineteenth-century Protestant missionaries. No other breed, certainly, left more voluminous accounts of themselves to posterity. The student has to read between the lines sometimes, relying with gingerly care upon the more commonplace insights of psychology to detect a likely meaning from texts which more often than not seem innocently unaware of deep self-revelation. The missionaries, by and large, were not very good at analysing their motives and actions; they came, after all, in an age which preceded Freud. They had been summoned to their work by a plain injunction from Scripture and each one of them believed he was plainly following it in Africa and elsewhere. Yet reveal themselves they did, because they were certain of their own rectitude. They had nothing to be ashamed of, it was virtually impossible to be ashamed with God's unquestionable blessing upon them, and so they did very little to conceal their activities, even though these seem hair-raisingly hypocritical on

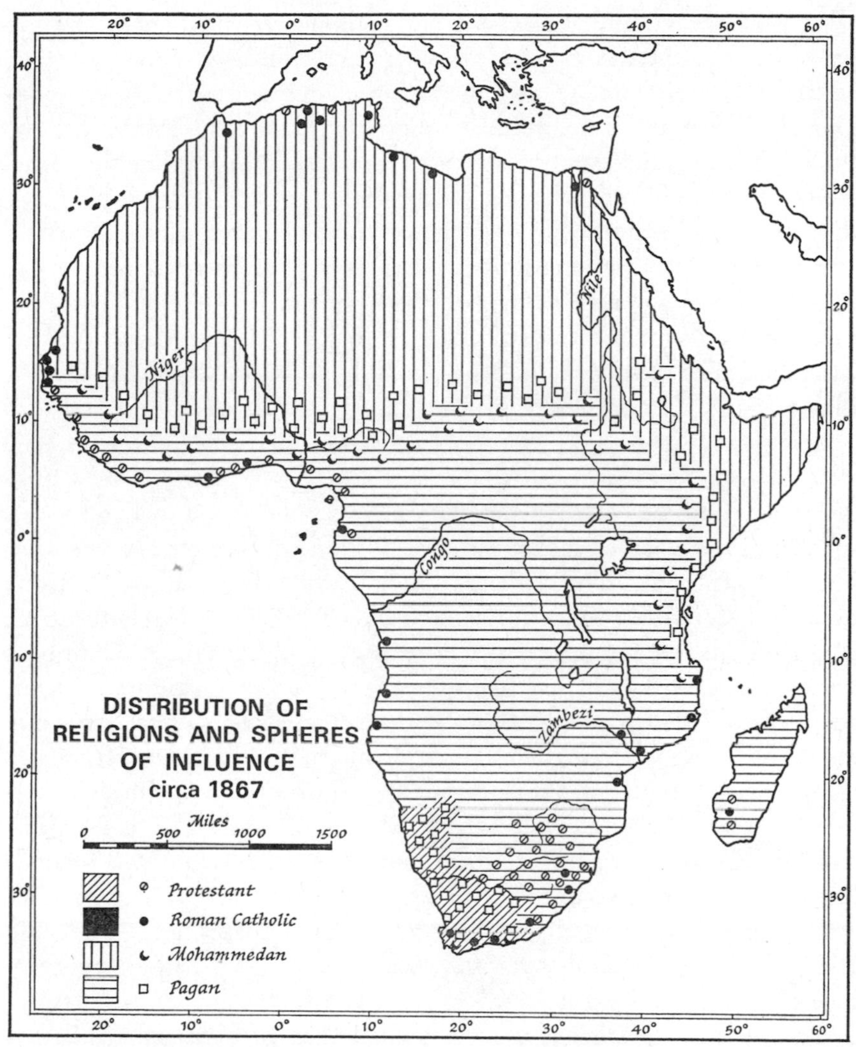

occasion to a generation which has long since ceased to accept the missionaries' own evaluation of their work.

They were, for the most part, tireless diarists and letter-writers. A large number of them published books about their experiences, which were eagerly taken up by those hordes of well-wishers at home, who were always avid for news from the mission field, and confirmation that the cause which they supported was a just and godly one. So full are these diaries, so great the detailed correspondence, that one sometimes wonders how the writers found time to pursue the activities of their vocation. One frequently has the impression that wherever the missionary went and whatever he was doing, it was with notebook perpetually in one hand and pencil in the other. And where this was not evidently the case, almost certainly the writer had spent some time each evening in scribbling up his journal. The result is a perpetual freshness about each volume that the reader picks up. However different the characters of the missionaries themselves – and there were wide variations, within certain narrowing limits – they convey the immediacy of their experience and with their daily attention to detail they transmit the variety of their circumstances. Here, for example, is an entry from the journal of Bishop George Tozer, the Lincolnshire rector who was nominated to succeed Mackenzie after the latter had died within a year of establishing his UMCA Mission on Livingstone's Zambezi Expedition. It is typical of the missionary experience only in so far as it records the day of arrival at journey's end, after the long voyage from Britain.

'Friday, June 26, 1863. I was standing with telescope in hand when suddenly I saw a gabled roof ahead. The mission station certainly is coming into view. It looked like a street, with certainly two gabled roofs. It was not long before I saw some movement, and almost immediately the street had its little crowd, gazing with all their eyes at the strange white boat with the English Jack flying from the mast. They stood thus an instant, and then rushed down to the water's side. We tried to make out the white faces; and when we thought we were within hail we began to cheer, and they answered, until I was able to rush to the bows and jump on shore and grasp and be grasped all round. "This is Waller" and "This is Rowley" and "This" – and a weak voice from a poor, dear sick face said "Procter". Alas! Alas! I needed no one to tell me that he was very, very weak and ill. And then I found which was Blair and which Adams, and "I am the Bishop", I said, which, by the way, was needful, for I had on only my blue sailor's jacket and holland trousers. Giving an arm to my newly-found sick friend, Procter, we made the ascent of the steep path . . . I made the tour of the place in company with Waller. Soon after, we went to the chapel, and had a special service, usual on all fresh arrivals . . . In the afternoon we all visited the graves of Scudamore and Dickinson.'

There were many arrivals in Africa like that one; with a warm welcome beneath a fluttering Union Jack, with handshakes all round, even from the man who was clearly dying at his post, with the little service of thanksgiving for a journey safely accomplished and a mission reinforced, with the melancholy introduction to the graves of two who had already perished in the awful climate. But then the melancholy would be shrugged away for a while, for this was part of God's inscrutable purpose for man.

There was work to be done and it would be done with a will at first, even if later some despair set in, with a sense of hopelessness in the face of very African difficulties of understanding and wholehearted commitment to the name of Jesus. Thoughts of home would never be entirely absent, but they would usually recede, and normality would consist of this land with its aching expanses of sky and bush, of these people with their pitifully primitive lives. They really were no more than children, beneath their sometimes shockingly vigorous customs, apart from their frequent outbursts of quite appalling savagery. You treated them as such; there was no other way. And slowly you enjoyed your small triumphs (but would they last?) as you painfully brought them inch by inch and day by exhausting day, a step or two closer to God. This is how Salter Price recorded one of the small triumphs of Christianity at his mission in Frere Town, near Mombasa, in 1875.

'Married fourteen couples of the freed slaves. It was an occasion of some little excitement and amusement. The men and women were grouped apart, and then the men, as their names came up, were asked to name the object of their choice. This, in most cases, they were unable to do, and there was nothing for it but for the would-be husband to enter the charmed circle and lead off the object of his affection. Generally there seemed to be a preconcerted arrangement between the parties, but not always. One unfortunate wight came forward and, on looking round on the galaxy of black beauties, was so bewildered that he was unable to fix his choice on any one in particular. With a peculiar nervous shrug and a crimson blush which was all but visible through his black skin, he said "I should be very happy to marry them, but don't know who will have me". He subsided amidst a roar of laughter from his companions, and his case was of course postponed . . . The number being completed, I took each couple separately and, joining their hands, required them to pledge their troth either to other. It is a pleasant thing to feel that one has made 28 people happy; for though in one sense their happiness is sublunary, it is in accordance with God's ordinances.'

One of the most meticulous and revealing diarists of the nineteenth century was Anna Hinderer, a missionary wife in Nigeria during those years when the Livingstone legend was being created in other parts of the continent. She had been born Anna Martin at Hempnall, in Norfolk, in 1827, and her mother died when she was five. Anna was always told that Mamma died murmuring the first few lines of a favourite hymn, 'I want, oh, I want to be there, Where sorrow and sin bid adieu'. By the time the child was twelve, her father sent her to live with a grandfather and aunt in Lowestoft 'for the benefit of her health', and she eventually went to live at the vicarage with the Rev. Francis and Mrs Cunningham. They seem to have been the only living people this little girl had so far felt close to. 'I loved Sunday above every day,' she wrote much later. 'The "Te Deum" carried me to heaven. I longed to be a martyr, to be one of that "noble army" . . . I longed to do something. I had a strong desire to be a missionary, to give myself up to some holy work, and I had a firm belief that such a calling would be mine. I think this was from a wish to be a martyr . . .'

She experienced, at this early age, an infantile mixture of joy and anguish that must have been common among the majority of Christian children in that age and place. 'I saw my need of a Saviour, and in the Saviour I felt there was all I needed, and I was by degrees permitted to lay hold on eternal life. Notwithstanding all my sinfulness and infirmities and shortcomings, the blessed hope of salvation in Christ Jesus was mercifully given, with the secret assurance that I was adopted into the family of God, made high by the blood of the Cross, and sanctified by the Spirit. This has been my comfort, joy and blessing, in sunshine or shade, prosperity or adversity, sickness or health. But grief, sorrow and shame must fill my mind in the remembrance of my sinfulness, the worldliness, the hastiness of temper, the pride, the evil that was within me, the temptation to run down the stream of life, whichever way it was going, and consequently denying my Saviour, not perhaps in word, but certainly not confessing, as I ought to have done, Him whom I had promised to serve.'

She had been introduced to the Cunninghams through her attendance at Sunday School. 'Dearest Mrs Cunningham,' who was a sister of the great social reformer Elizabeth Fry, started to invite Anna to tea on Sunday evenings. Then the child began to visit the vicarage regularly in the mornings and 'dear Mr Cunningham' asked her to copy letters for him and then to visit some of the sick people in his parish. But the best moments were spent on Sunday evenings, when friends would gather to sing hymns, with Mrs Cunningham playing the piano and leading the way with a high, clear voice, her face beaming with faith and joy, and Anna taking the second lead. Mrs Cunningham insisted on everyone joining in; she would allow no excuses. 'Oh! they were happy years!'

Anna was twenty-five when she met David Hinderer. He was one of the Germans, a Württemburger, employed by the CMS, and he had been working among the Yoruba for four years. He had returned to England partly to recuperate from illness, partly to report to the committee in Salisbury Square on the work in Nigeria. The year before, in 1851, he had been the first white man to reach Ibadan, some fifty miles above Abeokuta, and he was now going to press the committee to provide help in establishing a new mission there. He seems to have been a forceful man and he was certainly single-minded about the purposes of his mission to the Africans. There could be no half measures where the Chris-

tian God's will was concerned, whatever pain it might cause those who stood in its path. One of his colleagues has recorded the procedure followed when David Hinderer baptised James Oderinde, who had first been a heathen, then a Moslem.

Oderinde had joined the mission congregation at a time when he had three wives; one had died but the other two 'being both zealous disciples of Jesus', had been baptised by Hinderer. Oderinde had himself attended Sunday School and mission services regularly 'but he found it too much to dismiss his second wife, being much attached to both'. The missionaries explained to him many passages of Scripture and Luke XIV 26* apparently impressed him enormously. The second wife had been troubled for a long time that she was an impediment to his baptism and so she had agreed to

* 'If any man come to me, and hate not his father, and mother, and wife, and children, and brethren, and sisters, yea, and his own life, also, he cannot be my disciple.'

leave him. 'After much talking with him, and much consideration and prayer on his side, he agreed, and dismissed her in peace.' Oderinde was now considered in a fit state to receive Christian baptism, so Hinderer and his colleague Buhler 'did not hesitate to admit him'. Before the ceremony took place, Oderinde addressed the congregation of the mission and such heathen as had come to watch events. 'He shortly alluded to his past history,' writes Buhler, 'I never saw such attention, and the impression was very remarkable. It was a day full of joy and rich blessings from our Lord Jesus Christ.'

This was no more than the procedure laid down and reaffirmed that same year by the CMS, though Henry Venn's minute allowed a certain amount of local discretion. 'Serious difficulties,' he wrote, 'will doubtless sometimes occur, as in every transition from a wrong to a right course of action. These difficulties will vary according to the laws of marriage and divorce in different countries: cases must therefore be dealt with according to circumstances. Whatever unhappiness or injury may arise from the act of religious duty, must often be borne as the fruit of an original fault, though that fault may have been committed in ignorance . . . The present day has witnessed the fearful abomination of the Mormonites. These things are enough to warn Christians against any thing which tends to unsettle the original and universal law of marriage – "They twain shall be one flesh".'

This was the world that Anna Hinderer now entered from the warm security of her Suffolk vicarage. Her childish conviction had never deserted her through those happy years; 'though so much of my work at home was of a missionary character, yet I felt that to heathen lands I was to go, and that such would be my calling one day'. She had even suffered imaginary pangs of separation from the Cunninghams, long before David Hinderer appeared in her life. 'And in school, on a hot summer's day, when weary and dispirited, I would be roused and refreshed by the thought of the contrast between my present position and that of the missionary in other lands, under a burning sun and other trials; and then the thought of how soon I might be called to one of those lands, and have to give up those dear children, then entrusted to my care, would bring a tear to my eye, and give me a fresh stimulus to make use of my present opportunities in them; and that text Jeremiah XII 5* has given me fresh vigour and power . . .'

* 'If thou hast run with the footmen, and they have wearied thee, then how canst thou contend with horses? And if in the land of peace, wherein thou trustedst, they wearied thee, then how wilt thou do in the swelling of Jordan?'

The newly married couple sailed from Plymouth after a parting from the Cunninghams which made Anna sigh 'for the land where "all partings are o'er" '. It was not a comfortable voyage to West Africa. The weather was rough for a start, and Anna was intermittently seasick until the end. Apart from the Hinderers, there were eight other missionaries aboard, including the Bishop of Sierra Leone and his wife, and they held a service each Sunday, but the captain would not allow more than this. 'We had a sad and godless set of officials on board, and were greatly tried by it, but we were not without comforts in all our trials, and when for ten entire days the wind blew a gale, it was blessed to feel "He holdeth the wind in the hollow of His Hand" and the power to preserve His children!'

On Christmas Eve 1852 the ship dropped anchor along the coast of the Gambia and Anna was delighted by this first contact with the continent. 'I have really touched the African shore now! and seen and talked with Yoruba people. Yesterday we visited the little sandy town of Bathurst, where there is a mixture of people. My husband knew his own "kith and kin" by the marks on their faces, and saluted them in their own tongue, which delighted them immensely. They crowded round him and laughed and shouted. When I was introduced as his wife, and they learned that I was going with him to Ibadan, their delight seemed to know no bounds; and they came and shook hands most heartily.'

Within a fortnight the Hinderers were in Lagos, where Anna had the first of many bouts of fever. Then they began to move upcountry to Abeokuta, with Anna carefully noting all that was new around her: the people who sat and watched while the Hinderers ate outside their tent; the mobs of goats, fowl and dogs that encumbered every community; the fragrant and lovely water-lilies; and the many things 'that made a queer noise all night'. At Abeokuta they stayed in a missionary house much dilapidated by white ants, with spiders as big as the palm of your hand upon the walls. Anna went to the Sunday School that first weekend in Abeokuta and, at the thought of her own dear pupils at home, the tears flowed abundantly; and when the African children tried to comfort her, that only made things worse.

In all this strangeness, familiar things begin to occur. A harmonium arrives, a present from Mrs Cunningham, and Anna Hinderer begins to lead Sunday evening hymn-singing sessions, much as she had known them in Suffolk, though even that could be a two-edged blessing. 'I kept looking up at your dear picture and it made my eyes swim with tears to think how entirely it was a scene you would have liked and approved.' She begins to play games with the schoolchildren between five and six o'clock each evening, though her play is not half as energetic as it used to be in England. She prays to God she will meet her dear friends again in this lower world, but she is resolute in her vow to be of service to Africa. 'When I see what is the need, I feel that if I had twenty lives I would gladly give them to be the means of a little good to these poor but affectionate and well-meaning people who, though black enough their skins may be, have never-dying souls, which need to be led to the Saviour, to be washed clean in the blood of the Lamb.' Their black skins, she says, make no difference to her; to have them come to her, to see them pleased, makes her quite happy.

With David riding his horse and with Anna reclining in a hammock carried by bearers, the Hinderers moved to Ibadan. She speaks of the bearers quarrelling for the privilege of carrying her; and of the great welcome that awaited them when they reached the edge of the walled town, with shouts of 'The white man is coming' and 'The white mother is coming', with thousands of salutations and everyone staring open-mouthed at her. 'The people were good and kind enough to let us enter our house by ourselves, but many, many of them stood round about till sunset, just to catch a glimpse of the wonderful white woman; and every time I appeared, down they went on the ground, rubbing their heads and saying "Alafia, alafia"; that is, "peace, peace". We could but let them enjoy the treat, though we were not sorry when daylight fading warned them to depart . . .'

Their home was a mud-walled, thatched-roof building which they shared with Hinderer's assistant, Mr Kefer, the local schoolmaster, and the catechist; their own part of it was one long, narrow room which they partitioned off to make separate the sleeping and living quarters. Here, now, the Sunday night hymn-singing would take place round Mrs Cunningham's harmonium, with those tunes from the Lowestoft hymn book like 'Lydia', 'Comfort' and 'Arabia' much in demand, with Anna singing 'The Missionary Call' solo, and with everyone finishing in chorus with 'Praise God, from Whom all blessings flow'. The natives, said Anna, were much interested in the Cunningham pictures hanging over the harmonium, gratified to know that these two people in faraway England were singing the same hymns at the same time. In this home, Anna went down with fever again, not long after their arrival, and for three whole weeks she touched nothing but water, tea, a little raspberry vinegar 'and in very sinking moments, once or twice, I think they gave me weak brandy and water'. In this home she entertained her new flock of sixteen schoolchildren to dinner, serving a large bowl of palaver sauce with great quantities of beaten yams; and after the meal there were games and pictures, an examination of what the children had learned in school, and finally a present for each from the toy box, such as a knife or a box for cowries. School only lasted from nine until noon each day and Anna did not think this enough to keep little fingers busy, so in the afternoons she taught her pupils to knit and sew, boys as well as girls.

There were difficult times in Ibadan. Occasionally the people kept their children away because of some spasmodic fear that book-learning would make them cowards. One young woman was making excellent progress with her Yoruba primer and when she refused to yield it to her husband and father, she was put in chains for three days. Mr Kefer was twice disturbed when preaching, being ordered away from under the tree where he had taken his stand, with the admonition 'We will not have you, white man, you are the world's spoilers'. Anna confessed that, even when times were good, 'I am generally rather low on Sunday in heart; I can get hold of so little Sunday feeling. The scenes and sounds around us are so different from home; drums, guns, farms, markets, all the same as any other day, and though I can heartily mingle my "Amen" in our simple shed, yet all seems strange; but what a comfort our God is not confined to time and place.' At least, in that alien atmosphere, Anna could enjoy the homely sound of a church bell, which had been sent to them with the compliments of the Chelsea Juvenile Association.

Part of a missionary's duty was to write to the people in England who were supporting his station with their gifts and their prayers. Anna's share in keeping David Hinderer's supporters informed of their progress in Africa, was to correspond regularly with children in Lowestoft, who used to collect items for her toy box. In return, she would tell them about

the children of Ibadan. She described for them how you plaited an African child's hair; you had to use a great wooden comb, dragging it through the middle and in three or four places on each side, taking each little tuft and plaiting it as tightly as possible until the hair hung down in many short plaited tails which 'would hurt you and me, but their hard heads are used to it . . .' On another occasion she wrote, 'But who can wonder at their failings, when we think how they have been brought up? No clothes, no books, nothing to take care of, food easily procured and in plenty, without trouble or thought to themselves, and with very little to their masters or parents, so that eating is the principle thing with them, and in this, they have no order, no regularity.' Before the Hinderers had been in Ibadan very long, the inevitable happened; a child belonging to a converted couple was baptised Francis Lowestoft Akielle.

A baptism was guaranteed to bring out almost all the emotions in this sentimental and childless woman. One Advent Sunday, she records, eight adults were admitted to the Church by baptism. They were seated on the front benches before the service began, clad in white garments, and as they walked down the aisle to the font everybody in the congregation sang a hymn which David Hinderer had composed in Yoruba, called 'Be thou faithful', to the tune of 'Halesowen'. Anna found it very touching to see one old man at the font, leaning on his long staff 'as we might imagine Jacob to have done before Pharaoh, his lips quivering with old age and his eyes gleaming with pleasure and perfect child-like belief and trust, making the responses, of which he certainly put in some which were not in the book'.

By that time, the Hinderers had been on station some years. Anna's delight in all things new and the intoxication of being received as the wonderful white woman had long since passed. There had been a local war and Anna would suffer cruelly from anxiety pains in her left side whenever the noise of combat came within earshot. She was even obliged to record a human sacrifice, a man of twenty-five or thirty who was paraded through the markets so that the people might see what a fine fellow he was, for the whole town had been taxed to pay for the sacrificial expenses. On that day he was worshipped before his death and idolised after it, for it was believed that all kinds of glory awaited him in the next world, with great powers of intercession for the people left behind in this one. 'The moment he is killed, all prostrate themselves in prayer (what prayer!) then follow feasting and rejoicing, and before the body spoils, certain generals must be off on the road to the war. The head of the poor victim is left to the fowls of the air, but the body receives great honour from the women; they rub and decorate it with everything precious, believing that this same man is to return to the world again as an infant, but that he will then, when he grows up, surely be a king . . . Oh, the blindness, the darkness, the foolishness of heathenism, and in the midst of all this we are living; and when we are pressed down under the thought of these and a thousand other sorrows and horrors, we can hardly help asking sometimes, are we of any use in such a country?'

Anna never ceased to find the manifestations of the heathen repulsive. What subtly changed over the years, was her attitude to the converts. At first these had been shining examples in a dark land, as far beyond criticism as it was possible for an African to be. But after years of work among them, a note of disillusion creeps into her journals. 'These are troublesome people,' she writes in general terms of young native Christians. 'You must either let them go on as they please, or hold them with a strong hand; I think they like you better for the latter. At all events, they respect you more.' By then, the only things quite beyond criticism are 'our beautiful services' and 'the sweet English tunes' that went with them. Her ill-health was partly responsible, no doubt. Of the ten missionaries who travelled out from England together, only four were still alive after a couple of years. Anna was frequently sick with malaria and other diseases. In the end she succumbed, too. And when her journals were published, they were offered as an epitaph to 'one whose health had been utterly ruined by the pestilential climate of Africa, the dangers of which she had encountered for the love of Christ'.

By the time Anna Hinderer died, that much publicised and exemplary man, Alexander Mackay, was just about to begin his work as a missionary. He was born at Rhynie, Aberdeenshire, in 1849, the son of a Free Church minister; and, in spite of his sister's desire to promote in biography the mother's formative influence, it seems likely that young Mackay owed a great deal more to his father's guidance. Until he was fourteen, indeed, he took all his education from the older Mackay in that remote parish of the Eastern Highlands. At the age of three he could read the New Testament and at seven he was learning from *Paradise Lost*, Russell's *History of Modern Europe*, Gibbon's *Decline and Fall* and Robertson's *History of the Discovery of America*. His father was acquainted with a number of academics and scientists, one of whom was Livingstone's sponsor, Sir Roderick Murchison. When Sir Roderick stayed at the manse for a few days during a meeting of the British Association in Aberdeen, he remarked on the boy's skill as a map-drawer and typesetter, and presented him with a copy of *Small Beginnings; or The Way to Get On*. When Alexander was fourteen, and about to go to Aberdeen Grammar School, Mrs Mackay died.

He had always had a great taste for the world of machines and artisan crafts. He would walk four miles each way, just to see a railway engine as it stopped at the nearest station on its way to Huntly; and in the village he pottered round the smithy, the gasworks and the cording mill whenever he got the chance. The parents had hoped that he would follow his father into the ministry and he was enrolled in the Free Church Training College for Teachers in Edinburgh, doing a great deal of Sunday School work on the side. But he began to concentrate more and more on engineering and was soon studying higher mathematics and surveying and fortification at Edinburgh University, while spending his spare time learning the arts of fitting, turning and model-making in a Leith factory. In 1873 he went to Germany 'in order to acquire its language more thoroughly, that being the first step to becoming acquainted with the store of lore which that land contains'. He got a job as a draughtsman at the Berlin locomotive works and in the evening he translated Lübsen's *Differential and Integral Calculus*. When he was not otherwise engaged, he invented an agricultural machine which won first prize at an exhibition of steam engines in Breslau. At the teachers' training college in Edinburgh he had been noted as a youth who did not make friends easily. He did no better in Berlin, for a start. 'Here I am,' he wrote home, 'among all these heathenish people; almost all are infidels, but agree in so far acknowledging the existence of God as to continually use the expression "Ach, Gott!", often more than once in the same sentence . . . On this account, I am obliged to have as little conversation with them as possible, and hence cannot have the advantage of German conversation as I would like.'

However, 'it is extremely wonderful how in the greatest desert God always provides an oasis, an Elim for His people'. By this, Mackay meant that he had met a clergyman from the Protestant cathedral, Herr Hofprediger Baur, and had gone to lodge with the Baur family. There he met a lot of other active Christians, including Bismarck's sister, Grafin von Arnim, and the Rev. G. P. Davies, the British and Foreign Bible Society's agent in the city. Mackay was soon busy helping Mrs Davies to distribute tracts to the Berlin cabmen every Sunday morning.

At this point, Mackay's sister had written to tell him of a missionary talk she had recently heard about Madagascar, and Mackay decided 'if the Lord will, to go as an engineering missionary'. He conceded that this might seem a curious combination but he had his answer ready for the sceptics. 'I hope especially to connect Christianity with modern civilisation. In England it is true that as Christianity has made progress, so civilisation advanced; and as it advanced, Christianity became more deeply rooted and shines now as the light of an enlightened people.' He hoped to establish a college to train young men in religion and science but he also had a vision of himself deep in public works, such as railways and mines 'which, for one single-handed, is an enormous enterprise'. He started to learn Malagasy but there was one thing which had priority over even that. 'My first concern is to get quit of sin, or to know how God has provided for my extrication.' This was clearly a problem. Mackay had only just written to his father, deploring the fact that 'A community like Berlin sunk in licentiousness is difficult to deal with. If ever or anywhere, heathens are to be found, it is surely here . . . Oh, for a little of the power of the Spirit such as has of late been manifested in Scotland!'

It was all very well for this industrious young Scot to learn Malagasy in preparation for his great scheme of Christian public works across Madagascar; but no missionary society was willing to send him there. The CMS was interested in sending him to Mombasa, as overseer of a settlement for liberated slaves, but someone else got the job before Mackay's formal application went in. Then there was a suggestion from Edinburgh that he might go to Lake Nyasa as chief engineer aboard the steamer which the Church of Scotland had just launched there. It was while Mackay was thinking this over that the CMS made contact again, inviting him to join in a similar capacity the Lake Victoria mission which was being established with Robert Arthington's money in response to H. M. Stanley's clarion call. He accepted, and spent the next few weeks in London, getting a workshop to manufacture a boiler for the boat, to his own specifications. Then he dashed up to Edinburgh to see his father, and spent three hours of a long weekend at Leith Fort, learning astronomy and the use of the sextant from an officer there.

He found the voyage out to Zanzibar, by way of the recently opened Suez Canal, as trying as Anna Hinderer had found the journey to West Africa. When the Captain of the SS *Peshawar* read prayers before some of his passengers in the saloon the first Sunday morning, 'Of course, some of the nil admirari men stayed on deck smoking. Everyone knows – they knew themselves – that they only made themselves contemptible by so doing. O'Neill and I, however, with no feelings of Pharisaism, joined heartily in the service, however formal it might be supposed by some "ultras" to be, as we wished to join with everyone who inclined to echo Joshua's motto "As for me and my house, we will serve the Lord".'

There were other hazards on the way, and they were not climatic or navigational. As the steamer passed Cape St Vincent, Alexander Mackay spared many pious thoughts for the wretched folk in the hinterland. 'Ah, poor Spain and poorer Portugal! I see only a blind wall when I see thee . . . The loving Lord has given thee a sunny land with pretty mountain slopes, where every man in thee may sit under his own vine and lie in the shade of his own fig-tree. But the venomous blood of the Bourbons and the cursed leaven of Rome have undermined thy vital powers, and now thou art a corrupting mass, waiting, maybe, till, like thy fellow-victims in the East, thy sickness proves incurable and thou wilt cease to be.'

Malta, where the ship stopped long enough for an excursion ashore, appeared to be in an even worse plight. 'Oh, that foul leaven of thine which is hypocrisy! . . . to thwart thee in thine unprincipled actions, I shall, in the name and strength of God, set up my printing press on the shores of the Victoria Nyanza, and I shall not cease to toil till the story of the Cross and Christ be printed in the language of the Karague and Uganda, and every man be taught to read it and believe it, too!' The quaint language was only modified by a first sight of the North African coast: 'Now for the springing up of a new light in the dark land of dusky Ham! Is there any power that will elevate the degraded race? Yes, the Gospel – mighty power!'

Mackay arrived in Zanzibar in May 1876 and within a month the party that was to establish the new mission had assembled on the coast. Besides Mackay there was a clergyman, the Rev. C. T. Wilson, a naval officer in charge of the expedition to the interior, Lieut. G. S. Smith RN, a doctor, John Smith, a civil engineer, Thomas O'Neill, a blacksmith, W. M. Robertson, a shipwright, G. J. Clark and an agriculturist, J. Robertson.

The first task was to march the seven hundred miles inland to the proposed site, the second to establish a supply route. By November, Mackay was seriously ill with malaria, after having made some initial explorations up the Wami river with an ailing Lieut. Smith. By then, one of the Robertsons was dead and the other had been invalided home, together with Clark. Mackay himself was sent back to the coast to recuperate, while the rest of the party pushed on. By March 1877 he was on the move again and his task was now to cut a road 230 miles inland as the start of the supply route. By May he had cleared a wagon way for fifty miles, working with a gang of forty Africans, armed with 'the best American axes, English hatchets, picks and spades and saws'. He had also attacked a caravan of slaves and liberated 120 of the captives, but he was more conscious of his artisan role, perhaps, than of any other form of his vocation. 'We are Christian missionaries, and our work is the spread of the Gospel,' he noted in his journal, 'to the ends of the earth. Where we do not already find a way by which to enter unknown lands, we make a way ourselves. In doing so we make a way for others to follow after – a way for the trader to enter with his wares, and to return a richer man.'

Slowly Mackay pressed forward up his wagon road, tormented by mosquitoes, scribbling up his journal by the light of a ship's lantern, listening uneasily to the growls of hyena which had been attracted to his camp by the smell of the oxen, lying always with his Winchester repeater by his side. There was quinine in his medicine chest for the fever that the mosquitoes brought, just as there was Dover's Powder for intermittent dysentery and sulphate of zinc for use as an emetic. The Winchester was for possible use against hazards other than those of the hyena. Mackay records how one night a band of roving Wahehe turned up and performed a war dance in front of the camp fire. Then they demanded an ox and some small present from a package by Mackay's side. It contained nothing but books and papers, and in these they were not interested. The missionary then offered them several yards of cloth, at which the Wahehe leapt up and formed themselves into a line, ten paces from him, brandishing their huge red, white and blue hide shields, their spears and their bows and arrows. They prepared to charge and Mackay was uncertain whether this was in salute or in earnest. He restrained an impulse to reach for his gun, realising that it would have meant instant bloodshed and, after a leap into the air, the tribesmen knelt 'in the politest fashion' beside their upturned shields and arms. Then they drove off their ox and made their own camp for the night some distance away.

It took Mackay well over two years to get from the coast to the site of the new mission, in the kingdom of Mutesa, ruler of the Baganda. In that time he was frequently settled for weeks on end in the village of some tribal chief or other whose territory he had to pass through. He would set up his improvised workshop, and this would be the marvel of the local populace. 'When they see the turning lathe at work, or find me melting down the fat of an ox and turning out beautiful candles their wonder knows no bounds,' he wrote. '. . . again and again I have heard them remark that the white man came from heaven.' He did something, on such occasions, to modify this impression; he told them that the white men were once naked savages like themselves, carrying bows and arrows, but that God began to teach them, whereupon they became civilised. And thus, together with the judicious dispensation of presents – a dressing-gown for a chief, a few fish-hooks fashioned in the workshop for lower orders within the tribe – Mackay began to proselytise the heathen.

There was never a trace of Anna Hinderer's sentimentality in this man. He never ceased to react to Africans as he had reacted on first sighting the North African coast; they were a degraded race and he would elevate them with the power of the Gospel. Before he reached his destination among the Baganda, he was anathematising all tribes as congenital drunkards – 'go where you will, you will find every week and, where grain is plentiful, every night, every man, woman and child, even to sucking infants, are reeling with the effects of alcohol'. Because of this, he says, he became a teetotaller from the moment he left the coast. He had decided that it was prudent not to doctor all who came to the wonderful white man and his medicine chest for the relief of sickness. If the patient died, then it was he who was blamed, and if the white medicine did not appear to work fast enough, a native cure was used, which usually retarded or reversed whatever small progress had been made.

Mackay did not share Livingstone's instinctive regard for African virtues, and after he had lived among the Baganda for some time he would blaze with bitterness against their alien ways. 'Let one live in the land beyond the term of novelty of display and profusion of hospitality; let him express a horror of the barbarity of the practices he sees even at court; let him lift up his voice in condemnation of treachery, of lies, of lust and of cruelty and murder – then the spell is broken, and the character of the people comes out in its true light. Instead of hospitality he finds hatred; instead of food, he finds himself face to face with famine; instead of being received as he expected, as a welcome benefactor of the people, as a leader of truth and a leader in the way of light, a lover of law and love, he is denounced as a spy, as a bringer-on of foreign customs, and especially as a breaker-down of the national institution of religion!' He had been ten years with the Baganda at that point, and he was conceding that the missionaries were even then so far from the reaping stage that they could scarcely be said to be sowing. His anger was turned in another direction, too, by then. If he was bitter at the Baganda's inability to see him as a leader of truth and a welcome benefactor, he was sickened by the inability of Christians at home to forget their own sectarian differences in order to regenerate wholeheartedly the lost races of men. 'Millions untold,' he wrote, 'are surely more to be cared for than trifling peculiarities of creed.'

There were softer men than Alexander Mackay among the missionaries, and one of them was his colleague in the territory of the Baganda, Robert Ashe. He was to labour as industriously as the Scot, with as little apparent reward, but he was never embittered by his experience. He was an engaging fellow, as interested and full of relish as Bishop Mackenzie. He would note how the women of the Baganda distended their ear lobes with all manner of objects – a husk of Indian corn, a snuff box, the handle of a teacup, an empty cartridge case and the bishop from a chess set. He would observe wryly, but without anger, the deficiencies in equipment carried on those great extended marches across country, with five hundred porters bearing sufficient food, clothing, camping gear and tools to sustain seven white men from starting point to destination; they would have been provided with Epsom Salts in plenty by the missionary store in Zanzibar, but would find themselves without any common cooking salt, they would have a surplus of castor oil but no butter, and they would have an elaborate distilling apparatus but only one kettle.

It was Ashe who introduced the bicycle to Africa, doubtless in reaction against those marches. He had often thought, at any rate, that the machine could travel upon the more beaten tracks, though in the age of the penny-farthing, the velocipede and their immediate successors, he conceded that the built-in hazards of construction made this no more than an interesting theory. But when the safety bicycle was invented, with brakes and a low centre of gravity, he had one imported promptly. He had an accident or two, to start with, and natives fled in terror at first, for they assumed that Robert Ashe was mounted upon some new and deadly form of firearm. But eventually, and after having raced a couple of perplexed lions down a bush road, he had the satisfaction of proceeding easily on wheels where his companions panted much more slowly on foot.

Ashe had detachment. He could be critical of what the missionaries were doing as almost no one before him had been. The native converts at Frere Town, on the coast, were forbidden to wear trousers from the moment they were taken up as possible Christians, in the same spirit as Brother Haensel in Freetown had forbidden Samuel Crowther's friends from becoming too Europeanised, for fear that they might rise above themselves. Ashe thought this proscription a 'senseless piece of arrogant tyranny'. He could deliberate on the moral issues confronting any missionary from the moment he stepped ashore in Africa, without either the lofty certainty of a Mackay or the agonised torment that had been experienced by Francis Owen during his early years at the Cape. Ashe once had some difficulty in persuading a chief to allow his party to proceed through tribal lands, when it was important that it should do so rapidly. As an inducement to the chief, Ashe presented him with some small breech-loading guns. That night he wrote in his journal: 'There are some who blame the missionaries for giving a heathen chief firearms under any circumstances; but they belong to that select class who are given to fault-finding . . . The question, however, is perhaps a fair one as to how far the Christian Church is justified, in the first instance, in sending missionaries to countries which they cannot reach without being armed.'

This was a man standing thoughtfully on the edge of some vital emancipation. His reaction to the nakedness of African women was much less shocked than that of most missionaries, who usually found it so unseemly that it is the one commonplace of their experience which is not mentioned at all in their journals. Ashe, on the other hand, comes to terms with it. He wishes to purchase as a souvenir 'the little fringe both before and behind, attached to a string tied round the waist'. He has found it difficult to obtain one and mentions this to a group of natives. 'One of the bystanders immediately divested herself of the one she was wearing and brought it to me. I bought it. There was not the slightest immodesty. She had only made herself like many of her sisters standing by.'

And then, for the first time, he witnesses one of the erotic tribal dances of the Baganda women, in which the pelvis is jabbed forward to simulate coitus and the breasts bob and bounce and the arms are allowed to flow in sensuous patterns. 'The first time you see it,' writes Ashe, 'it looks a most disgusting and degrading exhibition; but in time one gets used to the sight. On this occasion it was performed by a number of young girls, who worked themselves up into an extraordinary state of excitement, and looked as if they were under the influence of some magician's spell. They gradually approach a stranger nearer and nearer, advancing slowly till they touch him with their hands. In my case, I broke the charm by giving them some beads, which sent them away quite satisfied, and left me even more pleased at their departure.'

Tales such as these, suitably diluted or merely hinted at, may have been responsible for the recruitment of more missionaries than Alexander Mackay, for one, would ever have wished to admit. For a study of missionary biographies and journals makes it clear that a large proportion of the people who spent their lives in Africa and elsewhere, spreading the Christian Gospel to the heathen, had decided to do so in childhood, consciously or not. Frequently this sprang from a desire to travel or 'to see wild beasts and bright birds'. In 1917 a survey was made of three hundred accounts by missionaries of the origin of their vocation and in almost half these cases, literature of one kind or another played an important and sometimes decisive part. High on the list of books was the literature of secular travel. William Carey had been stimulated by the accounts of Captain Cook's voyages, Lewis Krapf by reading about James Bruce's travels in Abyssinia; and there were many similar examples, particularly in the early years of the missionary enterprise. But gradually the missionary account of travel and the missionary biography superseded the secular editions, the biography becoming the most fruitful of all these stimuli to a vocation. Curiously, only one of the three hundred accounts surveyed seemed to suggest that the Bible was the original source of inspiration. Even missionary games had a greater formative influence than that.

The supreme influence, however, was that of parents and of individuals with whom a child might have come into contact. Missionary dynasties occurred, like the Scudders, the Humes and the Gulicks in America, the Isenbergs, the Pfleiderers and the Hochs in Germany. And where there was not an active missionary influence guiding a child into the same vocation, there was very often a missionary zeal in the parents that could be vicariously fulfilled by the child's eventual performance.

Robert Moffat had come to his life's work in this way. He had been working as a gardener, as a young man of twenty, when he saw a notice announcing a missionary meeting. At once he recalled stories that his mother had read to him as a child, of the Moravian missionaries working among the people of Greenland and Labrador; he went to the meeting on this impulse and he never again looked back.

James Chalmers, who was to spend his active life among the natives of New Guinea, describes another common form of personal influence. 'The Sunday school lesson was finished and we had marched back into the chapel to listen to a short address. I even now see Mr Meikle taking from his breast pocket a copy of the "United Presbyterian Record", and hear him say that he was going to read an interesting letter to us from a missionary in Fiji. It spoke of cannibalism and of the power of the Gospel, and at the close, looking over his spectacles, and with wet eyes, he said: "I wonder if there is any boy here this afternoon who will yet become a missionary and, by and by, bring the Gospel to the cannibals?" And the response in my heart was "Yes, God helping me, and I will." So impressed was I that I spoke to no one, but went right away towards home. The impression became greater the farther I went, and kneeling down I prayed to God to make me a missionary to the heathen. For some time I was greatly impressed: but at last I forgot all about it . . . After my conversion at the age of twenty-one, I soon remembered my vow in the Sunday school years before, to bring the knowledge of Christ to the heathen, and never again was it forgotten.'

Only a Briton or an American, perhaps, could have written that. For in the three hundred missionary accounts surveyed in 1917, one other striking fact was evident. Although a belief in the eternal perdition of the heathen was strong among the early missionaries of the English-speaking nations, missionaries who went out from the continent of Europe hardly ever mentioned it.

II
SCRAMBLING FOR AFRICA

The transformation which took place upon the map of Africa between 1879 and 1891 is one of the most remarkable in all history. At the beginning of that period it can be seen as an immense void of native tribal kingdoms with intermittent patches of European influence, each separated by great distances, around the perimeter. The most substantial of these by far is the area of Turkish suzerainty stretching from Tunis, across to Cairo and down to the edges of Abyssinia. The British occupy a solid wedge in Cape Colony at the foot of the continent and small blobs around the West African coast. The French are in Algeria, Senegal and the Gabon. The Portuguese are in Angola and along the East African coast at Mozambique. Otherwise Africa is in the possession of her own peoples, and her monarchs and chiefs are very local potentates indeed.

By 1891 the picture is enormously changed and, of all the outside influences, only that of the Turks has been diminished, being by then reduced to a strip of the coast in Tripoli. The Portuguese have remained much as they were. The French have expanded from Senegal down to the Ivory Coast and they have appeared in the Congo. The British have seeped inland from the West African coast, they have enlarged their holding in South Africa, they have a huge stake in East Africa and they occupy Egypt. To this bundle of original colonisers has been added a parcel of new ones. The Italians now control a large slab of territory above the East African British. The Germans have taken root in East Africa, South-West Africa and the Cameroons. The Spanish have dropped anchor opposite their Canary Islands. There is a colossal tract of the interior labelled Congo Free State, which is not very free and most certainly no longer Congolese, being the private estate of a Belgian King. The immense void of a dozen years before has been shrunk to the size of the Sahara desert and not much more.

The tribal chiefs have been encircled and they are rapidly being stripped of authority. About this time, the Matabele ruler Lobengula told the London missionary C. D. Helm just what this process felt like. 'Did you ever,' he asked, 'see a chameleon catch a fly? The chameleon gets behind the fly and remains motionless for some time. Then he advances very closely and gently, first putting forward one leg and then another. At last, when well within reach, he darts out his tongue, and the fly disappears. England is the chameleon and I am that fly.'

This was the period when trading companies were endowed with royal charters, the better to assert their imperial connections. The Royal Niger Company came first, in 1886, delayed somewhat because Mr Gladstone mislaid the charter itself on a train, so that a new one had to be drawn up. The Imperial British East Africa Company followed it two years later, the residuary legatee of that Livingstonia Company which had itself emerged from the great Doctor's plans to bring Christian commerce to Africa. With the trading charters came the treaties between the foreign powers, to settle their spheres of influence, and those men of freebooting instinct, like Cecil Rhodes and Carl Peters, who generally had one eye on patriotism and the other on the main chance. And, presiding over this scramble for Africa, was the unlikely person of Leopold, King of the Belgians.

Long before he ascended the throne of the least influential state in Europe, Leopold, as Duke of Brabant, had warmed himself upon a vision of empire. He had scouted out territory as far apart as Egypt, Formosa, Sarawak and the New Hebrides. On becoming king in 1865, he had already transferred his ambition to Africa, but with the limited resources of his inconsiderable realm, he had been without the means or opportunity to act there. He found an excuse when an expedition under the British Lieutenant Cameron, RN, which had originally left London to look for Livingstone, had instead proceeded upon a geographical exploration when it received news of the Doctor's death. This took Cameron and his party right across the continent, from east to west, and King Leopold promptly sent the Lieutenant his royal felicitations and an autographed portrait. So did Queen Victoria and the German Emperor. But when Her Majesty's Government declined to take up a ruling status in the Congo which Cameron had proclaimed before a succession of chiefs, Leopold decided that he could very well fill the vacuum. Sensitive of the imperial jealousies that might be aroused in nations more powerful than his own, however, his first step was to convene in Brussels a conference of explorers and scientists, which he did as a private patron and not as monarch. It resulted in an International African Association, with national committees in seven countries which vowed themselves to nothing more than the suppression of the slave trade and the exploration of Africa.

H. M. Stanley then drifted over the international horizon. He had just completed his own transcontinental journey, from the headwaters of the Congo down to the West coast and he was as anxious as Lieutenant Cameron had been for the British to annex this territory; he was, after all, a Welshman, even though he had been much Americanised. The British were still not interested, being preoccupied just then with matters in East and Southern Africa, so Stanley turned to King Leopold, who appointed him chief agent of a new committee which had been set up at a second Brussels conference – the *Comité d'Études du Haut Congo*. This, much more frankly than the product of the first Brussels conference, was dedicated to the commercial exploitation of the Congo basin. It represented commercial and financial interests from Britain, France, Germany and Holland as well as Belgium. It also promoted a great deal of international rivalry, for no one by now had any doubt that Leopold was bent upon controlling events in this quarter of the globe, even though he clung to the fiction of private patronage. Stanley, working for him, collided with the Frenchman de Brazza, who was making his own imperial excursions in the Congo; and because Stanley was still under suspicion of representing British interests, the Portuguese in Angola became uneasy at his presence. Meanwhile the Germans, though carefully keeping an official distance from their adventurer Carl Peters, were allowing him to make ground on their behalf in East Africa; which produced another source of tension for the British. And when the United States officially recognised Leopold's flag, now no more than nominally that of the International African Association, matters came to a head. A conference of the great European powers was summoned to Berlin in 1884; it was attended by almost everybody but the Swiss. Stanley turned up as technical adviser to the Americans, who were also represented. Bismarck presided. What occurred during the next three months was the end of the scramble for Africa and the beginning of the carve-up. It is suggestive of Leopold's responsibility in all this, that of the thirty-eight articles in the eventual General Act of the conference, no fewer than twenty-five were concerned with the Congo basin. Shortly after the conference ended, the King of the Belgians informed the Great Powers that the International African Association had been merged with a new independent state in the Congo, of which he was sovereign. He had his empire at last and, unlike most heads of state at the end of the nineteenth century, he did not even have to share it with a legislative assembly of his fellow-countrymen. The Belgian Parliament had decided that the Congo Free State was the exclusively personal property of the King.

The missionaries were not forgotten in the apportionment of the African continent. Article 6 of the Berlin Act, indeed, stipulated that 'Christian missionaries . . . shall likewise be the subjects of especial protection . . .' From now on the hazards of their life in Africa would be progressively diminished. There would be an increasing presence of European soldiery and police to protect them on their lawful occasions, to safeguard their converts against the reprisals of tribesmen who felt betrayed by the change of heart and faith, or merely envious of enlarged material opportunity. The more savage manifestations of tribal life, such as ritual murder and human sacrifice, against which the missionaries had preached with scant success, would now be eradicated by the same civilised secular authorities and the missionaries would thus be spared much tormented impotence, if nothing else. They could look forward to other benefits, and one of these would be improved communications. When Robert Moffat was in South Africa in the 1850s, he had taken two months to travel by ox-cart from Kuruman to the Matabele capital of Bulawayo; by 1897 a railway would carry a traveller over approximately the same ground in a couple of days or less. And soon it would no longer be necessary for messages to be transmitted laboriously by runners everywhere the missionaries went, for in many parts of Africa the miracle of the electric telegraph would have appeared.*

There were, on the other hand, liabilities to be faced in this new era. Hitherto, the reputation of the white man had rested very largely in the hands of the missionaries. True, the traders had followed them wherever they went, and consular officials had very often come trailing behind. But it was the missionary presence which had dominated, and the missionaries could rest assured that they would be judged by Africans mostly in the light of their own behaviour and standards, or those of their fellows. This would no longer be the case. The missionaries would always form a substantial proportion of the colonial population. But from now on they would be tainted by the standards and behaviour of other Europeans who had certainly not come to Africa with an overpowering wish to reveal the

* It had only just been introduced in Great Britain, where the CMS now had the telegraphic address Testimony and other societies were identified as Missionary, Gospel and Christian in the Post Office list available to subscribers.

light of the Christian Gospel to its people, however much they might pay lip service to its philosophy.

Now begins an age when values and responsibilities and objectives among Europeans in Africa overlap and become highly confused. What had been happening in Nigeria for more than thirty years, was now about to happen everywhere. The renegade missionary was not by any means unknown before this time, but there is something particularly symbolic now in the presence of someone like Charles Stokes in East Africa. He had at one time been a missionary for the CMS, but had abandoned this position in favour of a native wife and life as a trader in anything that made a handsome profit. When he was not garbed as an Arab, at the head of a slaving caravan, he was liable to appear in a German uniform, employed by Germans to convey gunpowder (at a profit of £250 per head load) in excursions against the British along the coast. Soon he would be gun-running for French Catholics in their struggle for Christian supremacy with his old Protestant comrades of the English Church Missionary Society.

The missionaries themselves were for the most part unaware of the liabilities inherent in this new situation. Indeed, more often than not, they seized the opportunity presented to them of expanding their own work under the protection of imperial power with a wholehearted relish which suggests that they were very largely indifferent to anything but European progress in Africa. They were certainly incapable of making a distinction between European and Christian values. The two things were for them synonymous. The mood is very obvious in the memoirs and activities of the English Baptists who now began to move up the Congo in the wake of King Leopold's ambitions.

It was a donation of £1,000 by Robert Arthington which had first turned the BMS in this direction; the Miser of Headingley very rarely gave his money away without specifying a purpose for it. A year after Leopold's first Brussels conference, a couple of the BMS men working in the Cameroons, George Grenfell and Thomas Comber, were told to sail down the coast and make a tentative exploration of the lower Congo. They spent a few months there and then reported back to England. Early in 1879, a reinforced party left Liverpool after a great farewell meeting in the Cannon Street Hotel in London, for which all tickets were sold so rapidly that hundreds of well-wishers were unable to get in. The missionaries sailed, a little uncomfortably, in a vessel carrying the despised 'Hamburg cargo'; that is, spirits and gunpowder. They had no comment to make on the gunpowder, but the rest of the merchandise moved one of them to write: 'Eleven hundred tons of vile trade spirit, as the month's supply for the trading houses of the coast by this line of steamers, besides that brought by other steamers specially chartered by the larger trading companies. Surely it is time this cursed traffic should be declared illicit?' Their own trading was limited to the purchase of six donkeys and a foal at Tenerife on the way out.

They landed near the ancient Congo capital of San Salvador. In the middle of the fifteenth century, Portuguese Catholics had settled here, they had even sent the most promising of the local Africans back to Lisbon for seminary training, but this Christian foothold had virtually died out. By the time the Baptists arrived there was but one Catholic priest in the district, and of the cathedral in San Salvador, only the ruined walls, the chancel arch and part of the Lady Chapel remained. 'It was,' wrote the Baptist W. Holman Bentley, 'to all intents and purposes a heathen land. King and people were wholly given to fetishism and all the superstition and cruelties of the Dark Continent.' A house in the king's compound contained a large crucifix and some images of saints, but Holman Bentley regarded these as fetishes too; they were, he said, sometimes brought out and carried round the town if the rains had been insufficient.

Suspicious as he was of these relics of Roman Catholicism, Holman Bentley had even greater reservations about the people on whom Christians of any denomination were prepared to bestow their blessings. After remarking on the Portuguese heyday in the Congo, when about seven thousand slaves were shipped out of their homelands each year, he adds: 'If the masters were sometimes cruel to the slaves, the slaves sometimes wreaked a terrible revenge on their masters . . . The slaves were often very provoking, and brought punishment on their own heads by their own wickedness and folly; no system, however draconic, will keep Africans from wrong-doing.' On the voyage to the Congo, the steamer had stopped at Freetown, and Holman Bentley reports a visit to the local cathedral where 'a black clergyman was uniting in holy matrimony two happy "niggers". But we must call them Negroes, for "nigger" is a most offensive word to an African.' This was advice which Holman Bentley himself was not inclined to follow. His party had brought with them the usual swag of presents for local chiefs, among which was a mechanical toy figure, painted black, which they gave to the king of the Congo, Dom Pedro V. 'As the steam got up and the wheel flew round, causing the agile nigger to cut wondrous capers, the King's laughter knew no bounds; his mirth was too large for his mouth and found expression in teardrops, which trickled down his cheeks; he clapped his hands, and rolled about in his chair, in a regular convulsion of laughter, and all dignity was completely forgotten.'

Dom Pedro allowed the Baptists to settle for a time in his area, while they made their plans for penetrating the hinterland up the river. The immediate objective was that small inland sea above the village of Kinshasa which had already been named Stanley Pool by the explorer who had discovered it at the end of his long journey westwards from the headwaters of the Congo. For five hundred miles or so above this misnamed expanse of water, the river Congo flows majestically around sandbanks, through gorges and between the edges of jungle, and it is nowhere less than two or three miles wide; sometimes the river is so broad that it is scarcely possible to detect the outline of one bank from the other. Because it is so wide along this stretch it is comparatively shallow, so that, today, steamers regularly go aground and it is very easy to run your dug-out canoe into trouble upon a sudden sandbar or upon one of those massive clumps of mauve water hyacinth which swirl downstream in their thousands. But the Congo here is navigable. Below Kinshasa it is not. A series of thundering cataracts, filling the air with their spray and their noise, stretch down towards the sea for the best part of a hundred miles, and still block the way to all navigation. This was the barrier the Baptists now had to ascend and they faced other hazards as well. There were hostile tribes between them and Stanley Pool, and de Brazza, who had recently been skirmishing in this area on behalf of France, had warned the people as he went to be on the lookout against Englishmen. Comber was injured in one encounter but the party managed to struggle on to friendlier territory. There was the everlasting sickness, and one of the wives in the party was dead within a month or two of arriving in Africa. It took the best part of two years to prospect a safe route from the sea to Stanley Pool, to secure it as a regular thoroughfare, to establish a station there and to be confidently based for the great project to Christianise the upper Congo. From here they would move by stages up one thousand miles of that mighty river, forging one by one the links in a great chain of missions that would bring the Gospel into the very heart of the Dark Continent.

Robert Arthington once more dipped prodigiously into his inheritance and produced another £1000 for a Baptist steamboat. She was built by Thorneycrofts on the Thames to very careful specifications. She drew only eighteen inches of water, an exceedingly shallow draught that would be important on the Congo. She had a new type of boiler, specially designed so that it could be carried by a number of bearers and capable, on installation, of raising steam from scratch within ten minutes. This was thought desirable for use among savage people, when it might be necessary to sail away rapidly in the event of sudden attack. The hull was made of Bessemer's steel and above this was fitted a series of wire screens, which unfolded from the mahogany sun-awnings to protect crew and passengers from missiles, the mesh being sufficiently close to prevent even the smallest

poisoned arrows from penetrating. Having christened this conveyance *Peace*, the builders dismembered it into eight hundred sections and shipped it off to the African coast, where a vast army of porters carried it through the jungle and past the cataracts to the Baptists waiting at Stanley Pool. In July 1884, George Grenfell set out in the new vessel, with five hundred brass rods for barter purposes aboard, to begin his long proselytising haul up the Congo.

The stations were to be spaced roughly one hundred miles apart, with two missionaries in each, and there would be ten stations when the chain was completed. Before the end of the year there was a mission three hundred miles upstream of the Pool, at Lukolela, but thereafter the going was much slower. For all its sophisticated construction, the *Peace* could not run non-stop, even if the missionaries had wanted it to. Every day it had to be tethered to the river bank in the late afternoon, so that a party could go ashore to look for fuel for the boiler. It was very often two or three o'clock in the morning before sufficient timber for another day's run had been sawn up and stowed away on board. The unexpected, moreover, was always liable to delay progress. Early in the first voyage, two or three of the crew went swimming on one of those blistering afternoons when the sun seems to burn itself into the top of your skull. The fireman was just climbing back over the gunwale when a crocodile seized the hand that was still trailing in the water. Two men grabbed the other arm and for a few frightful moments there was a tug-o'-war, with the fireman once being pulled back into the river by the reptile, before it let go and slithered away, leaving him with a very badly lacerated arm.

On another occasion, two natives came up in a canoe one afternoon, when the timber-cutting party was ashore, and demanded a toll. They were told that white men did not pay toll on the Congo and they paddled away. But next morning, as *Peace* was getting under way, a canoe full of men with guns put out from the bank just ahead and lay across the steamer's bows. At once Grenfell ordered full steam ahead and, with its whistles shrieking and the pet cocks puffing clouds of steam, the vessel prepared to ram the canoe, whose crew promptly dropped their guns and began to paddle frantically to the shore. They got there before *Peace* could catch them, and raced off into the jungle and, writes Holman Bentley, 'Everyone shrieked with laughter, and our crew chaffed their would-be assailants in an unsparing manner. It was a very droll escapade.' Engagements with hostile natives were not always so ludicrously one-sided. There was a time when fifty war canoes attacked the steamer, and the protective blinds proved their value. There was another time when an attack was made by snipers using bows and arrows from the treetops along the river bank, before canoes put out *en masse* and the *Peace* only escaped severe trouble by turning downstream and outdistancing the enemy.

It was four years before another station was set up, at Bolobo, where the Congo rolls, five miles across, around enormous sandbanks, and it took these Baptists a decade to establish only half their ten planned missions. Like every other party of Christians who had broken new ground in Africa, they were explorers as well as men of God. They would go pottering off the main river highway, up branches of the Congo, like the Ubangi river, which for four hundred miles from the junction is almost as mighty as the mainstream; and like the Sese river, which is so narrow and so flanked on either side by tall beds of reeds that you can almost imagine yourself to be paddling your canoe up the river Ouse above Ely on an uncommonly sweltering summer's day. Grenfell eventually produced a chart of the Congo river system which won him a Founder's Medal from the Royal Geographical Society. And King Leopold was so impressed by his abilities as a navigator, and his resourcefulness as a traveller, that he asked the BMS in London if they would allow Grenfell to serve as his commissioner during the settling of international boundaries in the region, for the carve-up which followed the Berlin conference. The BMS assented readily, and Grenfell temporarily abandoned his position in the wheel-house of *Peace* to travel more than one thousand miles ashore as a political agent of the Belgian sovereign. He discharged this task so effectively that Leopold made him Commander of the Royal Order of the Lion, and presented him with its insignia set in diamonds.

Where the missions were established there was the usual conflict between Christian and tribal values, with the usual shock waves being registered vehemently by the missionaries. Holman Bentley describes how, at Monsembe, five hundred miles above Stanley Pool, two men passed the mission house holding spears aloft. On one of these a human head was impaled, on the other an arm. They had scarcely gone out of sight when a party of warriors appeared, with one man carrying the mutilated trunk and two others shouldering a leg apiece. 'It was,' writes Holman Bentley, 'a sickening sight, the more so as we were assured that these would be cooked and eaten in the evening. Needless to say, we did not visit the scene of the feast. A few of the young men from the town went down for a share, but were too late, the flesh had been eaten; however, they were generously invited to partake of the vegetables still remaining in the water in which it had been boiled. Both Weeks and myself found it difficult to eat our evening meal, and you will hardly wonder that in our dreams for a few nights, men carrying mutilated limbs were the chief figures, and that these limbs were sometimes our own . . .'

As always, however, the missionaries did not attempt to interfere on such occasions. As always, a curious *modus vivendi* was worked out in which white and black men of totally alien cultures, involving a strong degree of repugnance on one side at least, could settle down in a form of community. It was an arrangement tolerable to each because both sides had something the other wanted. The black men wanted a share of the white man's wealth, and they were also much impressed by the white man's evident powers of sorcery. The white men wanted the black man's soul, that most priceless possession of all. And so these Baptists, once they had settled into a comparatively friendly village, could set up their school. In it they would teach the natives how to read and write, how to sew. The education they offered after a while became even more sophisticated; it included French for the senior boys, geography and ancient history for all; and when Mrs Holman Bentley joined the mission, she taught telegraphy to the sharpest pupils, for in the rear of King Leopold's colonisers was now coming the railway from the coast to Stanley Falls, and the Baptist missionaries thought that some of the natives might 'wake up to the possibilities of telegraphing as a means of livelihood'. After a time, the people around the mission became so enamoured of this new cult in their midst that they brought their old tribal fetishes to Holman Bentley, who records that 'My dinner on the Sunday . . . was cooked with the wood of a fetish image four feet high, which was publicly hacked to pieces without a word of dissent by one of our new Church members'. Presently there would be a clear distinction made between those natives who attended the Church and its school, and those who had not yet been seduced from their fetishes and their cannibalism. 'The Christian people of Tungwa are the pick of the town; there is a wide difference between the dirty, dissolute, superstitious "great man" of the old style, who may be found sometimes lying drunk in the squares of the town, and the kindly, well-dressed, cleanly, educated young native who keeps his bottle of quinine and a few simple medicines by him, reads his New Testament daily, and lives the Christian life. Even a heathen native can see the difference and wonder how it comes about. This is a new type of greatness.'

Holman Bentley was not indifferent to the material advantages that Europe might enjoy from the presence of the white man in the Congo. A commodity much prized by the people there was cloth. They were delighted when they could acquire indigo-blue drill, or white material with three or four bands of blue striping, or red bandana; and the missionaries very often kept up to £1,000 worth of these textiles in their warehouse in order to pay off their bearers. The native was keenest of all to be buried in great winding sheets of imported cloth, when he died. 'For this, he trades and works and sins, sparing no pains,' says the missionary. 'This custom is certainly good for commerce, for it forces the native to trade and work . . . So with the opening up of Africa, Manchester may take heart; not only are there thousands more to wear its cloth, but thousands more to be buried in it.'

There was no doubt at all in his mind that the arrival of the white man in Africa had brought anything but blessings upon its people, if one carefully forgot for a moment the excursions of those men who traded in vile spirituous liquor. 'What is there,' Holman Bentley asked himself one day, 'in the conditions of life or the character of the Bantu race, which would work otherwise than downward? Until the scramble for Africa set in, no outside influence for good has affected them apart from that of missions. The cruel superstitions and savage customs of the people could but debase; ten thousand years could not evolve anything better, they could only bring deterioration.' If Holman Bentley was aware of the atrocities that Leopold's European agents were by then beginning to commit in the Congo, he ignored them completely. There is no mention in his journals of the amputations that regularly occurred when a native worker failed to produce his expected quota in rubber and ivory upon this incredible private estate; though within a few years the British Government would have become so disturbed by the news coming out of the Congo that it would have sent its consul Roger Casement to investigate, and the British Foreign Secretary would have declared that the Congo Free State had 'morally forfeited every right to international recognition'.

Even when his journals were published, in 1900, Holman Bentley was writing, by way of postscript to his own time in the Congo: 'The Belgians may well be proud of the part which their small country has played in the opening up of Africa . . . But while we recognise the work that Belgians personally have done, we cannot fail to remember that the mind and energy, the personality which has been behind all through and through, has been King Leopold . . . his master mind has planned and worked, seized the opportunities, and led on the enterprise to its present successful issue.'

This English Baptist had only one small reservation to make about white men working in the Congo, and that was taken out against an American colleague. In 1886 Bishop William Taylor, of the Methodist Episcopal Church, had started in the Congo what the Baptist referred to as 'the best, or rather the worst, example of the manner in which a mission to the Congo ought *not* to be conducted'. And it was, indeed, a very curious enterprise. It was the brainchild of a curious man.

William Taylor had been a Methodist local preacher in his native Virginia, the grandson of an Irish immigrant from Armagh. He made a great reputation in California, after being sent there by his Church authorities, as a fervent evangelist at open-air meetings of gold-rushing miners, and was widely known as the Street Preacher. He had then evangelised in Australia and in South Africa before returning home. He had a considerable talent for raising money and it is perhaps surprising that with his combination of gifts and experience he was not made a bishop of the Methodist Episcopal Church until he was sixty-three years old, in 1884. He had just opened a Taylor Transit Fund, to pay the passages of missionaries bound for South America and it had been modestly successful in attracting the contributions of supporters. He now turned his attention to Africa again, and invited well-wishers to subscribe to a new enterprise in the Congo. He was operating, it must be remembered, in those generous days of American Revivalism that produced Dwight Moody and Ira Sankey. There was shortly to be launched a Christian and Missionary Alliance in the United States which promised, in the thirteen years that remained of the nineteenth century, to send twenty thousand missionaries to evangelise the world. In fact, it produced only 330 willing hands in this period, but such was the enthusiasm of the alliance's beginning that a single meeting one night, in the evangelistic Simpson's Tabernacle in New York, netted no less than 96,000 dollars.

William Taylor's appeal for possible supporters of a mission in the Congo was shrewdly calculated to play upon the emotions that were then running strongly through God-fearing American Protestants. 'The conditions are,' he wrote, 'first, that our friends in America, through our Transit Fund Society, may pay their passage outward. Second, that all our workers shall depend on God and the people they serve for daily bread. Third, that they shall receive their salary in full from Our Father in heaven after their arrival in the "heavenly Jerusalem". I can get more workers and better workers on these terms than I can get on any other. Glory to God, the race of heroes and heroines has not run out, and never will . . . I tried for months to intimidate the holy women who wanted to go into the wilds of Africa, for I did not think it suitable for them to go among naked savage cannibals on a line of such rigid economy and possible perils to life, but "they wouldn't scare a cent" . . .' Taylor also took space in the New York Church periodicals to make it clear what well-wishers could do to help the holy men and women planning to work in Africa without salary. He listed the items that his missionaries would need and they ran an extraordinary gamut, from Middlesex or Washington Mills indigo-blue flannel to gossamer underwear, from musical instruments to scented toilet soap, from Liebig's extract of meat to canned fruits of any kind. Taylor had already arranged contracts for good waterproof tents to be supplied at twenty dollars apiece and anyone wishing to contribute the cost of a tent would have his name inscribed along the side of the canvas – any excess monies sent for this purpose being hallmarked for the passages fund. A very big tent, price fifty-two dollars, would be required for worship and this was eventually paid for by the widow of a Methodist Episcopal predecessor of Taylor's, being stencilled by the packers 'The Bishop Simpson Tent'.

A handful of Americans who came within earshot of Taylor's exhortations were somewhat sceptical of his organising abilities, though no one doubted that his heart was in the right place. But for every sceptic there was always a ready reply, supplied by sympathetic journals like *Zion's Herald*, which declared that: 'He is a man of God, of an heroic mould, and full of resources as well as faith. There is no occasion for any of his many friends to fear that he will lack abundant pecuniary aid as it may be required. Already he has supplies for a year, and an open and direct line of sympathy with thousands of appreciative supporters.'

Taylor himself went ahead of his Congo party, to England, where their ship would pick him up *en route* to Africa. From Liverpool he wrote home to the authorities of his Church, respectfully calling their thoughtful attention to the status, relationship and rights of the Missionary Episcopacy. He speaks of an amount of compensation, due not to him personally but to his position, which he is willing to 'leave to your own godly judgment of the sacrifice and service to be rendered' but makes it plain that he would like to know as soon as possible just how much money will have been banked in his account during his absence overseas. The letter caused the Boston *Congregationalist* to wonder, just a little, 'why the apostle of self-support, who is leading out so many missionaries to live among heathens, and to live upon them, too, should ask for support, and . . . why he should not do as his fellow-workers are to do'. By the time that observation saw the public prints, Bishop Taylor was aboard ship off the West African coast, writing to the Church authorities: 'No room or time to speak of accounts, which Bro Withey will explain to you. We were induced from representations in England, to buy more than we had designed. The Lord has given the funds what you have and what I have to square all – but I will need all I have, so the Lord will help you to pay Fowler Bros.'

This financial cavalier was accompanied aboard the *City of Montreal* by nearly fifty men, women and children. They had been photographed *en masse* on the deck before the vessel left New York, and as the anchor was weighed they had sung in unison 'Sweet Bye and Bye' and 'Praise God, from Whom all blessings flow'. They included 'one or two more thoroughly trained financiers, two physicians, two or more experienced schoolteachers, mechanics, farmers, trained musicians, vocal and instrumental, some highly educated, some not, but all intelligent . . .' They held meetings aboard ship and converted several of the sailors and passengers to their faith; on one occasion 'I think one hundred rose to their feet, signifying that they wanted to go with us to glory'. Between New York and Liverpool, they had triumphed in one conflict with orthodoxy, when

Brother Ross Taylor's little boy Artie recovered from a brain-fever without the use of medicines; the ship's surgeon had told Brother Taylor that if he did not allow the child to be treated properly, and young Artie died, he would have the father arrested for murder in England; but Brother Taylor had replied that he was not accustomed to having anyone interfere with his family and preferred to trust in God rather than physicians or medicines.

In the Congo this philosophy was to be disastrous. Taylor had written, as an inducement to his recruits, of a salubrious climate, navigable streams, fertile soil, 'a chosen field for trade and missionary effort', though he had never once, at that stage, set eyes upon this Paradise. The recruits were now to discover how they had been gulled. Their Bishop led them inland as far as Stanley Pool. He found a deserted government building there which, he said, could be used as a base for their eventual mission to the interior. He stayed with them for a few days, then he went off to visit a party which had been dropped off on the voyage, some way up the coast. A few months later he returned. He stayed a few more days with the people at Stanley Pool. Then he went back to America to a conference and the Congo never saw him again.

His missionaries were totally unprepared, in any intelligent sense, for the life they had to lead. Not one of them spoke a word that could be communicated to the natives. And for all the frontier spirit of the propaganda, scarcely any of them was fitted by training or temperament for existence on the edge of Congolese jungle. When the tins of fruit and the Liebig's meat extract ran out, they supported themselves from a garden they created and by shooting hippopatami, whose meat they sold to the natives. The whole of their energies were required for sheer survival and they accomplished nothing at all of their missionary purpose. The Baptists and other missionaries in the area gave them some help, but they were doomed from the moment they stepped ashore. Some of them died where they were. The rest obtained passage money from their friends and relations at home and returned to the United States. Within a year or two, William Taylor's grandiose plan might never have existed, for all the mark it had left upon the Congo. And he had been quietly retired as 'non-effective' by a disillusioned committee of the Methodist Episcopal Church.

The English Baptist Holman Bentley, who had watched this wretched episode from his own mission just up the river, full of sympathy for the sufferings of the earnest people who had followed Bishop Taylor, would have held his tongue in criticism but for one thing, he said. This was that ill-organised ventures of this kind, run on unsound principles, promising great things on a minimum of outlay, tended to draw away support from the missions which were working on sound lines. 'Missions,' he wrote, 'are not to be conducted cheaply . . . Let those who wish to carry on such work beware of "cheap" methods.'

He could, in fact, see a much greater threat to the operation of the Baptist missions in the Congo by then and he did not mince matters when he came to set them down in print in his English retirement. 'The energy put forth by the Protestant Missionary societies in Africa,' he declared, 'had not escaped the attention of Propaganda in Rome. The Romish Church considered the advent of Protestant missionaries into Central Africa a greater evil to the natives than previous dark heathenism. The Pope issued a Bull, enjoining a most vigorous attack upon this Protestant enterprise. "The movements of the heretics are to be followed up, and their efforts harassed and destroyed." ' Holman Bentley, alas, did not offer the source for his picturesque quotation from the Papal Bull; it is doubtful whether any nineteenth-century Pope composed his utterances with the melodramatic terseness of a twentieth-century script-writer in Hollywood.

Nevertheless, there was something in the message which Holman Bentley wished to convey. The Catholic Church was, indeed, at this time awakening from comparative slumber in the missionary fields of Africa.

12

LAVIGERIE AND THE WHITE FATHERS

By the time Africa was on the threshold of its dismemberment by the European powers, the missionary initiative there had for nearly eighty years been overwhelmingly Protestant. It was now to be grasped much more firmly by Catholics. For a prince of the Church had appeared, who had dedicated his life to winning African souls for Christ and Rome, and he was Charles Martial Allemand-Lavigerie.

Catholicism, of course, had been the very earliest Christian influence in Africa, if one discounts the Coptic root that was never to be disturbed in Egypt and Abyssinia. Quite apart from the priests who were put ashore wherever the Portuguese landed around the African coast from the time of Henry the Navigator onwards – which meant that missions at one time or another were to be found at intervals everywhere between Gibraltar, the Cape and Somalia – there had been regular excursions along North Africa, in spite of Islam's secure hold on the Arab people from the middle of the eighth century onwards. St Francis of Assisi had visited Egypt during the Fourth Crusade, in 1219, and he had been courteously received by the Sultan. Cardinal Ximenes was even allowed to proselytise in Morocco in the sixteenth century; and, doubtless taking the view that time and the majority of the Arabs were not on his side, he indulged in mass baptisms by the expedient of trundling a wet mop of holy water over as many as four thousand bowed heads at once.

By the eighteenth century, these Catholic enclaves had virtually disappeared from Black Africa. Sometimes hostility had driven them out. More often than not, the religious orders which were responsible for them simply withdrew their manpower in the face of African indifference, and transferred it to more promising missionary work in the New World. This was particularly the case with the Jesuits, who at one time were active in Sierra Leone, the Congo and East Africa, as well as Loanda. The Dominicans, too, who had recruited Africans to their order from their bases in South-East Africa, had decided to concentrate their efforts upon the American natives from the moment that Spanish and Portuguese power was firmly established in Mexico and in the sub-continent to the south. By the time the Protestant missionaries came into Africa, from the beginning of the nineteenth century, there was almost nothing left of this Catholic heritage but the faintest birthmarks. Occasionally someone would detect, in a tribal myth, a curiously basic resemblance to one or other of the Gospel stories, which was almost certainly a transfusion into the local culture of Catholic teaching which had taken place many, many generations before. Or he would, as the Baptists did in the Congo, stumble upon the decayed ruins of much earlier Christian worship. As for the Catholic Church itself, it made a number of new gestures towards Africa in the first half of the nineteenth century. Lazarists and Capuchins from Italy went to Abyssinia in the early 1840s, but did not survive very long in the face of local nationalism. From 1837 onwards there was a Catholic settlement in South Africa that was to remain undisturbed by the growing turbulence between Boers, British and Bantu. But there was not anywhere in these years a dynamic drive from Rome comparable to that which possessed the various Protestant movements of Europe and North America.

A foretaste of things to come was the arrival of the Holy Ghost Fathers in East Africa in 1863. Bishop Maupoint of Réunion had been intent for some time upon establishing missions on the mainland. At the end of 1860, the French corvette *Somme* brought three priests, six nursing sisters, a naval surgeon and some craftsmen to Zanzibar, as a preliminary step. It thoroughly alarmed the British Consul there; he informed London that this was clearly an enterprise of the French Government and that 'the building certainly resembles a large fortified barracks rather than anything else'. Three years later, the Church in Réunion being too short of man-power to sustain missionary work elsewhere, Father Antoine Horner and a group of the Holy Ghost Fathers arrived to settle opposite Zanzibar, at Bagamoyo, with plans to start a chain of stations into the interior of the mainland. At once they established friendly relations with the local Sultan; he even gave them 1,000 rupees to assist their work. By 1866 they had 136 pupils in their school, all of them former slaves whose freedom had been bought by the priests on the open market. From the outset, the work of these missionaries was successful in every sense. They avoided friction with English Protestants working in the same area, and this was to be a unique achievement in the years immediately ahead in East Africa. The Englishman Sir Bartle Frere, indeed, who visited the area on behalf of the CMS, was so impressed that he gave the Fathers £200 from his own purse and commended their work to London as a model of what might be achieved in the liberation and instruction of slave children. By 1871 someone else had been captivated by Father Horner's mission, and he was H. M. Stanley, who stayed at Bagamoyo on his way inland to look for David Livingstone. 'The dinner furnished to the padres and their guest,' he wrote, 'consisted of as many plates as a first-class hotel in Paris usually supplies, and cooked with nearly as much skill . . . The champagne – think of champagne Cliquot in East Africa – Lafitte, La Rose, Burgundy and Bordeaux, were of first-class quality, and the meek and lowly eyes of the fathers were not a little brightened under the vinous influence. Ah! those fathers understand life and appreciate its duration.' The champagne was a Christmas present from the French Consul in Zanzibar and when Stanley's encomium was published, Father Horner felt obliged to write home to the Mother House in Europe that 'it is unneccessary to pay attention to this American pleasantry, which is little delicate and merely written down to amuse the reader'.

A real dynamic of modern Catholic missionary enterprise, however, did not appear until after the Holy Ghost Fathers had successfully taken root in East Africa. Two things triggered it off. One was King Leopold's ambitions in the Congo and the other was the energy and the inspiration of Cardinal Lavigerie.

His Eminence was a zealous Catholic and a French patriot, and there were times in his life when it would have been difficult to say which of these loyalties was uppermost. His father had been a Customs official and his mother was the daughter of a director of the Royal Mint in Bayonne, where Lavigerie was born. The boy evidently discovered a proselytising instinct very early in life, for he would save his pocket money as an inducement to Jewish schoolmates to convert to Christianity. There was clearly no doubt in the Lavigerie household that he would become anything other than a priest, and he went straight from school into the St Sulpice Seminary. He had a fine mind, with a gift for academic work, and within a year or two of ordination he was lecturing in ecclesiastical history at the Sorbonne. In 1856, when he was thirty-one, he was made director of *L'Œuvre des Écoles D'Orient*, which had been established to promote the reunion of the Eastern schismatic Churches with Rome. He continued with his Sorbonne lectures, but the new post released another flair in Lavigerie. It was discovered that he was a born fund-raiser, and on his first sweep around France he collected 60,000 francs; twelve months later, when the Turks attacked Christians in the Lebanon, he collected for their relief one million francs in August alone. This was obviously a man bound for promotion and before long he was serving in Rome as adviser to Propaganda on Oriental Rites. By the time he was thirty-eight he had returned to France, as Bishop of Nancy, and not many men in modern Church history had achieved a mitre younger than that.

There was a deep streak of dedication in this brilliant prelate; he was nobody's career man, and he was soon to demonstrate this in the most conclusive fashion. After only four years in Nancy he was offered the Archbishopric of Algiers by Marshal MacMahon, the French Governor-General. This was only nominal promotion, for Algiers was an outpost in which a man might labour without much notice being taken of him for the rest of his life, whereas Nancy was well in the mainstream of French Catholic hierarchy. Lavigerie accepted the job and, on arriving in his new diocese, delivered a charge to his clergy which vividly summarised his philosophy both as a Catholic and a Frenchman. 'In His providence,' he declared, 'God has chosen France to make of Algeria the cradle of a great and Christian nation; a nation like unto herself; her sister and her child, happy to walk by her side in the paths of honour and justice. He is calling upon us to use those gifts which are especially our own in order to shed around us the light of that true civilisation which has its source and its spring in the Gospel; to carry that light beyond the desert, to the centre of the continent which is still enshrouded in the densest darkness, thus uniting Central and Northern Africa to the common life of Christendom. Such, I repeat, is our destiny; and God expects us to fulfil it, our country is watching to see whether we show ourselves worthy of it – nay, more, the eyes of the whole Church are fixed upon us . . .'

It was a charge to build up the morale of priests who had always been severely discouraged by the French secular authorities from involving themselves in the world of the Arab natives; they were expected to act as chaplains to the French settlers, and not much more. It was a charge which so alarmed Napoleon III, with its clear intention to convert Moslems and others, which might cause more trouble for the French than they wished to have, that the Emperor promptly asked Lavigerie to come home again as Archbishop of Lyons. Had Lavigerie accepted that offer, a Cardinal's hat would have been almost his for the asking within months, for Lyons was one of the most prestigious thrones in Catholic Europe. Lavigerie refused it.

Instead he began to build, monumentally, where he was. Almost as soon as he had settled into his new palace, a famine hit Algeria, followed by an epidemic of cholera. He organised his priests for relief work, he set up orphanages for those children whose parents had died, and before long he had 1,700 under his care. He acquired an estate in the valley of the Chelif, where they could obtain work as they grew up, and he imported the Muscat grape from Spain which would eventually, in this new soil, produce the celebrated vin de Carthage. Everything that Lavigerie did was on a full-blooded and sometimes grandiose scale. He suffered from arthritis and his health, after several years in North Africa, had declined so much that he believed he would soon be dead. He at once had a great rococo mausoleum built for himself beneath the dome of a new cathedral in Carthage, and he composed the epitaph that was engraved upon its stone: 'Here rests in the hope of infinite mercy, Charles Martial Allemand-Lavigerie. Formerly Cardinal-Priest of the Holy Roman Church, Archbishop of Carthage and Algiers. And Primate of Africa. Now dust and ashes. Pray for him.' It was to be another ten years before he actually occupied it.

There had been a great deal of friction between French and Italians in the years leading up to the building of that cathedral and when Italian Capuchins in the town implied that Lavigerie had been responsible for the burning down of their church (which was, in fact, the result of carelessness in the sacristy) the Cardinal took them to court and sued. He could never be mistaken as anything other than an ardent Frenchman. The day would come when at a banquet in Algiers he would declare that Catholics should support the Republic, then gripped by Gambetta's anti-clerical campaign, sacrificing all that conscience and honour allowed for the sake of *la patrie*. This so impressed the Republican leader that he paid a neat compliment to the prelate from North Africa; 'Anti-clericalism, Monsignor, is for France; it isn't for export.'

Yet nothing that Lavigerie did or built was to be more wholeheartedly effective than the religious order he founded in 1869. He called it the Society of Missionaries of the Venerable Geronimo, in honour of a Moor who had refused to become a Moslem in the sixteenth century and who had then been walled up alive in the Fort Bab-el-Oued. But soon these men were to be known throughout North Africa as the White Fathers, because they were dressed in a white gandoura (robe) and burnous (mantle), with a chechia (red cap) on their heads. This choice of habit was not made on aesthetic grounds. Lavigerie copied Arab dress for his men because he wished them to form a Christian bridgehead in an Arab world; a later age might have said that he was providing them with a subtle form of camouflage.

There was no doubt at all, now, what his intentions were, in spite of latent hostility from his own French Government. In canvassing the French seminaries for recruits, Lavigerie made the point that European Christians seemed indifferent to the progress made by Islam in Africa. Since the start of the century nearly fifty million people, he calculated, had been converted to this creed in the Sahara and the Sudan alone – 'and so it comes about that while Islam sees its existence in Europe seriously threatened by the fall of the Sultan's throne, it is making vast strides in Africa, at the very door of our colonies'. He, Charles Martial Allemand-Lavigerie, had vowed himself to halt this advance. The British Consul in Algiers, Colonel Playfair, informed London that 'We have St Augustine amongst us again'.

Lavigerie picked as the drill sergeants of his new recruits a Jesuit and a lecturer from St Sulpice, his old seminary, both of whom had been sent to North Africa for the benefit of their health. These were his novice masters and through them he instructed his White Fathers in the new vocation they had adopted. Keen as he was on building his order as rapidly and substantially as possible, he was not prepared to accept men of easy enthusiasm. Anyone who thought that by becoming a missionary he would gratify his natural taste for adventure, was likely to finish up in some peril to his soul more even than to his life. He was not wanted by the White Fathers. They could only join this venture in a spirit of utmost self-sacrifice leading, in all likelihood, to death. Lavigerie was looking for potential martyrs, but he emphasised not so much the glories of martyrdom as the extremely unpleasant ways in which it had generally been achieved by Christians so far. The new men were told that they would have much to suffer – 'more, perhaps, than in any other mission on the face of the earth' – with poverty and fatigue, hunger and thirst, scorching heat and fatal fever and, as they proceeded into the deepest parts of Africa, the barbarous cruelties of savage inhabitants.

They were to undertake nothing that did not serve the paramount purpose of converting the pagans and Moslems of Africa. And in this mission they would be working to a set of rules that were so far unique in the history of missionary enterprise, either Catholic or Protestant. One distinguishing feature of the White Fathers was to be that they must share the exterior life of the natives among whom they worked, in language, food and clothing. Then came a most astonishing doctrine for the recruits to digest. Their founder told them that 'I not only forbid public preaching of the Gospel, but preaching of any kind, even to individuals. You must obey these orders strictly – no conversation about religion, under any pretext whatever. The time is not ripe for making converts. Your task is to win the affection and confidence of the Kabyles by works of charity. If you attempt to do anything more you will spoil all future prospects. Mohammedans invariably act in concert; before you begin to preach the Gospel, you must prepare the way for mass conversions. This period of preparation may last for a century.' Charity was the missionaries' best weapon, for it broke down the defences of the hardest heart; it must be the mainspring of all their endeavours. The maintenance of pharmacies to heal sickness was certainly permissible, and so was the running of schools in which secular subjects would be taught. But, at bottom, these White Fathers were to 'Love the poor pagans; be kind to them; heal their wounds. They will give you their affection first, then their confidence, and then at last their souls.' Their own lives must be dedicated to 'holiness, self-sacrifice and zeal . . . They must be all things to all men . . .'

No order of the day issued by any Christian commander on the eve of battle with the forces of darkness had ever been tougher upon his troops than this one. Lavigerie could be very tough indeed. He once told the Central Council of the order, when their funds were found to be in deficit, that if this ever happened again, two of them would have to go out begging until the amount was made up. At the same time, no Christian commander was ever more devoted to his troops than this one. Eight years after the foundation, the Cardinal asked the Pope if he might resign his see in order to spend the rest of his life entirely with his White Fathers. The Pope said he certainly might not. By then, Lavigerie had 125 of these men at his disposal. He had also founded a sister order for women, the Congregation of Missionary Sisters of Our Lady of Africa. He would add to these two squadrons a third, the Pioneers of the Sahara, whose job was literally to build places where travellers could be cared for, where fugitive slaves could be protected, where the sick could be tended. But the White Fathers would remain the dearest and the most potent force in his crusade.

By 1875 they had established a number of missions along the coastal strip of French territory, and around the edge of the desert. They had started to win from the Moslem Arabs something between that affection and confidence which their leader had prophesied, though it is evident that they were no longer following his orders as strictly as he had issued them. Father Paulmier wrote from one of the stations that 'Our school and pharmacy is our great stronghold. Whenever we can, whilst administering remedies for physical ills, we think of the sickness of the soul. Too often, the maladies from which our poor Moslems suffer are brought on by their reckless vice. When this is the case, we never fail to speak to them of an offended God, of the chastisement sin deserves, of the efforts they ought to make to conquer themselves in order to avoid those faults which even in this world bring upon us the penalty of disease and suffering . . . Oftentimes the Arab is not satisfied with expressing his gratitude in words; he kisses the missioner's hands effusively, and would, were he not prevented, prostrate himself at his feet. And in returning to his own people he proclaims loudly the benefits he has received from the Christian marabout.* Our influence is rapidly extending; our clientele not infrequently come from a great distance.'

Within a month or two, Father Paulmier was asked to join two other White Fathers in the most ambitious enterprise the order had so far undertaken. They were to attempt a crossing of the Sahara and, if possible, reach the still fabled city of Timbuctoo, which had been visited by only a small handful of Europeans so far. In the middle of January 1876, they left the desert outpost of Metlili, the southernmost mission of the White Fathers. Their brethren never saw them alive again. A long time afterwards, a group of ostrich hunters found their mutilated bodies among sand dunes some distance north of Timbuctoo. The White Fathers paid 1,500 francs for the recovery of the corpses. The order had its first martyrs.

Three years later, another attempt on the deep Sahara was made. Two of the Fathers, with Tuareg guides, left Ghadames and they were soon reporting remarkably good progress among the Azger Tuareg people. They had made friends with some of the most notable brigand chiefs of the desert, and they believed they were in a position to recommend that the town of Rat should be occupied as a mission station. They returned to Ghadames safe and well, and at the end of 1881 three priests left to open the new station, accompanied by guides. They had almost reached Rat when the guides suddenly turned upon them and left three more martyrs in the sand. It was to be quite a while before Lavigerie allowed his men to hazard themselves again in this area.

But by then he was deeply involved in expanding elsewhere and his ambitions as a Frenchman were at least as responsible as his zeal as a Catholic. In 1877 he had drawn the Pope's attention to King Leopold's African International Association and he had sent a memorandum on the same subject to the French Government in Paris. To the Vatican he pointed out that there had been a Protestant majority at the Brussels conference, that Protestants were even now marching on Central and East Africa in unprecedented numbers with missionary vigour. To the Quai D'Orsay he

* In Arabic, literally 'a hermit': generally used to indicate an ascetic holy man.

suggested that as a French bishop in Africa he could not remain indifferent to the prospect of Central Africa being opened up by European nations without French participation. To both he indicated, with differing emphases, that all the resources at his command would gladly be placed at the disposal of both the Pope and *la patrie* in this new field of spiritual and material combat. There is no evidence that the Quai D'Orsay made any positive move to take up the Cardinal's offer. The Vatican was much less inhibited. Lavigerie put forward a plan for a series of mission stations to be set up within the area that would now come under the influence of the African International Association. They would, of course, be manned by White Fathers. By the beginning of February 1878, the Pope had ratified the plan by decree and Lavigerie was entrusted with the whole operation of a Catholic drive on Central Africa.

Both memorandum and decree were drafted in secrecy, but the news leaked out. The immediate effect was consternation in London, at the headquarters of the Anglican Church Missionary Society, which had already started work in East Africa and which took the view that Catholics had no business poaching in its new province. It sent an emissary post-haste to see the Cardinal, a Dr R. N. Cust, who had once served on the Viceroy's Legislative Council in India and who was now lay secretary to the Board of Missions in the Province of Canterbury. Dr Cust was to represent the views of the CMS to His Eminence with the utmost vigour. He landed in Algiers in April and was conducted to the archiepiscopal palace. He presented his case and he was listened to with courtesy. The Anglicans, he was told, must not be too alarmed at the turn of events; the Catholics had no intention of provoking a clash with them in East Africa. There was, however, no question of the White Fathers abandoning a task to which they had set their hands. Indeed, the first party was already well on its way to Zanzibar, and a second was preparing to make the long journey.

It was true. By June, ten of the White Fathers under Father Livinhac would be marching inland from the East African coast at Bagamoyo, towards the Baganda kingdom of Mutesa, and a CMS mission which contained the explosively anti-Papist Alexander Mackay. Mackay would soon be reporting to London how these French missionaries had arrived, bearing presents of guns, ammunition and other articles of military equipment for the heathen king. The other articles of military equipment, in fact, were rather gorgeous redundant full-dress uniforms, full of gold braid and silver buttons, which the Cardinal knew would be much to the taste of any African chief. He had acquired them from the second-hand shops of Paris, which were always well stocked with accoutrements following every change of French regime. These were apt to be frequent; the uniforms came, he said 'with the compliments of our revolutions'. English Protestants tended to be less imaginative in their choice of presents for native chiefs; the London Missionary Society maintained, for this purpose, a regular order of brass bedsteads from the Army and Navy Stores.

The second expedition, which was on the eve of departure as Dr Cust arrived in Algiers, was equipped much more like a military unit. One of the Fathers, indeed, had been sent especially to Brussels to recruit retired Papal Zouaves, whose function would be to protect the missionary priests from hostile tribes and to be 'eventual founders of a Christian Kingdom'. He collected four Belgians and two Scotsmen, and these were with the twelve White Fathers of the second mission when the party was despatched from Algiers. First, a service was held in the Church of Our Lady of Africa. Lavigerie blessed the sword which he presented to each Zouave. Then he blessed the Papal colours they would fly at the head of their tiny column. He denounced the accursed trade in slaves. He told the missionaries that they were to teach the tribes they met that all men were brothers. Then he kissed the feet of the departing Fathers, and each member of the cathedral clergy did the same.

It had not been necessary for Dr Cust to point out the dangers to Christian expansion in Africa that would arise from any friction between Catholics and Protestants. Lavigerie was well aware of them before the CMS had sent its emissary from London. It had been with this in mind that, in March 1878, Lavigerie issued a special order to the first party of White Fathers bound for East Africa. They must on no account, he said, open any mission close to an existing Protestant mission. They must put at least eight or ten kilometres between the two. He was later to increase that distance to twenty-five kilometres.

His White Fathers had gradually become lax about his original orders that they must never preach the Gospel in any sense of the word for a long time to come. They were to become lax in their observance of this new instruction. It was one reason why, within a few years, Christians would be spilling each other's blood in the land of the Baganda, in front of the heathen they had all vowed themselves to convert with a message of peace.

13
THE RIVALS

King Mutesa was the autocratic monarch of nearly two million people and he ran his realm on feudal principles. Standing immediately below him in the hierarchy of the Baganda people* were a number of chiefs, each commanding the allegiance of thousands who were distinguished from one another by subtle differences of tribal ancestry. The chiefs had a degree of autonomy when they were with these clansmen of theirs, and they were awarded posts at Mutesa's court which gave them the powers and status in the nation as a whole comparable to that of a Minister in any European state. Mutesa, however, had full power of life and death over all the Baganda; he was the Kabaka, possessed of divine right, and he could do no wrong to any of his subjects, even if this meant that he put a man to death in the most frightful way conceivable. His position was not at all unlike that of an English monarch before the barons imposed Magna Carta upon King John in the thirteenth century. But this was East Africa towards the end of the nineteenth century. Indeed, it was representative of all Africa before Europeans imposed their own forms of rule upon the continent. And, although this native feudalism was about to be changed dramatically under the greedy pressures of the Great Powers, Europeans even now had to tread warily when they associated themselves with a ruler like Mutesa. They resided in his kingdom only on sufferance, and they knew very well

* There is a great confusion of proper names in this part of Africa, which I have attempted to avoid by referring, wherever possible, to 'the Baganda people', even where this reads a little awkwardly. Uganda is the name of the country as we know it today. Buganda is the name of the ancient kingdom, now one of four provinces in Uganda. Muganda is the name for a native of Buganda and Baganda is its plural form. Luganda is the name of their language. Ganda and Kiganda are adjectives relating to all these proper names.

that one offensive step on their part might be fatal; at the very least they would be sent packing in humiliation.

Mutesa's capital of Rubaga was part of what became the modern city of Kampala. It was a town of four hills, dazzlingly beautiful early in the morning when white mist filled the valleys, as it still does today, when from any hilltop the sun shines strongly over what looks like an Alpine snowfield. Spreading for six miles below the royal enclosure on Mengo Hill and for a couple of miles on either side of it, were the homes of the great Baganda chiefs and of the smaller chieflings, together with their retainers and their families, hundreds of them all told. Here, also, were the families of the royal bodyguard and the page-boys who were always in attendance on the monarch. Again, it was not unlike the subservient structure with which a ruler surrounded himself at home in medieval Europe. The CMS missionary Robert Ashe has given us a vivid picture of Mutesa's court in 1882, when he had just arrived in the country to join Alexander Mackay and his colleagues, who had already been there four years.

When word came down from the palace that Mutesa wished to see the new arrival, says Ashe, 'I . . . arranged myself in my largest black coat, in order to pay fitting respect to the great monarch'. Then he mounted the Muscat donkey which the king had presented to the missionaries, and trotted up the next hill. Mutesa's reception house was an enormous building, shaped like a beehive, supported on high wooden posts which ran in four irregular rows. Ashe was a bit disappointed at the lack of decoration in the palace, which was constructed of tightly woven and packed reedwork, a craft in which the Baganda have always excelled. It probably creaked a little in even a gentle breeze, as the similar construction over the Kasubi Tombs of the Kabakas does today. It was exquisite and perfect of its kind, but Ashe thought there was nothing enduring about it.

Mutesa was reclining upon a low couch, beneath a shabby canopy of dirty bark-cloth. He was clad in a white robe, and he held in his right hand a small round mirror, in which he could watch the courtiers grouped behind him. At the foot of the couch were two handsome page-boys, their bodies shining with what Ashe called a superabundance of oil. They were also dressed from head to toe in white robes. One of them clasped Mutesa's feet, warming them with his hands while 'the other held himself in readiness to brush away any miserable fly whose brain was too under-developed to comprehend the awful majesty of its fellow-mortal, upon whom it sacrilegiously dared to settle'. The couch was very close to a door-way. Half outside, but sufficiently inside to keep his ear close to Mutesa's head, was the kneeling figure of the chief storekeeper. He was in this curious posture because he was not considered noble enough to enter the royal presence completely; but he was a man of great influence and tribal power, so Mutesa liked to have him as accessible as sanguinary protocol would allow. Sitting on a mat, also near the king's head, was Mutesa's favourite chief, and opposite him was the royal chancellor. In a circle around the monarch were two or three rows of great chiefs and, at the back of the room, were seated a collection of beautiful women, the ladies of the royal household. In this claustrophobic atmosphere, two camp-stools had been set up between the king and the great chiefs, for the benefit of Ashe and a colleague who had just arrived in Africa with him. There, for just a few moments, pleasantries were exchanged. The missionaries presented the Kabaka with some fine red cloth, with the compliments of the CMS in London. Then they were dismissed.

Mutesa had the most brilliant delusions of grandeur. He once said to Mackay: 'Mackay, when I become friends with England, God in heaven will be witness that England will not come to make war on Uganda, nor Uganda go to make war on England. . . . Everyone will say "Oh, Mutesa is coming" when I reach England, and when I return "Oh, Mutesa is coming back again!" . . .' He wanted the missionary to obtain an English princess, so that he could add her to his already numerous collection of wives, and he was astonished when Mackay told him that in England no woman could be given in marriage without her consent.

Mutesa's polygamy was not the only thing that stood between him and Christian baptism; he also suffered from venereal disease and an Arab practitioner was regularly summoned to court to ease what Mackay fastidiously referred to as his 'stricture'. The Kabaka never did make his royal progress through London, but three of his emissaries once made the journey in the company of CMS men going home on leave. They returned with the most fantastic tales of their experiences. There were so many horses in London that no one could count them. The houses were built of stone in long, long fences, so long that no one could count the number of people living in one house; London was nothing but houses of stone stretching as far as . . . as far as from Rubaga to Bulemizi; which was twenty miles away. The emissaries had been taken to see the Queen, but when they reached her palace there were so many ladies dressed alike that they could not tell which one was the Queen. They had seen a place where cannons were made. And another place where beautiful guns were made. They had been to the zoo. And then 'after we had been many days in London, we went away to another place, where we stayed a short time. We did not walk, but went into a wooden horse, which went by itself, with us all in it . . .' There was no end to the marvels of England. But the thing that impressed these Baganda most of all, which they retailed to their Kabaka with greatest relish, was the fact that in England, every man had one wife, and every wife had thirty children. They had also, they believed, got to the bottom of something that had puzzled them ever since they had first encountered the white man in their own country. The missionaries who came to Buganda were notoriously without women of their own, 'but when they get back to England, they are made great chiefs and each one gets a wife as a reward for his services!'

As for Mackay, his reaction to the Kabaka was as variable as Mutesa's moods. Sometimes he believed that the work of God was in the black man's heart, and allowed that it was no small matter for such a fellow as this to leave the way of his forefathers and live like a Christian. But there were other times when he would become so angry and disillusioned that he would tell Mutesa to his face that he was merely playing with religion, professing himself a Christian one day, a Moslem the next, and then reverting to the superstitions of his ancestry the day after; and in his journal on such a night, the Scot would confide that 'Mutesa is a pagan, a heathen, out and out'. The sense of futility in the missionary was very often caused by some new excess of cruelty by the Kabaka.

Mackay was once writing his journal at the end of a day which had heard the drums of the royal executioners beating the news that fresh victims of Mutesa's displeasure had been secured and would be dead by morning. It was quiet as Mackay wrote but, 'Suddenly, a sharp cry in the road outside of our fence, then mingled voices; an agonising yell again, followed by the horrid laugh of several men, and all is still as before. "Do you hear?" says one of our lads. "They have cut that fellow's throat – hee, hee, hee!" And he laughs, too, the terrible Baganda grin of pleasure in cruelty.' Mackay knew that the throat had been cut on Mutesa's orders. Others would be put down in the same way by morning, while some would be slowly tortured to death – their noses, ears and lips cut off, the sinews of their arms and thighs cut out piecemeal and roasted in front of their eyes, before these were put out and the body itself was burnt alive. 'The wretch who orders all this to be done for his own gratification is he who is called in Europe "the enlightened and intelligent king of Uganda".' And Mutesa was indeed enlightened, compared with some African chiefs; a man was not executed among the Baganda without some form of trial, rough though its pretence of justice might be. But even when he was at his most biddable, Mutesa's record put a severe strain upon any missionary's charity.

At this distance it seems remarkable that such a potentate should have anything at all to do with Christian missionaries, let alone offer them hospitality and make them welcome to settle close to his court. The answer to that conundrum is the one which applies to every nineteenth-century African chief who was willing to accommodate the white man. Mutesa, though powerful, was highly insecure. He was also intelligent enough to enlist the potential aid of people whom he knew to represent greater power than ever he or his enemies could command. In Mutesa's case, these allies might be very necessary to help him retain his independence from the Arabs, who had long since moved into his kingdom from the coast. Mutesa had at first been as susceptible to the doctrines of Islam as any African. It offered him status in life and the prospect of sensuous marvels after death. It brought with it at first the protective presence of Arab slave traders, though he rapidly discovered that this might be a dangerous insurance. So Mutesa had received instruction in the faith of Mohammed, though he declined to be circumcised; and he ordered the building of mosques, though these were generally erected facing the wrong way; and he directed his people to eat meat slaughtered according to Islamic tradition, though he was less strict in his own diet. His executioners dealt with those Baganda who did not obey the Kabaka readily enough. The new religion developed in the land, however; indeed, most of its adherents far outstripped their monarch in the fidelity of their observances. Some became so fervent that they dared to criticise Mutesa's sloppy devotions. He had seventy of them burned alive in one pyre for their insolence.

When H. M. Stanley wandered into his realm in 1875, Mutesa was seriously worried about the influence of Islam. He therefore besought the explorer, with all the sincerity that he could invariably turn on and off like a tap, to have Christian missionaries sent to Buganda. Stanley at once composed that letter to the *Daily Telegraph* which prompted Robert Arthington to make the first of his financial contributions to missionary work, and the CMS obliged by recruiting Alexander Mackay and his colleagues to sail for Africa. For a little while, Mutesa felt happier with these white men on his doorstep. Their kinsman, the English Consul, was known to be on friendly terms with the Arab Sultan in Zanzibar and might prove an invaluable help in time of trouble. But then it became obvious to him that this might come in yet another form. There was now the threat of Egyptian imperialism looming from the north; moreover, it was Egyptian imperialism conducted with the assistance of Englishmen. First Sir Samuel Baker and then General Gordon had marched towards Buganda on behalf of the Khedive Ismail, with orders to put down the slave trade and annex the sources of the Nile to the Egyptian throne.

By the time Cardinal Lavigerie's White Fathers strode into sight in 1879, obliquely representing a second mighty European nation, the wily, uncomfortable Kabaka could obviously do no better for himself than to make them feel at home, too. They might be useful in the event of a hostile alliance being formed between the British and either the Arabs of Zanzibar or the Khedive's men from Egypt. The court was already divided into two strong religious factions, with one group identified with Islam, another with the CMS Protestants, both intriguing against each other, the Kabaka himself carefully blowing hot and cold upon each in turn. From now on there were three hats in the ring and Mutesa started to manipulate all of them with the uneasy skill of a juggler.

The first thing the White Fathers did was to disobey their founder's strict injunction to keep at least ten kilometres between themselves and the English Protestants. There were four hills in the capital. One was called Kampala and next to it, on Mengo Hill, sat the Kabaka's palace. Opposite, on Namirembe, was the CMS mission. The Catholics now set themselves up on Rubaga Hill itself, which placed them a little closer to the king than the Englishmen were. It meant that the distance separating the two missions was little more than a mile. Had the Fathers followed Lavigerie's orders precisely they would have been well outside the boundaries of the capital and their Protestant rivals would have had a clear advantage in exerting an influence upon the court and its followers. As it was, the chances of friction between the two groups were considerable. Alexander Mackay, for one, was not the man to take kindly to a Roman excursion into territory where he had already set up his own Christian standard. The friction began almost as soon as the White Fathers had unpacked.

Until the Catholics came Mutesa had, when the mood was upon him, gone through the dutiful motions performed by any rather distinguished adherent of the Church of England. Indeed, when the men of the CMS held their first service at his court, they had been pleasantly surprised by the volley of loud 'Amens' which had echoed round the building at the end of every prayer. The Kabaka, under their guidance, had started to lead discussion groups of impeccably Anglican felicity, had busied himself with distributing hymn sheets among his courtiers at the start of services, had behaved just like any God-fearing squire at home who subscribed equally to the divine right of landlords and the Thirty-Nine Articles. He was no longer to be such a reliable patron.

On the first Sunday after the arrival of the Catholics, Mackay went to the court early by himself. He found one of the White Fathers there, shook hands with him and then took a seat some distance away. Mutesa asked Mackay to pray as well as to read from the Bible. Mackay did so, noticing that the priest failed either to kneel during prayer or even to say 'Amen'. He also relayed to London his intelligence about the Frenchmen's presents to Mutesa – the five repeating rifles, the box of powder and shot, the 'embroidered military suits' and the cuirasses, helmets and officers' swords that went with these gaudy reach-me-downs from Paris. Before long there was open disputation at these services.

One Sunday, Mackay arrived at what Mutesa now seemed intent upon making a joint act of Christian witness, involving both Catholics and Protestants, without much sensitivity to the dogmatic differences and ritualistic tastes which separated them. Mackay was summoned by the Kabaka to come forward from this mixed congregation and read. 'They all knelt, and after opening the Prayer Book I said to M. Lourdel at my side, that we were going to pray, and perhaps he would kneel with us. He said he did not understand me, nor would he understand when told by one of the others in Swahili. So I went on and was not interrupted by the padres, only I heard one whisper to the other "Pater Noster" when I was reading the Swahili version of it. Prayers being over, I was asked to read the Scriptures as usual. I opened the book and commenced. The first sentence – "Ye know that after two days the Son of Man is delivered up to be crucified" – struck them by the accuracy of its prediction, and hence its testimony to the divinity of the "Son of Man". I never got farther. Mutesa, in his abrupt style, said to Toli; "Ask the Frenchmen if they do believe in Jesus Christ why don't they kneel down with us when we worship him every Sabbiti? Don't they worship Him?"

'M. Lourdel was spokesman. He became all at once very excited and said: "We do not join in that religion because it is not true. We do not know that book, because it is a book of lies. If we joined in that, it would mean that we were not Catholics, but Protestants, who have rejected the truth. For hundreds of years they were with us, but now they believe and teach only lies." Such was the drift of his excited talk, in a mixture of bad Arabic, Swahili, Luganda and French . . . Another asked me what I had to say. I felt sure that the moment was one requiring great coolness and great firmness, for my opponent's excited state might prove contagious; while his repeated denunciations of me as a liar (mwongo) could not be easily disproved on such an occasion – nor did I attempt to disprove it.

'I endeavoured to give the King a simple account of the history of the Church, and why we had left Rome. I stated as clearly as possible that our authority was the Word of God *only*, that the Romanists had the Pope as their head, while we had one head – Jesus Christ. I tried to smooth matters by saying that we had common belief in many things – one God, one Saviour, one Bible, one heaven and one law of life. But my friend would have no terms of peace. There was *one* truth, and he came to teach that, and we were liars! We were liars to say that they worshipped the Virgin Mary; we were liars to say that they regarded the Pope as infallible. The Pope was the king of "religion" in all the world. He was the successor of Peter, who was the successor of Christ. The Pope was the only authority to teach "the truth" in the world. Wherever we came to teach lies, the Pope sent his men to teach the truth. If what he said was not true, he would die on the spot, etc., etc.

'I listened calmly to all, and never replied to the padre. Only when the king asked me to speak, I quietly told him how "the truth" stood . . .

' "How can I know what is right and what is false?"

' "By appealing to the *Book*. You have the Gospel in Arabic and can read it."

' "Yes; and I have read it, and know that you teach only out of it."

' "Well, look and see if you find that Christ appointed a line of Popes as His successors to teach the truth."

'Never did I hear the word mwongo so frequently used. The padre was really, to say the least, not guilty of using too much of his native politesse. His Superior seemed to me at times to be persuading him to be quiet, and at others to be prompting him, but he spoke only in French. I could not but feel sorry for the king and his chiefs. Their feeling of hopeless bewilderment made them say "Every white man has a different religion".'

That sort of thing went on for years, while the Catholics acquired their own body of supporters in the land and their own nexus of chiefs at court, and the Protestants anxiously husbanded their converts and querulously registered their protests both in Rubaga and London at what they took to be this extremely unfair competition. The Baganda courtiers may or may not have been hopelessly bewildered by the variety of Christian experience they were invited to purchase; the intrigues which now took place in three different combinations at once were certainly enough to bewilder their Kabaka. He started to react as any man, black or white, might well do in such circumstances. He decided to get back to first principles and invoke the old pagan gods of his upbringing. He cried a plague on all the immigrant houses and began to make things unpleasant for Moslem, Protestant and Catholic alike. He was too intelligent, and fearful, to take direct action against the foreigners in his midst, beyond making it difficult for them to obtain all the supplies they needed. But he put a great deal of devious pressure on one group of converts after another and trusted that all proselytisers would get the message. They did. And in this unseasonably cold climate, the Catholics and the Protestants became friendly enough, in a suspicious sort of way, for the Frenchmen to help Mackay when he was ill. That downright anti-Papist found himself writing one night: 'The Frenchmen last evening sent a kind note saying that they heard that I was very ill, sending at the same time a bottle of wine and quinine in it, and offering us a milch cow.'

There were still severe limits upon this glimmering of Christian harmony. When Mutesa embarked upon a new series of executions the appalled Protestant missionaries sent a message to the Kabaka, beseeching him to be merciful and to remember the fifth commandment of the great God above, to believe that God would be very angry indeed if the butchery went on, that He would punish the Baganda and make their country very weak. At the same time, Mackay and his colleagues sent a message to the French Catholics, asking them to make a similar petition to Mutesa. The cautious reply from Father Livinhac was that 'The great idea which the people have here of the power of the English Consul at Zanzibar, and of the power of England in the whole world, permits you to hope that your words will be taken into consideration. For us, everybody knows very well that, coming from a country which has not even a king, we are only, in the idea of the Baganda, as little bagenyi (guests), without power, and we are sure that our intervention would be worthless. We cannot, therefore, interfere.'

Suddenly, Mutesa died. And it was perhaps the measure of the Christian success in his kingdom that he was the first Kabaka to be buried in European fashion. Previously, a Kabaka's corpse was borne a distance of eight hours' march from the capital. The lower jaw was amputated and put into an ant heap until the insects had picked it clean; it was then presented to the new Kabaka, covered with a woven pattern of beads, and kept by the old Kabaka's chief widow after that. The rest of the body was placed in the house of a peasant nearest to the terminal point of the cortege, the house was broken down around it and the thatched roof was pegged down over the remains to protect them from animals. But for Mutesa, Alexander Mackay produced a coffin more sumptuous even than the one he had made in his workshop years before for the Kabaka's mother. It took him a month to manufacture it, while the body was being mummified by squeezing out all the fluids with bark-cloth rags. The corpse was eventually placed in a large wooden box lined with calico. This was then put into a great coffin made of copper and bronze, which Mackay had laboriously created by beating out hundreds of trays, pots and drums into sheeting. So that the wooden coffin would lie snugly inside the copper one, it was packed tightly with thousands of yards of calico. Then the lids were screwed on; and the great metal case enshrining Mutesa was lowered into a pit, thirty feet deep, twenty feet long and fifteen feet wide, which had been lined with bark cloth.

The new Kabaka was the eighteen-year-old Mwanga and the choice of him from among Mutesa's multitude of sons was at first pleasing to the English and French alike. They had greatly feared the election of his brother Kalema, whose reputation for ruthlessness was such that Mwanga was comparatively nicknamed Mutefa (the Mild One). They soon discovered that this unstable young man had been badly misjudged. Mutesa had at least gone through long periods of mildness when it suited him. Almost the only sign of geniality which Mwanga exhibited was to have a pool excavated at the palace so that Robert Ashe could demonstrate the art of swimming to him, almost an unknown accomplishment in Buganda. From the moment he ascended the throne, Mwanga otherwise appeared to be nothing but a vicious barbarian through and through. He was also, to any Christian, infinitely more degraded than his father had been even when Mutesa had been wallowing most happily in concubinage. Mwanga had been much under the influence of the Arabs at court and he had become addicted to smoking bhang like them. Much worse, he had acquired a taste for sodomy.

The Arab faction now began to seed his readily suspicious mind with tales of Christian imperialism and, shortly after his accession, early in 1885, Mwanga acted. Three of the Christian boys at court, who had been baptised by the CMS missionaries, were tortured and then burnt alive.

'Our first martyrs,' wrote Mackay, 'have won the martyr's crown.' He and Ashe were knocked about by the palace guards when they attempted to intercede on the boys' behalf. There was nothing more they could do. There were even greater horrors in the offing.

Bishop James Hannington was on his way to Buganda. He had been chosen by the CMS to take charge of its expanding work in East Africa and he had decided to march inland to this important centre of operations by a route which would bring him into Buganda from the north. As everyone with some knowledge of the Baganda was well aware, this was folly. The Baganda had a deeply embedded tradition that if any foreigner entered their country from this direction, it would be the beginning of the end for them; they would be smothered by alien rule. Mackay and his colleagues had warned the Consul in Zanzibar that Hannington must on no account be allowed to travel along this route; the message evidently never reached its destination. The missionaries now sent runners who, they hoped, would be able to intercept Hannington before he reached a point of no return. They found him too late. He and his small party were seized on the threshold of Mwanga's kingdom, and Hannington's life was spared for some days while the border guards awaited specific instructions from Mwanga. The Bishop was in little doubt that he would soon be dead. The last entries in the diary which was later recovered from his body, a small volume with page after page covered in minute handwriting, are among the most moving documents ever to come out of Africa. They are the thoughts of a very frightened man who badly wants to muster the courage to meet his end with fortitude:

'October 21, 1885. To my joy I saw a splendid view of the Nile only about half an hour's distance, country being beautiful . . . when suddenly, about 20 ruffians set upon us. They violently threw me to the ground . . . Twice I nearly broke away from them, and then grew faint from struggling, and was dragged by the legs over the ground . . . my clothes torn to pieces, wet through, strained in every limb, and for a whole hour expecting death; hurried along, dragged, pushed, until we came to a hut, into the courtyard of which I was forced . . .

'October 22. I found myself last night on my bed in a fair-sized hut, but with no ventilation, floor covered with rotting banana peel and leaves and lice, in a feverish district, fearfully shaken, scarce power to hold up a small Bible. Shall I live through it? "My God, I am Thine."

'October 23. I woke full of pain and weak, yet they guard every move as if I were a giant. I don't see how I can stand all this, yet I don't want to give in . . .

'October 24. Thank God for a pleasant night. The day passed very quietly. I amused myself with Bible and diary.

'October 25. Still a great deal of pain in my limbs. When I was beginning to think of my time in prison as getting short, the chief has sent men to redouble the fence around me. What does it mean? Has a message arrived from Mwanga? The look of this has cast me down again. My guards and I are great friends, almost affectionate, and one speaks of me as "my white man". My men are kept in close confinement, except two, who come daily backwards and forwards to bring my food. This they take in turns and implore, so I hear, for the job.

'October 26. I am heavy and sleepy. If I mistake not, signs of fever creep over me. Today I am very broken down in health and spirits.

'October 27. I am very low in spirits, it looks so dark. I have been told that the first messengers would return at the latest today. I don't know what to think, and would say from the heart "Let the Lord do what seemeth Him good". I am very low and cry to God for release.

'October 28. A terrible night, first with my noisy, drunken guard and secondly with insects, which have found out my tent and swarm. I don't think I got one sound hour's sleep, and woke with fever fast developing. O Lord, do have mercy upon me, and release me. I am quite broken down and brought low. Comforted by reading Psalm 27 ("The Lord is my light and my salvation, whom shall I fear, etc"). Evening; fever passed away. News came that Mwanga has sent three soldiers, but what news they bring they will not yet let me know. Much comforted by Psalm 28; "Unto Thee, O Lord, will I call . . . The Lord is my strength and my shield, my heart hath trusted in Him and I am helped."

'October 29. I can hear no news, but was held up by Psalm 30, which came with great power. A hyaena howled near me last night, smelling a sick man, but I hope it is not to have me yet.'

The entries end there. That was the day they killed him.

At Rubaga the situation was so tense that Mackay had set up a native church council to take over the affairs of the Protestant mission in the event of all the Europeans being wiped out. The Englishmen had been refused permission to leave the land, just as they had been refused it when they wanted to go after the martyrdom of the three Baganda boys; they were reduced to sending messages to the coast by stealth, to describe their predicament to the Consul. Their murder was seriously discussed by Mwanga and his chief counsellors, but the CMS men were given warning by one of their converts and deflected the Kabaka by sending him the finest present they could manage, 'nearly a score of loads of our most valuable effects'. They did not mention their anxieties, but the bribe worked. And for several months the missionaries existed in fretful isolation, for Mwanga had now forbidden his people to have anything to do with them on pain of death. But his greatest outrage was yet to come. It sprang directly from a collision between Christian morality and the sexual habits he had picked up from the Arabs.

Mackay described it as 'an act of splendid disobedience and brave resistance to this Negro Nero's orders to a page of his, who absolutely refused to be made the victim of an unmentionable abomination. The lad was Christian and was threatened with instant death, but was ultimately only cruelly beaten.' In fact, the boy had been receiving instruction from one of the Protestant catechists when Mwanga desired his presence. The Kabaka went berserk with frustrated rage, summoned every page at court and asked these assembled boys which of them was Christian. Thirty of them stepped forward. The next fortnight was hideous with a series of atrocities. First a Protestant page was speared to death. Then three Catholic pages were beheaded. The next day two more Protestant lads were castrated and died, while a couple of Catholics were simply hacked to pieces. Others were picked off in ones and twos. For a few days there was a halt to this carnage. Then twenty-six of the pages, thirteen Catholics and thirteen Protestants, were taken sixteen miles from the capital and burned alive in one great pyre.

The immediate effect of this fresh series of martyrdoms was one which was to be noticed time and again wherever Christian missionaries worked throughout the world; indeed, it had been a curious reflex from the earliest days of Christian history in the Near East and elsewhere. Far from frightening off the existing converts, it evidently stimulated the recruitment of new ones. Within a week of the first Catholic death, the White Fathers had been begged to baptise 105 people who had just come under their instruction, while people who had previously shown little interest in the Christians began to come secretly to the mission at night. The Protestants could record a similar advance. The position of the missionaries themselves became more delicate than ever. Had Mwanga been more stable than he was, had he been strong as well as ruthless, there seems little doubt that they would have followed their slaughtered converts. But he was now rather a frightened man, with much blood on his hands that he believed might soon be avenged by the kinsmen of these white Christians. He announced that he regarded them as hostages. His hostility to them was so great that it is remarkable that Alexander Mackay was allowed to leave his kingdom just over a year later. The Scot travelled as far as Usambiro, on the southern shore of Lake Victoria, and there he stayed for the remaining three years of his life. A great deal of his time from now on would be taken up with urging the British Government, through its Consul on the coast, to press a division of the African interior upon all the European powers which might be interested – 'not for annexation, but for friendly negotiation with the natives and peaceful supervision . . . Each power, within the limits of its own supervision, will have a monopoly of trade and other means of investing and developing capital.'

Mackay had mellowed during his years with the Baganda. He could still be blistering about heathen degradation, but he could also express his shock at the apparent indifference of Christians at home to the martyrdom of black Christians in Africa when, at the same time, they could be roused to a fury at the murder of a white Christian like Bishop Hannington. Mackay was also now struggling to some understanding of Catholics. In the shared dangers of Mwanga's capital, he had discovered that the White Fathers were not quite as he had imagined such people years before, when he had been sailing past Spain and Malta. He wished now that Africans could understand that Christianity was cosmopolitan and not merely Anglican. But he never had time enough to close the emotional gap that had yawned between him and Rome since birth. 'The Papists are throwing a large force of priests into Uganda,' he wrote shortly before he died, 'and will now strain every nerve to win the land for Rome. I sometimes wish I were there to stir up our people to stand up for God's work and liberty, and save their country from the yoke of Popery.'

By the autumn of 1888 Mwanga's instability was such that he had reached the point achieved by his father before him. He planned to lead a pagan revival which would rid him of all the troublesome foreigners. But his was a curiously half-hearted strategy. He would entice all the Arabs and the Europeans, together with their supporters, on to an island in Lake Victoria, and there leave them to starve to death. The plot was discovered and, for once, all three alien influences united. Mwanga was deposed and sent packing to a distant part of the lake himself. A younger brother, Kiwewa, was enthroned in his place, a Catholic Muganda was declared chief minister, the other important offices of state were shared out between the victors, and freedom of conscience was offered to all.

It was a very brief coalition. Within a month the Arab leader in Rubaga, Selim Bey, a dropsical man so fat that he was unable to walk and had to travel everywhere by donkey, persuaded the new Kabaka that the Christians were hostile to him. That night the Arabs and their supporters stealthily surrounded all the Christians in the capital and drove them into the countryside. The missionaries of both parties were arrested and then they were expelled by boat across the lake. They travelled together for some distance and the hazards of the voyage (which included being capsized by a hippopotamus) improved their relationship considerably; the reports they sent home to Europe were mutually charitable. Nevertheless, the White Fathers settled at Bukumbi, some distance from the Anglican settlement at Usambiro.

The Arabs and their Moslem supporters were now to control Buganda for a year. One of the first things they did was to eject Kiwewa and replace him with their puppet, Kalema, his younger brother. Kiwewa had refused circumcision, for the Arabs now imposed their religion on everyone who was left in the capital. They also changed a number of customs in court; everyone now had to stand in their presence instead of sitting, which had been the tradition before. Mwanga, meanwhile, had arrived at the new mission of the White Fathers as a penitent and had been taken in as a refugee. Within a few months there was a concerted move by all the Christian Africans, now scattered around Lake Victoria, to restore him to his throne. The British Protestants at Usambiro declined to have anything to do with this, but the Catholic missionaries were agreeable. So was someone else, and he was the old CMS missionary Charles Stokes, who had long ago discarded Christian preaching for gun-running. It was in one of Stokes's boats that at the end of April 1889 Mwanga set sail for the borders of his old kingdom. Stokes landed the ex-Kabaka on an island only eight miles from Rubaga and, while Mwanga gathered about him an army to fight the Arabs, the Englishman returned down the lake to organise a supply of guns and ammunition. Mwanga passed the time by addressing a petition to Mr F. J. Jackson, who was known by then to be leading a caravan of the Imperial British East Africa Company towards Buganda from the coast.

The refugees at the foot of Lake Victoria had heard, a few months before, at the start of the year, that the company had just been given its royal charter by Queen Victoria. At the same time, news arrived that Britain and Germany had agreed upon a demarcation line for their respective spheres of influence in East Africa, which was to run from the coast to Lake Victoria. The effect of this intelligence upon the white missionaries was to influence forthcoming events in Buganda profoundly. To the British Protestants it was a signal that help in their great mission was at last imminent. No longer would they be facing the barbarities of any Kabaka in isolation, and no longer would they be obliged, in extreme situations, to look for immediate moral and physical support to a neighbouring handful of Europeans for whom they felt, in their bones, a deep and nagging aversion which embraced theology, morals and politics in almost equal proportions. Henceforth they could act more boldly, out of strength. As for the French Catholics, the news from Europe could only make them even more wary of their neighbours in God than before. The ancient heretical foe was now to be fortified by the vast power of its secular arm, which could only make the conversion of souls to the true faith more difficult than ever. In any confrontation which might take place here in future, European support could now come from only one direction. Germany, alas, was not a Catholic power like France. But at least the Germans would need no persuading that it might be expedient to counteract the spiritual imperialism of the British.

In the next twelve months one event succeeded another in rapid confusion; but by the end of that time the Christians of Buganda had manoeuvred themselves into fixed positions from which there would be no budging except by open war. In October, Mwanga led a joint army of African Catholics and Protestants back into Rubaga, without the help of a single white man. By the end of November, the Arabs and their Moslem supporters had driven him back to his islands again. While these battles were going on, Mwanga had managed to continue his correspondence with Mr Jackson. First, the Company leader had advised Mwanga that he was not entering the country at all; in fact, Jackson had instructions from his superiors not to get involved in the bewildering developments surrounding the Kabaka. On receiving another appeal for aid, Jackson had firmly suggested that the price would be not only material compensation from Mwanga but a treaty into the bargain. Mwanga prevaricated; he was well aware that treaties usually meant death to local kingdoms. Jackson sent, in return, the Company's flag. If Mwanga accepted this, it would mean help from the Company and a treaty from Mwanga. Then Jackson, to underline his supreme indifference to the outcome, tacked off on an excursion to procure ivory for the commercial interests he was chiefly representing. At this point, the Catholic and Anglican missionaries made their last united stand. They advised Mwanga to accept the Jackson offer. Even British Protestant domination was, to the Frenchmen, better than the totally inimical rule of Islam. Mwanga despatched his runners to the east and retained the flag.

It was now February 1890 and, almost at once, Mwanga's men defeated the Arab forces in a canoe battle on Lake Victoria. They seized a great quantity of arms and ammunition. Thus reinforced, they made another attempt on their capital and secured it conclusively. Two weeks later the

Christian alliance was once more in fragments. The German Carl Peters unexpectedly arrived in Rubaga. He was aware how things stood, for he had marched through Jackson's base camp a fortnight before, while the Englishman was away ivory-trading, and had read all the correspondence between Company and Kabaka. In Europe, the British and German Governments had reached their agreement about a demarcation line extending to the eastern shores of Lake Victoria but they had not yet committed this to a signed document; the Germans, in fact, were playing for time while Peters prospected as fast as he could in order to extend the boundary of German influence. He now proposed to Mwanga a treaty which he knew to be an improvement, in the Kabaka's eyes, on that which Jackson had offered. The White Fathers immediately advised Mwanga to treat with the Germans, and they could absolve their consciences with the reflection that Jackson's promised help undoubtedly had not materialised. The Kabaka and his Catholic chiefs signed without compunction; the Protestant chiefs added their marks with reluctance, finally persuaded by the knowledge that the Moslems were only a little distance away and known to be regrouping for another attack. The British missionaries were conspicuously not invited to be present at the treaty-making. They seethed at a distance. 'Nothing in the circumstances,' wrote Ashe, 'more clearly showed their hostility to the English Company than the action of Peters and the priests, and the attitude taken up by them towards the English missionaries.'

No sooner were the signatures dry upon the paper, than Peters and his men withdrew. The treaty, in fact, was to be invalidated by the Anglo-German Agreement ratified in Berlin that July. But locally it did enormous damage. Peters had decamped when news arrived that Jackson was at last only just over the horizon. When Jackson and his column marched into town, armed with 180 Snider rifles, the Company leader was very angry. He at once accused Mwanga of duplicity and now proposed a treaty which even Ashe thought 'certainly unreasonable in its demands'. The Protestant chiefs were eager to accept it, Mwanga was not and Ashe thought that Mwanga, for once, was in the right. Father Lourdel, now in charge of the White Fathers, inevitably sided with Mwanga, and the Catholic chiefs followed suit. The Protestant chiefs threatened to leave the country if the treaty with Jackson was not signed and in this notion they were encouraged by Jackson's second-in-command, Gedge. The Catholics, feeling that they could not hold Rubaga for Christendom alone, then said they would have to leave if the Protestants left. For the time being, the treaty was left unsigned, while Jackson returned to the coast to take superior advice on what to do, leaving Gedge and a platoon of soldiery in Rubaga.

For the next six months the mutual suspicion of the two Christian parties deepened, while that old Anglican Charles Stokes regularly ran consignments of arms and ammunition up the lake on behalf of Mwanga and his Catholic chiefs. Jackson never returned to the scene of his negotiations. But early in December 1890 his successor arrived without invitation. This was Captain F. D. Lugard, who had replaced Jackson as the Company's accredited agent in this bewildering sphere of influence.

Lugard marched into the capital of the Baganda at the head of a column consisting of 270 porters and one hundred good fighting men, which included fifty highly trained Sudanese and Somali infantry. They had brought with them a new device in armaments; a Maxim machine gun. It was a peremptory arrival, and even Robert Ashe reported it as such. 'Lugard, without permission from the king, and in spite of Mwanga's measures to prevent it, forced his way to the capital, and established an armed camp on Kampala Hill, within a rifle shot of Mwanga's enclosure.'

There was to be another new character on stage before the year's end. This was Bishop Alfred Tucker, who had replaced poor Hannington in East Africa. He was overjoyed at the size of his Christmas congregation in the CMS mission church on Namirembe Hill. But he was astonished to find that almost every man in his congregation had brought a rifle with him. Buganda, he said later, was like a volcano on the verge of an eruption.

14

THE BATTLE OF MENGO

Captain Lugard's brief was a ridiculous one. He was an unknown officer of thirty-two when he reached Buganda and, in the whole of the distinguished career that lay ahead of him, he would never again be working to a set of instructions which so combined supreme optimism with an unworkable basic assumption. He had been told by his superiors emphatically that the two Christian factions 'were animated by the most deadly hatred of each other, and that war had been imminent between them for some time'. He was invited to maintain order in this situation, while showing the strictest impartiality between the Catholics led by Frenchmen and the Protestants led by his own kinsmen. It would not be completely fair to blame the Company directors for this quaint order of the day, for they had been under much pressure from the Government and the public in Britain to send the column to Buganda in the first place. And they were conscious that they might be asking rather a lot of this promising young officer when they drafted his instructions. If he found it quite impossible to pursue a middle course through the morass of Ganda Christian politics, he should, they added, preferably 'consolidate the Protestant party'.

Lugard reached the capital after a long forced march which had taken it out of his column in more ways than one. It was low on ammunition and it bore all the marks of heavy going through jungle and bush. Lugard himself, in order to impress the natives of Rubaga, discarded his ragged uniform on the outskirts of the town and donned his rather splendid pyjama jacket, which happened to be adorned with brass buttons and gold braid. Then he led his troops past the swampy valley the Kabaka

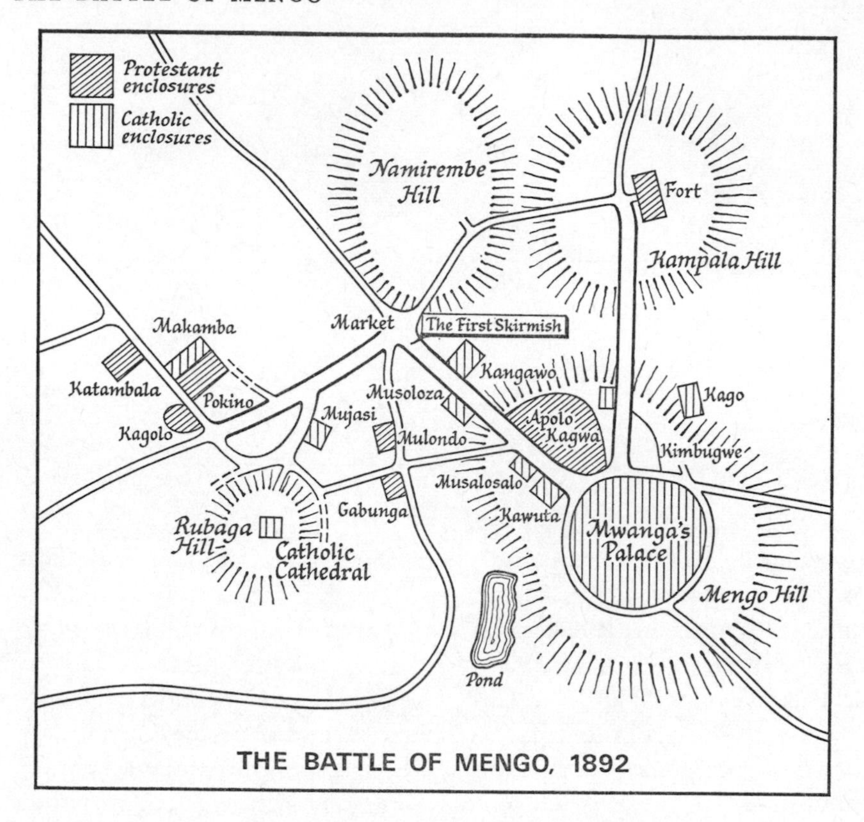

THE BATTLE OF MENGO, 1892

had reluctantly set aside for him, marched them to the summit of Kampala Hill and set up the Company flag, with the Union Jack in one corner and a large and rising sun emblazoned across the middle.

Whether or not his orders had been accurate in implying deadly hatred between the Christians, Lugard was soon in no doubt that they were not much inspired by Christian love for each other. The Frenchmen declined to attend his first interview with Mwanga, saying they would take no further part in politics; so two of the CMS men, Walker and Gordon, did all the translating. The question of the treaty was first broached a couple of days before Christmas and a large collection of highly excited chiefs had gathered at the court to hear the discussion. Each one of them was armed, the Catholics to support the Kabaka against the English and the Protestants to defend Lugard. One man actually levelled his rifle at Lugard's chest, but a Protestant chief beat it down angrily and it was not raised again. Lugard was a courageous man, but it may have been this hostile environment as much as anything which caused him to dilute the treaty he now proposed to Mwanga. One clause in it stipulated that the treaty would be rendered invalid, should a 'greater' European come later. The other conceded that the Company flag need not be flown anywhere in the capital other than over the Company camp on Kampala Hill. Lugard concealed any disappointment he might have felt by noting in his journal that it was not worth making a childish fuss about; but the concession was of great importance to Mwanga for, as Lugard knew, flying the flag over the palace would have meant a surrender of sovereignty. The concession did little to relieve the tension in the capital. On the first Sunday after Christmas, Bishop Tucker was even more astonished than he had been on Christmas Day; this time his armed congregation stumbled out of their pews before the service was over, in response to a false alarm that fighting had just broken out. Not long afterwards, His Lordship thoughtfully left Namirembe for some of the less belligerent corners of his vast diocese.

War scares occurred almost daily. One of the CMS missionaries, Gordon, wrote at this time that 'one day all is quiet and the principal chiefs of the opposite religions are paying each other friendly visits. The next day the chiefs and their followers are buckling on their cartridge belts and preparing for deadly conflict.' Lugard noted that the Protestant chiefs seemed keenest on provoking hostilities by making threats; and they used one crisis as an excuse for indiscriminate looting. The Catholics were not much slower to beat their own war drums, and their Muganda leader said on one occasion that he thought nothing would be settled until the two parties had fought it out. For the moment, there was little that Lugard could do except build a fort on Kampala Hill as rapidly as possible, and thus be ready for the worst. He was anxiously awaiting reinforcements, though the opportunist Charles Stokes offered to sell him arms at a price so exorbitant that Lugard briskly turned it down. At the end of January 1891, the reinforcements arrived, led by Captain Williams of the Royal Artillery, 'a typical specimen of the best class of British officer'.

Lugard now felt strong enough to try to settle some of the outstanding differences between the Catholics and Protestants. The greatest immediate bone of contention was the division of state offices among the chiefs of the two factions. When Mwanga had been restored to his throne, these positions of influence and power had been divided equally between Protestant and Catholic chiefs. At the same time it was acknowledged that if a chief changed his religious allegiance, he would have to vacate the office that had gone to him through his first religious affiliation. This would involve much more than a loss of status. A great deal of land, together with the allegiance of the peasants who tilled it, went with the office; it was not something that a chief took with him on an hereditary basis.

The fact that Mwanga himself, for the time being, was professing Catholicism, was a considerable attraction, for the Kabaka's patronage was the most important thing for any Muganda to secure. As a result, the Catholic party was distinctly in the ascendancy. A number of chiefs had converted to Catholicism in order to secure the Kabaka's favour and had submitted to the 'shamba eviction' from office, with its loss of land and peasant allegiance, as a result. A lot more would be prepared to follow suit if only they did not have to yield their office at the same time. The Catholics were now, therefore, pressing vigorously to have the arrangement altered, so that a man changing his faith could retain his office and the power that went with it. They were mustering behind the battle cry 'freedom of conscience'. The Protestants, knowing well that any such change would weaken them even further, were arguing fiercely that the original agreement should be maintained, and that all converts should be evicted from office.

The white missionaries were not aloof from this struggle. Bishop Hirth of the White Fathers, arrived in February and at once raised the question of religious freedom on behalf of his adherents. The CMS men naturally backed their own supporters and pressed for a maintenance of the *status quo*, though one member of the mission, Pilkington, started to tell some of the chiefs that they should abandon the thought of political power and seek the Kingdom of God instead. Lugard, in the middle of this argument, thought very little of either side. All the missionaries, he decided 'believed implicitly the statements of their own party. The Frenchmen wrote to Europe of . . . the heretical Protestants – and insisted that their own patient converts had suffered continuous injustice and violence from them. The English missionaries similarly believed that injury after injury had been patiently endured by their flock, who had done nothing by way of reprisal. My own belief was that the Baganda were par excellence the greatest liars of any nation or tribe I had met or heard of, and that it appeared to be a point of honour that each side should out-lie the others – especially to their missionaries . . .'

It was while this wrangle was proceeding, with Lugard concluding that he could not deal with religious freedom until a new treaty was signed, that the Moslems regrouped on the borders of Buganda for another attack on its divided Christian citadel. Differences were promptly forgotten in the face of a common enemy and a joint army marched to repulse the threat, the moment being marred only by the refusal of the Catholic troops to march under the Company banner. The Moslems were defeated in one battle. Whereupon Lugard, with a somewhat odd confidence in the

10. His Eminence Cardinal Lavigerie, founder of the most famous Catholic missionary order in Africa, the White Fathers.

11. The mausoleum which Cardinal Lavigerie built to contain his body, ten years before he actually died, in Carthage Cathedral.

12. The first party of White Fathers to go from North Africa to Buganda, in 1878. Father Livinhac is in the middle of the front row; Father Lourdel is next to him, to the right.

13. The church of St Paul, belonging to the Anglican CMS, on Namirembe Hill, Uganda, at the time of the Battle of Mengo.

14. The interior of St Paul's Church (above), with the communion rail running between the roof posts, and the communion table in the foreground.

15. Robert Ashe, the CMS missionary who introduced the bicycle to Africa, riding his machine down a track past three astonished lions.

16. Mwanga, King of the Baganda, who was Moslem, Protestant and Catholic in turn, and whose realm was a bone of contention for all three sects.

17. The martyrdom of the Christian Pages at Namugongo, Buganda, in 1886. An atrocity by a maddened king which became a chapter of Christian (and especially Catholic) hagiography.

18. The crucial charge of Sudanese troops under the command of Lugard's aide, Captain Williams, which settled the religious Battle of Mengo.

stability of the Christian alliance, marched out of the country with almost all his troops on an expedition to show the Company flag in Equatoria, and to recruit more soldiery. In Mwanga's capital he left Captain Williams and a small handful of native troops.

The next nine months were uncommonly trying for Williams who was, indeed, a fine specimen of the British officer class. He was brave, straightforward, totally reliable and rather obtuse. He was certainly not up to coping with the complexities of the situation he had inherited. He was open-minded enough to accept the arguments of Bishop Hirth in favour of religious freedom, which he doubtless thought was something every British officer had been gazetted to defend. He therefore began to advance the argument upon the Protestant chiefs. He proposed that after an interim of two years everyone should accept liberty of conscience and allow chiefs to shift faiths without loss of office. Grudgingly, the Protestant chiefs assented, taking the view that this quixotic young Englishman would by then be serving his Queen in some other outpost of God's Empire and that the Company itself would be so powerful in Buganda that their own position would be unassailable. Unfortunately, Bishop Hirth had an instinct for diplomacy which was totally lacking in the Captain. He now sent a very cordial message to Kampala Fort which pointed out that if, as he understood, the principle of religious freedom was accepted, what point was there in waiting two years before applying it in practice? The Captain, dutifully following the logic of this suggestion, hastened once more to the Protestant chiefs. They were even less enamoured of this proposal than they had been of its predecessor, but they could for the moment see no alternative to complying with it; on one condition. This was that British authority in the land should be unfeignedly proclaimed by the Kabaka flying the Company flag over his palace. Captain Williams obligingly went on that errand, too. He was rather surprised when Mwanga and his Catholic chiefs told him that it was just about the last thing they were prepared to do.

Williams now committed one more gaffe in the eyes of the Protestants – missionaries as well as chiefs. The Catholic chiefs were solidly behind Mwanga as long as it suited their purpose. But they had been sufficiently converted to Christian morality to become increasingly restless at his continuing sodomy; they had regarded it with some distaste even before conversion. They were also, of course, fearful of his traditional inherited power. They now seized a number of the page-boys with whom the Kabaka had been consorting and, according to Robert Ashe, had them put to death. Mwanga was at once furious and terrified of the repercussions upon himself. He therefore made overtures to the Protestants and offered to convert himself to their party. Possibly it was a matter of principle for Williams to receive this proposition coolly; maybe he was so confused by the deviousness he had found at every turn that he felt unequal to a solution. At any rate, he advised Mwanga to await Lugard's return before acting. 'Thus,' wrote Ashe, 'a golden opportunity was neglected, and the king was lost to the English cause.'

The war scares continued and skirmishes took place, while Captain Williams's energies ebbed. On one occasion Protestant tribesmen mustered with their arms in front of Kampala Fort and the Catholics asked Williams to disperse them. He replied that he was too tired to drive them away; and by then he probably was. He had spent weeks dashing round the countryside with his handful of askaris, to the scene of actions which were over and done with by the time he arrived. The bloodshed and the violence were not confined to Protestants and Catholics alone. Father Achté, of the Catholic mission, led a couple of hundred armed converts to the Sese Islands in Lake Victoria and there burned down a pagan temple. When pagans destroyed the house of a Protestant chief on another island, the Catholics were blamed and the Protestants took reprisals. When the Sese pagans struck back at the Catholics, the Protestants were blamed and the British Government eventually had to pay the Catholics compensation. Meanwhile, the French missionaries had started to construct a fort of their own on Rubaga Hill, a solid brick construction with bastions at the corners and loopholes for marksmen in the walls. The Frenchmen were also importing breech-loading rifles from the coast, smuggling them through the port of entry concealed in innocent loads.

This was the situation confronting Captain Lugard when he returned to Kampala Fort on the last day of 1891, loaded with his own extra supplies of arms and ammunition, heading a column which was reinforced by one hundred Sudanese troops. He was now in a position to act much more strongly than when he had left the capital in the spring. He was put in the mood for strong action by almost the first thing he observed on returning to the capital. Over the Kabaka's palace there was flying a new and much larger version of Mwanga's flag – two spears and a shield picked out in white on a red ground; Lugard described it as 'an ENORMOUS flag on a very high flagstaff'. The Kabaka had evidently become defiant in his absence. Conceivably it was this defiance which determined Lugard to ignore the first letter he opened on reaching the fort. It had been despatched by the Company in London in October and it ordered him to evacuate Buganda immediately. It was, in fact, to be countermanded by a new set of instructions which reached Lugard five days later; and these new instructions were issued largely as a result of CMS pressure in England.

The Government of Lord Salisbury had failed to get a subsidy for the Company through Parliament and in September 1891 the Company's head, Sir William McKinnon, had told the CMS that unless £40,000 could be raised by private subscription, Lugard would have to be withdrawn, as the Company simply could not afford to maintain a private army which seemed increasingly to be at the disposal of Anglican missionaries. McKinnon, who had always been a fervent supporter of missionary work, offered to produce £10,000 himself and to persuade friends to subscribe another £15,000; but the CMS would have to raise the remaining £15,000 from its own resources. For a month no money had come into the offices at Salisbury Square, in response to the CMS appeal, and the Company had issued its instructions for evacuation. But then Bishop Tucker, home on leave, had addressed a meeting of the Gleaners Union in impassioned terms about the need to fortify this Protestant bastion in East Africa. Within half an hour not only banknotes, but watches and jewellery, had been placed on the collecting plates by a thoroughly roused audience. A few days later the CMS had raised £16,000, and the Company was able to issue its countermanding order.

It is clear, however, that Lugard's responsibility for subsequent events was detached from the Company instructions and from the CMS efforts which produced them. He was evidently prepared to act as he did in defiance of orders. He was relatively unmoved by Mwanga's most recent accession of Catholic fervour; for after the rebuff by Williams, the Kabaka had thrown himself into his nominal Christian duties with renewed vigour, even attending mass on New Year's Day, with the Catholic chiefs competing for the honour of carrying him into the White Fathers' church on their shoulders. The symbolism of the flag, however, was much more important to Lugard than Mwanga's haphazard church-going. It was this subject that he brought up on his first communication with Mwanga, but the Kabaka would not budge from his independent stand. After a while Lugard dropped the matter. But his cast of mind seems clear from a message which he soon sent to the White Fathers, whose fortress on Rubaga Hill was still incomplete. He begged them that if war should break out they would come and take refuge in the Company fort on Kampala Hill. In short, he was prepared for action against Africans and he was anxious to protect the lives of Europeans whose creeds, hostile to each other, were responsible for the battle lines which would be drawn among the Baganda. The Frenchmen treated his offer with silence. Nevertheless, the missionaries of both denominations got on far better with each other than a cursory view of this mounting civil war might suggest. According to Robert Ashe, 'There were, of course, the religious differences between the Roman and Anglican Churches, which everyone knows, but that there was any personal prejudice or animosity between the missionaries of the two Churches I can happily most unhesitatingly deny.'

The crisis now escalated rapidly. Conflict was finally precipitated after a series of gun thefts which had lasted for several weeks. In the latest of these, a Catholic chief called Mugoloba went to complain that a rifle had been taken by a Protestant. He made his representations to the Protestant Chief Minister, Kagwa, and Kagwa agreed that restitution ought to be made. He was not particularly eager to speed this up, however, since he was himself trying to force the leading Catholic minister to yield a gun that had been stolen from his men earlier. After four days of inaction Mugoloba decided to take the law into his own hands. There was a beer stall on a nearby street and he posted one of his retainers close to it. When a group of Protestants stopped to buy beer, the retainer seized the rifle belonging to one of them and raced into Mugoloba's compound, pursued by the Protestants. As they approached the gates, Mugoloba opened fire on the pursuers and one of them fell dead. Immediately the news reached Kagwa, he sent a message to Kampala Fort, informing Lugard of the outrage and demanding that justice be done.

For the first time in months. Lugard went in person to the Kabaka's palace to demand that Mugoloba be dealt with as a murderer. Lugard was a very determined man when he arrived at Mengo and his reception there was not calculated to soften his feelings towards Mwanga. 'I was kept waiting,' he writes, 'a long time outside his enclosure in a boiling, hot sun. This waiting is a well-understood discourtesy, and when continued beyond a certain point, is an insult.' Worse, after he had made his point to Mwanga, he was kept waiting even longer while Mugoloba and the witnesses to the incident were summoned. For Mwanga had agreed that the Catholic chief should be tried at once. While the participants were being fetched, Lugard was made even more angry because the Kabaka and his Catholic chiefs were giggling and laughing between themselves. Lugard assumed they were laughing at him. He also assumed that the devious Mwanga had no intention of trying the case properly, turned on his heel and walked out of Mengo palace in the direction of Kampala Fort. He left behind his interpreter to report what happened and later was told that Mwanga had exonerated Mugoloba. The Protestants, it was decided, had taken the law into their own hands instead of reporting the theft and Mugoloba had fired upon them in self-defence when they were about to break into his compound. According to Baganda law, this was an impeccable judgment by the Kabaka.

Lugard was not disposed to accept it as such. Nor were the Protestant missionaries, who sent him a letter urging him to press Mwanga for the surrender of Mugoloba. Mwanga refused and Lugard concluded that the Kabaka and the Catholics were now ready for open war. That night he noted in his journal that the French White Fathers had been telling their adherents that 'we were only a trading company, and that one of them had said he could drive us out of Kampala with a stick, and not a gun would be fired'. Then he issued forty muzzle-loading rifles and a barrel of powder to the Protestant chiefs. The next day, Saturday, 23 January 1892, Lugard received a message from Mwanga. It told him that the Kabaka was well aware of the armaments distributed the night before – though it exaggerated the number of rifles issued – and protested that this would be taken as a sign that Lugard would be happy to see Mwanga slain in battle. Lugard sent a message by return, which told Mwanga that if Mugoloba were not yielded there would indeed be war. As soon as darkness fell, the Kabaka had eight barrels of gunpowder brought from an island in Lake Victoria to the palace on Mengo Hill.

There were no public church services in the capital that Sunday morning. War drums had been beating all night and everyone was in a state of high excitement. 'All felt that the day of battle had come,' writes Ashe, 'which was to decide the fate of the English Company and the Protestant faction.' The correspondence between Mengo and Kampala still continued, however, while the White Fathers said mass alone and Mr Roscoe of the CMS read the Bible with a few of his more earnest converts. First a letter from Mwanga begged Lugard to stop war from breaking out. Next, a letter from Lugard replied that he would surely do this if Mugoloba was sent to him, together with an apology for the insults Lugard had endured at the palace. As soon as he had signed this message, Lugard broke open his arsenal in the fort and issued something approaching five hundred guns to the Protestants, among them 150 rapid-firing Snider rifles. Then he once more invited all the European missionaries to take shelter in Kampala Fort. The Frenchmen declined, on the grounds that Bishop Hirth was 'indisposed'. The Englishmen replied that they could only come if their goods came with them; so Lugard sent forty porters over to assist the CMS party to his refuge.

At about eleven o'clock Mr Roscoe's Bible-reading was interrupted by the sound of shots. The Protestants brought in a wounded man. Lugard immediately sent another message across the valley to Mengo, demanding that retribution for this latest offence must also be added to his earlier requirements. Mwanga swiftly sent a reply that the culprit was on his way and a bound man soon appeared. It turned out that he was merely an unfortunate fellow who had been seized as substitute for whoever had fired the wounding shot. 'I therefore could not execute him,' said Lugard later; but he took the man's arrival as a sign that Mwanga was at last climbing down from his insolent position. He and Williams were congratulating themselves that the crisis might now be over when several more shots were heard. Then there was what Pilkington, of the CMS, describes as 'a terrible volley from the Protestants at the foot of Namirembe'. It was three o'clock in the afternoon and the Battle of Mengo had just begun.

It lasted for a couple of hours, in a series of sprawling sallies up and down the four hills of the capital. It started when a group of Catholics went to demonstrate their contempt for the Protestants by hurling insults outside the compound of the Protestant chief Kagwa, close to the Kabaka's palace on Mengo Hill. Insults were exchanged by both sides, then gunfire, and a Protestant fell dead. A huge crowd of armed Protestants, meanwhile, had grouped near the empty CMS mission at the foot of Namirembe Hill, about a mile away. On hearing the shots from the direction of Mengo, they started up the road towards Kagwa's enclosure and the palace. Their way was blocked by the compounds of two Catholic chiefs and they were fired upon from these. They replied with the thunderous fusillade that Pilkington and the other English missionaries heard in the Company fort on Kampala Hill. Yet the Catholics had them pinned down and, in an effort to break out of this stalemate, one of the Protestant leaders began to move round the Catholic emplacements with most of his men. They left behind a handful under the command of the leading Protestant elder, Sembera Mackay, who was later described by Ashe as 'simple saint and hero'. Mackay decided to rush up the road past the flanking Catholics. As he did so the Catholics opened fire again and he fell, mortally wounded, handing his gun over to one of his men and telling them to continue the advance.

The main party of Protestants may or may not have intended to attack the palace of Mengo. But their encircling movement had brought them close to the foot of the capital's fourth hill, Rubaga, on which stood another prize; the mission of the White Fathers and the great reed and wooden cathedral that was nearing completion there. At once they began to climb Rubaga. So did another squadron of Protestants which had set off from Namirembe after them. A handful of this assault force was wounded in the ascent, but the Catholic troops on Rubaga were small in number, the majority of their forces being grouped on Mengo to protect the Kabaka. The Rubaga Catholics were sent in flight and, ignoring the White Fathers crouched in their fort, the Protestant army put torches to the cathedral. Within minutes, flames had engulfed the building and it stood like a huge beacon, visible for miles out into the country and across the lake.

Now came the crucial engagement of the afternoon. The bulk of the Catholic forces, probably stirred to counter-attack by the sight of the burning cathedral, poured out of their emplacements around Mengo Palace and rushed upon Kagwa's enclosure. He and his men at once retreated in the direction of Kampala Fort, with the Catholics in pursuit. Robert Ashe, for one, was in no doubt that they made for Kampala rather than Namirembe or Rubaga because they wished to involve Lugard and his professional troops in the battle – 'naturally,' he writes, 'it was the policy of their prudent leader to put Kampala Fort between the enemy and himself, especially as Captain Lugard had shown signs of not interfering more actively than by arming the Protestant faction'. Lugard's account makes it obvious that he was spoiling for a chance to join battle. Kagwa's Protestants came pounding up Kampala Hill towards the fort and passed round the other side of it. The Catholic army came panting after them. They had reached the foot of Mengo and were about to cross the narrow strip of land that separated it from Kampala, when Lugard opened up on them with his Maxim machine gun, at 1,400 yards range.

'By a wonderful piece of good fortune,' he writes, '(for my estimate of the distance was a guess) my calculation and my sighting were correct, and my shots went in among the enemy even at this extreme range . . .' He was aiming for the narrow path down Mengo Hill, for on either side and in the valley were banana plantations which made concealment easy and firing a waste of ammunition. As two or three men fell, the Catholics leapt for cover among the bananas. If they were to continue their advance they would have to break across a potato field and they would be fully visible there. They did continue their advance and they did break cover, and again the machine gun opened up on them, and once more two or three men dropped. The gun had been liable to jam after every few shots, but Lugard was very proud indeed of the efficiency of this weapon. 'The moral effect of this long-distance shooting, and the apparent ubiquity of the Maxim, was incalculable . . . I don't suppose a dozen men were hit, and probably not more than half a dozen killed by my fire. Yet I had broken up their charge and dispersed and terrified them. And thus I maintain that the Maxim saved a good deal of bloodshed . . .'

It certainly had not saved the bloodshed which now took place in hand-to-hand combat among the banana plantations. Seeing their enemy in disarray, Kagwa and his Protestants went back down the hill to fight them without Captain Lugard's aid. Very soon it was clear that the Catholics were getting the upper hand with this variety of warfare. Once again, Lugard came to the rescue of the Protestants. 'I seized the critical moment to order our line forward under Williams, while I covered the advance with the gun. There was no holding our Sudanese and Zanzibaris! Down the hill they went with a rush, full of excitement and mad for a fight.' Those two hundred troops were so keen to get among the Baganda that Captain Williams had difficulty in keeping up with them. He was only just in time to stop them setting Mengo Palace on fire, the Catholics having fled up Mengo Hill and down the other side in the face of their frightening rush. According to Lugard, by now 'Flames were rising in every direction, in spite of my indignant orders, for the Katikiro* and chiefs were powerless to stay the excited rabble, who were scouring the country in every direction – mad to burn the houses of their detested rivals'. At last Mwanga's ENORMOUS flag was hauled down from the palace and the Company's standard hoisted in its place.

As for the Kabaka himself, he had escaped. Ashe put it this way, 'Mwanga, as soon as the fighting began, followed the dictates of one of his ruling passions, namely that of terror, and fled towards the Nyanza.' By the time the Protestants stood triumphantly in possession of all four hills in the capital, Mwanga and the dispersed Catholic forces had taken refuge on the island of Bulingugwe. Not so, the White Fathers. Somehow, they emerged from the smoking ruins on Rubaga Hill without injury though, according to Bishop Hirth, they had been fired upon by the Protestants and thought they were going to be burnt alive when the cathedral went up in flames. 'Some catechumens were there, who had not yet been regenerated. These were the young children who, after seeing their masters fall, had been able, through fire and flames, to reach our house. They were all cleansed in the saving waters, and I gave the last absolution to all the Christians and to the missionaries, and received it myself from the Father Superior. It only remained to die. Our aggressors, meanwhile, happily ignorant of our retreat amid the flames, withdrew to pursue our Christians. The firing altogether ceased . . . Through the black smoke which covered the capital-reduced-to-ashes, two of our children volunteered to go in order to carry to the fort a note, in which I made a last appeal to the humanity of Captain Lugard. An hour

* The Katikiro was the Prime Minister; i.e. Kagwa.

afterwards the captain arrived himself with a strong force. Our lives were saved. We had passed two mortal hours surrounded by the flames . . .'

Lugard arrived at a rapid trot, for he was seriously worried about the consequences that might have befallen him if the Frenchmen had been killed by any of his bullets. One man in the priests' party had, in fact, been killed. He was Francis Goge, the Catholic mission doctor, but as he was a Hausa his death was unlikely to create much of a stir in Europe, with plenty of other black corpses on the ground. Lugard was more troubled by the thought of the razed cathedral. To the White Fathers 'I expressed my bitter sorrow at the day's work, and indeed I felt well-nigh unmanned at the destruction in 12 hours of a year's hard work, and at the devastation I saw around me'. The Fathers, standing in the ruins of their mission, offered Lugard wine and said how delighted they were that at least their store had escaped the fire. They then taxed Lugard's offer of help somewhat beyond his expectations. They collected a mass of refugee women and children and shepherded them over to the fort and were not content, according to Lugard, that these should be treated like other natives; the priests wanted their Catholic adherents sheltered inside the fort 'and filled our dining-house with them to the exclusion of ourselves . . .'. Worse, the Catholic Baganda swaggered about as though the place belonged to them. 'We were ready to stand anything for the priests, to show our anxiety to make amends for their hardships, and the chagrin they must feel at the defeat of their party; but it was very trying, for the new store was full of wounded, as well as the bathroom, the verandah and every available corner. Our own men were lying out in the open (for the night was fine) but this was not good enough for the Roman Catholic refugees.'

Lugard sent a message to Mwanga, urging him to return to the capital. Two days after the battle, Bishop Hirth set off for Bulingugwe with his six priests in order to add his own pressure to Lugard's upon the Kabaka. Once there, he did nothing of the sort. In his own words, the Catholic fugitives now had a choice between apostasy, death or exile. He advised exile. After waiting for five more days, Lugard acted again. News came that a flotilla of Catholic canoes had attacked some Protestant boatmen on the lake, securing booty and prisoners. He ordered Captain Williams and one hundred Sudanese troops to march for the lake, taking the Maxim with them. It was now 30 January and, with Williams on the shore, covering his men with the machine gun, fifteen canoes full of askaris paddled towards the island. According to Bishop Hirth, who stood watching their approach, 'All of a sudden, the bullets began to rain upon the royal hut . . . The king seized me by the hand and dragged me away. If we were not riddled it was the Lord who shielded us. A crowd of women and children fled with us. How many fell! We had soon gained the other shore of the island; the bullets could no longer reach us. But what a sight! Just a few canoes and a crowd of three or four thousand throwing themselves into the water to cling to them. It was heart-breaking. What shrieks! What a fusillade! What deaths by drowning! The king was pushed into a boat; I had to follow him in without even thinking of my six colleagues I was leaving behind. We were soon in open water, whence we saw the flames that marked the presence of the enemy in the island . . .' The other White Fathers had surrendered to the askaris on the island, and were unharmed. Once more, they fared better than their African converts.

The Maxim had sunk six canoes, according to Williams, who estimated the Catholic death-roll at sixty. But Robert Ashe feared the tally ran into some hundreds of people, including a large number of women and children. And nasty tales began to creep back to Kampala Fort of atrocities committed by the Sudanese troops. At least, everyone assumed that the Sudanese (being Moslem) were responsible. Ashe declared that 'It is impossible to say what the utterly heathen adherents of either party might be capable of; but that the well-instructed chiefs of either creed would commit the atrocities charged against the Protestant leaders I feel sure is contrary to the whole tenor of their actions'.

Hirth, the Kabaka and a surviving flotilla of Catholics had escaped towards the Sese Islands, after a day and night on the water. From there they crossed the lake to the eastern shore and began a trek through Budu province towards the German frontier. 'It is not exile but rather new fatherland for us,' wrote Bishop Hirth, 'for an immense immigration . . . has followed us for several days. The whole of Budu has become a Catholic province. The Protestants, though ten times more numerous, have been driven out.' Soon there were refugees streaming in both directions across the borders of Budu province.

And soon, the White Fathers in Rubaga were quietly negotiating with Lugard for a peaceful settlement. Their Bishop, who had held hopes of German intervention on behalf of the Catholics, had been firmly told by Captain Langheld, the German officer in charge of the frontier district, that no such hope should be entertained. So Father Achté suggested to Lugard that perhaps there might be a denominational partition of Uganda,* with a British officer in charge of each area. In the event, a new treaty was to be signed, giving the Budu chiefdoms to the Catholics. But Lugard had only

* That is, of four tribal areas adjacent to each other, of which Buganda was one and Budu another.

agreed to this on condition that the Kabaka should return to the capital. Two Protestant chiefs were sent to collect him and eventually the hapless Mwanga re-entered Rubaga, 'dressed in a loin cloth and dirty white coat, a piece of calico wound round his head as a turban. Weary, travel stained, dirty, unshaven . . .'. No longer a tyrant, but a sorry penitent yet again, and about to undergo another conversion of religious faith for the sake of his throne and survival. Robert Ashe thought that he had taken this last road to his African Canossa, as much as anything, because he had grown tired of being ordered about by the Catholic priests.

The Europeans did not bear each other much ill-will even at this extreme stage of events. Robert Ashe was not to remain much longer in Buganda, and he left with kind words for his 'courteous opponents', in spite of what he called 'the serious political and religious differences dividing them'; and in spite of the fact that, in one of their periodic retreats, the Frenchmen had stolen his precious bicycle, together with a case of champagne which Mr Roscoe was supposed to have earmarked for medicinal use. In Britain and France, however, a rather more severe view was taken of the Battle of Mengo and its aftermath. Before long, the French Government was demanding compensation on behalf of the White Fathers for a variety of damages, which included the burnt cathedral, sixty chapels and twelve schools destroyed, and fifty thousand Catholics who were supposed to have been sold into slavery by the Protestants. Eventually the British Government settled for an ex gratia payment of £10,000 to the White Fathers.

The missionary propaganda machines at home, meanwhile, were doing their best to explain away these incredible happenings in the name of Christianity. The Catholic Union of Great Britain was stoutly asserting that 'through the troubled history of this time we can see only one reasonable account, and that is given by the White Fathers'. *The Gleaner*, the organ of the Church Missionary Society, improved upon this with a gesture towards Christian unity. It assured its readers that the bloodshed in Uganda was the work of heathens and nothing whatever to do with religious differences.

15

THE CRITICAL BACKLASH

In spite of missionary attempts to anoint these troubled waters, there was some uproar in England when the news of Mengo and its unsavoury context filtered home. A great deal of the noise was made in Parliament. At the very moment when the wretched Mwanga was stumbling back to Rubaga and Protestantism, Lord Salisbury's Conservative Government was making another attempt to channel £20,000 into the funds of the Imperial British East Africa Company. The money was described as a grant-in-aid for surveying the route of a railway which might run between Mombasa and Lake Victoria. It was justified as a project which might do much to end slavery in East Africa once and for all. No one, however, was in any doubt that the £20,000 was really a subsidy to a commercial enterprise which could not meet the cost of its political responsibilities. The Foreign Secretary made it clear that if the railway were not built, the Company would have to withdraw from Uganda and that the Anglican missionaries might well have to follow suit without its protection.

There were plenty of men in the House of Commons to resist both the implications and the effect of this. One of them was Mr Labouchere, who occupied with similar distinction the seat for Northampton lately represented by the agnostic Charles Bradlaugh. 'If we build this railway,' said Mr Labouchere, 'by going through the country of the bloodthirsty Masai, we shall have to send an army to defend these people from the inroad of a power as strong as that of the Mahdi, and then we shall have to prevent these very remarkable Christians from cutting each other's throats . . . I do not believe . . . it is the mission of the State to prevent these Protestant missionaries from cutting the throat of Roman Catholic missionaries, nor is it their business to prevent the Catholic missionaries cutting the throat of the Protestant missionaries.' There were, of course, plenty of men in the House who took the view that utterances like Mr Labouchere's were unspeakably and agnostically unjust, and one of them was Sir John Kennaway, the Liberal Member of Parliament and President of the Church Missionary Society. So the debate was at times fierce. It was also protracted long beyond the point immediately at issue. It was still continuing, whenever someone could catch the Speaker's eye with an excuse to bring it up, a couple of years later, when Sir Charles Dilke observed that the only person who had really benefited from the British presence in East Africa appeared to be Mr Hiram Maxim; and then went on to suggest to the honourable Members representing the interests of the CMS, that if St Augustine had landed in Kent with machine guns, they would probably all be pagans by now. That was the day when the Member of Parliament for Cockermouth, Sir W. Lawson, remarked that if recent events in Uganda continued, the place would soon become 'the Belfast of Africa'.

Parliament was not the only forum of debate about the rights and wrongs of missionary behaviour and Company activity and British presence in Uganda. It was carried on in the secular press, with *The Times* upholding all three manifestations and with both the *Manchester Guardian* and the *Daily News* asking variously pointed questions on specific issues. Nor could the Government be in much doubt that, whatever veneer might be placed upon events in Uganda by both the missionary and the Company lobbies, something had gone very badly wrong, and that people with a religious or political axe to grind were not the only ones to think so. Early in 1893, the Consul-General in Zanzibar, Sir Gerald Portal, had sent a memorandum to London on the subject of 'the miserable history of Uganda'. In it he said that 'I am extremely unwilling to enter into a discussion of the dangerous subject of Missionary interference in politics, but it is impossible to avoid an allusion to so important a factor of the whole question. That the missionaries on both sides are the veritable leaders of their respective factions, there can be no doubt whatever. The Romish Fathers would admit this to be the case; on the Protestant side it would not be admitted, but the fact unfortunately remains . . . It will from this be readily understood that the race for converts, now being carried on by the Romish and Protestant Missionaries in Uganda, is synonymous with a race for political power . . .'

The Parliamentary vote was won and the British mercantile, missionary and political presence in East Africa was secured in spite of all criticism, however. Quite apart from the pressure which interested parties could produce in the Commons and Lords, there was an enormous lobby outside Westminster. The Anti-Slavery Society sent its deputation to the Foreign Office. The directors and shareholders of the Company ambushed Ministers in the London clubs. Lugard came home and justified himself before packed meetings of provincial Chambers of Commerce. Cecil Rhodes offered to establish a telegraph from Nyasaland to Uganda at his own expense if the Government abandoned its clear duty. H. M. Stanley uttered moral threats about the results of 'a cowardly and disgraceful scuttle'. But the most widespread lobby of all, and the one which the Government reasonably took to be the voice of the nation, in so far as the nation was speaking on this issue, was the one organised by the CMS and the Church of England as a whole.

It was pressed forward on many fronts. Towards the end of 1892 the Liberals took office from the Conservatives and immediately told Sir Gerald Portal, in Zanzibar, to advise English missionaries on the coast that if they went upcountry it would be entirely at their own risk. This produced a very hurt response from Bishop Tucker, now back in Africa. Fifteen years earlier, he informed Sir Gerald, the missionaries had entered Uganda, 'carrying their lives in their hands', without seeking or expecting Government protection. Subsequently the Company had made treaties pledging itself to protect king and people in Uganda. 'Naturally the adherents of the English Mission supported the English Resident in the exercise of those powers entrusted to him by the English Government through the IBEA Company. The result was that they incurred the hatred and hostility of all other parties in the State.' At home the missionary supporters sounded not so much hurt as reproachful, and they were wonderfully well organised. The CMS itself made a fairly dignified statement about its 'special responsibility to communicate to the British public their sense of grave wrong' should Uganda be abandoned to paganism or (even worse, perhaps) Roman Catholicism, and left it at that. But then the Foreign Office became inundated with daily resolutions delivered from every branch of the vast Protestant network in Britain. They poured in from the Society for the Propagation of the Gospel, from Missionary Committees of the Scottish Churches, from Diocesan Conferences and Ruridecanal Chapters, from countless local committees of the Young Men's Christian Association and the Ladies' Negro Friend Society. As a crowning gesture the Archbishop of Canterbury, Dr Benson, prayed at the annual Church Congress in Folkestone that 'our country's course may be so shaped that the Christian converts of Uganda be not abandoned to imminent destruction'. Nineteenth-century British Governments found it excessively embarrassing to legislate against the prayerful interests of an Archbishop of Canterbury. And so Uganda, whether its people liked it or not, was taken into the protective custody of British officials, British soldiers, British tradesmen and British missionaries.

The agnostic and sceptical critics of Christian imperialism were defeated on this occasion. Significantly, however, their protests had been made more vehemently and more confidently than ever before. From now on the missionary interests in Britain would be well aware that there was a considerable and influential body of opinion in the country prepared to scrutinise every activity of the Church militant abroad with a gaze that was not at all sympathetic to its basic premises.

There had, of course, always been some criticism of the missionaries; this was no more than the natural order of things. In spite of his warm commendation of David Livingstone's book, Charles Dickens had taken at least a couple of sly digs at the missionary notion of philanthropy in his own works. In *Bleak House*, which began to appear within a decade of the Niger Expedition, the earnest Mrs Jellyby declares that 'We hope by this time next year to have from a hundred and fifty to two hundred healthy families cultivating coffee and educating the natives of Borrioboola-Gha, on the left bank of the Niger'. And in *Pickwick*, Mr Weller remarks on the habit of making coloured waistcoats for niggers. From time to time, similar sentiments had been expressed by people inhabiting a world much less rarified than that represented by Dickens and English literature. Generally, however, such comments had amounted to nothing more than caustic scepticism. In a nation that was so powerfully dedicated to the Christian ethic, that was socially organised so completely into a pattern of Christian behaviour it would have been fruitless, possibly reckless, to engage in open combat. Communities which were mightily beholden to the influences of the vicar, the elders and the deacons, and which supported missionary work so loyally with their alms and their efforts, would not have responded favourably to anyone declaring war upon their morality.

Thrice before Mengo, though, news of scandalous proportions had come out of the missionary field and had helped to stiffen the sceptics and arm them for any future campaigns. The first of these despatches had attended that gentle and boyish man Bishop Mackenzie. During his brief mission in the Shiré Highlands of East Africa in 1861, which he established with Livingstone's help, Mackenzie had taken the offensive against the Ajawa tribe, which was deeply engaged in slave-trading. The Bishop, indeed, not doubting for a moment that his cause was a just one, had rather enjoyed the experience. It had allowed him to enact many youthful fantasies of noble warfare, based upon an education in the heroic sagas of Classical Greece. Unfortunately for Mackenzie, one of his colleagues in that UMCA Mission, Henry Rowley, had a crippled wife in Oxford. Her life was made even more difficult by the minute income that was allotted to missionary dependants and Rowley had considerately sent his journal to her, so that she could raise some money by publishing it. It recounted, among other things, full details of the 'war' that Mackenzie and his missionaries had conducted against the Ajawa. The London secretary of the UMCA got wind of its impending publication and wrote to Mrs Rowley, begging her to desist. He wrote that 'although the committee have no desire to conceal the proceedings of the mission . . . circumstances have occurred . . . which need not with any advantage in all their details be brought before the public . . .'

Mrs Rowley dutifully desisted, but the UMCA had now placed itself in an agonising dilemma. If details of Mackenzie's war broke out, its new enterprise in Africa would be discredited. On the other hand, if the matter were hushed up, there would be the awful guilt of dishonest conduct attaching to the members of the committee. Honesty, and guilt, eventually won this moral struggle. The annual Church Congress of the Anglicans was shortly to be held in Oxford and the committee members resolved that Mackenzie's papers, giving his own account of the war, should be tabled. And there was, indeed, a great sense of shock running through that packed audience in the Sheldonian Theatre as the details were read out. The delegates heard how the Bishop's party had concluded that they could not defend their own stockade without attacking the Ajawa who were menacing them; how they had distributed powder to twenty men of the friendly Manganja tribe to go with guns already in their possession; how they had burned down two or three hundred huts belonging to the Ajawa; how they had marched and counter-marched across the land like a small army of freebooters, leaving a trail of smoking villages in their wake. It had seemed, to Mackenzie on the spot, something as excitingly irreproachable as the story of Thermopylae retold in a sub-tropical setting. To the temperate Churchmen in the Sheldonian it sounded less like the justification of a Christian mission than a commander's despatch after a successful military campaign. They recalled, uncomfortably, that the good Bishop had first arrived in East Africa with a crozier in one hand and a rifle in the other.

As soon as these revelations were finished, there arose on the platform the figure of Dr Edward Pusey, then at the height of his influence as leader of the Anglo-Catholic revival in the Church of England. Apart from his

19. A missionary's bedroom, East Africa. Photograph by Rev. R. H. Leakey.

Abide in Me.
and I in you.
My Redeemer

earnest desire to restore the deepest and most vivid Catholic traditions to his Church, Pusey was well known as a man with a profound belief in practising Christianity the hard way. It was in these terms that he now denounced Mackenzie's account from the mission field. 'There is no history perhaps during many years,' the Doctor declared, 'which has grieved me so much as this, and none which has more impressed upon me what I may call our common human frailty . . . It seems to me a frightful thing that the messengers of the Gospel of peace should in any way be connected, even by their presence, with the shedding of human blood . . . The Gospel has always been planted, not by doing, but by suffering . . .' After such a cry of anathema from such a towering figure in the Church, the repercussions outside the Sheldonian were predictable. Ecclesiastical newspapers like the *Guardian* and the *Colonial Church Chronicle* also denounced the mission. The governing structure of the UMCA was temporarily wrecked. It had been set up, in the first place, as an alliance between High Anglicans in the universities of Oxford, Cambridge, Durham and Dublin. Dublin now left it for good, and Durham abandoned the connection for a while. The central committee was stricken down the middle. Leading lay members, like Sir Roderick Murchison and Admiral Washington, resigned. So did some eminent Churchmen, like Dr Goulburn, who was headmaster of Rugby School and about to become Dean of Norwich. In the country at large there was a great deal of anger; somebody in the North of England wrote to Lord John Russell, threatening to prosecute the missionaries in a court of law.

Something much more unpleasant than Mackenzie's war was reported in 1880. In the wave of pious hero-worship which had engulfed the British Isles after the burial of David Livingstone in Westminster Abbey, the Free Church of Scotland decided to establish, as a testimonial to his memory, a mission station on the shores of Lake Nyasa, which he had discovered. It was to be called Livingstonia. This seems to have provoked some denominational jealousy in the parent Church of Scotland, from which the Free Church had long ago broken away in much the same way that the Methodists disengaged themselves from the Church of England. Livingstonia was already functioning when the Church of Scotland sent out a party to set up its own mission elsewhere along the lake shore. This one was named Blantyre, after Livingstone's birthplace. In 1879 a Fellow of the Royal Geographical Society, Andrew Chirnside, travelled extensively in the region on what appears to have been a combined sight-seeing and hunting expedition. He stayed for a while at the Blantyre mission and was thoroughly shocked by what he found there.

20. The Rev. G. K. Baskerville and a group of missionary ladies in Uganda.

For a start, there was the pit which had been dug at the back of the blacksmith's shop. You got to the bottom of it by ladder and there, in one side of the shaft, a tunnel had been excavated. It was fitted with a strong door which could not be forced and it was just large enough to contain a man. The ground above the tunnel was piled high with a pyramid of stones, so that no one could dig down into it. This was the mission station prison and it was regularly in use. Men were confined in that tunnel for three or four days at a stretch, Chirnside discovered, and they were not allowed either food or water while they were there in total darkness.

These Scottish missionaries had a very strong taste for administering punishment. Chirnside had heard a rumour, before reaching Blantyre, concerning the death of a native porter. The man had been suspected of stealing a chest of tea and, although he was ill at the time, he had been tied to a tree in the mission compound. With colleagues watching from the verandah of the mission house, one of the missionaries had then flogged the native with a buffalo hide whip. When it started to rain, the whip was handed over to three of the mission's Africans. They then took turns to flog the man, until he died after more than two hundred lashes. According to Chirnside, 'Flogging with this whip is an everyday occurrence, three lads in one day getting upwards of 100 lashes; and it is a fact that after being flogged on several occasions, salt has been rubbed on their bleeding backs.'

Chirnside was an eye-witness to something much more appalling than that. Some time before his arrival a couple of Africans were employed at the mission to do odd jobs. Between them they maintained a woman to give them both bed and board and to act generally as their female serf, which was quite in keeping with local tribal custom. She left them and complained to the Rev. Duff Macdonald and the other members of the mission, that they ill-treated her. The mission took her into its protection and the men were very angry about it. Other natives said they went about uttering threats to cut the woman's throat if they ever laid hands on her. Three months later, the body of another native woman on the station was found shot dead. According to Chirnside, who was by now at Blantyre, Macdonald and his colleagues immediately assumed that the culprits were their two former workmen. Without being told anything of these suspicions, the two were set to work making a set of wooden stocks. As soon as the job was finished, they were placed in the stocks and accused for the first time of murder. They protested their innocence emphatically and Chirnside was of the opinion that, according to local gossip, they were innocent. When he himself asked the missionaries what evidence there was against the men, no one could say that there was anything other than strong grounds for suspicion, because of the men's threatening behaviour over their shared woman.

The unfortunate pair were informed that the white man's God had ordained that whoever killed should himself be killed. That day, one of them managed to free himself from the stocks and got clear away into the surrounding hills. His friend was not so lucky. As Chirnside observed it, 'A grave having been dug on the other side of the stream, the next morning the wretched man was marched to the head of the grave, was then blindfolded and his arms and legs tied. Mr Macdonald again told him what "the white man's God" said, and the sentenced man again protested his innocence. Eight natives were then told off to perform the duty of executioners, and ranged in line at twelve paces. At the word of command the volley was fired, and when the smoke cleared the poor fellow appeared to have received shots in every part of his body but a vital spot, as he still stood upright but quivering in agony. There he stood while the guns were again loaded and, some firing again, one of the shots went clean through his right lung, and yet he stood there bleeding and maimed, a sight too sickening for the whites, one of whom, stepping forward, pulled him back by the head into the grave. Further description would disgust, but the man did not die, until one of the chiefs of a neighbouring village ended the tragedy by taking the breech-loading rifle of Mr Robert Henderson, an engineer of the Livingstonia Trading Company, who was standing by, and stepping up to the writhing form in the grave, blew the man's brains out at the muzzle of his gun.'

Chirnside published his news of what became known as the Blantyre Massacre in a pamphlet when he returned home. He pointed out that, as a result of this judicial execution by the missionaries, a great deal of fighting subsequently occurred between local tribesmen and the missionary party, 'the Missionary forces, being far better armed, generally getting the best of it and killing several of their opponents'.

He also reported 'an affair, very un-English in my opinion', which happened on the last day he was at Blantyre. A local chief, Chipitula, visited the mission with some ivory he was selling to the Livingstonia Trading Company representative there, and demanded that some of the African workers should be handed over to him. They had escaped from his authority and taken refuge on the station some time before. Hearing of his approach, they took to the hills, intending to return when the chief had gone away. Chipitula, however, persuaded the missionaries to retrieve the men for him, a party was sent out after them and brought them in.

'The last night I was at Blantyre,' writes Chirnside, 'the night was disturbed by the terrible cries of the poor fellows who had fallen into the hands of Chipitula. He had every intention of mutilating them and then torturing them to death. Surely the missionaries should either refuse to harbour refugees; or if they choose to do so, should rather assist them to fly than deliver them up to frightful deaths, and take the part of hunting them down for a chief when they make their escape?'

Apart from Chipitula's variety of friendship, there was little but hostility for these white men at Blantyre, and the repercussions extended beyond the station. Life was made more difficult for the Free Church missionaries down at Livingstonia. All their supplies from the world outside had to reach them along a route which passed through Blantyre, and now their supply parties were increasingly liable to attack by natives incapable of distinguishing between two different sub-sects of white men and their supporters. Chirnside quoted from the monthly journal circulated by the Livingstonia mission, under the editorial guidance of Mary Livingstone's old travelling companion, Dr James Stewart. 'At present,' wrote Stewart, in an edition which came out in December 1879, 'we can express no opinion on these unhappy collisions, except simply to say that their occurrence will seriously interfere with the work of the Blantyre mission and probably put it back by some 15 or 20 years . . . There appear to be several things at Blantyre which require a little rectification . . .'

Chirnside's pamphlet, *The Blantyre Missionaries; Discreditable Disclosures*, had scarcely left the presses in London when a Blantyre supporter, Alexander Riddel, leapt to the missionary defence with a pamphlet of his own. He asserted that he knew many of Chirnside's statements 'to be *false* and others *incorrect*', though Riddel confessed elsewhere that his own personal experience of Blantyre had ended in July 1878, a good twelve months before the events which Chirnside described. He called the report of the execution an exaggeration and was at some pains to dissect Chirnside's account, line by line, to demonstrate this. Of the two men placed in the stocks, Chirnside had written 'Between them, they owned one woman'. Of this, Riddel said, 'I deny that the woman was joint property, and assert that she was the slave of one of them'. Of the execution itself, Riddel remarked, 'An execution must at all times be a thing harrowing to the feelings and gladly would the missionaries have been free from all responsibility and connection with it; but what could they do?'

Riddel's rejoinder to Chirnside was a fairly typical example of the initial reflex of most missionary organisations when subjected to criticism, with its mixture of evasion and special pleading. In this case it was not sufficient to conceal what was obviously a dreadful episode. The General Assembly of the Church of Scotland could scarcely avoid setting up a commission of inquiry into Chirnside's allegations. It substantiated his main charges, though it accepted missionary evidence that some semblance of a trial had been held before the execution and decided that the confidence of local natives in the mission had not been damaged by what happened. Nevertheless, the Rev. Duff Macdonald, the mission doctor and two of the white artisan missionaries at Blantyre were dismissed for their joint behaviour in 1879.* The two artisans remained in the country, one becoming a trader, the other an Acting-Consul.

The sensation caused by Chirnside's pamphlet had scarcely subsided than another one arose. This one was caused by a scandal reported from Nigeria, which was printed in several English secular newspapers. It is doubtful whether such publicity would have been achieved if a question had not been asked on the subject by the Duke of Somerset in the House of Lords. His Lordship arose one day in April 1883 to bring to the attention of his colleagues the matter of some slaves attached to a CMS mission which 'occurred some years ago on the River Niger'. The society, he said, employed a number of coloured people and all of them had slaves. These were frequently ill-treated, and the local superintendent of police had often reproved the missionaries for their behaviour. The Duke said that three or four agents of the society were implicated and among them were a Mr Johns, employed as an interpreter by the CMS, and a Mr and Mrs Williams, a schoolmaster and his wife. Apparently some slave women had been punished by flogging for a misdemeanour. 'It appeared,' said the Duke, 'that some red pepper was put into the excoriated places caused by the flogging, after which the unfortunate people were supported or carried to their hovels, where they remained in agony all night. While this was going on, the native women heard their screams, and called out, and said to the Missionaries – "Surely this is not in accordance with your preaching". Upon which Mrs Williams came forward and said – "She

* Duff Macdonald returned to Scotland, to spend almost half a century as minister of a church in Motherwell and to receive an honorary degree from Aberdeen University. He had a reputation as a linguist and when he died, at the age of seventy-eight, the only reference to his days at Blantyre in the obituary notice of the Motherwell newspaper read as follows: 'In 1878, he was appointed the Church of Scotland's first ordained missionary to the East African Mission, and during his three and a half years there he published several translations in the native tongue. He was also the author of "Africana: or the Heart of Heathen Africa".' Even in 1954 a missionary historian was gliding past the Blantyre episode in these terms: 'Duff Macdonald resigned, though not personally involved . . . It was a calamity that such a man found his position untenable.'

had bought the girls and had a right to do what she pleased with them". During the night one of the girls died in consequence of the treatment to which she had been subjected, and after the body had been buried and the people enjoined to say nothing about it, the order was given to ring the bell for prayers.'

The Duke's disclosure in the House of Lords is perhaps more interesting for the response it produced among missionary supporters than for the details of the floggings and death. The CMS was not short of backers in the Upper House of Parliament and one after another they got to their feet. Lord Cairns pointed out that the matter had first been made public by a CMS representative, the Rev. J. B. Wood. This was not quite accurate. Mr Wood had, indeed, produced a report, for the CMS in Salisbury Square had heard rumours from traders and other Europeans that all was not well up the Niger and had asked him to investigate. But the report had been made confidentially to the Governor of Lagos. As a result, Bishop Crowther had held an ecclesiastical court, which meted no punishment; and the Bishop had left it at that. The Earl of Chichester, who in that year was President of the CMS, also spoke in defence of the missionaries in the House of Lords. After him came the Archbishop of Canterbury himself. His Grace began by saying that as long ago as 1857, and again in 1879, the CMS had produced memoranda forbidding their West African agents to hold slaves. He then ignored the allegations completely and spoke of steps which had recently been taken to strengthen the Niger Mission; a new archdeacon had been appointed to attend to administration; a steamer had been placed on the river to help the Bishop to travel more easily; an English secretary had been appointed to advise the Bishop, and the CMS was at that moment despatching a medical missionary to give more help to the Bishop. In short, the Archbishop of Canterbury was carefully implying that the real responsibility for any untoward occurrences up the Niger rested with the Nigerian Bishop Crowther and that his administrative weaknesses were being corrected by Europeans. And, indeed, as the Archbishop of Canterbury well knew (though he was certainly not prepared to let the House of Lords into the secret) a campaign to undermine Samuel Crowther's authority was then well under way in white missionary circles and had much to do with racial jealousy.

Yet the strangest aspect of the missionary defence case was the discrepancy between two accounts which were now offered to the public. In the Lords, the Earl of Derby, also a CMS defender, alleged that one of the two people accused of mistreating slaves had been sentenced to twenty years' penal servitude, the other to eighteen and a half years. Yet when the newspapers reported the disclosure in the House of Lords, the secretary of the CMS in London immediately wrote a public disclaimer, in which he explained that the persons involved were no longer in missionary employment, one having been dismissed by the Bishop three years before, the other having since withdrawn. As a matter of fact, he added, the offence had been committed five years before. That, at least, seemed to be true. The Duke of Somerset had offered the same date in the Lords.

The uproar which attended news of the Battle of Mengo in Uganda can thus be seen as a culmination of growing disillusionment with certain aspects of missionary behaviour and policy. From 1892 onwards, the missionaries would be liable to severe public censure whenever they were caught falling below their own professedly high moral standards. That this perhaps did not make such a great difference to the behaviour of missionaries in the field is suggested by the fact that, as late as 1904, the London Missionary Society felt itself obliged to pass a resolution that no missionary should allow himself to be involved in the flogging of adult natives for any kind of offence. Nevertheless, from now on, it would not be fair to assume that missionary failings only came to light when outsiders noticed them, as in the case of the Blantyre Massacre, or when the missionaries made such a monumental mess of things that they could hardly fail to attract general attention, as at Mengo. There would now be a spirit of self-criticism abroad, and its first and most splendid manifestation came in a pamphlet published in 1894 by Dr Robert Needham Cust, the gentleman who had hastened to Algiers, on behalf of the CMS, to beg Cardinal Lavigerie not to send his White Fathers to East Africa.

Dr Cust was a fussy man with some sense of his own importance. 'I have,' he wrote, 'for many years helped to rule vast Provinces in British India . . .'; which was no less than the truth, for at one time he had served on the Viceroy's Council there. His pamphlet described him, in capital letters which almost filled the title page, as 'An observer in the field, a member of committees, an all-round reader of missionary literature in five European languages, and one whose heart, and intellect, have been devoted to the subject for 50 years, independent of Church, denomination or nationality'. Then followed two quotations in Latin and one in Greek, and a dedication to the delegates who would be assembling for the annual conference of the CMS that year. He carefully produced another two quotations, in English, in the course of his Prefatory Remarks, the burden of which was that the truest friend of any institution is the man who criticises it fearlessly, the man who is prepared to swim calmly against the pleasant and profitable current of popular opinion.

Pompous Dr Cust may have been, but there was no denying his bluntness or his apparent indifference to ostracism by the company he had kept so closely for half a century. Almost the first thing he wrote in his text proper was 'No class, and no individuals, have such a narrow view of human affairs as the Missionary'. Speaking as one who was conversant with five European tongues, he lamented the fact that those less well-equipped than himself were usually, as a result, restricted to one field, one set of opinions, one environment of experiences and ideas. The missionary to China would be wonderfully improved if he could spend three years in Africa; the problems of the opium trade, which tormented every missionary in China, would seem very small when replaced by the problems of Cannibalism, Witchcraft, Slave-Trade, Murder, 'and the entire Nudity of both sexes . . .'

Dr Cust was able to quote from a missionary manual to substantiate another point he wished to make about the narrowness of missionaries. Written by a man who had served abroad it said that 'Quarrels are specially rife at small stations: missionaries, accustomed to command natives, become dogmatic, and desirous to have their own way; thus a Mission ceases to be a model of Apostolic zeal and self-denial, and becomes a hot-bed of jealousy; small men contending bitterly with each other for the exercise of a feeble power. Missionaries are notorious for littleness, narrowness and puny mental character; a record of their disputes would form a humiliating chapter in the History of the Missions.' One other thing that Dr Cust added from his own experiences in two foreign continents, clearly had much to do with the entire Nudity of both sexes, visible in Africa as nowhere else in the missionary field. 'In the length and breadth of British India,' he wrote, 'during a quarter of a century, I never heard a breath of scandal against any Missionary, Protestant or of the Church of Rome. But in Africa my experiences are sadly different.'

His criticisms were mostly about missionary policy. He believed that the sending of young women to Africa 'merely to die, is a cruelty which cannot be too severely condemned. How many young wives lie buried in Africa, valuable lives needlessly thrown away! . . . Some Missionary Societies and Training Colleges have become mere Matrimonial Agencies.' The CMS, he recalled, had created a Children's Home, on which 'money collected to convert the Heathen is squandered on maintaining children, chiefly the result of early, improvident and thoughtless marriages'. He was also against the establishment of industrial farms attached to missions, which was an important aspect of missionary policy. The duty of the missionary, Dr Cust believed, was to preach the Gospel and nothing else.

'Augustine did not teach our Anglo-Saxon forefathers the art of building ships, or starting manufactories, or breeding oxen . . .'

He was especially critical of the organisation and outlook of the missionary societies in Britain. The structure of the CMS particularly incensed him. Dr Cust had been associated, in his time, with a remarkable range of institutions which included the SPCK, the SPG, the Bench of Magistrates, the Board of Guardians, the Council of the Royal Geographical Society, the Council of the Royal Asiatic Society and the Anti-Slavery Society – 'yet in none have I found the position of the paid secretaries so markedly and really objectionably prominent as in the CMS'. And, indeed, CMS secretaries did tend to remain in office for a very long time and to shape much of the society's policy while they were there; Henry Venn's period stretched over three decades and almost everything the society did in that time originated in his mind. This was not to Dr Cust's taste. To him, a secretary was appointed on a salary to fulfil certain clerical duties, to edit periodicals, to keep accounts, to hold his tongue, and most certainly not 'to get up and speak without being called upon by the Chair on every possible subject just because he is a self-asserting individual'. Dr Cust had a very lofty, almost a Viceregal view of administration, and it was not confined to the duties of a secretary. He was not enamoured, either, of the little men and busybodies who formed the Home Committee of the CMS. He was scathing about the continued re-election of old and worn-out men, with little to offer except a lifetime's fidelity to a cause. 'It is not edifying,' he said, 'to see decaying remnants of vitality on the benches of a committee which administers the affairs of a spiritual kingdom . . .'

The annual reports emerging from this suspect appliance had also engaged the Doctor's withering attention. They seemed, he thought, to be fashioned to catch the taste of a peculiar emotional class of people; 'in some quarters a hit against the Church of Rome, the Ritualist, or the Opium-Taker are essential ingredients calculated to draw subscriptions, or perhaps the absence of such remarks would injure the society financially'. For a man who had been so close to the imperial levers of power in British India, Dr Cust was quite remarkably averse to the creeping imperialism which had stained the missionary movement, exceedingly astute in his observation of the national character which had produced it. He had very little time, almost none at all, for those committee members of the CMS who encouraged relatives and friends in the English provinces 'to pass frothy resolutions calling for Expeditions and Annexations and Protectorates and "Jingo generally". Is the Gospel of Christ to be preached by such methods?' he asked. 'We are a great, strong, self-asserting, arrogant Nation; let us restrict these qualities to our Commercial and Political transactions, and conduct our Mission work as simple Christians: we can expect no blessing on Gospel-teaching when in close contact with Calico-bales and Rifles, not to say tuns of Liquor, cases of firearms and barrels of gunpowder and Maxim-guns, as at Uganda.'

Had he not spent all those years in India, of course, Dr Cust would not have brought his rather large cast of mind to this somewhat narrowing subject. It was his detached experience in the East which had made him so receptive to the best of other traditions; missionary workers at home were not often so well endowed; and returned missionaries had usually been so seared by some personal experience or other in the mission field, that generosity towards the people they had worked among was not their most notable characteristic. Dr Cust was thus enabled, as very few people within this confined and confining circle were, to express shock at the derision, sometimes the open laughter, which he had heard in many home missionary meetings whenever other religious beliefs were mentioned and objects of worship other than Jesus Christ were caricatured. His particular experience, moreover, allowed him caustically to remark that while every missionary society in the land was constantly clamouring for funds and pleading the poverty of its workers, not one missionary society's annual report had made any reference to the fact that the recent devaluation of the Indian rupee had produced an instant windfall in British pounds, to any organisation with dealings in India.

It says much about the spirit of the time that Dr Cust's essay produced little reaction in missionary circles. Very probably many people felt that he could be disregarded as a disappointed office-seeker; the Doctor obviously believed that he could do better in the higher levels of the CMS than most of the existing incumbents, yet he had never been used as more than an emissary abroad and was ordinarily just a provincial secretary in the movement.

No such excuses could be made on behalf of Miss Mary Kingsley, who was answerable to no one but her own conscience and who was in the middle of her first solitary expedition to West Africa when Dr Cust's pamphlet was coming off the printing presses. A niece of the clergyman novelist Charles Kingsley she was, apart from her high intelligence, most notable in an age of demure and generally domesticated young ladies for her insatiable appetite for experience, her forthright delivery of opinions and her intolerance of humbug. Her first taste of foreign travel had taken her to the Canary Islands and there she had conceived her plan to 'see for herself' the legendary continent stretching away on the eastern horizon. The books which she published as a result of her two journeys up and down the West coast could not by any means be regarded as anti-missionary tracts – though a great number of missionary supporters identified them as such – for her interests were wide and intense. She had a taste for biology and she could be absorbed by local economy; she was a great collector of specimens and she sketched all manner of things wherever she went. She was, above all, interested in people, in their individual and communal relationships, in their traditions and their habits. Had she been born fifty years later she would very probably have become a trained social anthropologist of distinction. As it was, she contributed something of lasting value to the discipline in one small field, by her habit of acute observation and coherent thought. Though her range was much smaller and her skills less developed, she stands somewhere in the company of Richard Burton.

Given that her field of study became West Africa, she could scarcely avoid the missionaries. On preparing for her African trip she had been advised on all sides to read the missionary accounts for invaluable assistance. 'So to missionary literature I addressed myself with great ardour; alas! only to find that these good people wrote their reports not to tell you how the country they resided in was, but how it was getting on towards being what it ought to be, and how necessary it was that readers should subscribe more freely, and not get any foolishness into their heads about obtaining an inadequate supply of souls for their money.' That was the general flavour and tone of Mary Kingsley. It is easy to see, without reading farther, how missionary supporters generally would find it a little difficult to digest her without rising irritation. She herself relished one piece of advice from their direction, however. It was to 'Abstain from exposing yourself to the direct rays of the sun, take four grains of quinine every day for a fortnight before you reach the Rivers, and get some introductions to the Wesleyans; they are the only people on the Coast who have got a hearse with feathers'.

She was not reluctant to give credit to the missionaries. She was full of unqualified admiration for the Mission Evangelique at Lambarene, down in French Gabon, where Albert Schweitzer was soon to set up his famous hospital. She was highly impressed by the formidable Mary Slessor, whose influence as a Scottish Presbyterian missionary was so great in Calabar that she had already been appointed Vice-Consul for the region. Mary Kingsley reported how the red-haired Scotswoman's 'unbounded courage and energy' had deterred tribesmen from slaughtering a pair of new-born twins and their mother in accordance with local superstition. 'Had it not been for the fear of incurring Miss Slessor's anger she would, at this stage, have been killed with her children, and the bodies thrown into the bush'; as it was, the mother was merely hounded out of the village. In the same area, Miss Kingsley came across 'a very noble and devoted Scotch gentleman named Thomson', a wealthy missionary supporter, who had come out to set up at his own expense a sanatorium where the missionaries working in Old Calabar could recuperate from fever without having to voyage back to Britain. At the end of her travels in West Africa, she had come to the conclusion that 'taken as a whole, the missionaries must be regarded as superbly brave, noble-minded men who go and risk their own lives, and often those of their wives and children, and definitely sacrifice their personal comfort and safety to do what, from their point of view, is their simple duty . . .'

None the less, she thought that the technical training offered by the Protestant missions to their African adherents – in printing, book-binding and tailoring – thoroughly ill-advised. True, the Wesleyans were better than most of their colleagues in that they also offered training in blacksmithying, carpentry, bricklaying and wagon-building. But only the Catholic missions taught what Mary Kingsley believed were the most important skills for the natives to acquire in the conditions induced by European influence; namely, improved methods of agriculture and plantation work. She was, above all, critical of the effect of missionary methods upon the Africans; she was certainly not grinding an agnostic axe for use against Christians. She thus condemned the notorious Hubbard because it seemed to her to be 'one of the factors producing the well-known torpidity of the mission-trained girl; and they should be suppressed in her interest, apart from their appearance, which is enough to constitute a hanging matter'. The Hubbard was the shapeless garment introduced to missionised Africa in the interests of female modesty, and produced by the thousand at working parties of pious ladies throughout Europe. It consisted of a yoke round the shoulders, fastened at the back with three buttons, two of which were usually lost. From the yoke protruded dwarf sleeves and round its lower rim, on a level with the armpits, a flounce was sewn on, which fell to the heels. If someone wearing a Hubbard leant forward, to mend a fire, or stir a cooking pot, the dress fell forward so loosely that it dragged over the ground or into the cooking pot, soon becoming thoroughly grubby and at all times impeding rapid movement. Mary Kingsley wondered what conception the pious Christian ladies of Europe had of the average African female figure. She had measured a couple of Hubbards on the spot. One was thirty inches deep and forty-two inches in the beam; the other was thirty-six inches deep and sixty inches across. 'It is not,' she said, 'in nature for people to be made to fit these things.'

The shortcomings of the Hubbard, however, were small compared with some of the missionary attitudes Mary Kingsley encountered. She noticed that wherever she went, when missionaries felt frustrated in their attempts to convert the heathen to the Christian Gospel, they generally ascribed their failures above all either to polygamy or the liquor trade, or to a combination of both. She was not exaggerating. Every missionary account coming out of Africa contained its sidelong gesture of acute distaste for a plurality of wives; it was generally no more than this because sexuality was not a thing to be mentioned bluntly to Victorian readers. Possibly as a compensation for this frustration, every missionary account contained at least one hearty broadside on the evils of drink. When the CMS could boldly send a deputation to the Foreign Office, as it did in 1884, pressing for an abolition of the liquor trade in Africa, the subject was thoroughly mentionable in cold print. The liquor the missionaries were most incensed about was imported spirits, which they usually described as poisonous raw alcohol. Mary Kingsley took the trouble to return to England with a bottle of Van Huytemer's trade gin, one of the most widespread of the imports. There she had it analysed by a chemist. It contained just 39·35 per cent of alcohol.

She believed that the missionary lobby used the liquor trade as a means of whipping up support at home where, as they well knew, the temperance movement was popular. There was much support to be gained from people who liked to think of the African as an innocent creature who had been led astray by the bad white trader, who could be rescued from his clutches by their noble endeavours and their generous subscriptions. 'I do not say,' she declared, 'that every missionary on the West Coast who makes untrue statements on this subject is an original liar; he is usually only following his leaders and repeating their observations without going into the evidence around him; and the missionary public in England and Scotland are largely to blame for their perpetual thirst for thrilling details of the amount of Baptisms and Experiences among the people they pay other people to risk their lives to convert, or for thrilling details of the difficulties these said emissaries have to contend with . . . I have no hesitation in saying that in the whole of West Africa, in one week, there is not a quarter the amount of drunkenness you can see any Saturday night you choose in a couple of hours in the Vauxhall Road; and you will not find in a whole year's investigation on the Coast, one-seventieth part of the evil, degradation and premature decay you can see any afternoon you choose to take a walk in the more densely populated parts of any of our towns.'

As for polygamy, it was not an unmixed evil for Africans and it was not to be ended at the present level of African culture. For one thing, it was quite impossible for one African woman to do all the work of cooking, fetching water, attending to the house, cultivating the plantations and looking after the children, expected by one man. She might, if she had the capacities of an English or Irish charwoman, but she simply was not built that way. And, anyway, an African lady, according to Mary Kingsley, was remarkably indifferent to the extent of her husband's amorous adventures, provided he gave her as much cloth and beads as anyone else received.

This highly emancipated English lady believed she had detected the fundamental reason for missionary failures in Africa. It was, she felt certain, largely a failure to recognise that the difference between themselves and the African was not a difference of degree but a difference of kind. The black man, in her view, was no more an underdeveloped white man than a rabbit was an underdeveloped hare. She thought that the mental differences between the two races was somewhat similar to that between the sexes among Europeans. 'A great woman, either mentally or physically, will excel an indifferent man, but no woman ever equals a really great man. The missionary to the African has done what my father found them doing to the Polynesians – "regarding the native minds as so many jugs only requiring to be emptied of the stuff which is in them and refilled with the particular form of dogma he is engaged in teaching, in order to make them the equals of the white races".' An African who had been truly converted to Christianity was a very beautiful form of Christian. But in Mary Kingsley's experience, the majority of converted Africans, who were paraded through the annual reports as evidence of missionary success, were in a different category. In them, the missionaries had eliminated those parts of the native fetish which placed a wholesome restraint of fear upon them, and had not succeeded in replacing it with the greater restraint of love. 'The missionary-made man is the curse of the Coast, and you find him in European clothes and without, all the way down from Sierra Leone to Loanda. The pagans despise him, the whites hate him, still he thinks enough of himself to keep him comfortable. His conceit is marvellous, nothing equals it except perhaps that of the individual rife among us which the "Saturday Review" once aptly described as "the surburban agnostic"; and the missionary man is very much like the suburban agnostic in his method . . . he removes from it all the inconvenient portions . . . on the West Coast he frequently sets up in business for himself; on the South-west Coast he usually becomes a sub-trader to one of the great English, German or French firms. On both Coasts he gets himself disliked, and brings down opprobrium on all black traders, expressed in language more powerful than select. This wholesale denunciation of black traders is unfair, because there are many perfectly straight trading natives; still the majority are recruited from missionary school failures, and are utterly bad . . .'

She had closely observed the reaction of missionaries to these converted failures of theirs. The missionary, she had noted, would be disgusted and pained by his pupil's bad habits. But at the same time he remained convinced of the excellence of his method of instruction and of the spiritual equality, irrespective of colour, of everyone. And he laid the blame for failure squarely on the shoulders of the white traders.

This was not a conclusion to be swallowed easily in missionary circles, either at the time Mary Kingsley was writing or much later. Even in the middle of the twentieth century, one of the most highly respected missionary historians would be caught advising his readers to approach her books with 'the customary caution – cum grano salis'. Possibly he had been stung painfully by her most resounding rebuke. It was an admission, she said, that went against all her insular prejudices. But one was bound to say that the Protestant English missionaries were chiefly responsible for rendering the African useless.

16

THE BOOM YEARS

No amount of criticism, internal or external, could stop the missionary armies from marching forward now, it seemed. Not even the most shocking disclosures, such as those of Blantyre or Mengo, seemed to have the slightest impeding effect upon their joint advance. The Battle of Mengo, indeed, almost coincided with the beginning of the most re-remarkable expansion in the history of missions, before or since. This lasted nearly a quarter of a century, from 1890 to 1914. In this period a score of new Catholic missionary orders were founded to join the old ones and to move into Africa and elsewhere under the direction of Rome. At the same time, and even more numerously, the Protestants of Europe and North America set sail for the Dark Continent to put down the heathen in unprecedented waves.

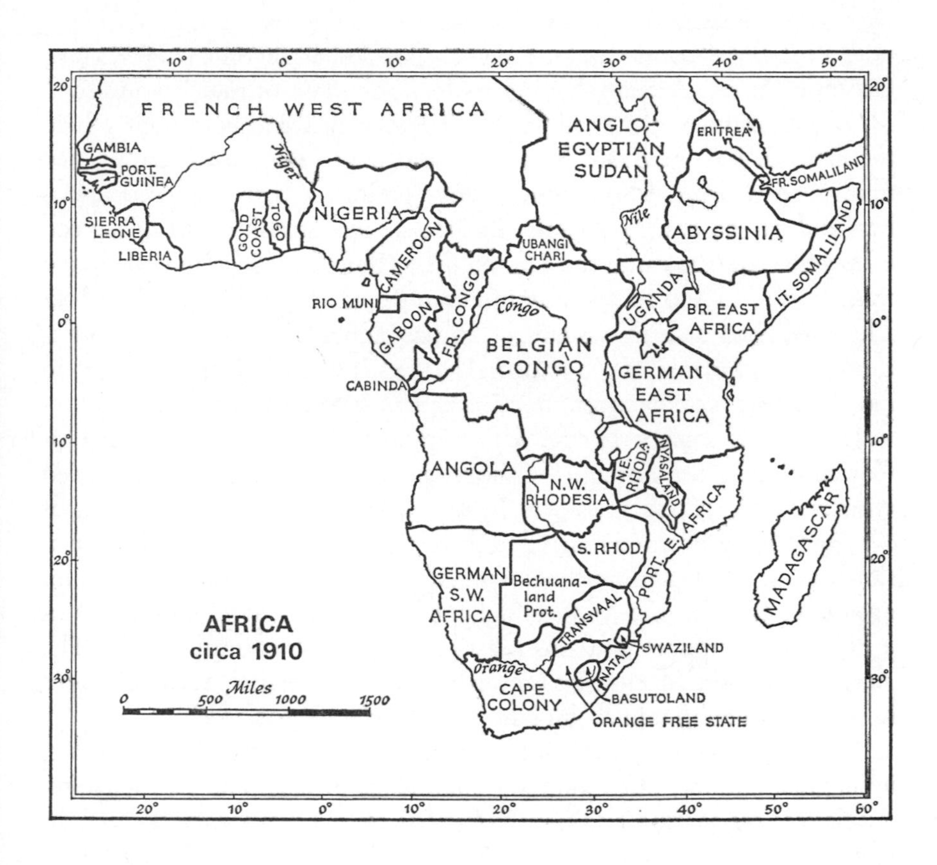

Between 1800 and 1860 there had been no decade in which the entire Protestant world had started more than nine new missionary enterprises in Africa.* Between 1860 and 1870 the figure rose to twelve, from 1870 to 1880 there were twenty-three, from 1880 to 1890 there were thirty-two. Between 1890 and 1900 the figure had climbed to fifty-four and from the turn of the century until 1914 there would be another sixty-two. Throughout this period the missionary societies of Great Britain maintained an enormous lead over those of all other nations. By 1901 the British had 2,750 male missionaries in the field somewhere in the world and 1,700 unmarried women, and the total income of these societies was £1,500,000. At the same time North America (including Canada) was

* i.e. the CMS in Sierra Leone being one unit, the CMS in Nigeria a second, the American Board at the Cape a third, and so on.

fielding 1,630 men and 1,200 unmarried women, from an income of £850,000. The third most highly mission-conscious nation was Germany, with a total of 880 men and women abroad and an income of £250,000. Generally, it was Africa which took the lion's share of these resources.

Of the British societies it was the CMS which had consistently held the national lead. It could by 1901 boast of 510 male missionaries, 326 unmarried women, 365 ordained native pastors, 270,000 baptised members and 71,500 communicants; its income was steadily over £300,000 each year. After it came the United Free Church of Scotland, with 330 missionaries, 41,500 native communicants and an income of £120,000. The LMS had 200 missionaries, 171,000 adherents, 50,730 communicants and an income of £137,000. The Baptists had 160 missionaries, 70 native pastors, 55,000 communicants and an income of £75,000.

The largest society in the United States, the American Board of Commissioners for Foreign Missions, fielded 177 men, 186 unmarried women, with 55,000 members in full communion and an income of £135,000. The Presbyterian Church of the United States had 290 missionaries, 31,000 communicants, with an income of £150,000. Wealthier even than this was the Methodist Episcopal Church, with an income of £237,000 to support 250 missionaries and 62,000 communicants. The American Baptist Missionary Union had 180 missionaries, 120,000 people in full communion and an income of more than £100,000.

At whatever point the missionary enterprise is examined in these years, it suggests nothing but bounding confidence in itself and its capacities. All figures are soaring and new variations on old missionary themes are being initiated. In 1890 the CMS starts its Sowers Band for young folk wishing to help the missionaries with their pennies and their prayers; five years later there are 230 branches all over Great Britain. By then, in 1895, the Gleaners Union has 79,000 workers in 653 branches, producing £4,000 a year for missionary funds. A CMS centenary appeal in 1899 raises £212,000 and the year 1900 produces, for the only time in history, 100 new recruits to the mission field. Both the Baptists and the LMS excel themselves, in that last decade of the nineteenth century, with centenary funds which raise well over £100,000 apiece. In one respect at least, the world has been transformed to a sense of mission in a hundred years.

On every side there were clarion calls to be off to the mission fields, and they were not answered grudgingly now; nor were the men who came forward those who subconsciously hoped, perhaps, to better themselves socially by exchanging hard manual labour at home for perseverance with a Bible overseas. This may have been a pattern in missionary recruitment during the tentative years at the start of the nineteenth century, but only the brightest and best talents available were required for God's work in these burgeoning years at the start of the twentieth. Particularly phenomenal was the increase in women who went to Africa at this time. In the past, women had gone out to help the men as their sisters or their wives. But now the cry went up for unmarried ladies to work as missionaries in their own right. An advertisement in the CMS *Intelligencer* started the rush in May 1887. 'Wanted immediately,' it said. 'Three ladies for East Africa. Must be wholehearted missionaries, physically strong, and thoroughly understanding the principle "In honour preferring one another".' This somewhat ambiguous message (doubtless lost upon the majority of God-fearing Victorian spinsters) had originated in the mind of Bishop Parker in Frere Town and been sanctioned by the committee in Salisbury Square. Within a fortnight three ladies had offered themselves, and in the next twelve months another four had been accepted by the CMS. In 1899 seventeen women were sent overseas and ten of them travelled at their own expense, which a contemporary chronicler of the missions seemed to feel a matter requiring some explanation. 'Perhaps if so many had come forward to go at the society's expense,' he wrote, 'there might have been some hesitation about sending them . . . But the Lord Himself, we cannot doubt, was leading the Society step by step along a path marked out by His own Providence – leading . . . the blind by a way that they knew not; and so He raised up Christian ladies with private means as the pioneers of perhaps the most important development of the work which recent years have witnessed.' Between 1887 and 1894 no fewer than 214 Christian ladies sallied forth alone on behalf of the CMS.

By the time the dust had settled after the Battle of Mengo, they were being invited to venture to Uganda. In 1894 the *Intelligencer* was writing that 'It is Bishop Tucker's distinct opinion that, assuming the country will now be reasonably safe, we must no longer delay in sending up Christian women . . . In the present circumstances of Africa women must be ready, as so many men have been ready, to go with the distinct and solemn purpose of remaining single for a few years for the Lord's sake. The time is not distant when the beauty of English family life may be exhibited in Uganda, but the time is not yet . . .' Such was the instinct of young English ladies to prepare, in the most solemn way possible, for the forthcoming exhibition of beautiful English family life in Uganda and elsewhere, that the CMS had to set up a new training structure especially for their benefit. To the men's training school at Islington was now added Miss Pennefather's establishment, The Willows, later to be superseded by The Olives, run by Mrs Bannister. And soon the CMS was producing, from its new Women's Department, advice on how to clothe and conduct oneself fittingly in foreign parts.

The Women's Department made out a list of different outfits that lady missionaries might care to consider for their baggage, pointing out first that 'Through an arrangement made with a large wholesale firm, the Women's Department is able to procure for outgoing women missionaries woollen underclothing, *unshrinkable* and of beautiful quality, at more than 25 per cent under ordinary prices'. The advised Regular Outfit for (A) The Road consisted of: '*Underclothing* – 3 Combinations, wool ("some take 2 woollen nightdresses"), 2 cholera belts, woven and shaped, 3 pairs of stockings, wool. *Dresses and Blouses* – 1 walking costume, blouse and skirt of thin woollen material. "Skirt not long, brown a good colour. To be worn with woollen knickers, no petticoat." 1 Change of Dress for camp wear; "any dress worn aboard ship will do. An extra serge suit is useful in bad weather. A little Brandy in case of need." ' For (B) The Destination, the Regular Outfit should consist of: '*Underclothing* – 2 or 3 thin Petticoats, 2 or 3 pairs thin woollen knickerbockers if liked, 6 woollen combinations, high necked, short sleeved, 6 pairs thin Cashmere stockings, 4 pairs canvas or other corsets, 4 or 6 cotton bodices, 2 cholera belts, woven and shaped, 2 dozen pocket handkerchiefs (quantity more than quality), 1 dressing-gown, flannel generally preferred, 4 woollen nightdresses, a few yards of extra flannel, useful in case of illness. *Dresses and Blouses* – Some like fairly thin woollen dresses, others prefer skirts and blouses. Coats and skirts not recommended, as it is generally too warm to wear a coat over a blouse. 12 cotton blouses, or materials for making them, also, two or three of thin flannel for walking; make with a turn-down collar, no stiff collars to be worn. 3 or 4 skirts to wear with the blouses, including a cycling skirt. 1 plain evening dress, or silk blouse for evening wear. 1 better dress. "A Sunday frock" if liked.'

A lady missionary, it was suggested, might care to solicit useful presents from friends before leaving home. These might include: bicycle, sewing machine, Commentary, tea-basket, cushions for easy chair, Manifold writer, baby organ, eiderdown quilt, small wringing machine, eau de cologne, picture frames, clock, Chinese afternoon tea sets. She might also consider taking with her suitable presents for the natives. Things that would not come amiss in that quarter included: coloured cotton handkerchiefs, large size, small looking-glasses, small bottles of scent, large beads, coloured pictures (much prized), picture 'scraps', knives and scissors, pens, pencils and paper, small cakes of fancy soap 'etc., etc.'. There was, finally, a suggested list of useful foodstuffs for consumption on the trek to the missionary's destination. Plenty of substantial biscuits were needed for lunching by the roadside in the middle of a march. For this, potted meat was nice. Each lady was also supposed to supply herself with plenty of toilet soap. And, by way of afterthought, 'Insist on having Huntley and Palmer's Biscuits, and avoid all tinned meats of the Army and Navy's own makes – they are not good.'

Missionary gentlemen had long been accustomed to such lists which, in their case, were comprehensive enough to suggest the requirements of an army quartermaster planning for a major expeditionary force. Besides a pith helmet from the Army and Navy Stores, a Willesden canvas tent by Edgington and a White African tin box by Farwig, every man was expected to muster a billhook, a hatchet, a fishmonger's knife and an 'old, cheap Snider rifle, plus 50 cartridges'. He would have a travelling tin bath, an umbrella with three white covers, four pairs of sleeping trousers, a small meat-mincing machine, two white tablecloths and seven yards of mosquito netting. A standard list of the time included 66 other different items of clothing and hardware, apart from these. There were, in addition, foodstuffs calculated to last the new missionary for a couple of years, like the 24 tins of Brand's or Mason's concentrated beef tea, the 12 tins of Edwards desiccated soup, the 12 lb. of Johnston's cornflour, the 4 lb. of curry powder (by Vencatachellum of Madras) and the 10 tins of Bartlett pears. There were the quantities of medicines and medical instruments, like one dozen bottles of opium tablets, ½ lb. of sulphur (an antidote to itching), five bottles of Eno's Fruit Salts, forceps, hypodermics and bedpan. By 1893, 'Livingstone's Rousers', from the pharmaceutical house of Burroughs Wellcome, were being advocated as laxatives, rather than as antidotes to malaria, as the eponymous Doctor first offered them.

Experienced missionaries were prolific in the advice they sent to headquarters in London for the help of the new men. One of the CMS representatives in Uganda, the Rev. R. H. Walker, must have spent several nights composing his long foolscap essay 'A few hints for a march to the Victoria Nyanza by the Old Road through Ugogo'. The great object, he promised, was to march in comfort; and to do this the march should never last for more than four hours at a stretch. It was a good plan to have breakfast before setting off about 6.45 am, to march for four hours, then stop for cooking and a rest lasting two hours, before proceeding. This method, he reckoned, should put about fifteen miles behind the marching missionary each day, which would be good going. 'On getting into camp, the first thing to do is to give orders for cooking, to send off men for firewood and water, and then to have a warm bath and a change of clothes . . . In half an hour after getting into camp on most days it is possible to have a warm bath and a cup of tea . . . The "boys" are particular about their own water, and often it is as well to take a drink of theirs to see if it is really as bad as what they may have brought you.'

Mr Walker declared that the sun was the greatest enemy in Africa by this time. Therefore a pith helmet and an umbrella should always be used. He had found it advisable to take ten grains of quinine if feeling other than 'perfectly well', a good idea to wear tweed after sunset and an overcoat after a wetting. 'A good general rule,' he added, 'is to avoid all hardship as much as possible; not to lose sight of the remnants of the last meal until the next one is in view; to begin in good time to make a comfortable bed for the night; never to walk in the rain and to avoid getting the feet wet.' It was also important to keep the porters together and to avoid straggling, never to leave the caravan on the march 'in pursuit of game, etc.'. Mr Walker promised newcomers to the mission field that he had tried all the above suggestions 'and hope to do so again'.

There were 'Notes on Barter and keeping a Barter Store' to be digested by the novices now, the fruits of one hundred years of hard-earned experience by the pioneers. Its author began with the observation that 'The native has no conception of our social life and mode of thought, and cannot understand how a white man can live in his country for the good of the natives and make a profit out of them at the same time'. This particular white man had seen missionary service in the Congo, where the natives by now were particularly exposed to this quaint combination, under the authority of King Leopold of the Belgians. Typical barter goods which had always been used by missionaries in exchange for foodstuffs were brass rods and pieces of iron roughly fashioned into spear heads; this was currency almost anywhere in Africa. In the Congo there was a local market in blue pipe beads, which were threaded on strings, one hundred at a time; they cost a farthing from the English factory which produced them, but they were worth a penny by the time they were offered to the natives in the Congo. One string of beads would buy an egg and ten strings would buy a chicken. Also acceptable was 34-gauge brass wire: and guns. The pay of a porter for carrying a 70 lb. load from the mission station at Tunduwa to San Salvador in the Lower Congo was two guns; a pig was valued at between five and ten flintlock guns, a goat at between two and four. But gradually, as the missions became well established, the range of their barter stores became wider and the tastes of their customers much more sophisticated. Where, in the early days, they had been confined to cloth, looking-glasses, spear-point knives, machetes, beads, iron spoons, tin plates and brass nails, by the beginning of the twentieth century they were trading with soap, candles, matches, lamps, chimneys, enamel ware, hinges, padlocks, corned beef, tins of tea, coffee and condensed milk, shirts, straw hats, Oxford shirting and best calico. Guns, curiously, were not allowed for trade over the counter; and alcohol was most certainly prohibited. 'Tawdry rings and jewellery should also be eschewed ... in some districts it would be disastrous to have in the store dolls or toy animals as a part of the barter stock. I have known such to be regarded as fetishes ... We should jealously guard our mission barter store from containing any article that will minister to the superstition, vanity and bad customs of our parishioners.'

Armed with these and many other sage counsels, the newcomers marched on Africa, out of the nineteenth century and into the twentieth. They joined an army now thoroughly secured in its emplacements, under the leadership of men like Bishop Tugwell in Nigeria, who would roar for recruits to fill any gap or any wavering in the missionary line. Writing in 1898 from Benin, which had just capitulated to British rule after a rather bloody campaign, he declared that 'it is heartbreaking work to visit such scenes and realise that Christian England cannot send forth a single man to undertake such a work in Christ's name ... There can be only one right attitude for the Church of England to adopt at this moment, and that is one of profound humiliation; shame and confusion should cover her face. Her sons dare not venture for Christ what every soldier will gladly venture for his Queen and country; viz., his health and his life ...'

A similar drumbeat had echoed across the laggard congregations of England once before, in the days in Melville Horne, and had produced a rush to the Christian colours. It was no less successful now. And, marching onwards as to war with the men, came the women to join ladies like Mrs Fisher, the first missionary Englishwoman among the pygmies of the Congo border, who was being conveyed across rivers in her hammock, surrounded by half-naked savages, with a gleam in her eye that did not seem wholly devoid of enjoyment.

In spite of the need still to march at fifteen miles per day through the bush of Africa to get to your base of operations, how different this world was from that of Melville Horne and the other early nineteenth-century missionaries, is suggested by a contemporary account of the Rev. Dennis Kemp, who belonged to the Wesleyan Mission on the Gold Coast. His baggage was almost as weighty as that listed for any missionary of the CMS, though he personally had found a flannel belt of great service in warding off dysentery, and he had a preference for the tinned foodstuffs of Messrs Crosse and Blackwell who 'are always most obliging in executing orders'. A man going out from London to West Africa by now would have sent all his heavy baggage to Messrs Elder, Dempster and Co. at Liverpool three days before his departure. After that 'it is possible to take the light luggage as late as the midnight train on any Friday from Euston, and after breakfast in the neighbourhood of Lime Street, to find our way to the Prince's landing stage in comfortable time for the tender which is to take us to one of the "African" or "British and African" companies' vessels. We must not raise our expectations too high. Our vessel is neither an Atlantic liner, a P and O, nor a Cape boat. But the line is being made increasingly comfortable; and, with the very genial captains, it is possible to have a very comfortable voyage, as far as the companies are concerned.' There were still missionary reservations about the passengers, however, though they were made rather more lightly than in previous decades. When Kemp went out 'our companions were not of the most select. One, a lady of the theatrical profession, who left us at Grand Canary, has lately been compelled to release her husband from his matrimonial vow. Another, a gentleman, has since died, leaving *two* wives and families in England to mourn his loss. And a third, a few years ago, was sentenced to two years' imprisonment for embezzlement.'

Once in Africa, however, you still travelled the hard way, though in Kemp's case this meant that 'we have to submit ourselves to the humiliating process of being borne about the country in a hammock, on the heads or shoulders of four men'. There was an unwritten rule that you changed your hammock bearers every ten miles or so; but the Germans economised on this expenditure by merely paying their carriers for the time a missionary was actually in the hammock. You also had to be prepared for the worst from malaria, though Kemp was writing in the year that Ronald Ross was to end the mystery of its cause; you regularly took Warburg's Fever Tincture – 'the most vile drug that man ever invented' – and unless you wanted to court disaster, you avoided standing by newly upturned earth in the wet season; you heard that your colleague, who had gone down with fever yesterday, had died today and would be buried tomorrow. You had to beware of other hazards. 'The most scrupulous total abstainers,' wrote Kemp, 'are of the opinion that alcohol, in one form or another, though perhaps not necessary in this land, cannot always be dispensed with . . . But the man who has not the grace to control his appetite should certainly avoid the Gold Coast; for in that thirsty land the temptations naturally are very great; and without the restraining influences of wife, mother or sister, a man's life may become such as to cause those of his old home to blush.'

Most of the missionary attitudes were unchanged by the procession of one century into another. An annual report of the Wesleyans at the time brought warming news of increased attendances at Sunday Schools on the Gold Coast, of progress in scriptural knowledge 'and influence for good upon the lives of heathen children'. A Fanti Gospel-singing band and choir had been formed to spread the Word around the land and was meeting with much success, though the missionaries thought they detected lurking dangers even here. 'A fear is expressed,' according to the report, 'that our numerical increase may ultimately prove costly. Our Sunday School anniversaries are in danger of lowering the standard of Christianity. If it is a fact that the processions headed by drum and fife bands ultimately lead to the ball-room, the heathen dance, and other worldly amusements, there can be no question as to what our action must be. In our anxiety for numerical success, we must not encourage methods which, however proper in themselves, create a relish for unholy and degrading pleasures.'

Kemp himself was quite prepared to generalise loftily about the heathens under his tutelage. He was fair enough to note that these Africans had a profound respect for their old people, and evidently loved their children – 'but we look in vain for that generous integrity of nature and honesty of disposition which always augurs true greatness, and is usually accompanied with undaunted courage and resolution; manliness. Cowardice is one of their most serious defects. In warfare they have become a byword among those who have commanded them; they are ever ready to obtain an advantage over the weak. Their savagery becomes manifest in their outrages upon their dead foes. Untruthfulness is transmitted at birth . . . Their supreme concern is grovelling sycophancy . . .' As for Kemp, 'I should consider myself worse than despicable if I failed to declare my firm conviction that the British Army and Navy are today used by God for the accomplishment of His purpose.' Then followed an anecdote, related with approval, about a gunboat which had conveyed two missionaries to some destination in the South Seas, in the course of which the naval officer in charge had promised a cannibal chief that if the two professional Christians were harmed, he would blow the islanders to bits with a broadside. 'I unhesitatingly declare my belief,' wrote Kemp, 'that these means were used by God for the preservation of the Missionaries from the cannibal cooking pots.' Kemp had quite an appreciation of the military arts. He attended a murder trial held under British jurisdiction and remarked upon the pathetic demeanour of the accused man. 'How nervously he fumbled the clumsy flint-lock gun while reloading it! He seemed to be at least fifteen minutes in completing his arrangements. We could not but reflect that any British officer with a spark of manliness must have felt devoutly thankful that events were so ordered as to spare him the necessity of wholesale butchery of these savages by Maxim gun.'

The same cast of mind, patronising at best, something more nearly vicious in its extreme forms, was to be found in missionaries throughout Africa. While Dennis Kemp was warily watching his Wesleyan Sunday Schools grow on the Gold Coast, the Rev. Colin Rae, of the Church of England, was marching as chaplain with a military force in South Africa. It had been despatched to punish a Tsoana chief, named Malaboch, who had refused to pay taxes because, he argued, the Europeans were systematically stealing land from his people. Many of them were eventually blown up in the caves where they had sought refuge, but Malaboch was captured and taken to Pretoria prison. In the course of the campaign which preceded these two dispensations of justice, Rae had observed the effect of a mission which had been working among the Tsoana. He was himself a missionary, though seconded briefly by the Bishop of Bloemfontein to the Army, but he was not much impressed by the efforts of his colleagues in the northern outpost. 'I do not entirely agree with their *modus operandi*,' he wrote, 'for I am in entire sympathy with the policy of the Government with regard to the native tribes. In bringing the natives out from their strongholds, and thus dispossessing the petty chiefs of their powers, the Government is doing a much better work than any Christian missionary has yet accomplished ... The missionary's object should be ... to teach them that great lesson which was practised and taught by the Great Master Himself, and of which the greatest of His Apostles commanded, "That if any would not work, neither should he eat ..." When the native is taught to *want*, then he will work; it is no use setting him a good example, which he will not follow; something more forcible must be done. He must be kept under control, and subjected to discipline, and the keynote must be work! work! work!'

In short, the racialism which had never been far from the surface whenever a white man contemplated a black one in Africa, was beginning to flow more freely than ever before. Missionaries had generally been no more exempt from this feeling than traders, though their professional ethic had given them a vocabulary and gestures which allowed them to camouflage their racialism with unlimited euphemism. The camouflage would never be abandoned, but in some places it was now applied very thinly indeed. Nowhere was this more the case than in the circumstances attending the last years of Bishop Samuel Adjai Crowther, in Nigeria. As a target for what was basically racial animosity, he was a particularly ironic choice. His rescue from slavery as a child, by the Royal Navy, had left him with an abiding sense of gratitude to the British and he never ceased to proclaim it. He had been so thoroughly Anglicised that in his early years as a bishop he ridiculed talk of Africa for the Africans as much as he later deplored attempts by some European missionaries to identify with the natives by dressing in similar fashion and eating the same food. He did nothing at all to put into practice Henry Venn's great and enlightened scheme for a self-governing native pastorate in the Niger diocese. At the same time, he could never shed his own African nature and sympathies completely. He tolerated a number of tribal customs which Europeans would have smashed because he believed that they were not necessarily antagonistic to Christianity. And in the whole of his half century as a bishop he did not celebrate a single marriage in his diocese, because he believed that the Anglican requirements for marriage were too demanding for the people of the Niger region.

By 1879, however, a number of things were beginning to change. Henry Venn was no longer in control of the CMS. In his place there now stood Edward Hutchinson, who began to reverse a long-standing policy. Hitherto, missionary activity up the Niger had been conducted by Africans under Crowther, on the grounds that the country was too unhealthy for Europeans. Hutchinson decided that the Niger Mission must be Europeanised, whether the climate was dangerous for them or not. A new steamer had just been presented to Crowther by his admirers in England, to enable him to move about his vast diocese more easily. Hutchinson, against the Bishop's wishes, placed a layman, J. H. Ashcroft, in charge of the steamer. More than this, he instructed Ashcroft to take control of all temporal affairs connected with the mission. This alone was enough to undermine Crowther's authority severely. Ashcroft's own arrogance completed the damage. There were times when Crowther wanted the steamer in order to make a visitation. It would not be available; very often this was because Ashcroft had gone trading in it. He also dismissed some of Crowther's men working up the river, without consulting the Bishop. And he regularly wrote to London, pleading with Hutchinson to send out more Europeans. 'I feel more and more convinced that it will have to be a mixed Mission,' he wrote on one occasion, 'and that Europeans must lead if there is to be any genuine substantial Christianity in the Niger.' Usually, however, these letters tended not to use the word European. One piece of correspondence contained the word 'white' fifty-two times. Very soon a report was being concocted upon the shortcomings of Crowther's administration. It was instigated by Hutchinson, most of its evidence came from Ashcroft and in the end it seriously backfired upon its authors. A committee of the CMS in London decided that many of its observations were grossly exaggerated, and the upshot was that Hutchinson resigned.

Crowther, however, was still to be harried by his European patrons. He was not, indeed, a very good administrator. For more than nine months of the year he lived in Lagos, which was a couple of hundred miles from the nearest station of the Niger Mission. It was very easy for an incompetent or corrupt African missionary agent to get away with anything up to murder, without the Bishop being properly aware of what was going on; as, indeed, a couple of them did in the notorious flogging to death of the slave woman, which was debated in the House of Lords. Moreover, Crowther was too gentle and forbearing a man to rule with a rod of iron. He tended to give his agents the benefit of any doubt that might be going about their conduct. He stood by them, unwisely, far too often. But Crowther's administrative failings were not the chief reason for the campaign that was now fully mounted, Hutchinson's resignation notwithstanding, to remove him.

In the late 1880s a clutch of new Europeans descended upon the Niger, hot from the evangelical meetings of Moody and Sankey in Britain. They belonged to that student army which mustered behind the battlecry 'The evangelisation of the world in this generation'. Among their novel ideas was the conversion of Sudanese Moslems by means similar to those used by the Catholic White Fathers in Algeria; they would dress in local fashion and go as completely native as a decent Christian dared. Yet their philosophy was, at bottom, based on white racial supremacy. They were very well educated young men, mostly the products of Cambridge University, and on arrival in Africa they expressed a great contempt for the under-educated Africans who were carrying out missionary work. One of them, J. A. Robinson, had a taste for markedly anti-Negro choruses in rousing student songs; and he was soon writing home that

'The Negro Race shows almost no sign of "ruling" power'. Another of them, G. W. Brooke, reported to Salisbury Square that the Niger Mission was a den of thieves, that the people from Sierra Leone working on it were 'swarms of ragamuffins' who were in reality conducting 'a charnel house'. Brooke very candidly set out their basic aims in one of his memoranda to London. 'We came here,' he wrote, 'hoping to carry on and expand the work of twenty years in the place, and now after two months we are driven to admit that there is no hope of success until we have first taken down the whole of the past work so that not one stone remains upon another. I mean that the pastors . . . must be changed, the message preached must be changed, the schoolchildren must be changed and the course in the school must be changed.'

They established what was virtually a local Inquisition. If what Mary Kingsley was soon to write was at all accurate, then some of the charges they brought against African members of the Niger Mission had a basis in fact. They were, however, presented in wildly sweeping generalisations about debauchery, cheating and slaveholding. They were also excessive. Archdeacon Dandeson Crowther, the son of the Bishop, was accused of deliberate lying and robbery. The Bishop himself was called a liar and was told to his face that his mission was the work of the Devil, because it had been financed from money that came out of the liquor trade. In documents that were sent to London, one of the white newcomers described the Sierra Leonians as the worst species of Africans, the descendants of people sold as slaves by their tribes because they were scum. The Inquisitors went so far as to suggest that Henry Venn and everyone who had been responsible for making Crowther a bishop had 'allowed zeal to outrun discretion and sentiment to have greater weight than sober facts'. At which point the CMS decided that the official history of the Niger Mission must now be rewritten. They gave the task to an Archdeacon Hamilton, whose views were known to coincide with those of the new men. And the new history asserted that the exclusive use of Africans up the Niger had been an accident, that the appointment of Crowther was unintentional and regrettable.

By this time African feeling, essentially nationalist in character, had placed itself vigorously behind the black Bishop. There were public demonstrations in his favour throughout Christianised Nigeria. The editors of Nigerian newspapers showered protests and articles upon Salisbury Square. Whether it liked it or not, the CMS was clearly required to adjudicate upon a matter which, morally, politically and territorially, was entirely within its province. It set up a committee, sprinkled with men like Dr Cust, who was sympathetic to Crowther, to examine the allegations. Cust and like-minded colleagues were heavily outvoted. The committee's report concluded that the Niger Mission was thoroughly corrupt and could only be redeemed by white supervision in future. Everything that Brooke, Robinson and their colleagues had argued for would be done, with one exception. It was damnably difficult to remove a bishop of the Church of England for anything save immorality and not even a black bishop could be dismissed for any smaller reason. So he would stay, though no apology was ever offered him for the offensive attitude of the white missionaries. His son Dandeson, lately Archdeacon and the Bishop's right-hand man, was demoted to a vicarage in Bonny, under a white supervisor.

It was now that the faithful Crowther at last turned on his old patrons. He had patiently endured the cross-examinations and the vilifications, he had even urged his agents to co-operate fully with the white missionaries in their investigations. He had long since accepted the fact that he was carefully and slowly being stripped of all his real authority, being reduced to nothing more than a confirming and ordaining machine. The pressure on him had been mounting for so long that it had produced a paralytic stroke and made him into a sick man. All this time he had kept his peace. But now, in the face of this ultimate rebuff from London, he spoke out against his tormentors. He accused Salisbury Square of 'fanning up the flames of race antipathies'. He went even further. When African nationalists asked him to declare the independence of the Church in the Niger Delta, he complied. It was the last shred of power remaining to him and he made it with a final genuflection towards European authority. He justified himself to the CMS on the grounds that this would promote Henry Venn's great strategy for Africa. Ironically, Henry Venn's successors had a new strategy and Crowther's act was merely a defiance. He refused to be moved from it, however, even when those successors sent a deputation from London to make him change his mind. A few weeks later, on the last day of 1891, he was dead.

The Christianising process survived Crowther's betrayal and the indignation of Nigerians which accompanied it, just as it survived other failures of the white missionaries elsewhere in Africa. Indeed, there was nothing more remarkable in these years than the events in Uganda after the upheavals which followed the Battle of Mengo had subsided. That portion of the country allotted to Protestantism in the post-war settlement was suddenly consumed with galloping evangelism, in which the people themselves took as much initiative as the missionaries. The origins of the movement, however, can be traced to one of the CMS men in Mwanga's capital, George Pilkington. He had undergone one of the more dramatic conversion experiences himself when he was an undergraduate at Cambridge and sailed for Africa as a missionary with a reputation as a linguist. He spent three years in Uganda, largely in translating the Bible, before removing himself to one of the islands on Lake Victoria, to rethink his vocation. There, he claimed, he had a vision. It was of 'a lost Truth, the loss of which gives Satan his opportunity of introducing both Mohammedanism and Popery'. Returning buoyantly from the lake to Mengo, he immediately held a series of revival meetings, in which people were invited to stand up and tell the rest of the congregation how they had come to know the Lord. The effect was astonishing, and no one was more nonplussed than Pilkington's colleagues in the CMS mission house.

In the next few weeks, people would dash up to the missionaries in the street, interrogating them about words and passages in the Bible. What was a tare, they asked? How far was it from Jericho to Jerusalem? And what precisely was the relationship between the Pharisees and the Sadducees in the Judaic social structure? A number of the missionaries had to send messages off to London, post-haste, requesting reference books and commentaries that might enable them to slake this sudden thirst for Biblical knowledge. Such texts as were already in the country, rapidly disappeared from the missionary store shelves and were devoured by the populace as avidly as any bestseller in the white man's world. One of Pilkington's colleagues, G. K. Baskerville, has described the growing exuberance with which the missionaries tried to cater for this sudden and rather unexpected demand for their literature: 'Talk about siege – if ever there was a siege it was yesterday, and this morning it seems likely to be renewed tenfold. I mentioned that our two canoes had come, and I gave out on Sunday that the Gospels of St Matthew would be sold Monday morning. I was roused up before it was light by the row of voices, and after dressing hurriedly, sallied out to the – I had almost said fight. Close to my house is a slight shed used for the cows to stand in, in the heat of the day. This was barricaded, keeping the people outside; but the barricades were useless – in came the door and we thought the whole place would have fallen. In ten minutes all the 100 Gospels were sold. We now returned for some breakfast. I had just opened another box, which I strongly suspected to be books, and I found beautiful little reading books, arranged by Samwel when at the Coast, about 800 in all. Here was a find! I had barricaded my house front window and we sold through it;

the doctor selling to the women in another place. Now was a scrimmage and the shells came pouring in. I have in the house six or seven loads of cowries. In the evening we opened two other boxes, which proved to contain Prayer Books and large wall reading sheets. I am going to try and get some breakfast now before we begin selling.' After a very industrious day, Baskerville added: 'We have survived and taken 36,000 shells for the Prayer Books. But I should think 1000 or more people are waiting about, each with shells, mad to buy a book, but we have none to sell.'

Early in 1894, eighty native evangelists went into the country from Mengo. They travelled like the evangelists of old, in twos, bearing Gospels and reading sheets. Soon, they were being received with open arms by the district chiefs, being given banana plantations from which they could support themselves, as an inducement to settle in a particular area. By the end of the year the number of churches and Gospel reading rooms in the land of the Baganda had risen from twenty to two hundred; every day they were attended by about 4,000 people, with perhaps 20,000 on Sundays. When Pilkington's translation of the Bible was published 1,100 copies were sold in twelve months, together with 4,000 copies of his New Testament, 13,500 copies of one or other of the Gospels and 40,000 copies of Bible stories. Professor Roland Oliver has identified this as 'one of the most remarkable and spontaneous movements for literacy and new knowledge which the world has ever seen'. And although similar trends on a smaller scale could be observed elsewhere in Africa at this time, it is significant that the movement was particularly powerful among the Baganda.

The Baganda stood, in relation to the other peoples of Uganda, in much the same position as the Ibo among Nigerians, and the Bengali among Indians; sharper and quicker witted, hungrier for self-improvement, more adept and more arrogant than their fellows. The confusing changes of sectarian allegiance among the Baganda in the years before the Battle of Mengo, the rapid switches from Islam to Protestantism and then to Catholicism were fundamentally, perhaps, a result of their ability to spot an opportunity for advancement and a desire to make the most of it. They were the subject of such envy among the tribes of East Africa that Bishop Tucker discovered, when making a tour of the country in 1899, that the neighbouring Basoga people did not want to be taught in their own language, but in Luganda. For Luganda had become the language of promotion.

The Baganda now became not only evangelists in the surrounding territories but colonisers in the wake of their British patrons. Wherever

21. Mrs Fisher, 'the first Englishwoman to the Pygmies', being carried across the Malaku river, Central Africa, in 1903.

22. Eventually travelling became rather more sophisticated. Miss Taylor being conveyed by mono-wheel, East Africa, 1926.

23. Anglican missionary preaching to a sun-dazzled group of tribesmen in East Africa, early twentieth century.

24. A priest of Cardinal Lavigerie's order, the White Fathers, proclaiming the Gospel in the Central African bush, early twentieth century.

25. Josiah Olunowo Oshitelu, founder and first Primate of the Church of the Lord (Aladura) – one of the many separatist Christian sects that have emerged in Africa in the twentieth century.

British officials opened up new country, they brought in Baganda to fill key posts in native administration. It was Baganda who organised native labour for public works, who built roads and rest camps for European officers on tour; at the same time they built churches and schools for the Baganda evangelists who were spreading through the same areas. Visiting Europeans were soon remarking on the contrast between the well-kept and cultivated lands where the Baganda were lodged, and the bedraggled wilderness around them. By the turn of the century Archdeacon Willis of the CMS was writing that 'you will see them at every centre of importance on the Nile, down the railway, far north of Mount Elgon; the whole country for a radius of hundreds of miles is today being travelled by the Baganda'. By 1905, twenty Baganda evangelists had started work with the Gordon Memorial Mission in the southern Sudan. When the census of 1911 was taken, with a population of 660,000 Baganda, some 282,000 claimed to be Christian.

This was by far the most impressive advance of Christianity in Africa. But on almost all fronts the missionary armies and their supporting native troops were moving steadily forward in these years. They advanced so rapidly and from so many different points of the denominational compass that there was a danger of them colliding in the field. 'Without co-operation,' said one missionary, 'the struggle against heathenism cannot be carried to a successful issue.' So they began to enter into agreements about respective spheres of influence, in much the same way as the Great Powers had done a little earlier. The United Presbyterians of North America and the CMS of Great Britain thus agreed between themselves that in the Sudan, where both were established at the turn of the century, the education of girls should be left to the Anglicans, while the education of boys should be regarded as the sole province of the Americans. The Catholics, of course, proceeded independently, setting up their missions around the continent wherever they saw an opportunity, keeping themselves to themselves and praying that the whole world, Protestant and pagan alike, might soon see the true Light.

It was in the spirit of divide and rule that the Protestant societies, from every European and North American country, proposed a World Missionary Conference, which was eventually held at Edinburgh in 1910. The societies attending this conference were sufficiently aware that the differences between them were potentially damaging to the Christian cause, that they agreed beforehand upon an agenda in which 'no expression of opinion should be sought from the Conference on any matter involving any ecclesiastical or doctrinal question on which those taking part in the Conference differ among themselves'. The matters which they were prepared to discuss were therefore prearranged in a common front, which would provoke little of self-criticism. They talked about carrying the Gospel to all the non-Christian world, about the Church in the mission field, about education in relation to non-Christian religions, about the preparation of missionaries, about the missionary message in relation to non-Christian religions, about the home base of missions, about missions and Governments, about co-operation and the promotion of unity. Given that the world was somewhat altered by the passage of a century and a quarter, that matters of education and relations with Governments had become real issues, it was an agenda not markedly dissimilar from those of the meetings held in the days of William Carey and the founding fathers of the three original British missionary societies.

It was an agenda and a conference which saw little blemish in Protestant Christianity, which wilfully ignored those stains that were tacitly acknowledged as being there, and which still saw Christianity and its missionary purpose as a shining light surrounded by darkness. The Conference was warned by a leading German Lutheran, Professor Gustav Warneck, that the chief priority for the missionary societies of Christianity was the race against Islam for the conversion of the pagan world. The German missions springing up along the East African coast had been confronted with the counter-attractions of Islam, just as the CMS had experienced them in Uganda three decades earlier. The Conference took note of the Professor's warning, and bent its collective mind to finding a solution.

But an even greater threat to the claims of Christianity before the pagan world was just then beginning to take shape on the horizon.

17

PARADISE LOST

The Great War for Civilisation, as the British military medal-strikers were eventually to call it, was bound to have a profound effect upon missionary work in Africa. Apart from any other considerations, Africa was second only to Europe as a battlefield from the moment that hostilities broke out in 1914. In the scramble for imperial possession of the continent during the penultimate decade of the nineteenth century, the Germans had acquired territory in Togoland, the Cameroons, South-West Africa and East Africa, while the British surrounded them on almost every side. In the first three of these areas, the fighting was over within a few weeks of the opening shots being fired; Togoland, indeed, was occupied within a fortnight. In East Africa, the conflict was much more sustained, lasting as long as the warfare in Europe itself. Bounded by British East Africa and Uganda to the north, the Belgian Congo to the west, Northern Rhodesia and Nyasaland to the south-west and Portuguese East Africa to the south, this was by far the largest of Germany's African possessions in 1914, with an African population of over seven millions, spread across 384,000 square miles. It was a prize to be fought for and, in von Lettow-Vorbeck, the Germans had a local commander equal in skill and courage to any colleague who was simultaneously thrashing around northern France and Flanders. A very small proportion of his army was German – he started with 5,000 troops, of whom no more than 260 were Europeans – but, first in open battle, and then with guerrilla tactics, he kept British and Allied soldiers fully occupied for four years. Until December 1915 he controlled Lake Tanganyika and, in spite of the fact that his enemy ruled the sea routes by which he might hope for supplies and reinforcements, it was not until General Smuts took command of the Allied forces opposing him, early in 1916, that the tide of the campaign began to go against him. Von Lettow-Vorbeck, indeed, was never actually defeated in Africa. He voluntarily emerged from the hills when news of the European armistice came through, and laid down his arms. By then he had just over 4,000 Africans and 155 Europeans at his disposal. The Allies had employed, from start to finish of the East African campaign, 52,000 Indians, 43,000 South African whites, 3,000 Rhodesians and 27,000 black Africans as fighting soldiers.

The missionaries of almost every nationality were sucked into the Great War, whether they liked it or not. If they were French, and of combatant age, they were conscripted into service and not even priests were exempted. Thirty-one priests of the Lyons Society for African Missions, which by 1914 was working in French West Africa, in the Gold Coast, Nigeria and Egypt, were mobilised for service in Europe the day war broke out, and another forty-one were pressed into local military service. The White Fathers were drastically reduced in numbers; they lost thirty-four men to the colours in Uganda alone. Although the British were placed under no such statutory obligation, a great number of their missionaries volunteered to fight for King and Country; in 1917, the CMS in Uganda reported that seven of its missionaries were actively on war service. When ordained, such men generally found a place as chaplains to the forces, while the medical missionaries went to doctor the troops. Others officered the various native carrier corps that were established to do the donkey work for the fighting soldiers on African soil.

For Africans, too, were pitched willy-nilly into this white man's war. Many of them were pressed into service at home and overseas; many more volunteered. They were dragooned into established colonial regiments like the West African Frontier Force, which had been created as the military arm of the Royal Niger Company in 1897 by Lugard, who had been despatched to Nigeria after his conspicuous success with the Maxim gun in Uganda. They were marshalled into new battalions, like the King's African Rifles, which fought the askaris of von Lettow-Vorbeck around East Africa. Most of them became military porters in the carrier corps. Northern Rhodesia alone recruited 41,000 natives for such duties in East Africa. France had something approaching half a million Africans among her colonial combatant troops, almost all of whom saw service outside Africa. Lugard estimated that the British African contingents numbered 700,000 men, and thought he knew why most of the volunteers fought for their colonial masters. 'It would, I think, be untrue to say that they gave their lives to uphold the British Empire, for that was a conception beyond their understanding . . . their chief motives were, I think, personal love of their officers, the terms of pay offered, the decorations they hoped to win, ignorance of the conditions of warfare to which they would be exposed, and their natural courage and love of adventure.'

Wherever Africans were mustered, missionaries took the lead in explaining the needs of the contending armies, in acting as recruiting sergeants for the military. Most of the carrier corps were run by regular army officers, but the missionaries began to create corps of their own. One of them was the Kikuyu Missions Volunteer Carrier Corps, commanded by Dr J. W. Arthur, of the Church of Scotland. Eight of its eleven officers were missionaries and half of the two thousand carriers belonged to stations of the CMS, the other half coming from stations run by the Church of Scotland, the Africa Inland Mission and the Gospel Missionary Society. They divided into denominational groups for daily prayers, but held united services every Sunday. Bishop Frank Weston of Zanzibar was another who raised a private army; for some months he led his two thousand men in person and did such sterling work that General Smuts commended him warmly. 'May I thank you,' wrote the South African, 'for your great services at the head of your Carrier Corps in G.E.A. The Archbishop of Canterbury was much interested in my picture of you marching with an enormous crucifix at the head of your black columns.' A lot of Africans died in this wartime service to the white men. Out of a total of 162,000 recruited for the purely military Carrier Corps in East Africa, fifteen per cent were known to have died by the time the war was over; slightly more, 25,600, were listed as deserted or missing, and over half of them were presumed to have perished also.

Of the missionaries, it was obviously the Germans who suffered most, in one way or another, from the Great War. Their treatment varied from area to area as the Allies advanced into German territory; generally speaking, it was lenient to begin with, becoming progressively tougher as the war continued in East Africa and Europe. At Blantyre, which became the chief Allied military base in Nyasaland, the principal Church of Scotland missionary, Alexander Hetherwick, publicly preached a new form of racialism; the Germans, he declared, were Huns, and German missionaries, if they had any pretence to Christianity, ought to condemn the warfare of their countrymen. There were Germans of the Berlin Konde Synod in the district – twenty-three men, twenty-one women and forty-four children. Under the combined influence of Hetherwick's attacks and von Lettow-Vorbeck's irritatingly persistent campaign, they were consigned to a succession of prison camps between Blantyre and Egypt, finally reaching Germany in 1919.

This was a fate shared by many of their colleagues up and down Africa. The most celebrated missionary prisoner of all was Albert Schweitzer. He had sailed with his wife for Gabon in 1913, in the service of the Paris Missionary Society. He had scarcely settled down to work in his clinic at Lambarene when war was declared. That night the Schweitzers were informed that, as Alsatians, they were prisoners of war, and were promptly put under African guards at the mission house by their French colleagues. Schweitzer's intellectual resources were somewhat greater than that of most missionaries and the next day he began to write a book of philosophy that had long been swilling around in his head. Three months later he was allowed to get on with his medical work among the natives and the truce lasted for nearly three years. But in September 1917 the Schweitzers were removed to Europe and interned in an old monastery in the Pyrenees, before being placed in a special camp for Alsatians. There they remained until repatriation through Switzerland in 1918. It was 1924 before Lambarene saw them again.

The Germans in South Africa fared best. Many were interned there but they were treated with more sympathy than in other places; there were none of the wholesale removals that occurred in East Africa. At one place in the Union a missionary named Pakendorf was interned in 1914. At once, his African congregation advanced upon the local magistrate's office, where this conversation took place.

'Where is our minister?'

'He is in Maritzburg.'

'Who has taken him off and what is he doing there?'

'He is under arrest.'

'What has he done?'

'He has not done anything, but he is a German.'

'We have never yet heard that a man who has done nothing gets placed under arrest. Besides, it's no crime to be a German. He can't help having been born a German. We must urge our request that at the earliest possible moment he return to us, for he is our father and shepherd.'

Pakendorf was released.

When an order was made for the internment of Moravian missionaries in Cape Province, their superintendent, von Calker, went to the magistrate with the original letters written by Lord Somerset in the 1840s, inviting the Moravians to settle in the district. He asked the official whether the promise of a British Governor was to be broken so easily. And the magistrate, having read these inconvenient documents, cancelled the internment order.

There were several instances of German missionary work being taken over sympathetically by missionary societies of the Allied nations. In Togoland, Germans of the Bremen and Basel Missions were well established at the outbreak of war. The fighting there was over almost as soon as it had begun and for some time the missionaries were allowed to continue on their stations, apart from the handful of men who had signed on for service with the German forces, and been taken as prisoners of war. Indeed, a consignment of Bibles in the local Ewe language, which had been printed in Berlin and was ready for despatch at the outbreak of hostilities, was allowed to reach its destination by way of Amsterdam. But in 1916, with anti-German feeling at home running high, the British authorities took a harder line and the missionaries were deported. As they left, members of the Presbyterian United Free Church of Scotland, who had long been based nearby in eastern Nigeria, moved in to take charge of the schools and the churches that the Germans had painstakingly built up, on the mutual understanding that they would not change the principles on which the work had been based. Something similar happened in the Cameroons, where the Paris Missionary Society took over from the Basel Mission. In East Africa, the CMS took charge of stations evacuated by the Bethel Mission on the western shore of Lake Victoria and American Lutherans accepted responsibility for stations in the foothills of Mount Kilimanjaro, which had been run by the Leipzig Mission. Americans, being neutral for much of the war, found themselves repeatedly in the role of custodians throughout Africa. As for Catholic missions run by Germans, transfers of manpower were made by the Vatican. In Togoland, German Fathers of the Divine Word were replaced by Frenchmen of the Society of African Missions; in the Cameroons, Pallotine Fathers gave way to Fathers of the Holy Ghost; in East Africa, where German Benedictines of the St Ottilien Congregation ran a number of missions, after 1916 these were taken over by Swiss Capuchin friars and Italian Consolata Fathers.

The upheaval in missionary life, the break in continuity and the general difficulty in carrying on work as normal in abnormal conditions, formed only a small part of the damage done by the Great War in Africa. The displacement of a few hundred European workers was nothing compared with the moral consequences upon the African imagination of the war itself. Fighting was anything but a foreign experience to these black people.

For their manhood it had always been a primary instinct. They might have some reservations about the white man's method of engaging in combat, and a Matabele tribesman once expressed them thus: 'With your weapons you shoot from far, far away and do not know whom you are killing; that is unmanly. We prefer to fight man to man.' But battle was a necessary engagement from time to time in order to survive, in order to prove virility, in order to demonstrate loyalty to a chief or a king. For a century and more, however, they had been told persistently and vehemently that fighting and all the savage instincts which it released were both fruitless and wicked. The white people who for generations had preached this curious and alien doctrine had, indeed, justified their presence in Africa as messengers of gentleness and love; they could have no other justification for being there. They had invoked a new god who went under many names, but one of the names most frequently repeated by these missionaries had been Prince of Peace. All the prizes of that fabulous world outside Africa which were dangled before African eyes, had been offered suggestively in His name. True, the white man had occasionally gone to war himself, but this had been against black men unwilling to accept his message. Such warfare could be justified, by an effort of will and a large degree of open-mindedness, as a necessary destruction of evil forces; this, at least, was another part of the white man's message.

But now, without any warning at all, the white men had turned upon each other on a scale which the African could only imagine, from the rumours available to him, was infinite. No longer was the Prince of Peace benevolently guiding the white man's hand. And from the evidence before the African's eyes, the white man was to be seen as a fellow not very different from himself. He, too, could behave with tribal savagery in order to demonstrate his loyalty to a regional leader. He could also be cowardly and weak, where his legend had always insisted that he was courageous and strong. As an Englishman wrote to *The Times*, when the war was drawing to a close, 'I could mention cases where black men standing steadfast in a fight have seen white men turn and run'. This man was acutely conscious of the damage done to the European's prestige in Africa as a result of the Great War. 'Our consistent and universal teaching has been that it was sinful to fight,' he wrote. 'Any transgression of this law by the native has been almost universally followed by punitive measures on our part. Casting this teaching to the winds, and without any apparent reason to him, we have suddenly called upon the native not only to kill his fellow-native, but to kill the white man.' There had been instances at the start of the war of British native patrols, encountering

German native patrols led by a German officer, sending a message down the line for their own white man to come and shoot at the enemy white man, while the black men shot at each other. 'The sudden, and to the native, reasonless reversion from our teaching has without question weakened the white man's prestige, while at the same time the native has gained – and justifiably so – the knowledge of his own indispensability to us and his prowess generally as a soldier.'

There were other effects. In Northern Rhodesia, uneasy whites noticed how the authority of chiefs and headmen, which they had been laboriously undermining for years as part of what they called a pacifying process, had been fortified by the war because the chiefs had been required to use their ancestral powers of persuasion on behalf of the war effort, to recruit natives into the forces. There were occasions when Africans, suddenly aware that their powers were not as inferior as they had been given to understand, turned on their European superiors and taunted them with a future in which power would no longer reside where most recent traditions had placed it. When a Belgian officer caught one of his askaris in a mild piece of looting, and ordered him to replace a book which he had just taken from a German mission shelf, the African burst out angrily, 'You Europeans just don't want us to know what is in your books, for once we could read them we should become as bad as you are – even worse – and it would be you who would then have good reason to be afraid of us.'

The seeds of nationalism, which had started to sprout intermittently in Nigeria and elsewhere on the West coast almost before the colonising process was completed, were to be much nourished by the discoveries of the Great War, and gradually given a sense of direction in the years immediately after it, as black men who had watched the white men betray their own teachings in several quarters of the world, shared these discoveries around camp fires in the jungle, the bush and the high and endless veldt. The missionaries who returned to their task, when the fighting was finished, frequently transferred their own deepest perplexities about the war into the minds of their pupils, struggling to perceive clarity where there was none and justifying by obscurities. 'The conflict,' wrote an Englishman in Nyasaland, 'has had its lessons for our boys. "Christian nations are at war: is that the fault of Christianity?" This question came to them, and in its answer they learned that there are still Europeans who do not owe allegiance to Christ. That still puzzles some of them, and troubles some of them; but it also strengthens them, for it shows them that there is no colour line in the Church of Christ, and that if a man is not necessarily in the Church because he is white of skin, neither is he necessarily outside of the Church because his skin is black.'

Only the very wisest of these missionaries admitted their own defeat in the face of the questions which the Great War flung in their face before their African converts. One of these was Albert Schweitzer, who said that 'We are, all of us, conscious that many natives are puzzling over the question how it can be possible that the whites, who brought them the Gospel of Love, are now murdering each other, and throwing to the winds the commands of the Lord Jesus. When they put the question to us we are helpless. If I am questioned on the subject by negroes who think, I make no attempt to explain or to extenuate, but say that we are in "front" of something terrible and incomprehensible. How far the ethical and religious authority of the white man among these children of nature is impaired by this war we shall only be able to measure later on. I fear that the damage done will be very considerable.'

Part of the damage was that the Christian victors appeared rather slow to forgive the Christian vanquished. The Treaty of Versailles not only seemed intent on bleeding Germany to the bone; it obviously had no intention of allowing German missionaries to resume their work in Africa. Its Article 438 declared that German mission property should be handed over to trustees 'composed of persons holding the faith of the mission whose property is involved'. Immediately after the war, a Conference of British Missionary Societies sent a deputation to the Government, led by the Archbishop of Canterbury, asking for favourable treatment of German missionaries. It was told that their work in Africa and elsewhere could not be continued where it had been broken off 'for a period to be defined hereafter'. The embargo was not lifted until the middle of 1924 and it was not until the following year that the Germans began to dribble back to their old stations, not until 1930 that the last settlement was completed and the last mission restored to its former owners.

Another part of the damage was done in Europe, to the enormous machinery that had been laboriously constructed over a century in order to keep the missionary enterprise running. The Great War shattered faith in a number of values which had been handed on firmly and unquestioned from the nineteenth century to the twentieth, almost all of them identified with the institutional Christianity which had both blessed them and been strengthened by them. No one had thought to question imperialism when it had been seen and advertised not only as a patriotic benefit and adventure but as a Christian responsibility. But the end product of imperialism had come home to Europe in its most ghastly form in the decimations of Passchendaele, in the hungry streets of post-war Berlin, in the spectacle of gallant officers and gentlemen eking out their genteel poverty upon a range of chicken farms which were soon collapsing from one end of southern England to the other. Not even the victors, it appeared, had achieved much out of their Great War for Civilisation. The Church which had tacitly sanctioned the causes of this war was thus tacitly discredited for the first time in many generations. And the missionary enterprise, which was symbolically the Church at its most militant, its very own form of imperialism, was discredited before a growing army of Europeans for the same reasons that caused disillusionment in Africa. It had been founded specifically to bestow the benefits of civilised man upon the degraded heathen. After the revelations of the Western Front, no sane man could fail to wonder precisely what civilisation consisted of and just who was degraded.

The effect of this disillusionment took some time to be worked out in the mission field. With the exception of the hamstrung Germans, the missionary societies of Europe and North America carried on just as before, the moment the war was over. The number of missionaries continued to grow for a couple of decades; where there were 4,102 white Protestants working in Africa in 1911, there would be 5,556 in 1925 and 7,514 in 1938; and the Catholics could show a similar advance. But support dwindled on an increasing scale now. The income of the missionary societies began to fall, as a growing number of Gleaners, Sowers and kindred souls discovered more pressing requirements for their pennies nearer home; and the central missionary funds of the Catholic Church were to decline by half between 1931 and 1935. Never again would a missionary lobby in Great Britain hold a meeting with the sure feeling that the eyes of almost all the nation were upon it. In the glorious days at the start of the enterprise, *The Times* had spent a full page, six densely packed columns of minute type, upon reporting the first anniversary meeting of the Society for the Extinction of the Slave Trade and for the Civilisation of Africa. No missionary meeting now could hope to rate more than a single column in the national press.

Yet the greatest damage of all to the cause of Christian growth in Africa was perhaps done by missionaries themselves, after the war was over, when they returned to their task with all their old assumptions and their professional sense of purpose. The damage occurred all over Africa, but it was most obvious in East Africa, where missionary work had been most disrupted by the fighting between German and Allied forces.

This has to be seen against a background of what has since become known politely as paternalism. Historically, both the Catholics and the Church of England had long maintained that, wherever they proselytised, the development of native churches was of prime importance. Ever since the early seventeenth century the Vatican had insisted that a local clergy should be developed as quickly as possible, in the wake of Jesuit, Dominican and other European teaching. In 1845 a synod of Catholic missionaries in India had been told that they 'must realise that the fundamental objective of their work was the creation of strong local churches controlled by native priests and bishops. To produce catechists and auxiliaries was not sufficient; an education of high quality must be given to the indigenous inhabitants to fit them to occupy the highest positions in the Church.' Shortly after settling in East Africa, the Holy Ghost Fathers had opened a junior seminary at Bagamoyo in 1869, in order to begin this side of their work. And the White Fathers in Uganda, with Cardinal Lavigerie's reminder that they must on no account attempt to produce black Frenchmen ringing in their ears, had done likewise as soon as conditions after the Battle of Mengo had settled into a form of stability. The Anglican CMS had been given a similar injunction by its great secretary Henry Venn and had been ordaining native ministers all over Africa since the middle of the nineteenth century. The policy had been played down after Venn's death by his successors in Salisbury Square, but a number of Anglican bishops in the missionary field had continued to urge it upon their workers. Bishop Weston, whose private carrier corps of Africans was much better cared for than any comparable body organised by the Army during the war, had said in 1898 that native clergy must be regarded as equals by whites, for 'we must remember that they, and not we, are the permanent leaders of the African Church'. Bishop Tucker was another who subscribed to this view.

By 1914 the White Fathers had just ordained the first two black Catholic priests in East Africa. By then the CMS had ordained fifty-four Africans as priests of the Church of England and the missionaries of the UMCA had added another small handful to this Anglican tally. The difference between the Anglican and Catholic performance here could not fairly be taken as an indication that the Catholics were so much less zealous than the Anglicans in creating a native clergy. The fact was that they required far higher standards of education among their priests than the Church of England missionaries. The Anglicans were sometimes happy to ordain an African who had been regular in his church-going for years, after only a few months of special training. Ever since the Council of Trent in the sixteenth century, the requirements of the Catholic Church had been infinitely stiffer for ordination to the priesthood and had been inflexibly observed; and in an African context, the demand for a celibate priesthood alone was a great obstacle to recruiting. It was for a combination of these reasons that the Holy Ghost Fathers had abandoned their seminary by 1880, training their pupils after that date as catechists rather than priests; the material they had been tutoring, to put it bluntly, had been unequal to the demands made upon it. And the Catholic policy was somewhat vindicated by the experience of the Anglicans, who lost twenty per cent of these early ordinations, through backsliding into other sects or for a variety of moral offences.

Nevertheless, Anglicans and Catholics had made some attempt to create an African priesthood which might in theory one day lead these two branches of Christianity in Africa. Not one of the other very numerous missionary societies working in East Africa – Protestants from a number of European countries as well as America – had made the slightest attempt to do this. They were all evangelical in their cast of mind; they believed in something called 'spreading the Gospel', which meant preaching a code of conduct and a mythology but doing nothing to elevate the African pupil to the status of his white teacher. There were plenty of Anglicans in the ranks of the CMS with this same cast of mind; it was much more obvious among them, evangelically-inclined, too, than it was among their Anglican High Church colleagues of the UMCA. In 1899 Bishop Tucker had proposed a constitution for the Church of England in Uganda which would have put white and black men on an equal footing before God and man. It was roundly rejected by the Bishop's white missionaries, a majority of whom preferred not to contemplate a situation in which any of them might one day be placed in a subordinate position to an African. This vote, in fact, was the beginning of a decline in Anglican fervour for a native priesthood in East Africa. Almost half of the fifty-four who had been ordained by the outbreak of the Great War, had been made priests in the six years which preceded the Bishop's proposal; the rest came in the fifteen years which followed.

The war itself made demands upon the black Christians of East Africa that had been unknown before. They had not, to any great extent, been trained to take charge of any Church work but they frequently found now that they had to run the Church in their localities. White missionaries had either been deported (if they were German) or had gone off to fight (if they were Allies) and those that remained were often attending to the missionary work of the absentees in addition to their own, which meant long periods away from any group of converts. In these circumstances the black Christians of every denomination performed small wonders. The Catholics of Uganda at the outbreak of war had been building a new cathedral at Rubaga. Hostilities did not mean only that many of the White Fathers vanished into the ranks of the French Army; it also brought work to a standstill for lack of money from Europe. At once the local Catholic chiefs collected £900 on their own initiative so that work could be resumed, and when that ran out men continued to labour on the building without payment. Africans were sometimes obliged to fend for themselves much more than that.

There were a number of missionary stations run by the CMS in German East Africa. The Englishmen who had not managed to get over the border on the declaration of war were interned, just as German missionaries were interned in British Africa. The Africans who were left behind on these stations suffered a great deal in their absence. Fourteen teachers and two deacons, who were imprisoned by the Germans and put in chain gangs, died as a result of their treatment. Three African priests, however, remained free until 1916 and, apart from keeping their church going, they led their community as a whole through a period of great deprivation; most of the grain harvest was requisitioned by the Germans to feed their troops and there was famine in the land. When the British missionaries returned in 1917, after the territory had been occupied by Allied forces, they found that although a number of church buildings were in a state of disrepair, Christianity was in surprisingly good heart. According to the annual report of the CMS for 1917–18, 'In spite of what they had suffered at the hands of the German askaris . . . most of the African agents had continued their work, and in many places the schools as well as the Sunday services had been carried on. Some, but only a few, cases of backsliding occurred, and Canon Rogers wrote: "The work has undergone a test of the severest possible kind, and has stood better than anyone would have anticipated" . . . The church, school and teachers' house at Buigiri have been burnt, but the spiritual work has been fairly maintained . . . At Zoyisa, an outstation in the district, work has been continued ever since the war began, save once when the teacher and his flock had to flee to the mountains for safety. "There is great keenness and spirituality" among the people, it is said; "the congregations number about 500; classes are being taught by the catechumens, who also help in the schools and there are many desirous of becoming enquirers." A somewhat similar account is given of Cilonwa, another outstation, where Mr Banks found many candidates for baptism.'

The reference to 'African agents' in that report is significant of the general attitude of the white missionaries to what were, after all, ordained priests of the Church of England. And the subsequent annual reports of the CMS are significant of the grudging regard the white missionaries had for the black man's ability to carry on Christian community life without a European overseer. First of all they speak of the work having come to a standstill, a very strange contradiction of what had evidently been discovered at the end of hostilities. Then they stress the failures rather than the successes; and a lot of these, the cohabitation among Christians without the benefit of marriage, could be attributed to the lack of enough African priests to get into outlying districts and perform marriage ceremonies. It is also clear that the missionaries are bent upon introducing the old order exactly as it was on the outbreak of war; there is much talk of restoring 'discipline' among their African converts.

The attitude was not a purely British phenomenon. It was to be found among Protestant missionaries from Germany as well, when these had returned to their interrupted work. What happened in the district of the Lutheran Bethel Mission, in Tanga Province, is a case in point. Most of the missionaries left in 1917, in the face of the British advance across German East Africa, leaving a handful behind in charge of a hospital. The British allowed these Germans to continue this work until 1921, but it meant that all the work of the mission outside the doctoring and nursing had to be conducted by Africans. At that stage there was not a single ordained African and the work was taken over by teachers, led by a man called Luka Jang'andu. He was a man with an instinct for leadership, who organised the congregations into self-supporting work-forces and punished those who were lazy. An observer of the events taking place at the time remarked that 'In 1917 the word of God was further spread when the church was being run by natives. Those who had accepted Christianity were helped by the Holy Spirit and had a burning zeal without being forced.' He said that 'During that time there was a true manifestation of love. At funerals many came from far and sang hymns and played trumpets. One day during a baptism a pagan was so moved that he wanted to be baptised on the spot – but he was asked to receive instruction first.' By then, Jang'andu and six others had been ordained hastily by the remnant of German medical missionaries, for the British had decided that they, too, must be deported in the wake of their colleagues.

For the next few years Jang'andu and the other African ministers, working without any pay, built even more firmly upon the foundations laid by the missionaries. They baptised great numbers of new converts. They extended the influence of the old mission to workers on sisal plantations who had not been reached by the Europeans. Everyone who was involved in this venture at the time seemed to feel that here was something authentically Christian in its sense of community, of mutual care, of mutual growth. But back in Germany, news filtered through of the high rate of conversions since the Africans had been left to their own devices. Instead of applauding this, the people at the headquarters of the Bethel Mission expressed concern. They seem to have been under the impression that the Africans were behaving irresponsibly in their absence. Eventually, the Germans returned in the somewhat more relaxed atmosphere of the late 1920s. They found that their fears of African irresponsibility were almost entirely unjustified. In spite of this, they simply marched in and took control of something that had evidently been growing without their help. 'When the missionaries came back,' wrote the observer of these events, 'there were signs that the Holy Spirit had left, for the desire to cooperate for the work of the Lord was no more seen. Trouble started when they started grading workers. Hatred started.'

Something less downright than hatred was to be a general pattern in Africa wherever white missionaries continued where they had left off after the interruptions of the Great War. But brooding resentment can damage a man and all his works even more than hatred. Of this period a historian of the Church in East Africa has written that 'Many new hospitals and schools were opened, it is true, and large numbers of people were baptised, but there was little progress in handing over any real responsibility to Africans'. Not until 1939 was a black man made a bishop in East Africa. And he, Joseph Kiwanuka, was significantly a Catholic who had been educated and trained by the White Fathers. No African was allowed to approach similar status among the Protestant Churches until 1947, when the Anglicans made Aberi Balya an Assistant Bishop in Uganda. It is very difficult to avoid the conclusion that in the years following the Great War the Europeans in general were rather desperately trying not to answer a question which had been raised by the non-combatant events of 1914–18 and which was crucial to their own future. If Africans could run the Christian Church at least as effectively as the Europeans, and the evidence seemed to be that they could, what was the point of having missionaries any more?

18

A BLACK REFORMATION

A lot of Africans now began to do what white Christians had been doing ever since Martin Luther nailed his ninety-five theses on Wittenburg church door in 1517. They began to break away from a parent body which seemed indifferent or even hostile to their growth both in faith and as human beings, and which apparently wished to maintain them in a form of subjection. They started to form what have since become known as Separatist Churches, in a movement of secession from the main current of African Christianity which has continued intermittently up to the present day.

This was not a new phenomenon, although it had not before occurred on the scale which developed from 1918 onwards. West Africa, and Nigeria in particular, had been the scene of a growing nationalist movement for the better part of half a century before that, and which went under the name of Ethiopianism.* This was very closely connected with the spread of Christianity in the area; its ideological origins, indeed, have been seen paradoxically in the principles enunciated by Henry Venn of the CMS for an Africanised Church. The Ethiopian leaders were African Churchmen who had been educated by missionaries and given a vision of the future by missionaries, but who felt that in the final analysis they were regarded by the missionaries in the same way that young Samuel Crowther had been patronised by his teacher in Sierra Leone; as nothing more than very useful instruments of an alien purpose. It was from the ranks of the Ethiopians that the great wave of support

* The word was derived from Psalm 68, verse 31: 'Ethiopia shall stretch forth her hands to God.'

came for Crowther in the years of his betrayal by the CMS, when Henry Venn's principles were no longer acceptable in Salisbury Square. One of the movement's leaders was Edward Wilmot Blyden, the West Indian preacher of pan-Africanism, who lost a scholarship to an American college because of racial discrimination, and who lost a teaching post with the Presbyterian Missionary Society of America because he had an affair with the Liberian President's wife.

Another was James Johnson, who became an Anglican bishop, who preached the Annual Sermon of the CMS in London in 1900 and was fêted just as Crowther had been fêted before him (including a reception by Queen Victoria), but who at the same time was a perpetual thorn in the flesh of his white English patrons. Twenty years before the missionaries wooed him with all the blandishments at their disposal in London, the then Archdeacon Johnson expressed precisely the feelings of most Ethiopians, which he was never to lose himself. 'You in England,' he wrote to a friend there, 'cannot fancy how some of those who come here inflated with the idea that they are the "dominant race", do treat with something like contempt the natives of the country. The truth is that they regard us this day in pretty much the same light as our forefathers were, who were rescued from the ironpangs of slavery by the philanthropists of a former generation. We are not over sensitive, but at the same time we are not unduly pachydermatous . . . But does anyone think we have no feelings at all, or no rights which are to be respected? . . . Having educated us, you will not allow us to think and speak and act like men.'

Besides conducting that lobby against Salisbury Square on Samuel Crowther's behalf, the Ethiopians formed a Society for the Promotion of Religion and Education in Lagos, whose avowed intent was to supplant the educational machinery of the missions and provide teaching which would equip Africans for social equality with Europeans. They revised the Book of Common Prayer in those Delta churches whose semi-autonomy had been Crowther's last creative act as bishop, so that prayers for the Queen were excluded and prayers for the local Nigerian king were substituted in their place. They changed their names from those bestowed upon them by white missionaries to ones which their African ancestors would more easily have recognised. The Rev. J. H. Samuel thus became Adegboyega Edun, Joseph Pythagoras Haastrup became Ademuyiwa Haastrup and David B. Vincent became Mojola Agbebi. James Johnson, curiously enough, was content to remain James Johnson.

It was Agbebi who led the first native Church to secede from a parent missionary body. A large majority of the Ethiopians had been reared upon the variety of Christian belief practised by the English CMS, but this first breakaway was from an American mission. Southern Baptists had established stations in Yorubaland from 1850 onwards. Being hard-pressed for white manpower during the years of the American Civil War, they had sent Negroes to pioneer their establishment in West Africa but by 1875 a pastor from Mississippi, the Rev. W. J. David, had taken charge of the operations in Nigeria. He was a man who could describe with relish in his journals how he had whipped local labourers in Abeokuta to stimulate the building of a church there, but who was much more practical than any English missionary in his approach to the tormenting question of polygamy; he was not at all averse to baptising men with a number of wives. And he was in favour of creating a training school to produce local African workers, which was not a thing the Southern Baptists generally at that stage favoured. At the same time he firmly believed that all black men had to be kept in their place under the direction of white men. With his background, it would have been remarkable if he had come to any other conclusion.

Strains eventually developed in David's relations with one of his trained local Africans, Moses Ladejo Stone, who had been ordained by the American in 1880. Stone had pressed frequently to be allowed to go to America for higher education and David had consistently turned him down. Moreover, he employed Stone on the mission for a pittance, even judging by the standards of the time. Stone's salary from the Southern Baptists was only twenty-five shillings a month, and even the CMS paid its lowliest African ordained employees £5 a month. Stone had to take part-time work as a trader in order to live decently and on this issue David seized the excuse to sack a man who was for ever challenging his authority, with assertions that black men should control their own Church affairs in their own land. Why, said Stone, the death-roll of whites from malaria was Providence's clear demonstration of this Divine intention. Revolt was in the air, and Ethiopians of all denominations were not slow to add their weight to that of Stone's supporters among the Southern Baptist converts. In April 1888, a new Native Baptist Church was announced. Its membership consisted of all Nigerians connected with the Southern Baptists, apart from a faithful rump of precisely eight men.

The organiser of the revolt was D. B. Vincent, just then on the threshold of his translation into Mojola Agbebi. He had already made his nationalist mark with a number of pamphlets and articles, for he was a journalist by instinct and craft, editing at one time or another every newspaper that was published in Nigeria between 1880 and 1914. It was he who argued more volubly than most for the retention of native names, native dress, harmless native customs and habits, who demanded that native languages should be used in worship. 'Prayer-books and Hymn-books, harmonium dedications, pew constructions, surpliced choir, the white man's style, the white man's name, the white man's dress, are so many non-essentials, so many props and crutches affecting the religious manhood of the Christian African. Among the great essentials of religion are that the lame walk, the lepers are cleansed, the deaf hear, the dead are raised up, and the poor have the Gospel preached unto them.' This was Agbebi's manifesto as a Christian product of the missionaries. What it denounced was, moreover, inseparable in his view from much greater dangers to the dignity and the wholeness of the African. They were part of a general threat to African survival which had been apparent to any black man with a sense of racial pride since the missionaries had led the white exploitation of his continent. 'When we look for no manifesto from Salisbury Square,' said Agbebi, 'when we expect no packet of resolutions from Exeter Hall, when no bench of foreign Bishops, no conclave of Cardinals, "lord over" Christian Africa, when the Captain of Salvation, Jesus Christ Himself, leads the Ethiopian host, and our Christianity ceases to be London-ward and New York-ward but Heaven-ward, then will be an end to Privy Councils, Governors, Colonels, Annexations, Displacements, Partitions, Cessions and Coercions. Telegraph wires will be put to better uses and even Downing Street will be absent in the political vocabulary of the West African Native.'

Agbebi travelled extensively outside his own country, preaching his cultural nationalism wherever he went. Like many an African who came after him, he was invited to visit the very lands of which he was most critical. He lectured on African customs in the United States, reported back to the *Lagos Standard* that its civilisation was a snare and its Christianity counterfeit, and was hailed by the Negroes of upstate New York as a blood brother and a black hope for a distant future; in Yonkers they promised that the occasion of his visit, 11 October, should for ever afterwards be observed as Agbebi Day in remembrance of Africa for the Africans and his own part in spreading this new Gospel. In London he addressed a Universal Races Congress at the University Senate House in 1911 and went so far as to defend African secret societies, human sacrifice and cannibalism. After the secession of the Native Baptist Church he refused to work for any Christian mission, although Bishop Herbert Tugwell of the CMS attempted to seduce him into the ranks of the submissively faithful with offers of various high positions among the

Anglicans of Nigeria. A much greater triumph than anything the Bishop could have placed before him awaited Agbebi in 1914, however. By then the Native Baptist Church had more than twice as many churches and churchgoers as the Southern Baptist Mission in Nigeria, and the rueful American missionaries conceded their independence and their traditional superiority by joining forces in a united Baptist Yoruba Association. Mojola Agbebi was chosen as its first President. In spite of his tub-thumping against all forms of colonialism, from the commercial to the spiritual, he had never denounced Christianity itself, wishing only to reconcile it with Nigerian culture and institutions. It was, he said, the 'grandest of all revolutions'.

There were a handful of other secessions in West Africa before the end of the nineteenth century, like those of the United Native African Church and the Bethel African Church, both breakaways from the Anglicans of the CMS. It was not until 1913 that the first of the prophetic movements began, forerunner of many independent sects which were to be created periodically in the years following the Great War, and which generally resulted from the visionary experiences of a single individual who believed he had a call from God to stride through the land like a Testamental colossus, gathering followers as he went. In this case the man was William Wadé Harris, who had taught in schools run by American Protestant Episcopalians in Liberia, at the same time being imprisoned on a number of occasions for political disturbances. After his vision he began to move out of Liberia, first into French and then into British territory, an impressive figure wearing a white gown and turban, carrying a large cross and a Bible, preaching against idolatry, urging repentance and baptism with all the rolling fervour of any evangelist known to the hot-Gospelling tabernacles of the deep southern United States. Wherever followers gathered around him Harris set up a church, appointed twelve apostles to lead it, and moved on. It has been reckoned that something like 100,000 people joined his movement, and the majority of them had been resistant to the appeals of white Christian missionaries over many decades; on the French Ivory Coast, Harris was much more successful than the immigrant Catholic priests had ever been in making converts. The trouble was that the congregations he left dotted around West Africa expected Harris to be followed by equally inspiring teachers of his faith, and none ever came. His biggest achievement was to create a receptive atmosphere in which orthodox Christian teachings could later flourish, and many of his congregations were eventually absorbed by Methodists, though the Church of the Twelve Apostles on the Gold Coast was to remain a legacy of his distinctive approach.

The prophets appeared all over Africa. In the Congo, a Baptist catechist called Simon Kimbangu had a series of dreams and visions, at least one of which left him unconscious after a kind of fit. He decided that he was required to heal the sick and his reputation soon became such that mission hospitals in his area found that their supply of patients dried up, as people took themselves to Kimbangu's house instead. He made no attempt to deflect people from their established Christian allegiances, claiming that he had come to supplement the teachings of missionaries, not to rival them. Nevertheless, the defections grew to such a scale, the cases of African workers abandoning their jobs in order to visit Kimbangu's village as pilgrims became so numerous, that missionaries and Belgian civil authorities alike saw in Kimbangu a distinct threat to their own stability. In 1921 he was arrested and imprisoned for thirty years. This did nothing at all to stifle the Pentecostal movement he had started. His Church of Christ on Earth through the Prophet Simon Kimbangu, flourished as never before in the wake of what his followers saw as a martyrdom. A couple of decades after its founder's death in the prison cell at Elisabethville, it had three million adherents, and had received the highest accolade of twentieth-century Protestantism in affiliation with the World Council of Churches.

Rhodesia produced Alice Lenshina. She had been a reliable mission Church worker until she had a serious illness, on recovering from which she announced that she had just returned from the dead. Angels, she declared, had given her a new Bible to celebrate this resurrection, and she began to send out her own missionaries to spread the good news. Her Lumpa Church* had very strict rules for its adherents, forbidding racial discrimination, immorality, pride, anger, polygamy and 'drinking or smoking in church'. It avoided any conflict with civil authority until, paradoxically, white Rhodesia was dismembered and the African state of Zambia was created. Alice had forbidden her followers to have anything to do with politics, but they demonstrated against the new Independent Party, five hundred of them being killed in one riot with the cry 'Jericho' upon their lips, a word which they had been given to understand would render them impervious to bullets. And Alice was finally banished to a distant part of the country, where her influence could be kept under strict control. Her followers sometimes returned to the older churches from which she had attracted them, but in handfuls here and there continued to practise the prophetic doctrines she had offered them. In the same fashion, the teachings of the Zulu Isaiah Shembe have continued to

* Lumpa means the Church 'which excels all others'.

be practised with all their Old Testamental zeal in the Ama Nazaretha Church of South Africa. The permutations of the black prophets now pattern Africa from end to end.

So do the marks left by the other secessionists. Sometimes the origins of an independent Church can be seen as less the result of prophetic self-indulgence, more a reaction against white domination, as much an overt expression of nationalism as Agbebi's creation of the Native Baptists. It was so in the creation of the Bantu Methodist Church – popularly known as the Donkey Church, because it used the donkey as its sign manual – on the South African Rand. It was so in the case of the Ajawa Providence Industrial Mission, which appeared in Nyasaland just before the Great War. The African who started it, John Chilembwe, had come under the influence of an Australian evangelist named Joseph Booth, who sympathised with African grievances against the white man and who helped him to go to America for a college education and ordination.

At first, Chilembwe dissociated himself from nationalists who publicly incited rebellion against the white man's system of taxation and against the lack of compensation offered to widows of black men who were killed fighting white men's wars. But he secretly advised his followers not to pay taxes and when the British dragooned thousands of men into the Carrier Corps and other units at the start of the Great War, he sent a message to the Germans, asking them to support a local rising. No support came, but the rising took place early in 1915. It was on a small scale and it resulted in the deaths of three Europeans. One of these was the detested W. J. Livingstone, a relative of Doctor Livingstone, a land-grabber who superintended the Bruce Estates in Nyasaland and who had even been fined by a white man's court for assaulting an African. His head was cut off and mounted on a pole during a church service conducted by Chilembwe the next morning. Chilembwe's church was demolished by the authorities and he was shot. His followers drifted back into the Churches from which they had first come to him, nursing their unresolved grievances and their memories of something that had briefly seemed to offer a kind of salvation.

Sometimes a secession was more obviously the result of bewilderment in the face of so many different varieties of Christian teaching offered to the African by missionaries, mixed up with a resentment against white superiority. This thread is to be seen in the formation of the African Greek Orthodox Church in Uganda by Reuben Spartas in 1929. Spartas had been brought up by the CMS Anglicans; it was while he was at Bishop Tucker College that he had abandoned the name Mukasa after being commended by his headmaster for certain Spartan virtues. He had served in the Native Medical Corps during the war, had worked for a time in the Post Office and had then enlisted briefly in the King's African Rifles. During the war he had for the first time pondered the curiosity of three different missions established round Kampala, those of the CMS, the White Fathers and the Holy Ghost Fathers, all claiming the same Divine inspiration, each clearly separated from the others by something which Spartas took to be unfathomably decisive. Which of them, he wondered, was offering 'the true Church'? His confusion was temporarily increased when, just after the war, he came across some literature published by Marcus Garvey, that remarkable Jamaican who was starting to lead a Back to Africa movement among the blacks of Harlem, whose pamphlets were promoting among other things the Negro Orthodox Church in America. Spartas, who had just become politically involved in the African Progressive Association, quickly responded to Garvey's racial call, hearing at last in Negro Orthodoxy a sound that had been conspicuously missing from the missionary Churches of East Africa. One can imagine that, a generation or so later, he might well have been attracted by the propaganda of Malcolm X and the Black Muslims of the United States.

Soon he was corresponding with Archbishop McGuire, head of the Negro Orthodox in America, whose Church had already put down a root in South Africa. By 1928 he was writing to the Archbishop 'I am prepared to go from field to field throughout Africa . . . Encourage me and empower me whether I may start work'. A year later he publicly announced that he had broken with the Church of England and had started an Orthodox Catholic Church 'for all right-thinking Africans, men who wish to be free in their own house and not always being thought of as little boys'. He called himself the Archpriest, began to build churches and schools and by the start of the Second World War had about five thousand followers in Uganda. His Church never grew much beyond that point, in spite of the fact that he made many contacts with both Greek and Russian Orthodox Churches and collected funds from them to help expansion. This can, to a great extent, be explained by the political commitment of the Spartas movement. Much of its energy was spent on working for an independent Uganda, and for four years after the war Spartas was in prison for taking part in riots against the British colonial Government. When Independence came, a lot of the motive steam was taken out the Archpriest's followers. But the Church lingers on.

In all the independent Church movements that were to creep across

Africa in the first half of the twentieth century, two common denominators were present. One was the adherence to some form of belief in the God of the Christians. The other was a strong sense of African racial identity, a reaction against various manifestations of white racial superiority. Beyond those two points the differences were very often wide, emphasising the prophetic qualities of the leader sometimes, being more obviously the emotional outlet for suppressed nationalist feelings at others, frequently owing something of both religious flavour and racial pride to the influence upon Africa of the United States. Where an independent movement was not stimulated to action by a sense of brotherhood with American Negroes, whose own morale was fortified by feelings of kinship with restless Africans, it was often given a sense of religious direction by the example and the propaganda of various American evangelistic organisations, whose style of Christian worship was much more in tune with the nature of Africans than anything a European missionary had ever exhibited. No representative of the Anglican CMS would ever have allowed himself to display the almost carnal emotions that had regularly shifted mountains of faith in the person of Dwight L. Moody, for example.

The complexity of derivation can be seen in the history of the Church of the Lord (Aladura), which emerged in Nigeria in the years following the Great War. The aladura (or praying) movement was detectable from 1918, when a post-war influenza epidemic which killed thousands throughout the world had particularly disastrous effects in West Africa. There was a strong feeling locally that the established missionary Churches had not done nearly enough to help Africans through this plagued time. A Nigerian was later to describe them as 'houses of death', in which not even spiritual aid was made available to the people. 'They were being locked up, closed altogether during the time of pestilence and influenza, through lack of God's power to withstand these. Are these churches? . . . Where will the members of such church run to at the time of influenza or pestilence in the near future . . .?' A result of this disillusionment was the formation of private prayer groups near Ibadan; they did not for the moment sever themselves from the Anglican Church, forming themselves into a band of zealots within the traditional congregation supervised by missionaries. But then a young woman belonging to one group declared that in a vision she had been told that anyone who used medicines when sick would die, that they would be healed only if they relied upon pure rainwater. By the middle of 1920, these people had started to call themselves the Precious Stone Society.

No sooner had the society been formed, than its members began to encounter literature which was then reaching Nigeria from the evangelistic Faith Tabernacle in Philadelphia. These Americans never sent money or missionaries to Africa, but they were prolific in their distribution of propaganda. The people of the Precious Stone Society discovered that there were white Christians who also rejoiced in prayer and divine healing, in a way that Englishmen apparently did not. More to the point, the Americans rejected the baptism of infants. A number of newly baptised children had recently died round Ibadan during the epidemic, and the conclusion was inescapable in the circumstances. The Precious Stone people abandoned the Church of England and established their own offshoot of the Faith Tabernacle. By 1925 it had attracted Christians at a number of other places in Nigeria, and not all of them had been deflected from the Anglicans. 'My family,' wrote one new adherent, 'had always been Methodists and objected strongly when my older brother joined the Faith Tabernacle in Lagos. They then noticed changes for the better in him, in his character. He was less worldly, and stopped going to ballroom dances . . . He ceased drinking, and was more loving towards us in his actions in the house . . . He bought my (younger) brother and myself clothes, such as shoes and ties, which we had not had before. My brother and I decided we must wear these new clothes first at his church, on the first Sunday. The congregation was only about a hundred and fifty, but we observed something strange. We had banged our heels on the floor when we walked in, to draw attention to ourselves, but no one paid us the attention we desired. They also lent us hymn books. Odubanjo preached on God's power to protect, heal and bless. All this was new to me – that God was still doing this today. I'd never heard this in a Methodist church, nor that God meets our financial needs also, and protects us from all dangers and perils . . . Our mother followed us into Faith Tabernacle. I was baptised by immersion, and was about twenty-one then. I had found Christ was not only a saviour, but also a healer.' And although the Nigerians dissociated themselves from the nominal headquarters of their new sect, when scandal broke in Philadelphia which ended in the chief pastor being divorced, their own Faith Tabernacles continued to flourish, producing a number of variants which eventually took other names.

One of these had no more than a brief flirtation with the Tabernacle, in 1930, when the leaders of the movement heard of a young man called Josiah Olunowo Oshitelu who had apparently been having visions and collecting disciples. Oshitelu had been baptised as an Anglican and had been employed by the Church as a teacher and catechist. He was well on the way to a secure future as an ordained Anglican minister when, in 1925, there began an extraordinary sequence of dreams. At first he saw an eye 'reflecting as a great orbit of the sun', surrounded by figures which he took to be witches, and which frightened him very badly. A week or two later 'assistance came through a Holy man in my dream, who dealt the witches with heavy blows until they were turned into cows, horses, rats, cats and some deformed creatures'. Oshitelu began to fast, as a friend had advised him to, and for the following six months he heard a series of disembodied voices. They gave him a number of messages, which Oshitelu carefully wrote down in an exercise book. One was 'Your prayers are heard. After many afflictions I will uplift you. Be not afraid, I am with you.' Another voice said, 'I will anoint you as my prophet, even as Elijah anointed Elisha with oil in the olden days, so it shall be unto you'. And another, 'I will build new Jerusalem in you. You are the one whom Jesus Christ has sent like the last Elijah to repair the Lord's road and make his way straight.' There were many other injunctions, all with the same burden, that Oshitelu would be given authority, power and leadership. Soon there would be visions of 'holy writing', which Oshitelu also committed to his exercise books, a queer amalgam of Syriac and Greek scripts. Later still, when Oshitelu had been given to understand that his holy name was Arrabablalhhubab, there would be a Great Seal of authority, which bore a remarkable resemblance to the heraldic devices of Freemasonry.

All this was too much for the Anglicans. Oshitelu was summoned to appear before a group of ministers and dismissed. The reason generally put about by the Church for the breach with this promising young agent was his refusal to accept the Christian ideal of monogamy, and there was almost certainly something in this charge. At the time, Oshitelu was unmarried; he had, in fact, just broken off his engagement to a young woman who had become alarmed by the prospect of union with a black messiah. By the time Oshitelu died in 1966, however, he had acquired no fewer than seven wives. Yet he had no intention of fostering a polygamous Church. A number of bishops in the Church of the Lord (Aladura) were to be allowed more than one spouse, though no one ever rose to the tally of the Primate and Founder; lesser ministers and laymen tended to be disciplined with enforced fasting, prayer and physical jerks for sexual irregularity, and something of the Church's philosophy on women is revealed in a lecture given by Bishop Orebanjo in a correspondence course he ran for postulants. 'God made Eve to be a helpmate, and now a helper becomes an obstacle. But spiritualists should have ways of dealing with women . . . A womaniser . . . can never be successful in spiritual development . . . In the days of your special prayer, consecrate yourself highly and avoid women entirely . . . Menstruating and fornicating are deadly enemies to the Angels, who fly away at the slightest smell of them . . . When you are inclined to think much of women to instigate your private nerves, read Psalm 53 three times and you will be free.'

The Faith Tabernacle now made its approach to Oshitelu. One of its leaders was Joseph Babalola, who had also abandoned membership of the Anglican Church (as well as his job as a steamroller driver) in order to become a faith healer. Hearing of this rival prophetic figure, he travelled a hundred miles to see him and over the next six months tried to draw Oshitelu into the organisation of the Faith Tabernacle. There were many meetings and Oshitelu participated in several Tabernacle revival campaigns. His new companions were somewhat disconcerted by his habit of identifying witches among the women attending meetings, who were invited to come and confess their sins to him. They were perhaps more impressed than they would have liked to be by the man's magnetism and power to attract a personal following. During one campaign in Abeokuta no fewer than 607 people brought their ailments to him, rather than to long-standing members of the Tabernacle, in the space of a fortnight; and it was discovered that services of baptism conducted by Oshitelu or one of his lieutenants, which were apt to be all-night affairs, might handle as many as four hundred potential converts. There was also Oshitelu's addiction to special language and holy names, which was not at all to the taste of the Tabernacle people. 'I enquired from Mr Ajayi (one of Oshitelu's men),' said Babalola, 'how they got at these names, and I could gather nothing save that they were in the bush for some years tormenting themselves from whence they emerged with these names . . . Pastor Akinyele once wrote me that there were interpretations to these names. Why can't we use these interpretations, as God can hear us in our language without bothering ourselves with these strange names which are, of course, of foreign origin.' There was almost certainly jealousy on the part of the Tabernacle leaders towards a man who was clearly capable of weaning their supporters away from them. The upshot was that Tabernacle and Oshitelu decided to part company.

By 1931 what had been a single mud-walled building in the bush town of Ogere had increased to three congregations, and converts to this new Church of the Lord (Aladura) were being attracted from established Christian denominations. Most of them had been Methodists, but almost as many had been drawn from the Anglicans, and there was a surprisingly high proportion of Catholics; seventy-five per cent of the members were to come from these sources. At first Oshitelu offered them a rudimentary form of Pentecostal faith, with its emphasis on possession and healing. Gradually, sophistications of authority, of ritual, of theology were evolved, as the Primate had more visions which gave him guidance for the future. The time came when there were Prophets and Acting Prophets, Apostles and Captains, as well as Bishops in his Church, when the rank of Crossbearer immediately preceded that of ordinary member. This particular function resulted from a revelation in 1937 and, according to the Church's *Book of Rituals*, 'the position of Crossbearer is higher than that of a communicant member in other Churches . . . It is next to the Church Minister, anointed to preach, to heal the sick, raise the dead, and to work miracles, looked upon to operate a Church where Minister is not available, then what an honourable position! . . . The anointment is the SIGN that confers the Power, the Cross is the "key" that carries the power about. That is why we feel special power and confidence whenever we hold the Cross in our hands.'

Much of the ritual was merely lifted from the Anglican Book of Common Prayer, with indigenous additions. These involved the good Pentecostal habits of dancing, clapping and shouting, but also a number of delicious combinations in the rubric. Part of the marriage service, for example, runs:

> *Question:* Wilt thou have this man to be thy wedded husband, to live together after God's ordinance in the Holy estate of matrimony? Wilt thou obey him and serve him, love, honour and keep him, in sickness and in health, and forsake all other, keep thee only unto him as long as ye both shall live?
> *Answer:* I will, the Lord being my helper.
> *Question:* Wilt thou be a noisy or quarrelsome wife in the house?
> *Answer:* God forbid! I shall pray always to God to make me as meek as a dove.

As for God, he was seen much more as a Jehovah-figure from the Old Testament, than a Christ-figure from the New. One of the constitutions which Oshitelu drew up for his adherents, indeed, indicated the hymns and ceremonies which 'conduce to the worthy praise of Jehovah-God'. Christ was little more than a teacher of prayer, fasting, trust in God, an intermediary through whom messages might be passed to God, a spirit to be invoked for healing and exorcism. Yet Oshitelu frequently described himself as a forerunner of the Lord, a sort of second John the Baptist. The Church of the Lord (Aladura) was to be 'the last church, the one that Jesus Christ would come and meet at the second advent'.

The response of the well-established missionary Churches to this new outcrop of seductive Christianity, was remarkably cool, considering its appeal to some of their members. Shortly after Oshitelu's break from the Church of England, the Anglican Bishop Melville Jones of Lagos was writing, of the aladura movement generally, that 'Such movements are generally begun by some earnest spirit with little education and a not very balanced grasp of the truth, who desires to see a reform of the Church and an ingathering of . . . converts. His preaching may be earnest enough at first, but he soon begins to resort to unscriptural ways of winning the multitudes . . .'

For the most part, the missionaries were supremely ignorant of what was happening. Until the Second World War, after all, Oshitelu's followers were numbered in hundreds rather than thousands; as far as the vast majority of Europeans were concerned, this was no more than one of many small fringe sects and they felt no great threat from it at an ecclesiastical level. It is likely that none of them had even read some of Oshitelu's pamphlets, which prophesied the eventual destruction of the established Churches 'down to the foundations, because they know nothing but money' and which declared that 'the white man takes another's property by force' and would perish from smallpox. There was a small brush with the colonial Government early on, because police had encountered a booklet containing 159 warnings and promises. Most of them were a mishmash of vague admonitions about the conceivable perils that might follow 'if the people of this town do not turn away from their evil ways'. Only three appeared to be directly critical of Government. Warning 139 vowed that 'The day is coming when the Government will be demanding taxes on goats and sheep every year. As a result domestic animals will be at liberty to feed in the open places without anybody to claim their ownership.' No. 149 promised that 'Epidemic of smallpox is coming to the land of Africa, so much that all the Europeans in the Continent will die of it'. No. 150 offered the terrible possibility that 'Those who collect taxes and money on land, and other things, MONTTFFGRATION, the judgment of God is awaiting them'. But even a sensitive and suspicious white constabulary found it difficult to make a court case out of these and, apart from the confiscation of the booklet in question, no further action was taken.

So the Church of the Lord (Aladura) prospered. By 1947 its congregations stretched throughout western Nigeria. The day was not far off when the Federal Minister of Education himself would be opening a new church building in Lagos. In the same year the Church's first representatives travelled to Sierra Leone, traditional landfall for all forms of Christian expansion in Africa. They were not entirely welcome even to the local Africans and, just before setting off for a hilltop service above Freetown, a crowd gathered to jeer at them. Help, however, was at hand. 'God rained down showers of blessing in the form of a violent storm and heavy down-pour of rain which thrashed and drove away the mockers who had gathered to exhibit their blindness and twenty minutes later, when the rain abated, there was a great calm (not a single mocker was about) the lorries moved on to the foot of the mountain . . . in a procession . . . they proceeded with lighted candles and palms of victory in their hands, singing . . . "Onward Christian Soldiers" and interrupted by no mocker climbed to the mountain top and arrived at the Holy Spot.' After that, there was no looking back.

There was another setback awaiting these proselytisers when they ventured into Liberia. They happened to pass President Tubman's official residence with a bearer who was carrying their luggage on his head. A guard turned them back at gunpoint 'as it was against the rule of the country to pass before the Mansion with loads on head'. Within a year the climate had so improved that the President himself made a donation of fifty dollars to Church funds. By 1953 the Church had not only secured its outposts in both Sierra Leone and Liberia; it had obtained a footing in Ghana as well; before long it numbered local Cabinet Ministers among its congregations.

Springing up in a Black Reformation of African Christianity, the Church of the Lord (Aladura) had traversed a full circle within the lifetime of its founder. It, too, had become a missionary Church. And the crowning, ironic glory of its missionary zeal came in April 1964. That was when it opened its most distant outstation: in London.

19
THE ACHIEVEMENT

By the time the world plunged into its second great war of the twentieth century, white missionaries had been active in Africa for the best part of 150 years. They could produce figures which showed that the Protestant Churches between them by then mustered 2,131,000 communicant members throughout the continent. Much more impressive was the tally of communicant African Catholics – 4,613,000, after a period of determined missionary effort by the Church of Rome amounting to approximately half the time spent by the Protestants in the salvation of black souls. It has been reckoned that the number of Africans who by then acknowledged some form of Christian belief came to about twenty millions. The population of the entire continent in 1938 was something approaching two hundred millions. There were about sixty million Moslems. The rest of the people, perhaps 120 millions, were as pagan as their ancestors had been on the day the first Protestant missionary stepped ashore in Sierra Leone. Considering the amount of effort and expenditure, the degree of self-sacrifice and heroism that had been spent by generations of God-fearing Christians across a century and a half, the statistical returns were perhaps a little thin.

It is, indeed, one of the most striking things about the history of the missionaries in Africa, that the pioneers achieved almost nothing at all in terms of their primary aims; that is, in conversion of people to a steady belief in the Christian faith. And the pioneer period cannot really be said to have ended until the nineteenth century was almost over. Even in the twentieth century new ground was regularly being investigated by the professional bearers of Bible and goodwill. It is quite possible that, of them, some traveller of the future will find himself echoing the melancholy report made by Sir Bartle Frere in 1874. This former Governor of Bombay had been asked by the CMS to make a fact-finding tour of East Africa during his retirement. In the course of it he stumbled upon Johannes Rebmann, the German who had served the CMS during its infant struggles and who had been the first European to set eyes on Mount Kilimanjaro. He was, astonishingly, still alive, though he was very frail, surrounded by piles of translated manuscripts upon which he had worked for decades. 'He has been unable,' wrote Frere, 'of late years to take much active part in more direct missionary work; and we found but eight converts at Kissoludini, and five of them belonged to two families which had joined from the African Orphanage at Nassick, near Bombay . . . his influence has been limited to the example of a holy life of ascetic self-denial and indifference to all worldly enjoyments and employments, which have had the usual effect of exciting the admiration, without securing the imitation of the people around him.' That was the product of thirty years' work as a missionary.

Rebmann was perhaps unique but, on a smaller scale, apparently fruitless endeavour was commonplace. When Bishop Tozer arrived up the Zambezi in 1863 to take over Mackenzie's place at the head of the UMCA venture, he was astonished to find that the colleagues awaiting him had taught the Africans nothing that he could identify as the Christian religion. Mackenzie, they told him, had been loth to start teaching until he could speak the language coherently; and he had died before reaching that stage. Scudamore had been near to teaching but he, too, had died before he could begin. Under Tozer's irritated interrogation, one of the old hands, Rowley, surprised two colleagues who had been there from the start with the news that he had taught the people some Bible stories and a few parables. But that was all the UMCA men had to show Tozer for two years on their station; the rest, they declared, had been a continuous fight for life. And so it had. So it was for most of those first few generations of missionaries. If it was not a fight for life against hostile tribesmen, which was not the most frequent hazard of Africa, it was a fight for life against disease, it was a fight for something approaching life merely in the day-to-day business of penetrating new territory, building dwellings out of the bush, organising supplies and recruiting labour to carry them in. Such converts as were made came very expensively in terms of missionary manpower and the money that was poured behind it by faithful supporters in Europe. The Central Africa Mission of the LMS was fourteen years old when its first convert was baptised. By the time the twentieth baptism had been registered, twenty missionaries had died on the station and £40,000 had been spent on the venture by the society.

When one considers how ill-equipped many of the missionaries were, it is surprising that anything was achieved at all. The early recruits to the British societies, apart from a few exceptions like Lewis Krapf and Francis Owen, were people who had learned their own Christianity by rote in an artisan environment and who had neither the imagination nor the intellectual flexibility to translate it into the terms required for reception into another. They were almost incapable of seeing anything positive and valuable in the life and culture of the African. They had been trained to apply derogatory labels to him and unless he surrendered himself to them entirely on their own terms, the labels were allowed to remain and obscure the reality beneath. Even when the artisans had given way somewhat to the genteel products of university education the result was more often than not the same. The Christian fervour was as narrowly fanatical, as unwilling to make any concessions to other forms of belief in the supernatural, and in place of doggedly obtuse suspicions that the black pagan was an inferior being there came a more dangerous form of patronage. The educated missionary could rationalise his prejudices with a variety of crude anthropological statements that were either unscholarly in origin, irrelevant or downright vicious. The *Anthropological Review* in 1866 dismissed David Livingstone's sympathetic consideration of the African as sentimental rubbish which would appeal only to 'Nigger Worshippers, missionary exporters and other Exeter Hallitarians'; it was, the author of the article asserted, the product of a 'poor, naked mind bedaubed with the chalk and red ochre of Scotch theology, and with a threadbare, tattered waistcloth of education hanging around him'. Travellers with high qualifications and extensive experience of the Negro races, like Richard Burton and Winwood Reade, could also be adduced in evidence of black inferiority to support the observations of the armchair anthropologists at home. Reade was convinced of the 'absolute futility of Christian missions among savages. Even the culture of the much-vaunted converts of Sierra Leone remained basically unchanged, basically corrupt.'

It was not until the last two decades of the nineteenth century that the tone of scientists in Europe began to change, that someone as distinguished as Sir Francis Galton could be heard saying that 'the English do not excel in winning the hearts of other nations. They have to broaden their sympathies by the study of mankind as they are, and without prejudice.' And even in the 1890s distinguished men of opinion could be found offering attractively alternative theses; in the journal of the Anthropological

Institute, Sir Bartle Frere was declaring that the history of India, Assyria, Egypt, Rome and Britain all showed the conquest of inferior by superior people. In this climate it was exceedingly difficult for a missionary, convinced that his faith alone contained the Truth and the Light of the world, to resist the assumption that those who did not immediately share his ecstatic awareness had nothing of any value to offer him in return. There were men deeply and honourably situated in his own profession whose whole lives were a denial of this attitude. Henry Venn is an outstanding example. David Livingstone is another. But such men were always a small minority. In his own day, Livingstone was unique among the men who actually set foot in Africa. His acknowledgment of and respect for African virtues were his supreme and enduring greatness, transcending his manifest deficiencies. But even in the twentieth century it was rare indeed for a missionary like T. W. W. Crawford to be so receptive to the African that the Embu people of Kenya invited him to join their tribal council of elders. Much more common was a man like Albert Schweitzer, who laboured long and devotedly in unpleasant conditions, who became a white deity among Europeans rather more than among Africans, who was sufficiently broad in his interests to write a book on Indian philosophy, but who from start to finish of his extended mission at Lambarene never showed any intellectual response to the traditions of Africa.

Even the bare bones of communication with the African were neglected more often than not. The missionary societies were certainly not slow to engage in linguistic work. From the outset, men went out to Africa with the fixed intention of picking up the native languages as rapidly as possible and the earliest missionaries spent a great deal of their time in translating the Bible, or at least the Gospels, into local tongues; sometimes, as in Rebmann's case, they did very little else. By the middle of the nineteenth century some portion of Scripture was available in almost twenty different languages; between 1879 and 1896 some fifty-eight fresh versions were added; and the twentieth century saw a tremendous increase in translation. By 1954 the Gospels at least were available in no fewer than 399 African languages; the New Testament had been completed in 161 of them; the full Bible could be read in fifty-two different versions. The trouble was that the acquisition of a native language was seen far too frequently as nothing more than a means of translating Scripture. Comparatively little effort was spent, either by individuals or by the societies employing them, in ensuring that a missionary could speak to a native in his own tongue with the fluency that alone can produce deep understanding between two human beings. Every missionary would pick up a smattering of local vocabulary; he could scarcely avoid doing so. Beyond that, communication was generally made in the appalling and stultifying cadences of so-called pidgin English, with its implicit assumption that the African native must submit himself to the norms of the English visitor. At its worst, this was yet another manifestation of racial superiority. At the very best, the attempts of English missionaries to persuade Africans to communicate in the language of Shakespeare and Chaucer could only increase the confusion of a man presented with this sudden access of alien culture.

Some missionaries were well aware of this, and Bishop Tozer was one of them. 'There was Kellaway,' he wrote home to his sister, 'teaching Devonshire of the broadest kind, Sivill the most undoubted Lincolnshire, and Adams indulging in low cockney slang where "grub" stands habitually for "food" and "kid" for "child". The effect was that the boys who heard all this jargon were naturally puzzled and, with the exception of a few such sentences as "O, my Eye" and the like, made but a small advance in speaking English.' But, again, the Tozers of the missionary world were not a majority. Most missionaries were men like Bishop Tucker, who spent eighteen years in East Africa, who has been reckoned to have actually walked 22,000 miles in the service of the Church there, yet who in all that time and distance never learned one African language. In 1922 the School of Oriental and African Studies in London, which had been invited to survey the problem of teaching languages to missionaries, reported that 'as far as our experience and information go, we are of the opinion that the average level of proficiency attained by missionaries in the vernacular at the present time is regrettably and even dangerously low'.

The communication gap was never as wide between the African and the Catholic priest as it was in the case of the Protestant missionaries. It is tempting to find a reason for this in the much higher standard of education generally required of Catholic missionaries than of the Protestants, and to suggest that justice was eventually done in the comparative number of converts each branch of Christianity produced in Africa. There were obviously other factors at work, however. One of them is perhaps that Catholic ritual, with its high and sensual emphasis on decoration, colour and even smell, was more appealing to the African temperament than the drabber worship of Protestantism; that the Catholic could offer a pantheon of figures, all gaudily represented in plaster or wood, which was more readily attractive to an imagination already suffused with a tradition of innumerable divine beings which were depicted just as colourfully in the form of fetishes. The fact is that if the Catholic was indeed given a headstart over his Protestant rival by the very nature of his creeds and liturgy, he generally increased the distance in the field merely by his way of living there. He lived, as a rule, much more simply than the Protestant, without the complexities of a family to attend to. He was usually sent out to Africa by his missionary order on the understanding that if he returned to Europe more than once for the rest of his life, his case would be exceptional. He had little psychological alternative in these circumstances but to involve himself as deeply as he could in the life of the people around him. Professor Roland Oliver has suggested that, certainly in East Africa, only the Anglo-Catholic missionaries of the UMCA could be compared in this respect to the average Roman Catholic priest.

'They, too, planned their parish centres in such a way that they could be handed over to Africans without any material alterations. The European parish priest of the Universities Mission, living beside his church in a house of mud and thatch without wood in the doorways or glass in the windows, often quite alone and without speaking English for weeks on end, represented indeed the very extreme of missionary assimilation to the environment. At other Protestant stations, missionaries lived in comfortable bungalows set in spacious gardens and furnished, though modestly, in unmistakeably European fashion. They travelled in motor-cars, albeit old ones. Their wives and families necessitated large domestic staffs and regular visits to Europe. They presented an example of Christian family life, but in an economic setting which was far beyond anything to which an African minister could aspire, and in a family and racial privacy which only their domestic servants could penetrate.'

The financial difference in the condition of the Catholic and Protestant missionaries was important, too, to the process of identification with the life of the African. The Catholic belonged to a religious order which had obliged him to take a vow of poverty; and though this did not mean penury, it meant an existence not very far above that of any African tribesman, given the difference of habitual basic requirements. The Protestant missionary, though by no means wealthy according to the standards of Europe, was placed in a far superior position even to those Africans who were nominally encouraged to regard him as an equal. In 1930, the CMS paid its African lay evangelists £5 a year; its African clergymen received between £10 and £25 a year. A married European missionary received £650. The Vatican, at the same time, allowed £35 per head of its missionary workers overseas.

The largest inhibition of all upon missionary activity in Africa, however, was always the insistence of the Europeans, and particularly the Protestants, upon imposing their own standards of morality in this alien milieu, rigidly and inflexibly. As we have seen, an inspired leader at home like Henry Venn might even dare to suggest that the most apparently savage habits of the African should sometimes be regarded with tact and sympathy. Somehow, the message was scarcely ever practised by the missionaries in the field. It is significant of a peculiarly Protestant missionary cast of mind, that a quite disproportionate amount of time and energy was spent in attempting to correct African sexual morality. The indignation of these Europeans at the slave trade in Livingstone's time was never equalled by their response to the brutalities inflicted by whites upon black in the Congo during King Leopold's, but it certainly rose to a similar pitch over the issue of female circumcision among the Kikuyu in 1929. When the three Protestant organisations in the area – the Church of Scotland, the Africa Inland Mission and the Gospel Missionary Society – found that even their African supporters and congregations were mostly unwilling to accept a European imposition at this point, they applied the most powerful sanctions at their disposal. They suspended their workers and they closed the schools they were running. They paid the penalty in catastrophically reduced church memberships.

The missionaries were curiously incapable of rethinking their own morality, even when such experiences with their own converts might have suggested that they should at least attempt a form of compromise in the values they had imported from Europe and the Americas. Time after time Christianised Africans demonstrated that some of the standards demanded by their white tutors were beyond their reach except for limited periods. During one visitation to Masasi early in the twentieth century, Bishop Weston, of Zanzibar, had to adjudicate upon no fewer than five hundred cases of what were euphemistically called 'marriage offences'; when he returned the following year the number had risen to one thousand and half of them were thought to be so serious that the offenders were not allowed back into Church communion. In 1910 the German missionaries of the Leipzig Society reported that most of them were convinced that 'an African who had passed the age of puberty and who was left in his accustomed environment could never become more than a nominal Christian'. The Anglican Synod of 1913, in Uganda, was so concerned about the state of morality among converts that it threatened to excommunicate anyone breaking the Church's rules for sexual behaviour. 'Since that discussion,' said Archdeacon Lloyd in 1921, 'there seems to the casual observer but little improvement in the state of the

Church. The two great evils against which there is constant warfare, drunkenness and immorality, are as flagrant as ever; indeed, the latter is more open to the world than ever it was. Plurality of wives and concubinage are everywhere, and the whole Church is riddled with this sin, while drunkenness follows in its train.'

To catch precisely the flavour of the morality which missionaries wished to inspire in the African at that period, one can do no better than to listen to Dr Donald Fraser reporting from a village in Nyasaland in the year of the Archdeacon's invective. 'The noise of play had attracted the village seniors, and groups of men and women stood looking at and instructing the young people in the rules of the game. Now in the heathen villages the older women are the leaders in the vilest dances. I have seen them break into the children's rings and teach them and incite them to more and more loathsome posturings. But this night I have the Christian women with me suggesting forgotten games, guiding the merry folks how to follow the rules . . . The slow, rather uninteresting wedding dance is given; then more vigorous solo or double dances within the circle. From both rings a perpetual chorus is going on vociferously to the accompaniment of rhythmical clapping of hands. Once or twice in the excitement of the dance, actions which are not pretty or pure are attempted, but the girls stop them. These are not allowed tonight. The fun must be as clean as God's moonlight.' And Africans, it is inviting to add, must be patronised as children, seen at their most attractive when playing clean and merry games. Neither the sense nor the tone of that report from Nyasaland in 1921 suggest much of a change in outlook from the sentimental and enclosed entries which Anna Hinderer was making in her diaries at Abeokuta and Ibadan in the 1840s. Both Dr Fraser and Mrs Hinderer would almost certainly have found very shocking indeed an observation involving morality which was made by an African Christian upon a parallel between one of his old ancestral traditions and his new theology. It had been blithely ignored by missionaries for a century, though it was central to their creed, but Mojola Agbebi, leader of the Nigerian Native Baptist Church, offered it as a solemn thought to the delegates attending the Universal Races Congress in London in 1911. 'In administering the Lord's Supper to converts from cannibalism, I have,' he said, 'often felt some uneasiness in repeating the formula "Take, eat, this is my body . . . This is my blood." '

The capacity of the Protestant missionary movement not to budge an inch from its principles and its prejudices, from its most vital thinking, over long periods of time, was only paralleled in Africa by the evident incapacity of most natives to adapt themselves to the standards of these white people and to stick to them except in the short term. As for the capacity of Africans to turn themselves into black reproductions of European Christians, with identical responses to the theology that was offered them, a survey made within the past twenty years of the Mende people of Sierra Leone – who have been exposed to Christian teaching longer than almost anyone else on the continent – came to this forlorn conclusion. 'Most chiefs who are professing Christians also have an ancestral shrine in their compounds . . . A number of other individuals who are nominally Christians continue the ancestral practices at the same time . . . Many of them turn instead to magic. They rely quite often on special talismans. Others are regular clients of medicine men whose help they seek in love affairs and to further personal careers.' Dr K. A. Busia, a distinguished sociologist as well as a politician, has recently remarked of his own people that 'It is commonplace to describe Christianity in Ashanti and the Gold Coast generally as a thin veneer. The description is not inaccurate or superficial if it means that the people have not taken over the concept of the universe and of the nature of man within which Christianity finds its fullest meaning.'

No detached observer of Africa under the influence of the missionaries, who views with some sympathy the essential message which the missionaries attempted to convey, can fail to be depressed by the largely negative balance of the account they left after a century and a half. It is not even a crude over-simplification to suggest that they were, as often as not, their own worst enemies. They were sometimes even incapable of learning from the most idiotic mistakes of their predecessors. No organisation, and particularly none from the United States, should have repeated the wretched performance of the Methodist Bishop William Taylor, who set up his missionaries in the Congo in the 1880s and then abandoned them to starvation and totally inadequate means of survival as preachers of the Gospel. Yet, as recently as 1955, the American writer John Gunther was reporting that 'One of the worst sights I saw in Africa was . . . an American mission run by backward folk from Tennessee, practically without funds and hopelessly handicapped by various factors. A dysentery epidemic had swept the school. Children slept in cages curtained with chicken wire – orange crates or similar boxes piled up on top of one another against a wall, like a sectional bookcase. In these tiers, babies whimpered, groaned and cried, in pools of their own making.'

Yet no movement as dedicated as this one, as massively organised and as heavily supported by outside agencies of Government and trade, could fail to achieve much that was positive after such long activity. The missionaries achieved a great deal, even if most of it was not the thing that lay nearest their heart's desire. It is indisputable that the conscience of Europe was roused to a pitch of concerted and determined action to put down the African slave trade, largely because of pressure from the missionary lobby at home and because missionaries alone in the early nineteenth century were in a position to offer eye-witness accounts of the slave trade. It is doubtful whether the history of any continent can produce any instance of enormous and honourable effort resulting from the single observation of one man, comparable to that which followed David Livingstone's harrowing account of the massacre of slaves he witnessed at Nyangwe in 1871. And the number of Africans who escaped infanticide, execution and torture because some courageous white missionary like Mary Slessor bullied and threatened the tribal authorities off, is incalculable but probably considerable. The evidence of any European visiting Africa and reporting favourably upon the activities of other Europeans there, particularly in the context of conflict with African tribal values and African behaviour, ought properly to be received with some caution. But there is the ring of truth in reports made to the Foreign Office in 1900 by the diplomat Sir Harry Johnston, who was agnostic but who declared that the teaching of Anglican and Catholic missionaries was to a great extent responsible for the improvement in Uganda when one compared the country at the turn of the century with the barbarous kingdom of King Mutesa.

The missionaries were somewhat less successful in transforming the various barbarities of white men in Africa. There were very few occasions, indeed, when they made any attempt to rouse the conscience of Europe at such points, as they conspicuously did in the case of Arab and African slaving. One notable exception was their performance in Kenya in the years immediately following the Great War. That it occurred then was evidently the result of some soul-searching by the Churches, in the wake of disillusionment with European notions of civilisation that the war had promoted.

Immediately after the war, a campaign was mounted by a variety of secular interests to encourage British ex-servicemen to go out and settle permanently in Kenya colony. White settlers meant black servants and labourers, and it was obvious to the colonial authorities that these would be in short supply; Africans in the area had suffered badly during the East African campaign, with high casualties in the army and the Carrier Corps, largely resulting from disease and bad service conditions. The influenza epidemic had also reduced the potential labour force drastically. General Northey, the Governor of Kenya, issued a series of instructions to 'exercise every possible lawful influence to induce able-bodied male natives to go into the labour field'. In the polite language of British colonial rule, this meant that Africans were to be virtually pressganged into service under white bossmen. With very little delay, the Anglican bishops of Mombasa and Uganda, together with the Church of Scotland's Dr Arthur, who had formed a missionary Carrier Corps in the war, wrote to the Imperial Government in London and pointed out that Governor Northey's instructions laid the African open to the widest abuses and exploitation. Bishop Weston, indeed, was soon to publish a pamphlet enlarging on these views, entitled *The Serfs of Great Britain*. London's immediate response was very cool. Lord Milner sent a despatch to Northey which advised that 'the Protectorate Government would be failing in its duty if it did not use all lawful and reasonable means to encourage the supply of labour for the settlers'.

The Conference of Missionary Societies in Great Britain and Northern Ireland, however, possessed in Dr J. H. Oldham a new and vigorous young secretary with something of Henry Venn in him. Prompted by the growing anxiety of missionaries in Kenya, he set about organising a lobby against the very strong ex-servicemen's and settlers' supporting groups in Britain. He canvassed the youthful Labour Party. The weight of the 1920 Lambeth Conference of Anglican Bishops was brought to bear upon the subject. The Archbishop of Canterbury, Randall Davidson, helped to enlist the support of public figures as diverse as Lord Balfour, Gilbert Murray, R. H. Tawney and Beatrice Webb. Then the Archbishop cornered Lord Milner at Canterbury and obliged him to receive a memorandum on the matter of Governor Northey's land legislation. It demanded a Royal Commission to inquire into a very wide variety of affairs in East Africa, including the supply of native labour for European benefit, the effect of Western civilisation upon the tribal system, the economic and moral advancement of the native population, and the training of natives in responsibility for their own affairs. The Government turned it down.

For the moment, both Oldham and the Archbishop held their fire. In the next few months, while Northey was issuing new orders to discourage natives from growing cash crops on their reserves (and thus competing economically with the white settlers), Lord Milner was succeeded by Winston Churchill at the Colonial Office. Oldham now wrote a new memorandum on native affairs in East Africa. It produced evidence that the compulsory labour of natives was beginning to do serious harm, it quoted a recent report of the Belgian Royal Commission, which had looked into the dreadful conditions of native labour in the Congo, and it pointed out that if the Imperial Government was going to allow things to slide into a similar situation in Kenya, it must not be surprised if it was eventually faced with native political agitation on an ominous scale. The Archbishop acted as runner between the missionary societies and the Government once again; and towards the end of 1921, Churchill ordered an end to Northey's compulsory recruitment of native labour.

This was one of the finest battle honours of the missionaries in Africa. Yet nothing that they did quite equalled their long campaign in the fields of medicine and education. As a matter of organised policy, they came rather late in the day to the first. Missionaries trained as doctors had occasionally gone to Africa since the time of Livingstone. But it was not until 1885 that the CMS set up a sub-committee to look into the establishment of distinctly medical, as opposed to preaching, missions. Even then, and for some years afterwards, the medical missionary was regarded as a form of propaganda for the Christian way of life, a more impressive rival to the tribal witch doctor, able to outdo any practitioner of juju with a sophisticated range of pharmaceutical and surgical skills. The CMS sub-committee decided that doctors would be an advantage 'where the Gospel could not easily be preached by ordinary evangelists or among aboriginal and uncivilised people likely to be impressed by the kindly influence of medical work'.

By the beginning of the twentieth century, however, the medical commitment of the missions was more of a genuine desire to eradicate disease by the promotion of hygiene, and to alleviate sickness with the establishment of hospitals. A balance was tipped, so that where once a man's medical skills were auxiliary to his chief vocation as a preacher and converter of souls, a mission doctor would now spread the Christian Gospel almost incidentally, after removing his surgical gloves at the end of a day in the operating theatre, or when he had finished yet another stint with the queues of people bringing their elephantiasis and their leprosy, their yaws and their strangulated hernias. Albert Schweitzer went to the Gabon as a medical missionary so that 'I might be able to work without having to talk. For years I had been giving myself out in words . . . this new form of activity I could not represent to myself as talking about the religion of love, but only as an actual putting into practice.' For decades, the missions would run the vast majority of hospitals in Africa. Many thousands of black men would never know a care more disinterested than that offered in a ward staffed by nuns, or by nurses sent out from Europe and America by the well-wishing organisations of young Protestant spinsters.

From the outset, education had been seen as a primary function of the Christian missionary. Again, it was no more than a means to a white man's end for many generations. The missionary school was the first building to be constructed after the missionary chapel and the missionary house, and here the young heathen were to be trained first in the language which would reveal the white man's truths, divine and otherwise, to them. And though the growing towns of Africa gradually acquired grand academic institutions, like Bishop Tucker College in Uganda, with syllabuses resplendent with Classics and other disciplines which theoretically ought to produce upstanding and clean-living black Christians, out in the bush the schools remained as primitive as anything that the pioneers had laboriously constructed in the middle of the nineteenth century. 'Imagine a rough shed, built of mud and wattle . . . On the inside of the roof hang innumerable hornets' nests, and possibly a few bats. On the walls, suspended from little pegs, are sheets displaying the alphabet, or rows of syllables, some of them nibbled by intrusive goats or fretted by the ubiquitous termites. Look in at about 8.30 in the morning and you will see groups of readers, of mixed ages and sexes, seated on the floor in front of the sheets, saying over the letters of syllables in a sing-song voice . . .' The description comes from northern Uganda in the 1920s, but it could equally be from Nigeria in the 1840s or the Congo in the 1970s. It is in surroundings such as these that the vast majority of educated Africans have always acquired their first competence in literacy.

That it was for a long time designed to instruct them in the values of imperialist immigrants to their continent is undeniable. A visitor who toured a great number of missionary educational establishments in 1922 reported that 'the pupils were asked to sing any song they pleased. They always brightened up at this request, for the African loves singing. The chances were strong that we would hear "The British Grenadiers". Perhaps there was a desire to please the strangers, but when they were asked to sing an African song, a boat song, or any chant used in their own plays, a laugh invariably went through the whole class and only in a few instances, even when we declared our love for their own music, could they give us a single African chant. Sometimes, if we asked about history, we soon discovered what happened in 1066, but of their own story – nothing.' The chances are strong that twenty years later the visitor might still have had much the same experience. But at least, the soul-searching which followed the Great War in some quarters caused the missionaries to review educational policies.

On the initiative of the American Baptist Foreign Missionary Society the Phelps-Stokes Fund was approached for a study of education in Africa. The fund had been established by an American philanthropist, Miss Caroline Phelps-Stokes, to encourage the education of Negroes both in Africa and the United States, but this was its first venture overseas. Between 1920 and 1924 a commission produced two reports after extensive fieldwork in Africa. It was perhaps expecting too much, when three of the seven members most closely involved in the work were missionaries themselves, for the commission to come to conclusions which would be radically upsetting to the missionary movement. It did, nevertheless, make the point that missionaries basically followed the educational ideals prevalent in their own countries, with the implicit suggestion that this was less than wise in the face of an Africa which was rapidly developing an independent mind about the sort of future its people wanted.

Within a few years, a high official of the CMS in London was admitting that 'From the point of view of secular education, hundreds of our schools are practically useless'. And from this time onwards, a new policy of missionary purpose began to shape itself in those European centres where colonial rule had followed the advances of Christianity into Africa. Almost everything written by J. H. Oldham – to name the outstanding apostle of the new philosophy – pronounced the necessity of the white man's obligation to help the African to political independence. He criticised the existing state of affairs in South Africa where even the most open-minded of the whites, exemplified by General Smuts, believed in their divine right to rule the blacks for ever and a day. He conceded that all over the continent, missionaries had perhaps misunderstood the nature of religion as much as they had mistaken the purpose of education. In Oldham's view, it was no longer enough for a missionary to spend his time teaching the contents of the Bible. 'What a missionary can do for Africa by preparing Africans for positions of trust and responsibility, and laying responsibility on their shoulders, is immeasurably greater than anything that he can accomplish by himself.' Oldham recognised that 'The fundamental issue is whether the policy of Europe in regard to the native peoples of Africa is to be one of repression or development. Will the dominant white race look on them primarily as instruments of its own economic advantage or recognise that its duty and responsibility is to guide and assist them to the highest development of which they are capable?'

The same tone was evident in many of the papers read at the international missionary conference held at La Zoute, Belgium, in 1926. It was increasingly heard in the directives of Catholic leaders to their missionaries in Africa. The architects of missionary policy, Protestant and Catholic, soon became the major pressure upon colonial governments to prepare their black subjects for political independence. It is arguable, indeed, that so dedicated to this purpose did the missionary leaders become that they were much slower than they might otherwise have been in transferring the control of the Church in Africa from white to black hands. In addressing his bishops and missionaries, at Dar-es-Salaam in 1928, upon this new joint purpose of Church and colonial state, Monsignor Lechaptois, the Apostolic Vicar of Tanganyika, said, 'Collaborate with all your power; and where it is impossible for you to carry on both the immediate task of evangelisation and your educational work, neglect your churches in order to perfect your schools.' In the field, missionaries were often much slower to recognise their new responsibility than the leaders at home; it had been so in the days of the visionary Henry Venn. In these years between the two great wars a man like Bruno Guttman, who worked among the Chagga of Kenya and who devoutly believed that the African in some ways grasped more clearly the true meaning of life than the European, was still a very rare missionary.

Yet even under the order of things which existed before Oldham and like-minded men appeared on the missionary scene, the missionary schoolteachers had made an important bequest to Africa. It had been offered ever since they had first set up their blackboards and easels, and hung their alphabet sheets upon those mud and wattle walls. As in the case of the British in India, it was the greatest legacy of colonial rulers to their subject peoples. The missionaries who taught their black pupils the history of Great Britain to the exclusion of African history or the history of any other land, were teaching them the history of a people who had always demonstrated a determination to be free of alien sovereignty, even if this very often meant that they bought their freedom at some expense to others. Although a missionary might be sublimely unaware of the potential consequences of this teaching, no intelligent black child could fail to be similarly stirred to put down oppressors and to reject invaders, when he was asked to admire Magna Carta and – more frequently, perhaps – to applaud Oliver Cromwell's Protestant annihilation of an overweeningly Catholic King. Some of these children were eventually stirred very deeply indeed. Almost every one of the men who led the countries of black Africa to Independence after the Second World War was educated by missionaries. For their generation, there was no other source of education. Hastings Banda, of Nyasaland/Malawi, was reared by the Livingstonia missionaries. Kenneth Kaunda, of Northern Rhodesia/Zambia, whose father was a Protestant minister, came up under the guidance of Church of Scotland missionaries; so did Jomo Kenyatta, of Kenya. In Tanganyika/Tanzania, Julius Nyerere was educated in a government school, but he taught at a Catholic mission and remained a good Catholic. In the Congo, Joseph Kasavubu was schooled by Catholic Scheut Fathers and Moise Tshombe by American Methodists. Kwame Nkrumah was taught by Catholics in the Gold Coast/Ghana and Leopold Senghor by Catholics in Senegal. In Nigeria, Nnamdi Azikiwe came out of an Anglican school, while Obafemi Awolowo had his education in turn from Anglicans, Baptists and Methodists. There were others – like President Tubman of Liberia, brought up and trained by American Methodists – whose first grooming for national leadership came from the same sources.

What these men preached in their maturity meant the end of a great deal that the missionaries had always cherished. It meant the end of European supremacy on the once Dark Continent. It meant the rejection of many European values, like the one about the inherent superiority of the white man over the black man. It also meant the beginning of the freedom to control one's own life, to stand up in the congress of nations with the right to speak as an equal upon the affairs of the whole world. The missionaries were agents of that freedom. This was not a small gift.

20

EPILOGUE

The missionaries, of course, are still in Africa today. It says a great deal for their positive contribution to the continent that, a generation after Independence, they are still playing an important part in the shaping of its future. They no longer dominate even its Church life. In no independent country does any white man remain as a bishop of the Catholic Church. There is now only one white Anglican bishop, and he was invited by Africans to take charge of a diocese in Uganda a few years ago because either of two alternative African choices would have split the congregations from top to bottom in ancient tribal rivalries. Africans, therefore, now control their own Christian affairs even in those Churches which owe an ecclesiastical allegiance to the fountain-heads of Europe. Yet the missionaries are still there in quantity, even though a great deal of the resources that traditionally sustained their movement – in manpower, in money and in moral support – have been deflected in a secular age into such channels as those represented by Oxfam, Voluntary Service Overseas and the foreign aid programmes mounted by a variety of governments in Europe and North America. They are much reduced in numbers, where they have continued to be sent out from the white man's world, to something around the level of the mid-nineteenth century. If it were not for the great legacies of the past, from people like Robert Arthington, which allowed organisations like the BMS to build up considerable capital and a steady income from its interest, it is doubtful whether many of the European Protestant societies would still have the money to send emissaries abroad. As it is, the British Baptists could afford to accept thirty-three missionary recruits in 1971, to be deployed on BMS work throughout the world – in India, East Pakistan, Ceylon, Nepal, Hong Kong, Jamaica, Trinidad and Brazil, as well as in the African Congo.

It is important to notice how the missionaries, indeed, have survived the various political upheavals that have disturbed Africa over the past two and a half decades. They have been occasionally ejected during some desperate local conflagration, as in the Congo or in Biafra. But invariably, when the local horror has been ended, when tempers have cooled down, they have been allowed to return to their work, even when (as in the case of Biafra) they were closely identified in their sympathies with the defeated faction. The reasons for their staying power are manifest in every independent country. They still provide certain medical and educational facilities that the independent Governments cannot maintain out of their own resources. At the Baptist mission station of Bolobo, high up the river Congo, there is a hospital, staffed by five Europeans and a larger handful of African assistants. In 1970, more than 850 operations were performed there by the one missionary doctor, and almost three thousand in-patients were treated. There is no comparable form of medical service within two or three hundred miles; and people are very likely to bring their relations in to the Baptists after their local witch-doctor has failed to relieve the sickness.

When the Congo became independent of the Belgians in 1960, three-quarters of a century of colonial rule had left the land without a single Congolese trained as a doctor. Congolese doctors are still very few and far between. And while the situation is much better in the field of education, the missionaries are still so important as schoolteachers that the Congolese Government pays their air fares between Africa and Europe or America.

Conditions left by the Belgians in the Congo have produced an extreme reliance upon missionary resources. But the same tale can be told, on a smaller scale, elsewhere in Africa today. You find missionaries whose whole time is spent not upon preaching Christianity but upon teaching native farmers how to increase their agricultural yields. You find them deep in the middle of public health schemes. You even find American missionaries of the Mennonite Brethren running a travel agency along Kinshasa's widest and most flashy boulevard.

The Americans alone seem to exude a sense of unbounded confidence in what they are about, a certainty that it is God's palpable will for both Africa and themselves that they should be there. One can imagine the same feeling projected by the British at the turn of the twentieth century. The British today project a feeling of deep uncertainty, more than anything else. Partly, no doubt, this is no more than the uncertainty of many Christians in Europe and North America, who have come to question the articles of their faith more in the past generation than ever before. But there is also an uncertainty about their missionary purpose. They belong to organisations in which it was a deeply embedded principle first that Africans were of their nature degraded heathen, later that Africans were decent human beings like everyone else, but who needed guidance from the white man and the paternal instincts of someone inherently wiser. Only in this past generation, again, have the doubts about this principle been growing among the mass of missionary workers; in the years between the two great wars they had been confined to the upper ranks of the missionary leaders. And in a growing desire among many missionaries to serve the African genuinely as he feels he can be served, not as the European feels he ought to be 'served', a deadweight of the old tradition remains at home among the people who still give support to the missionary movement.

A young Anglican worker in Uganda reports that when she returns to England on leave, she is expected to spend most of her weekends visiting the parishes whose contributions help to maintain her at her post. She takes a boxful of colour slides from Africa to show these good people just where their thrifty offerings are spent. Invariably, she shows them a picture of the main Post Office in Kampala, which is a very modern building, rather more splendid than the majority of Post Offices in the British Isles. This, she tells them, is representative of Africa today, just as much as the other pictures showing half-naked tribesmen and clearings in the bush. The reaction of the parochial English, she says, generally goes through two stages. The picture of Kampala Post Office is first received with downright scepticism. After that, the feeling seems to be that it is not quite in the natural order of things for Africans to be possessed of such modern marvels. And, indeed, it is sometimes hard to avoid the conclusion that the modern missionary movement is very largely maintained by white people who have never been near Africa, who still feel a deep psychological need to patronise the African.

The feeling rubs off on to many of the missionaries at times. Because missionary funds, except in the case of the Americans, are now very thin upon the ground, a number of missionaries are to be found living in circumstances of what can only be described as genteel poverty. When one of them goes home on leave, and is obliged to clear out his larder, he is to be detected selling his half-used pats of butter and his unused tins of baked beans to his colleagues, rather than giving them away. He needs to do so, you discover, because he is heavily in debt to his missionary society. The people on that station, moreover, do not appear to be practising anything that could be described as genuine Christian love, but something called charity, which is a rather different and sometimes a very tight-lipped thing. And they are really rather bitter (though, of course, they try not to show it) that the Africans around them do not fall over themselves with gratitude at the sacrifices the missionaries believe themselves to be making on their behalf.

Some sacrifices are clearly made, though perhaps not quite as many as the missionaries think. One very striking thing about the Protestant workers the traveller is liable to meet in Africa, is their relatively low standard of education, certainly compared with that of the Catholics working for missionary orders. The Catholic stations are well staffed with priests carrying one or more university degrees apiece, covering philosophy, anthropology and sociology, as well as theology. The Protestant station which contains more than a medical degree or a brace of teacher's training certificates appears to be something of a rarity. It is difficult to see how many of these people, were they to seek employment in their own lands, could obtain positions which would give them greater security and very much more economic support, how they could hope to aspire to anything which would give them a comparable status either in their field of work or when they are at home among their own countrymen. Nor does it seem likely that a different manner of individual will now emerge into the Protestant missionary field. The training schedules of the missionary societies offer crash courses in some specialised fields; in, for example, tropical medicine, or in French-for-use-in-the-Congo. Otherwise they are much overloaded with the study of missionary history, very thinly served with a new theology of mission, scarcely served at all with more than interjected comments by old hands upon African sociology and African tribal custom.

These people can sometimes startle you with observations which seem to be neither Christian in origin nor of the mid-twentieth century in time. A Southern Baptist from the United States can suddenly say – with a vague gesture into the darkness, which is meant to encompass every African in the continent – 'When these people have received the Lord, they're the most beautiful people in the world. When they haven't they're the rottenest people on earth.' A minister of the Free Church of Scotland can write from his missionary outpost in South Africa: 'As was the case at the time of the Reformation, when the Church of Rome tried to inseminate their insidious doctrines of self-salvation, so is the case still.

The powers of darkness are at work in the Colleges, Unions and even in the Churches to overthrow whatever is pure, virtuous and of good report. In a very different sense from that of the writer in the Acts of the Apostles, "the people who have turned the world upside down have come here also". But as yet, the South African Government, which, let it be said in their praise, is authoritative, has managed quite effectively to keep order . . . Though the Church in this Country, as in other countries, presents a dark picture, the State somewhat relieves the situation. Calvinistic principles prevail in the National Party. These principles are mainly authority, morality and liberty . . . Patience must be exercised with the present state of affairs. "Apartheid" or "separate development" is not such a formidable thing as it is made out to be.'

The Catholic missionaries seem to be in rather a different case, in spite of the fact that they have come from the most deeply paternalistic Church of all, with Inquisitorial noises still to be heard occasionally from the confines of the Vatican and elsewhere. In Africa, they appear to have tuned in sensitively to the spirit of changing times, both theological and secular, much more deftly than the Protestants. In the Cameroons and elsewhere they have admitted the dance to the liturgy of the Church, because at last it has been understood that the African uses his body to express emotion in a way that the European scarcely ever does. In Uganda, the White Fathers of the Pastoral Institute of Eastern Africa have for some years been producing some very tough-minded essays in pastoral anthropology, trying to work out at the deepest level just where the indigenous culture can by synthesised with Gospel rather than institutionalised Christianity, not only to enhance the life of Africa but to provide a feedback that might do the same for the spiritually starving millions of Europe. Cardinal Lavigerie's old order has even been prepared for conflict with the Vatican itself on the question of its missionary purpose, showing a rugged independence that His Eminence would most certainly have approved.

In 1971, its Dutch Superior General announced that the White Fathers were no longer prepared to work in the Portuguese colony of Mozambique and that the forty priests on station there would be withdrawn. This was in spite of the fact that nowhere else in Africa had these missionaries enjoyed such a privileged status, nowhere else had they been given so much material help from a Government. The withdrawal was being made because the order felt it could no longer be associated even obliquely with colonial rule. 'On the one hand,' said the Superior General, 'there was the fundamental ambivalence in a situation where our presence ended by bearing witness to untruths; on the other, there was the sincerity of a mission in Africa which refuses to be two-faced.' The White Fathers had, for a long time before this, asked the Vatican for permission to leave their work in Mozambique but the inquiry had been ignored. 'Confronted by a silence which we do not understand, we believe that in all good conscience we have no right to appear to be party to the official support that the bishops seem to be giving a regime which so cleverly makes use of the Church to consolidate and perpetuate in Africa a situation both anachronistic and, in the long term, hopeless. A silent Church, a gagged Church, can stand for something worth while in a regime where it is officially persecuted. But in a country which proclaims itself Catholic and protector of the Church for ends which have nothing to do with the Gospel according to Jesus Christ, silence would be merely bearing false witness.'

It was a White Father who, in Uganda one night, said: 'You know, the trouble with most so-called Christians in Europe is that they don't realise that the so-called pagans in Africa have a hell of a lot to teach them.' What the Africans may have to teach the white nations above all else seems very obvious if the traveller visits one of the Separatist Churches on its home ground. Someone has recently estimated that at the turn of the next century there may well be 350 million Christians in Africa. No one with a sense of history and an instinct for the fruitfulness of mankind can doubt that, if the prophecy comes true, all but a scattered handful of those Christians will be found in congregations like that of the Church of the Lord (Aladura), which stands at the top of a dirt road beneath those bush-covered hills that encircle Freetown like an embrace.

Every Sunday morning, the rickety old building is packed with Bishops and Apostles and Cross-bearers and rather fat ladies in white or green robes. They pray in great rolling periods of fervour and passion, their supplications seasoned with many cries of 'Hallelujah'. Their hymns contain lines which might startle more sober souls who labour each Sabbath through the Metrical Psalms; lines with a splendid vernacular tang to them like 'Congrats to the Church in Sierra Leone'. Their singing might be considered undignified, perhaps a shade irreverent, in any parish church used by the English. But the singing comes out of faces which are open, relaxed, allowing something precious and vital to stream out of the soul. It comes bounding out of bodies which swing and throb with the pleasure of life itself. There comes steaming off these people a very palpable sense of joy. This, perhaps, is what they can teach the Christians – so-called and otherwise – who inhabit the white man's world. It is one of the two great Christian virtues, and we lost it for too long.

No one who travels round black Africa today, and who carefully takes his sense of history with him, can fail to be stirred by the fingerprints the missionaries have left upon the continent. Every land he passes through has been marked by their presence, in some places much more indelibly than others. It requires but a small effort of the imagination, in the modern city of Kampala, to picture it as it was when Mwanga was vacillating between Moslems, Catholics and Protestants in turn, when Alexander Mackay and Father Lourdel acrimoniously went through a form of Christian worship together in the Kabaka's palace, and when Captain Lugard came marching upon the scene in his fancy pyjama jacket. The two great bastions of Christian faith, cathedrals built of solid brick now, in place of the reed and wooden structures of eighty years ago, still dominate the old capital from the tops of their adjacent hills. And on a smaller hill, forming a triangle with the other two, small boys scramble and shout around the empty structure that was Lugard's Company fort, with its surrounding ditch that is not quite deep or wide enough to be called a moat.

At the back of the Anglican Cathedral, on Namirembe Hill, the visitor can inspect the almost sacred relics which have been carefully preserved in glass cases. Here is one of the first bricks ever made in Uganda, Mackay's work, of course, and beside it the little wooden box containing the Scotsman's dividers, parallel rulers and other tools of his trade. Bishop James Hannington's last diary is here, opened at an entry made just a month before he died, with tiny writing in ink, describing ostriches and a rogue elephant which was too far away for him to shoot and a plain covered with antelopes, jackals and pigs. His Bible is opened at Psalm 16, where the Bishop had underlined the word 'hell', with the marginal annotation of 'unseen world'. They also have his chalice at Namirembe, fashioned from a coconut shell, with a short rope thong round its base. And the nameplate of the *Daisy*, the boat the missionaries used on Lake Victoria; a polished brass oval inscribed with the name and with 'J. Messenger, Boatbuilder to Her Majesty, Teddington'. The missionary alliance with the Queen really was rather close.

Sometimes the relics the traveller stumbles upon are much more remarkable and very much more moving than these. He will, perhaps, have taken himself up the Congo river, to follow the line of H. M. Stanley and of the trail-blazing missionaries like George Grenfell, who laid that string of Baptist stations into the interior in the 1880s. At Bolobo the boiler of Grenfell's vessel *Peace*, specially constructed to raise steam rapidly for escape from hostile tribesmen, lies rusting quietly beneath a collapsing verandah in an old missionary garden, a piece of Africa's Christian archaeology. From here the traveller will push on by dug-out canoe up that mighty river, with its enormous sandbanks and its myriad clumps of mauve water hyacinth which are always swirling downstream, and its side creeks in which ancient and derelict steam launches – descendants all of the *African Queen* – can occasionally be observed waterlogged among the reeds. One evening he will arrive at a village, hundreds of miles above Kinshasa, feeling like a million miles from the sophistications of Europe. The smoke of wood fires will be drifting down to the water's edge. The people will be waiting there, drums having announced the traveller's coming long before his canoe has been sighted. They will take his possessions from the boat and they will lead him in cavalcade, half dignified, half scrambling with excitement into the central clearing surrounded by their mud and thatched dwellings. They will gather round him while he stands a little awkwardly, wondering just what is to happen next. Suddenly, they start singing 'Auld Lang Syne' in their local dialect. It was taught them many generations ago by a missionary called MacBeth, and this is their welcome and their first gift to any white man who now comes their way. As the traveller stands there, moved almost to tears by this kindness and by the very nature of this gift, he becomes a little intoxicated by the concentration of all the faces around him, shining in the firelight, willing him to be pleased, bent upon his pleasure and upon him alone. He realises how a white man, exposed to this great flow of warmth for too long, might easily believe himself to be a demi-god of sorts.

SOURCE NOTES

CHAPTER 1: *To Spread Mild Truths*

p. 21, line 22; *The Times*, 3 June 1840
All other quotations in the chapter come from the extensive report of the Exeter Hall meeting published in *The Times* of 2 June 1840

CHAPTER 2: *To Convert the Heathen*

p. 33, line 32; Leipoldt p. 189
p. 34, line 11; Stock Vol. 1, p. 20
p. 34, lines 29 & 33; Thompson p. 23
p. 35, line 11; Ibid. p. 66
p. 37, line 38; Warneck p. 75
p. 38, line 22; Carey p. 8
p. 39, line 5; Ibid. p. 63
p. 39, line 9; Ibid. p. 63
p. 39, line 16; Ibid. p. 65
p. 39, line 40; Ibid. p. 74
p. 40, line 18; Ibid. p. 87
p. 41, line 6; *Evangelical Magazine*, September 1794
p. 41, line 20; Lovett p. 13
p. 41, line 33; Ibid. p. 43
p. 41, line 40; Ibid. p. 70
p. 42, line 4; Ibid. p. 73
p. 42, line 20; Ibid. p. 48
p. 42, line 29; Ibid. p. 48
p. 42, line 36; Ibid. p. 156
p. 43, line 4; Ibid. p. 156
p. 43, line 21; Ibid. p. 62
p. 43, line 26; Ibid. p. 63
p. 45, line 14; Stock Vol. 1, p. 85

CHAPTER 3: *The German Salvation*

p. 47, line 14; Stock Vol. 1, p. 72
p. 47, line 24; Stock Vol. 1, p. 73
p. 48, line 2; Ibid.
p. 48, line 34; Stock Vol. 1, p. 84
p. 49, line 29; Ibid. p. 95
p. 49, line 36; Ibid. p. 91
p. 50, line 27; Krapf p. 2
p. 50, line 35; Ibid. p. 7
p. 51, line 22; Ibid. p. 14
p. 52, line 8; Ibid. p. 86
p. 52, line 34; Ibid. p. 127
p. 53, line 18; Ibid. p. 133
p. 54, line 8; Ibid. p. 149
p. 54, line 37; Ibid. p. 151
p. 55, line 12; Ibid. p. 158
p. 56, line 19; Ibid. p. 232
p. 57, line 12; Ibid. p. 235
p. 58, line 12; Ibid. p. 403
p. 58, line 29; Ibid. p. 428
p. 59, line 30; Ibid. p. 405
p. 59, line 36; Ibid. p. 512
p. 61, line 6; Ibid. p. 405

CHAPTER 4: *To the Cape*

p. 62, line 17; Stock Vol. 1, p. 132
p. 63, line 24; Knutsford p. 122
p. 64, line 25; Stock Vol. 1, p. 176
p. 65, line 13; Lovett p. 585
p. 66, line 21; Owen p. 38
p. 66, line 27; Ibid. p. 14
p. 67, line 4; Ibid.

p. 67, line 29; Ibid. p. 30
p. 70, line 3; Du Plessis p. 227
p. 70, line 21; Owen p. 91
p. 71, line 10; Ibid. pp. 40–41
p. 73, line 11; *Memorial Volume* of ABC, p. 43
p. 74, line 7; Report of ABC 24th Annual Meeting, 1833, p. 142
p. 74, line 21; *Life and Times of Daniel Lindley* p. 49
p. 75, line 32; Ibid. p. 53
p. 76, line 17; Ibid. p. 162
p. 76, line 38; Ibid. p. 160
p. 77, line 11; Ibid. p. 308
p. 77, line 33; Ibid. p. 294
p. 78, line 22; Ibid. pp. 316–7
p. 79, line 19; *Memorial Volume* of ABC, p. 283
p. 79, line 27; Ibid. p. 239

CHAPTER 5: *The Advance in the West*

p. 82, line 20; Coupland p. 288
p. 84, line 21; McWilliam p. 73
p. 85, line 39; Buxton p. 573
p. 86, line 2; Stock Vol. I, p. 455
p. 86, line 9; Proceedings of the CMS, 1842, p. 40
p. 87, line 18; Ibid. 1855, p. 56
p. 89, line 34; Hope Waddell, 28 April 1846
p. 92, line 12; Ayandele p. 26
p. 92, line 18; Ibid. p. 23
p. 93, line 12; Ibid. p. 24
p. 93, line 23; Letter Gollmer-Venn, 7 January 1852 (CMS file CA2/043)
p. 94, line 32; Agnes Waddel p. 43
p. 95, line 3; Ayandele p. 26

CHAPTER 6: *A Very Useful Instrument*

p. 97, line 8; Cust p. 25
p. 97, line 17; Page p. 24
p. 97, line 28; Ibid. p. 39
p. 97, line 32; Ibid. p. 34
p. 98, line 31; Ibid. p. 78
p. 99, line 24; Ibid. p. 100
p. 100, line 20; Ibid. pp. 103–4
p. 102, line 9; Ibid. p. 177
p. 102, line 25; Ibid. p. 147
p. 102, line 36; Ibid. p. 165
p. 103, line 34; CMS *Intelligencer*, May 1864
p. 104, line 7; Quoted from *The Record* by Page, p. 189
p. 106, line 11; Stock Vol. II, p. 457
p. 107, line 14; Ayandele p. 77
p. 107, line 31; Sir H. H. Johnston, quoted Ayandele p. 78
p. 108, line 4; Page p. 205
p. 108, line 33; Ibid. p. 264
p. 109, line 31; Ibid. p. 308

CHAPTER 7: *The Greatest Missionary*

p. 113, line 11; *Private Journals* p. xvi, comment by I. Schapera
p. 113, line 5; Debenham p. 21
p. 114, line 8; Seaver p. 40
p. 114, line 12; *Family Letters* Vol. I, p. 198
p. 114, line 14; Ibid.
p. 114, line 30; *Family Letters* Vol. II, p. 81
p. 115, line 6; Debenham p. 22
p. 115, line 9; *Family Letters* Vol. I, p. 14
p. 115, line 38; Groves Vol. II, p. 123
p. 116, line 9; *Family Letters* Vol. II, p. 29
p. 116, line 26; *Missionary Correspondence* p. 59
p. 117, line 5; *Private Journals* p. 272
p. 117, line 33; *Family Letters* Vol. I, p. 257
p. 118, line 15; *Family Letters* Vol. II, p. 9
p. 118, line 32; *Family Letters* Vol. I, p. 12
p. 119, line 4; Du Plessis p. 445
p. 119, line 11; *Family Letters* Vol. I, p. 261
p. 119, line 31; *Family Letters* Vol. II, p. 152
p. 120, line 17; *Missionary Correspondence* p. 188
p. 120, line 25; *Missionary Correspondence* p. xxii
p. 120, line 26; Ibid. p. 107
p. 121, line 2; Campbell p. 241
p. 121, line 34; Report of the Directors, 1852, p. 15
p. 121, line 37; *Missionary Correspondence* p. 188
p. 122, line 10; *Family Letters* Vol. II, p. 191
p. 122, line 16; Ibid. p. 230
p. 122, line 20; Ibid. p. 200
p. 123, line 1; *Missionary Travels* p. 39
p. 124, line 33; Ibid. p. 229
p. 125, line 8; Ibid. p. 284
p. 125, line 33; Groves Vol. II, p. 168

p. 126, line 19; *Missionary Correspondence* p. xxii
p. 126, line 21; Ibid.
p. 126, line 35; Campbell p. 232
p. 127, line 22; Ibid. p. 234
p. 127, line 31; Ibid. p. 23
p. 129, line 34; *Missionary Correspondence* p. xxiv
p. 130, line 7; Campbell p. 244
p. 130, line 13; LMS Board Minutes, 1857, p. 373
p. 130, line 36; Campbell p. 238
p. 131, line 18; Ibid.
p. 131, line 34; *African Journals* p. xv

CHAPTER 8: *To Create an English Colony*

p. 134, line 22; Debenham p. 130
p. 135, line 27; Kirk Vol. I, p. 309
p. 136, line 15; Debenham p. 130
p. 136, line 36 *et seq.*; Kirk Vol. I, pp. xvii, 13, 48
p. 137, line 26; Ibid. p. 309
p. 137, line 32; Ibid. Vol. II, p. 538
p. 138, line 4; Debenham p. 155
p. 138, line 15; Chadwick p. 25
p. 138, line 18; Kirk Vol. I, p. 310
p. 138, line 24; Ibid. Vol. II, p. 469
p. 138, line 34; Ibid. p. 560
p. 138, line 39; Ibid. p. 546
p. 139, line 2; Kirk Vol. II, p. 547
p. 139, line 30; Campbell p. 253
p. 140, line 20; Coupland p. 182
p. 141, line 22; Goodwin p. 216
p. 141, line 29; Chadwick p. 39
p. 142, line 39; Ibid. p. 50
p. 145, line 2; Ibid. p. 219
p. 145, line 12; Ibid. p. 220
p. 146, line 9; Ibid. p. 83
p. 146, line 40; Kirk Vol. II, p. 568
p. 147, line 2; Ibid.
p. 147, line 19; Blaikie p. 251
p. 147, line 30; Kirk Vol. II, p. 475
p. 148, line 11; Coupland p. 271
p. 148, line 21; Chadwick p. 81
p. 148, line 31; Ibid.
p. 148, line 35; Ibid. p. 220
p. 149, line 6; Ibid. p. 221
p. 149, line 21; Ibid. p. 171
p. 150, line 22; Blaikie p. 293
p. 150, line 33; Ibid. p. vi
p. 151, line 4; Debenham p. 221
p. 151, line 9; Blaikie p. 309
p. 152, line 9; *Last Journals* Vol. II, p. 132
p. 154, line 12; Stanley p. 410
p. 154, line 19; Ibid., p. 440

CHAPTER 9: *The Flood Tide*

p. 156, line 16; Stock Vol. II, p. 392
p. 157, line 35; Ibid. Vol. III, p. 56
p. 158, line 12; Holman Bentley Vol. I, p. 372
p. 158, line 39; Stock Vol. III, p. 58
p. 160, line 6; *Daily Telegraph*, 16 November 1875
p. 161, line 5; Chirgwin p. 25
p. 161, line 25; Ibid. p. 31
p. 162, line 9; Ibid. p. 32
p. 162, line 18; Ibid. p. 22
p. 164, line 32; *The Story of Mackay* p. 32
p. 166, line 36; Findlay p. 26
p. 167, line 28; Ibid. p. 359
p. 168, line 21; CMS *Intelligencer*, December 1894
p. 169, line 13; Moir p. 43

CHAPTER 10: *The Christian Soldiers*

p. 172, line 15; Chadwick p. 201
p. 173, line 15; Stock Vol. III, p. 87
p. 173, line 38; Hinderer p. 6
p. 174, line 4; Ibid. p. 7
p. 174, line 12; Ibid. p. 6
p. 174, line 35; Ibid. p. 8
p. 175, line 11; CMS Annual Report, 1857, p. 49
p. 176, line 12; Ibid. Appendix Minute
p. 176, line 25; Hinderer p. 13
p. 177, line 2; Ibid. p. 22
p. 177, line 7; Ibid. p. 23
p. 177, line 14; Ibid. p. 25
p. 178, line 6; Ibid. p. 30
p. 178, line 16; Ibid. p. 34
p. 178, line 24; Ibid. p. 41
p. 178, line 35; Ibid. p. 54
p. 179, line 16; Ibid. p. 79
p. 179, line 34; Ibid. p. 84
p. 180, line 12; Ibid. p. 194
p. 180, line 13; Ibid. p. 293
p. 181, line 7; Ibid. p. 316
p. 181, line 23; Ibid. p. 212
p. 181, line 38; Ibid. p. 224

p. 182, line 39; Mackay p. 13
p. 183, line 7; Ibid. p. 17
p. 183, line 22; Ibid. p. 21
p. 183, line 33; Ibid. p. 22
p. 184, line 19; Ibid. p. 37
p. 184, line 28; Ibid. p. 38
p. 184, line 38; Ibid. p. 39
p. 185, line 25; Ibid. p. 58
p. 186, line 17; Ibid. p. 70
p. 186, line 3; Ibid. p. 78
p. 188, line 3; Ibid. p. 217
p. 188, line 20; Ibid. p. 381
p. 189, line 16; Ashe, *Chronicles* p. 9
p. 189, line 24; Ashe, *Two Kings* p. 33
p. 189, line 35; Ashe, *Chronicles* p. 364
p. 190, line 4; Ashe, *Two Kings* p. 21
p. 190, line 19; Ruth Rouse, *International Review of Missions* Vol. 6, 1917, p. 244
p. 191, line 8; Ibid. p. 246

CHAPTER 11: *Scrambling for Africa*

p. 193, line 6; Groves Vol. III, p. 52
p. 197, line 1; Holman Bentley Vol. I ,p. 91
p. 197, line 13; Ibid. p. 35
p. 197, line 25; Ibid. p. 48
p. 197, line 31; Ibid. p. 94
p. 197, line 37; Ibid. p. 126
p. 200, line 23; Ibid. Vol. II, p. 139
p. 201, line 20; Ibid. p. 213
p. 202, line 6; Ibid. p. 394
p. 202, line 10; Ibid. p. 365
p. 202, line 15; Ibid. p. 378
p. 202, line 30; Ibid. Vol. I, p. 174
p. 202, line 39; Ibid. p. 228
p. 203, line 16; Ibid. Vol. II, p. 426
p. 203, line 26; Ibid. p. 414
p. 204, line 14; Davies p. 106
p. 205, line 4; Ibid. p. 124
p. 205, line 14; Ibid. p. 125
p. 205, line 18; Ibid. p. 132
p. 205, line 23; Ibid. p. 175
p. 205, line 33; Ibid. p. 151
p. 206, line 10; Ibid. p. 109
p. 207, line 2; Holman Bentley Vol. II, p. 414
p. 207, line 7; Ibid. Vol. I, p. 372

CHAPTER 12: *Lavigerie and the White Fathers*

p. 209, line 31; Versteijnen p. 11
p. 210, line 10; Stanley p. 42
p. 210, line 19; Versteijnen p. 14
p. 211, line 19; Clarke p. 33
p. 212, line 14; Ibid. p. 222
p. 212, line 29; Goyau p. 170
p. 213, line 8; Clarke p. 115
p. 213, line 13; Ibid.
p. 213, line 28; Ibid. p. 93
p. 213, line 39; Ibid. p. 94
p. 214, line 12; Bouniol p. 72
p. 214, line 37; Clarke p. 97
p. 217, line 21 *et seq.*; I am indebted to Dr M. Louise Pirouet for the information about the distance to be maintained between the missions of the White Fathers and those of Protestants in East Africa. It is drawn from her research for a work which has not yet been published.

CHAPTER 13: *The Rivals*

p. 220, line 11; Ashe, *Two Kings* p. 48
p. 221, line 7; Ibid.
p. 221, line 27; Mackay p. 101
p. 222, line 10; Ibid. p. 205
p. 222, line 30; Ibid. p. 186
p. 222, line 36; Ibid. p. 182
p. 225, line 26; Ibid. p. 120
p. 227, line 19; Ibid. p. 225
p. 227, line 30; Ibid. p. 191
p. 229, line 1; Ibid. p. 257
p. 229, line 26; Ashe, *Chronicles* p. 73
p. 230, line 39; Mackay p. 267
p. 231, line 7; Mackay p. 276
p. 232, line 5; Ibid. p. 350
p. 232, line 20; Ibid. p. 403
p. 235, line 20; Ashe, *Chronicles* p. 144
p. 235, line 31; Ashe, Ibid. p. 145
p. 236, line 15; Ibid. p. 150

CHAPTER 14: *The Battle of Mengo*

There are several eye-witness accounts of the Battle, and none of them agree with each other in detail or even upon the general course of events. Apart from the sources noted below, I have drawn most extensively upon a recent analysis of all the available material – *Lugard at Kampala: Makerere History Paper 3* by John A. Rowe (Longmans of Uganda, 1969)

p. 237, line 6; Lugard, *Rise* Vol. I, p. 17
p. 239, line 29; Ibid. p. 61

p. 240, line 23; Ibid. p. 69
p. 242, line 6; Ashe, *Chronicles* p. 198
p. 242, line 35; Lugard p. 303
p. 244, line 3; Ashe, *Chronicles* p. 207
p. 244, line 26; Lugard p. 325
p. 245, line 9; Ibid. p. 340
p. 245, line 23; Ashe, *Chronicles* p. 224
p. 246, line 6; Lugard, *Diary* Vol. III, p. 31
p. 247, line 14; Ashe, *Chronicles* p. 232
p. 247, line 24; Lugard, *Rise* p. 342
p. 248, line 6; Ibid. p. 343
p. 248, line 14; Ibid. p. 344
p. 248, line 21; Ashe, *Chronicles* p. 231
p. 248, line 29; Ibid. p. 233
p. 249, line 9; Lugard, *Rise* p. 344
p. 249, line 39; *The Tablet*, 4 June 1892
p. 250, line 17; Ashe, *Chronicles* p. 251
p. 250, line 25; *The Table top. cit.*
p. 251, line 3; Ashe, *Chronicles* p. 312
p. 251, line 12; Ibid, p. 415

CHAPTER 15: *The Critical Backlash*

p. 252, line 20; Hansard, Col. 57 4 iii, 1892
p. 253, line 17; Hansard, Col. 243 1 vi, 1894
p. 253, line 29; Cust p.58
p. 254, line 9; Oliver p. 154
p. 254, line 20; Stock Vol. III, p. 445
p. 254, line 29; Minute of CMS General Committee, 11 October 1892
p. 254, line 39; Stock Vol. III, p. 444
p. 256, line 11; Chadwick p. 189
p. 257, line 4; Ibid. p. 191
p. 258, linc 19; Chirnsidc p. 20
p. 259, line 8; Ibid. p. 14
p. 259, line 30; Ibid. p. 16
p. 260, line 1; Ibid. p. 19
p. 261, line 18; Hansard Lords, 12 April 1883
p. 267, line 19; Kingsley p. 3
p. 268, line 1; Ibid. p. 473
p. 268, line 5; Ibid. p. 618
p. 268, line 10; Ibid. p. 659
p. 268, line 26; Ibid. p. 220
p. 269, line 29; Ibid. p. 661
p. 270, line 22; Ibid. p. 659

CHAPTER 16: *The Boom Years*

p. 272, line 13 *et seq.*; The statistics are taken from Warneck p. 140 *et seq.*
p. 274, line 19; Stock Vol. III, p. 736
p. 274, line 30; Ibid. Vol. II, p. 449
p. 276, line 7; CMS file W/A2
p. 277, line 34; Ibid.
p. 278, line 21; 'Notes on Barter' by John H. Weeks. *International Review of Missions* Vol. 6, 1917
p. 279, line 23; Stock Vol. III, p. 727
p. 280, line 7; Kemp p. 4
p. 280, line 21; Kemp p. 6
p. 280, line 29; Ibid. p. 68
p. 281, line 1; Ibid. p. 38
p. 281, line 16; Ibid. p. 181
p. 281, line 28; Ibid. p. 57
p. 281, line 35; Ibid. p. 232
p. 282, line 7; Ibid. p. 254
p. 282, line 27; Rae p. 104
p. 284, line 3; Ayandele p. 208
p. 285, line 1; Ibid. p. 214
p. 285, line 4; Ibid.
p. 285, line 6; Ibid. p. 215
p. 285, line 27; Ibid. p. 216
p. 287, line 7; Harford Battersby p. 235
p. 287, line 27; Stock Vol. III, p. 449
p. 289, line 9; Oliver p. 192
p. 289, line 20; Groves Vol. III, p. 283
p. 289, line 38; Ibid. p. 279

CHAPTER 17: *Paradise Lost*

p. 293, line 1; Groves Vol. IV, p. 71
p. 293, line 20; Ibid. p. 69
p. 294, line 26; Ibid. p. 34
p. 296, line 3; Ibid. p. 75
p. 296, line 31; *The Times*, 16 April 1918
p. 297, line 20; Groves Vol. IV, p. 75
p. 297, line 34; Ibid. p. 77
p. 298, line 6; Schweitzer p. 138
p. 300, line 7; This, and subsequent quotations in the chapter, is drawn from Dr Pirouet's unpublished research into this period of Church history in East Africa.

CHAPTER 18: *A Black Reformation*

p. 306, line 5; Ayandele p. 184
p. 308, line 3; Ibid. p. 255
p. 308, line 15; Ibid. p. 174
p. 312, line 23; From a paper on Spartas by J. R. Kigongo Dam-Tibajiua, privately circulated.

p. 313, line 28; *The Present-Day Prophets*, by J. Ade Aina (Lagos, 1932) p. 12
p. 314, line 14; Turner Vol. I, p. 11
p. 315, line 4; Ibid. p. 38
p. 315, line 11; Ibid. p. 39
p. 315, line 40; Ibid. Vol. II, p. 43
p. 316, line 6; Ibid. Vol. I, p. 23
p. 317, line 11; Ibid. Vol. II, p. 10
p. 317, line 24; Ibid. Vol. II, p. 251
p. 318, line 9; Ibid. Vol. I, p. 26
p. 318, line 23 *et seq.*; Ibid. pp. 28–9
p. 319, line 8; Ibid. p. 117
p. 319, line 21; Ibid. p. 137

CHAPTER 19: *The Achievement*

p. 320, line 5 *et seq.*; Statistics taken from *Data on the Distribution of the Missionary Enterprise*, by M. Searle Bates (International Missionary Council, New York, 1943)
p. 321, line 9; Frere p. 59
p. 322, line 23; *Anthropological Review* IV (1866), p. 144
p. 322, line 31; *Journal of the Anthropological Society* III (1865), p. clxiv
p. 322, line 36; *Journal of the Anthropological Institute* XV (1885), p. 337
p. 324, line 11; Chadwick p. 222
p. 325, line 13; Oliver p. 242
p. 326, line 34; Ibid. p. 209
p. 326, line 39; Groves Vol. IV, p. 222
p. 327, line 9; *International Review of Missions*, January 1921, p. 110
p. 327, line 34; Jarrett-Kerr p. 289
p. 328, line 8; Groves Vol. IV, p. 343
p. 328, line 15; Ibid.
p. 328, line 32; *Inside Africa* (Hamilton, 1955) p. 300
p. 330, line 2; Oliver p. 248
p. 330, line 14; Ibid. p. 250
p. 331, line 21; Oliver p. 211
p. 331, line 35; Schweitzer p. 27
p. 332, line 15; Kitching p. 31
p. 332, line 30; Phelps-Stokes Report Vol. I, p. xix
p. 333, line 18; *International Review of Missions*, January 1925, article by Garfield Williams
p. 333, line 31; Oldham and Gibson p. 145
p. 333, line 34; Oldham p. 4
p. 334, line 12; Quoted by J. Mazé in *La Collaboration Scolaire des Missions et des Gouvernements* (Algiers, 1933) p. 14

CHAPTER 20: *Epilogue*

p. 339, line 38; Rev. A. A. MacDonald in *From the Frontiers* Vol. V, No. 10, January 1970
p. 340, line 38 *et seq.*; *Le Monde*, 17 June 1971
p. 341, line 20; Estimate by David B. Barrett in *International Review of Missions* Vol. LIX, No. 233, January 1970

BIBLIOGRAPHY

The literature of Christian missions to Africa is colossal. This selection is confined to those books upon which I drew directly.

AMERICAN BOARD OF COMMISSIONERS FOR FOREIGN MISSIONS. *Memorial Volume of the First Fifty Years* (Boston, 1861)

ASHE, R. P. *Chronicles of Uganda* (London, 1894)

Two Kings of Uganda (London, 1889)

AYANDELE, E. A. *The Missionary Impact on Modern Nigeria* (London, 1966)

BATTERSBY, C. F. HARFORD. *Pilkington of Uganda* (London, 1895)

BENTLEY, W. HOLMAN. *Pioneering in the Congo* 2 vols (London, 1900)

BLAIKIE, W. G. *The Personal Life of David Livingstone* (London, 1880)

BOUNIOL, J. *The White Fathers and Their Missions* (London, 1929)

BUXTON, C. *Memoirs of Sir T. F. Buxton* (London, 1851)

CAMPBELL, R. J. *Livingstone* (London, 1929)

CAREY, WILLIAM. *An Enquiry into the Obligations of Christians to Use Means for the Conversion of the Heathens* (London, 1792)

CHADWICK, OWEN. *Mackenzie's Grave* (London, 1959)

CHIRGWIN, A. M. *Arthington's Millions* (London, 1935)

CHIRNSIDE, ANDREW. *The Blantyre Missionaries: Discreditable Disclosures* (London, 1880)

CLARKE, R. F. *Cardinal Lavigerie and the African Slave Trade* (London, 1889)

COUPLAND, R. *East Africa and its Invaders* (London, 1938)

CUST, R. N. *Essay on the Prevailing Methods of the Evangelisation of the Non-Christian World* (London, 1894)

DAVIES, E. *The Bishop of Africa: a Life of William Taylor* (Reading, Mass., 1885)

DEBENHAM, FRANK. *The Way to Ilala* (London, 1955)

DU PLESSIS, J. *A History of Christian Missions in South Africa* (Cape Town, 1965)

FINDLAY, J. E. *Dwight L. Moody: American Evangelist* (Chicago, 1969)

FRERE, SIR BARTLE. *Eastern Africa as a Field for Missionary Labour* (London, 1874)

GOODWIN, H. *Memoirs of Bishop Mackenzie* (London, 1864)

GOYAU, G. *Le Cardinal Lavigerie* (Paris, 1925)

GROVES, C. P. *The Planting of Christianity in Africa* 4 vols (London, 1948–58)

HARRISON, J. W. *The Story of the Life of Mackay of Uganda, Pioneer Missionary. By his Sister* (London, 1898)

HINDERER, ANNA. *Seventeen Years in the Yoruba Country* ed. by R. B. Hone (London, 1872)
JARRETT-KERR, M. *Patterns of Christian Acceptance* (London, 1972)
KEMP, DENNIS. *Nine Years at the Gold Coast* (London, 1898)
KINGSLEY, MARY. *Travels in West Africa* (London, 1897)
KIRK, JOHN. *Zambezi Journals and Letters* 2 vols, ed. by Reginald Foskett (London, 1965)
KITCHING, A. L. *From Darkness to Light* (London, 1935)
KNUTSFORD, LADY. *Life and Letters of Zachary Macaulay* (London, 1900)
KRAPF, J. LEWIS. *Travels, Researches and Missionary Labours* (London, 1860)
LEIPOLDT, C. L. *Jan van Riebeck* (Cape Town, 1936)
LIVINGSTONE, DAVID. *Missionary Travels and Researches in South Africa* (London, 1857)
The Last Journals 2 vols, ed. by H. Waller (London, 1874)
Family Letters 1841–56 2 vols, ed. by I. Schapera (London, 1959)
Missionary Correspondence 1841–56 ed. by I Schapera (London, 1961)
Private Journals 1851–53 ed. by I. Schapera (London, 1960)
African Journals 1853–56 2 vols, ed. by I. Schapera (London, 1963)
LOVETT, RICHARD. *History of the London Missionary Society* (London, 1899)
LUGARD, F. D. *The Rise of Our East African Empire* 2 vols (London, 1893)
Diaries 2 vols, ed. by Margery Perham and Mary Bull (London, 1959)
MCWILLIAM, J. O. *Medical History of the Expedition to the Niger* (London, 1843)
MOIR, F. L. M. *After Livingstone: An African Trade Romance* (London, 1923)
MYERS, J. B. *Centenary Volume of the Baptist Missionary Society* (London, 1892)
OLDHAM, J. H. *White and Black in Africa* (London, 1930)
and GIBSON, B. D. *The Remaking of Man in Africa* (Oxford, 1931)
OLIVER, ROLAND. *The Missionary Factor in East Africa* (London, 1969)
OWEN, FRANCIS. *Diary* ed. by Sir George Cory (Cape Town, 1926)
PAGE, JESSE. *The Black Bishop: Samuel Adjai Crowther* (London, 1908)
PHELPS-STOKES REPORTS. *Education in Africa* 2 vols (New York, 1922 & 1924)
RAE, C. *Malaboch* (London, 1898)
SEARLE-BATES, M. *Data on the Distribution of the Missionary Enterprise* (New York, 1943)
SEAVER, GEORGE. *David Livingstone: His Life and Letters* (London, 1957)
SCHMIDLIN, J. *Catholic Mission History* (London, 1933)
SCHWEITZER, ALBERT. *On the Edge of the Primeval Forest* (London, 1922)
SMITH, EDWIN W. *The Life and Times of Daniel Lindley* (London, 1949)
STANLEY, H. M. *How I Found Livingstone* (London, 1872)
STOCK, EUGENE. *History of the Church Missionary Society* 4 vols (London, 1899)
STRONG. W. E. *The Story of the American Board* (New York, 1910)
THOMPSON, T. *An Account of Two Mission Voyages* (London, 1758)
TURNER, H. W. *African Independent Church* 2 vols (London, 1967)
TUCKER, ALFRED. *Eighteen Years in Uganda and East Africa* (London, 1911)
VERSTEIJNEN, FRITS. *Zangueber through Contemporary Records* (St Peter's Seminary, Bagamoyo, 1968)
WADDEL, AGNES. *Memorials of Mrs Sutherland of Old Calabar* (Paisley, 1883)
WADDELL, HOPE M. *Twenty-Nine Years in the West Indies and West Africa* (London, 1863)
WARNECK, GUSTAV. *Outline of a History of Protestant Missions* (Edinburgh, 1901)

INDEX

INDEX